# GENSHIKEN

**2**

## KIO SHIMOKU

TRANSLATED AND ADAPTED BY
**David Ury**

LETTERED BY
**Michaelis/Carpelis Design**

BALLANTINE BOOKS • NEW YORK

*Genshiken*, Volume 2 is a work of fiction. Names, characters, places, and incidents are the products of the author's imagination or are used fictitiously. Any resemblance to actual events, locales, or persons, living or dead, is entirely coincidental.

A Del Rey Books Trade Paperback Original



Published in the United States by
Del Rey Books, an imprint of
The Random House Publishing Group, a
division of Random House, Inc., New York.

DEL REY is a registered trademark and the Del Rey colophon is a trademark of Random House, Inc.

First published in Japan in 2002 by
Kodansha Ltd., Tokyo
This publication rights arranged through
Kodansha Ltd.

Library of Congress Control Number:
2005922043

ISBN 0-345-48170-4

Printed in the United States of America

www.delreymanga.com

9 8 7 6 5 4 3 2 1

Lettering—Michaelis/Carpelis Design

# げんしけん

THE SOCIETY FOR THE STUDY OF MODERN VISUAL CULTURE

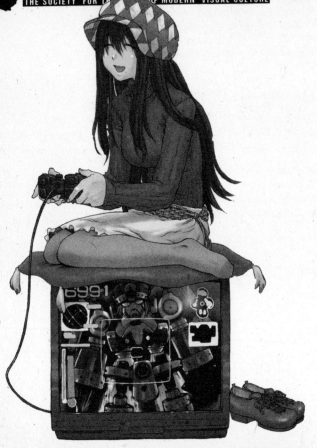

**KIO SHIMOKU**

# Contents

**THE GENSHIKEN MEMBERS PICK
THE MOST NOTABLE SCENES
FROM "KUJI-UN."**

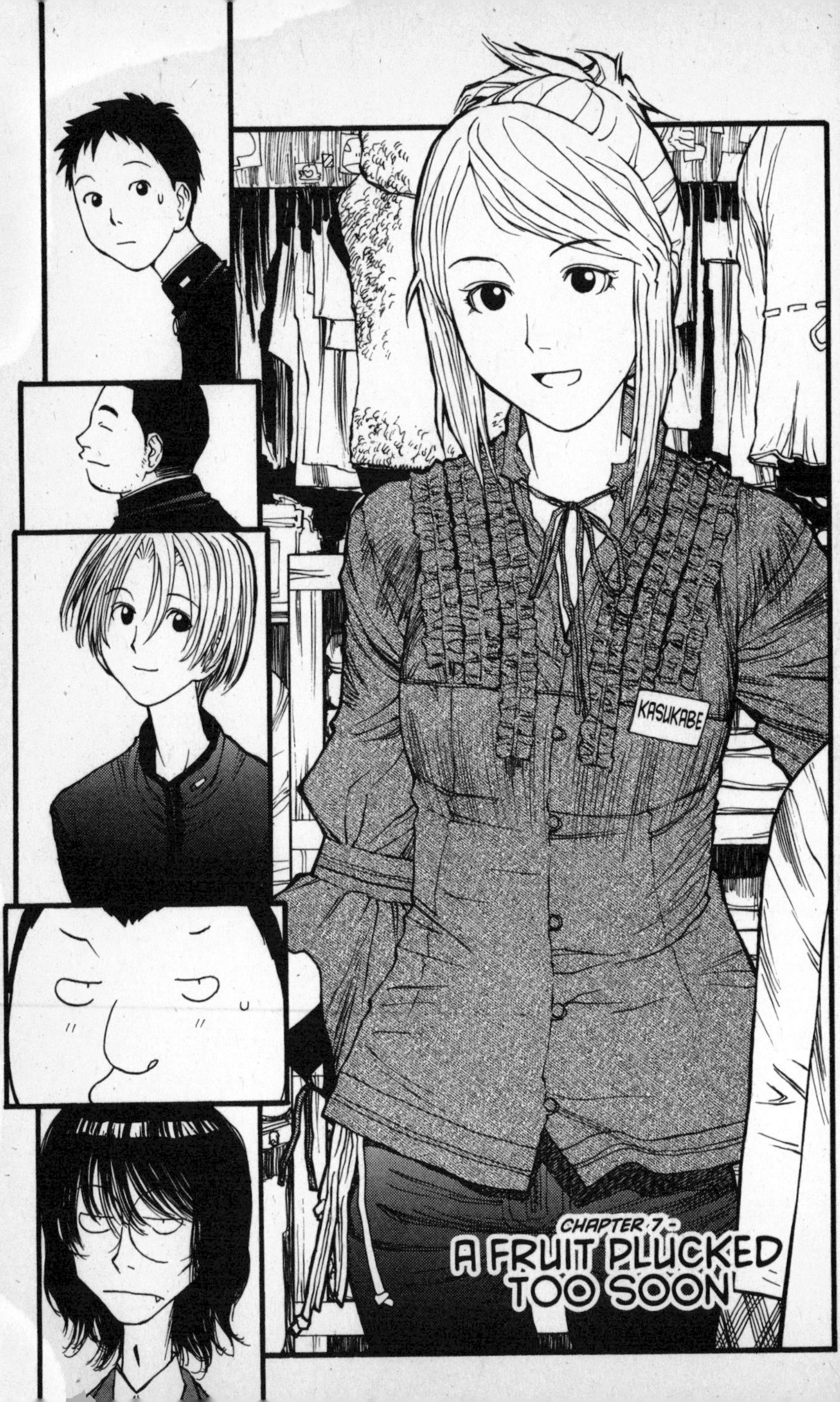
KASUKABE
CHAPTER 7 -
A FRUIT PLUCKED TOO SOON

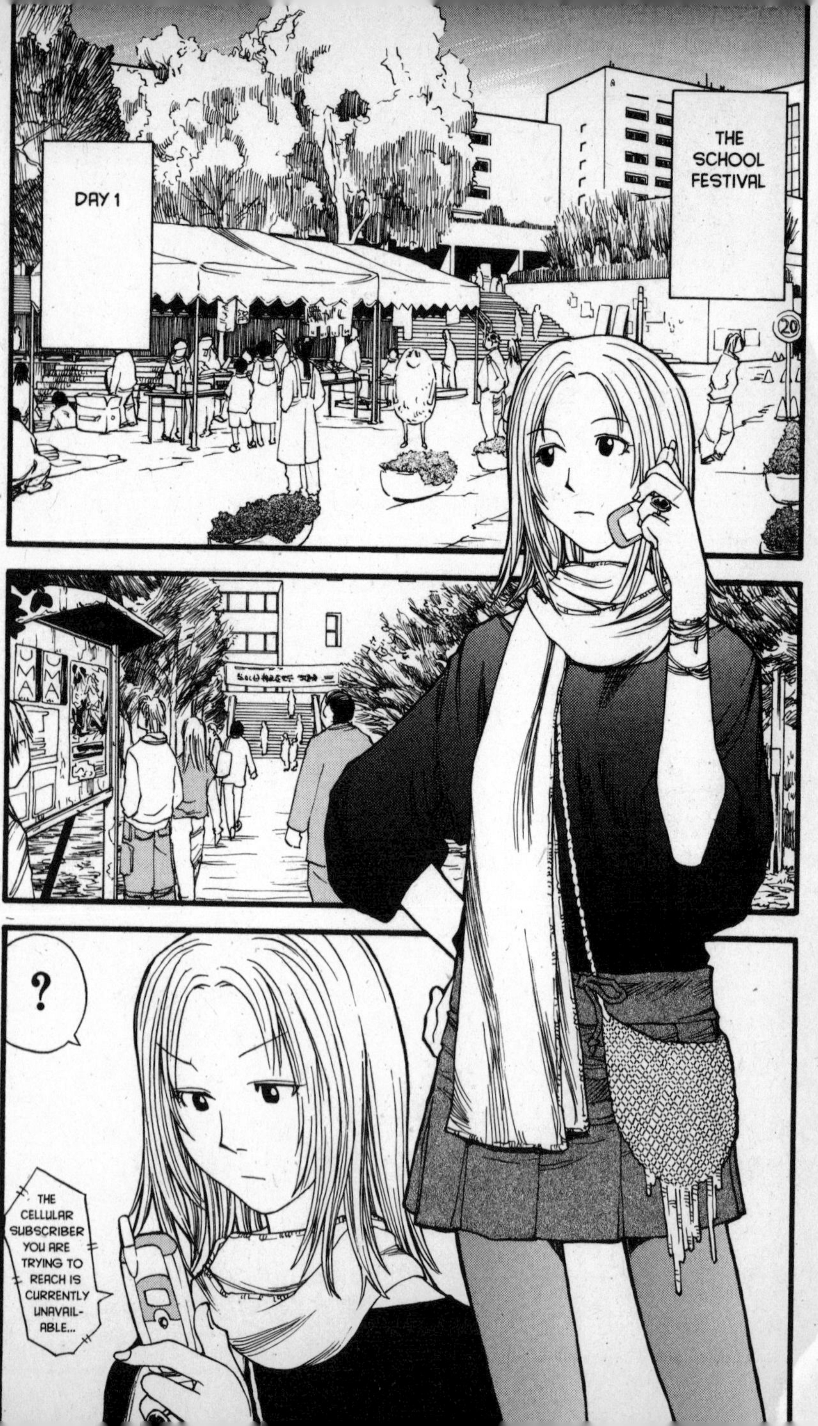
THE SCHOOL FESTIVAL
DAY 1
?
THE CELLULAR SUBSCRIBER YOU ARE TRYING TO REACH IS CURRENTLY UNAVAIL-ABLE...

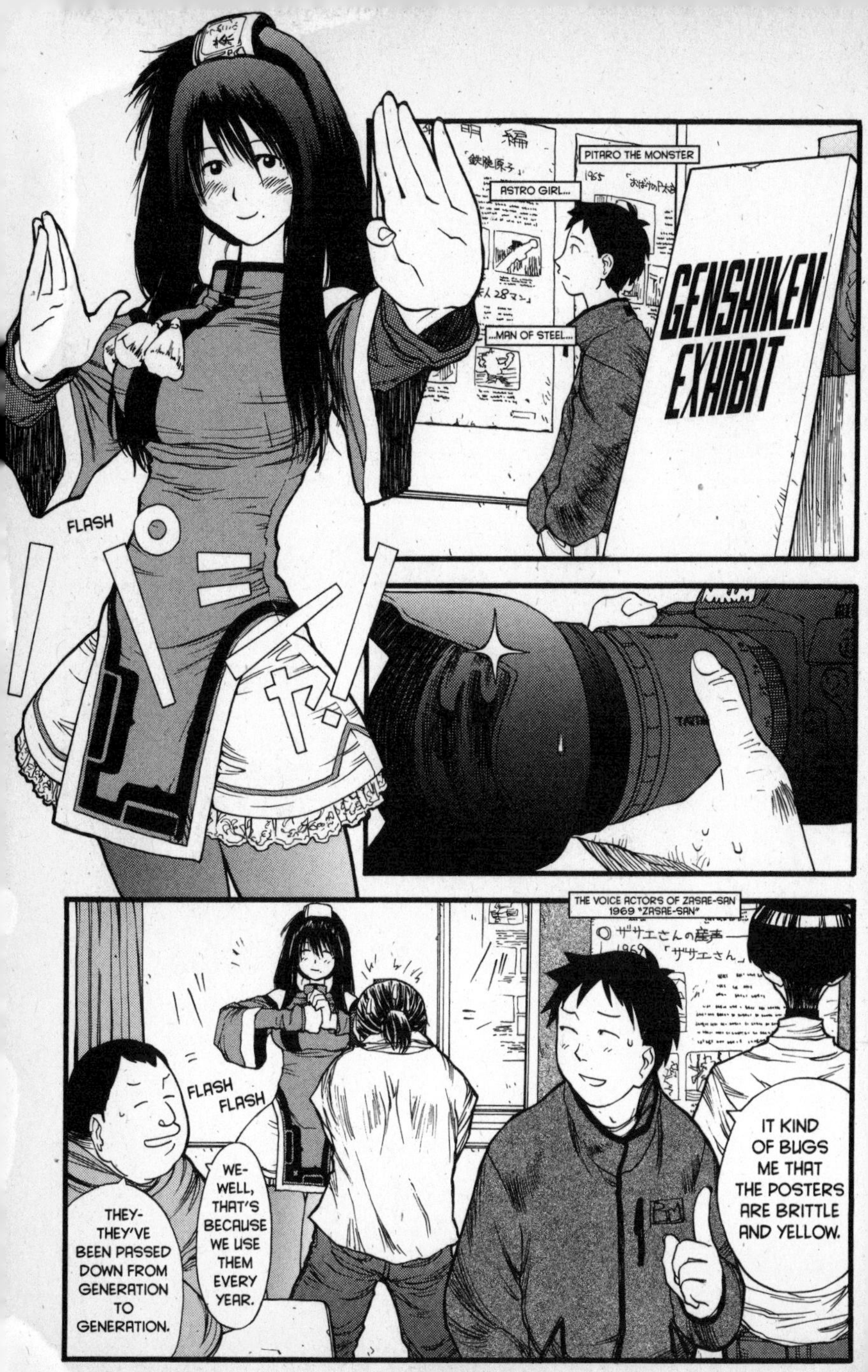

PITARO THE MONSTER
ASTRO GIRL...
...MAN OF STEEL...
GENSHIKEN EXHIBIT
FLASH
THE VOICE ACTORS OF ZASAE-SAN 1969 "ZASAE-SAN"
IT KIND OF BUGS ME THAT THE POSTERS ARE BRITTLE AND YELLOW.
FLASH FLASH
WE-WELL, THAT'S BECAUSE WE USE THEM EVERY YEAR.
THEY-THEY'VE BEEN PASSED DOWN FROM GENERATION TO GENERATION.

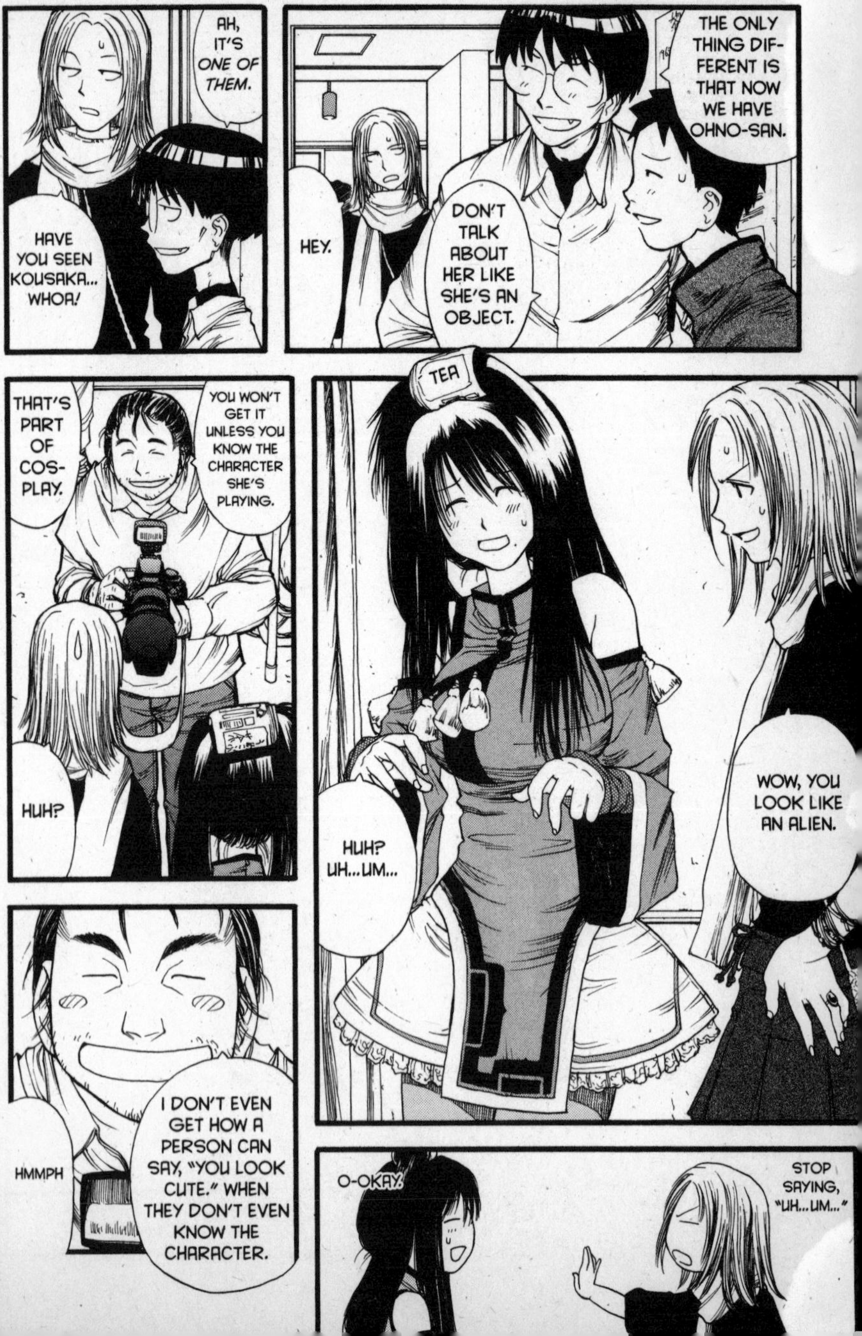
THE ONLY THING DIF- FERENT IS THAT NOW WE HAVE OHNO-SAN.
DON'T TALK ABOUT HER LIKE SHE'S AN OBJECT.
HEY.
AH, IT'S ONE OF THEM.
HAVE YOU SEEN KOUSAKA... WHOA!
TEA
WOW, YOU LOOK LIKE AN ALIEN.
HUH? UH...UM...
YOU WON'T GET IT UNLESS YOU KNOW THE CHARACTER SHE'S PLAYING.
THAT'S PART OF COS- PLAY.
HUH?
I DON'T EVEN GET HOW A PERSON CAN SAY, "YOU LOOK CUTE." WHEN THEY DON'T EVEN KNOW THE CHARACTER.
HMMPH
STOP SAYING, "UH...UM..."
O-OKAY.

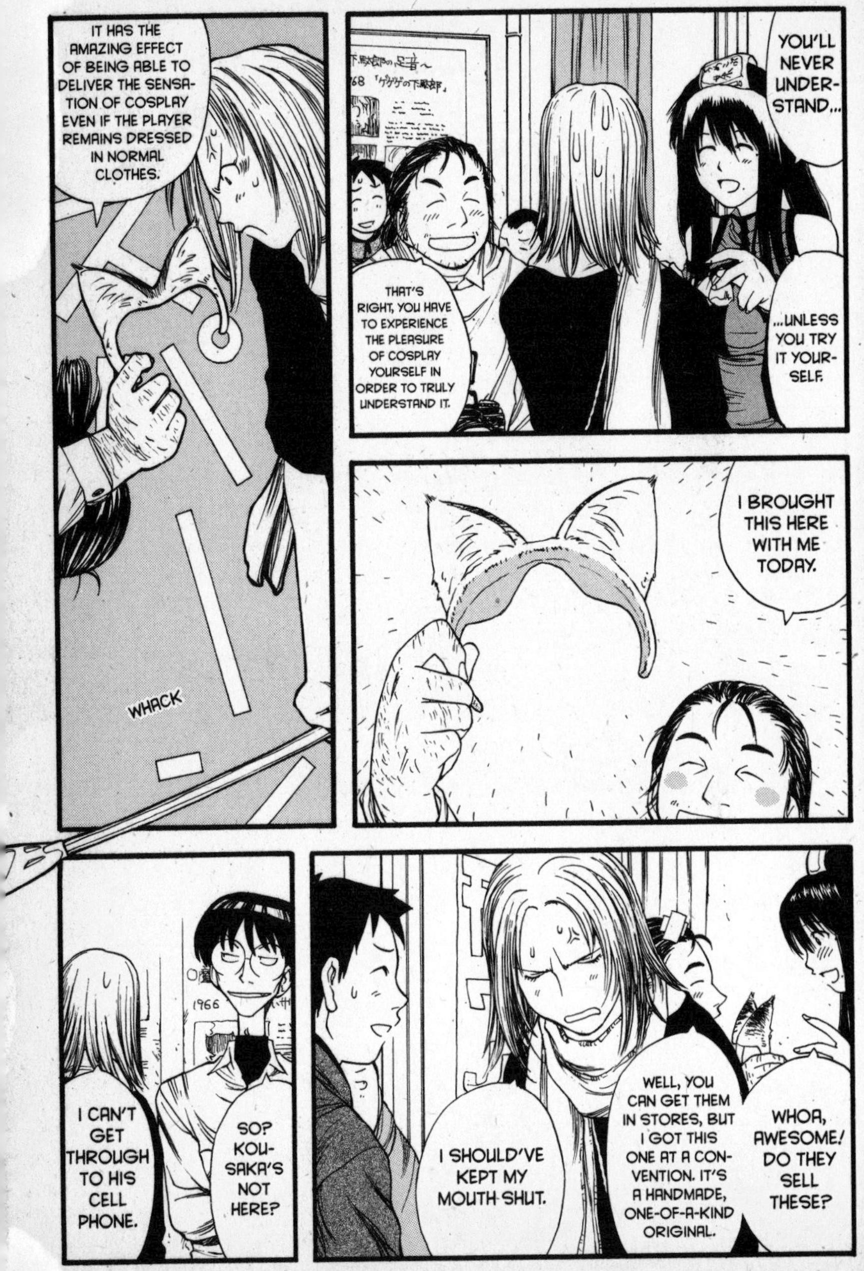
YOU'LL NEVER UNDERSTAND...
...UNLESS YOU TRY IT YOURSELF.
THAT'S RIGHT, YOU HAVE TO EXPERIENCE THE PLEASURE OF COSPLAY YOURSELF IN ORDER TO TRULY UNDERSTAND IT.
I BROUGHT THIS HERE WITH ME TODAY.
IT HAS THE AMAZING EFFECT OF BEING ABLE TO DELIVER THE SENSATION OF COSPLAY EVEN IF THE PLAYER REMAINS DRESSED IN NORMAL CLOTHES.
WHACK
WHOA, AWESOME! DO THEY SELL THESE?
WELL, YOU CAN GET THEM IN STORES, BUT I GOT THIS ONE AT A CONVENTION. IT'S A HANDMADE, ONE-OF-A-KIND ORIGINAL.
I SHOULD'VE KEPT MY MOUTH SHUT.
SO? KOUSAKA'S NOT HERE?
I CAN'T GET THROUGH TO HIS CELL PHONE.

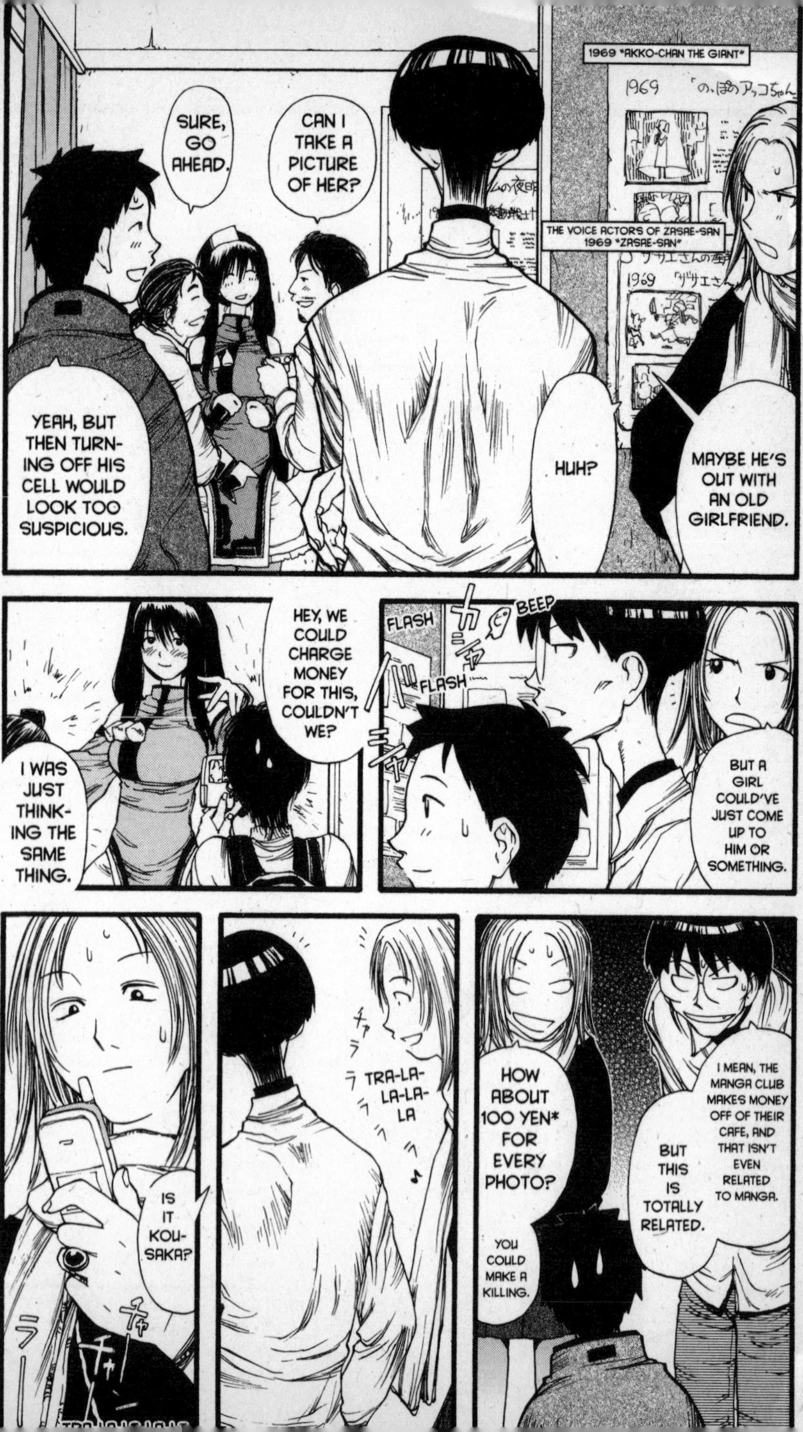
1969 "AKKO-CHAN THE GIANT"
THE VOICE ACTORS OF ZASAE-SAN
1969 "ZASAE-SAN"
MAYBE HE'S OUT WITH AN OLD GIRLFRIEND.
HUH?
CAN I TAKE A PICTURE OF HER?
SURE, GO AHEAD.
YEAH, BUT THEN TURNING OFF HIS CELL WOULD LOOK TOO SUSPICIOUS.
BEEP
FLASH
FLASH
BUT A GIRL COULD'VE JUST COME UP TO HIM OR SOMETHING.
HEY, WE COULD CHARGE MONEY FOR THIS, COULDN'T WE?
I WAS JUST THINKING THE SAME THING.
I MEAN, THE MANGA CLUB MAKES MONEY OFF OF THEIR CAFE, AND THAT ISN'T EVEN RELATED TO MANGA.
BUT THIS IS TOTALLY RELATED.
HOW ABOUT 100 YEN* FOR EVERY PHOTO?
YOU COULD MAKE A KILLING.
TRA-LA-LA-LA-LA
IS IT KOU-SAKA?

*$1

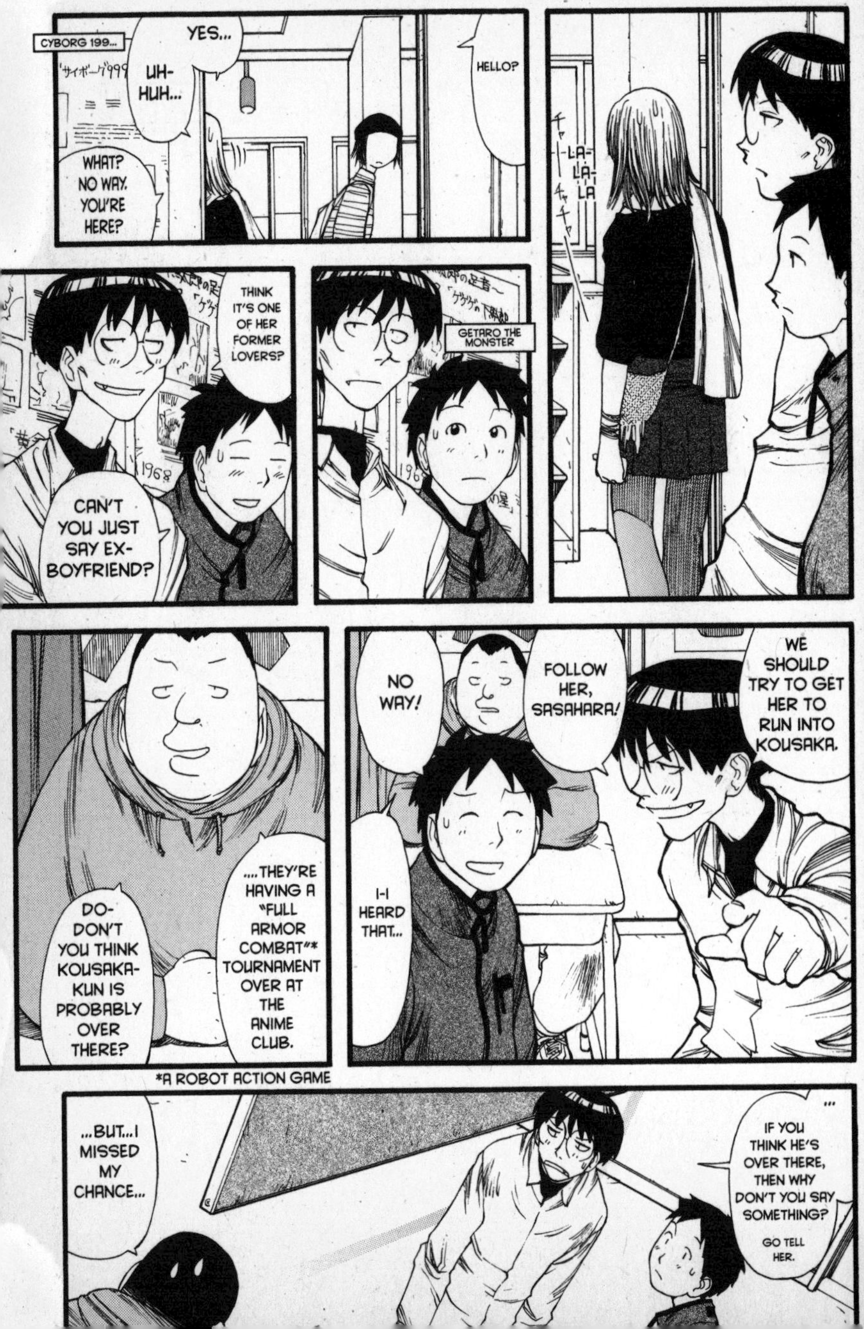
LA-LA-LA
チャーチャチャ
HELLO?
YES...
UH-HUH...
CYBORG 199...
"サイボーグ999
WHAT? NO WAY. YOU'RE HERE?
GETARO THE MONSTER
THINK IT'S ONE OF HER FORMER LOVERS?
CAN'T YOU JUST SAY EX-BOYFRIEND?
WE SHOULD TRY TO GET HER TO RUN INTO KOUSAKA.
FOLLOW HER, SASAHARA!
NO WAY!
I-I HEARD THAT...
....THEY'RE HAVING A "FULL ARMOR COMBAT"* TOURNAMENT OVER AT THE ANIME CLUB.
DO-DON'T YOU THINK KOUSAKA-KUN IS PROBABLY OVER THERE?
...
IF YOU THINK HE'S OVER THERE, THEN WHY DON'T YOU SAY SOMETHING?
GO TELL HER.
...BUT...I MISSED MY CHANCE...

*A ROBOT ACTION GAME

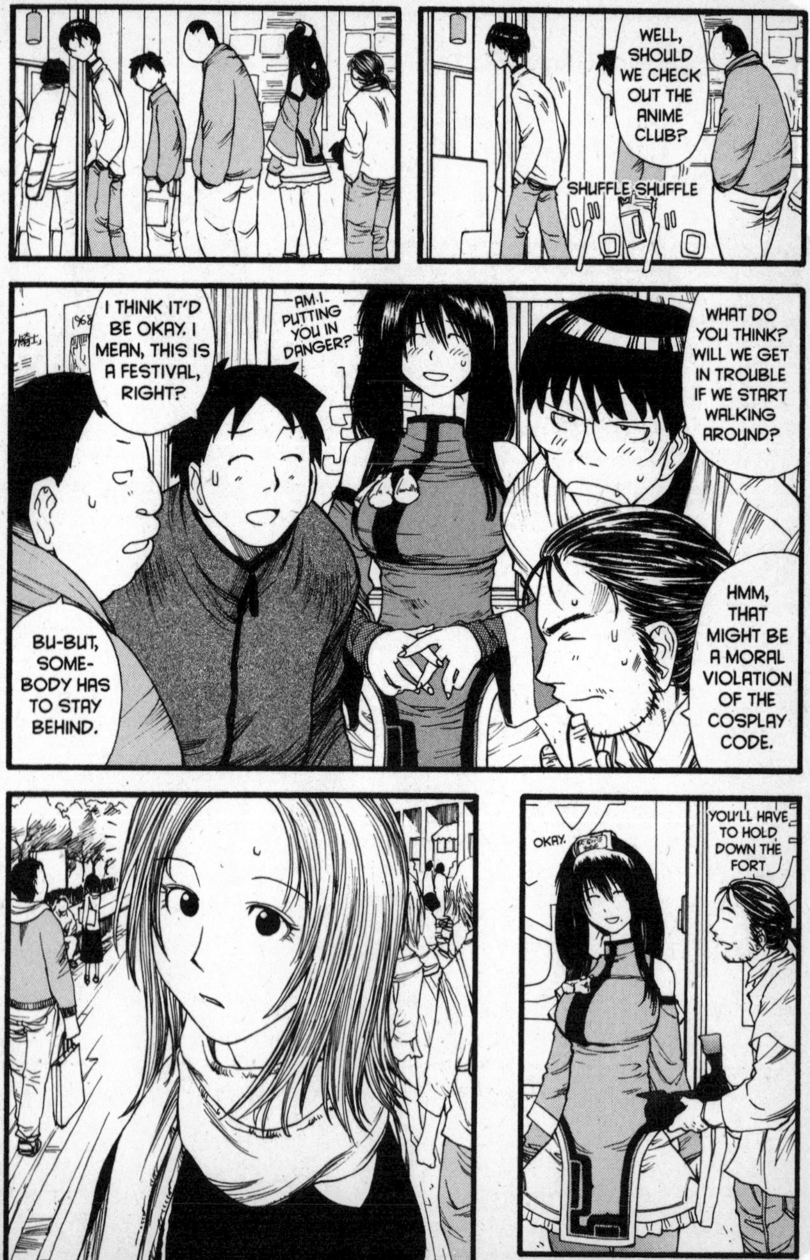
WELL, SHOULD WE CHECK OUT THE ANIME CLUB?
SHUFFLE SHUFFLE
WHAT DO YOU THINK? WILL WE GET IN TROUBLE IF WE START WALKING AROUND?
AM I PUTTING YOU IN DANGER?
I THINK IT'D BE OKAY. I MEAN, THIS IS A FESTIVAL, RIGHT?
HMM, THAT MIGHT BE A MORAL VIOLATION OF THE COSPLAY CODE.
BU-BUT, SOMEBODY HAS TO STAY BEHIND.
YOU'LL HAVE TO HOLD DOWN THE FORT
OKAY.

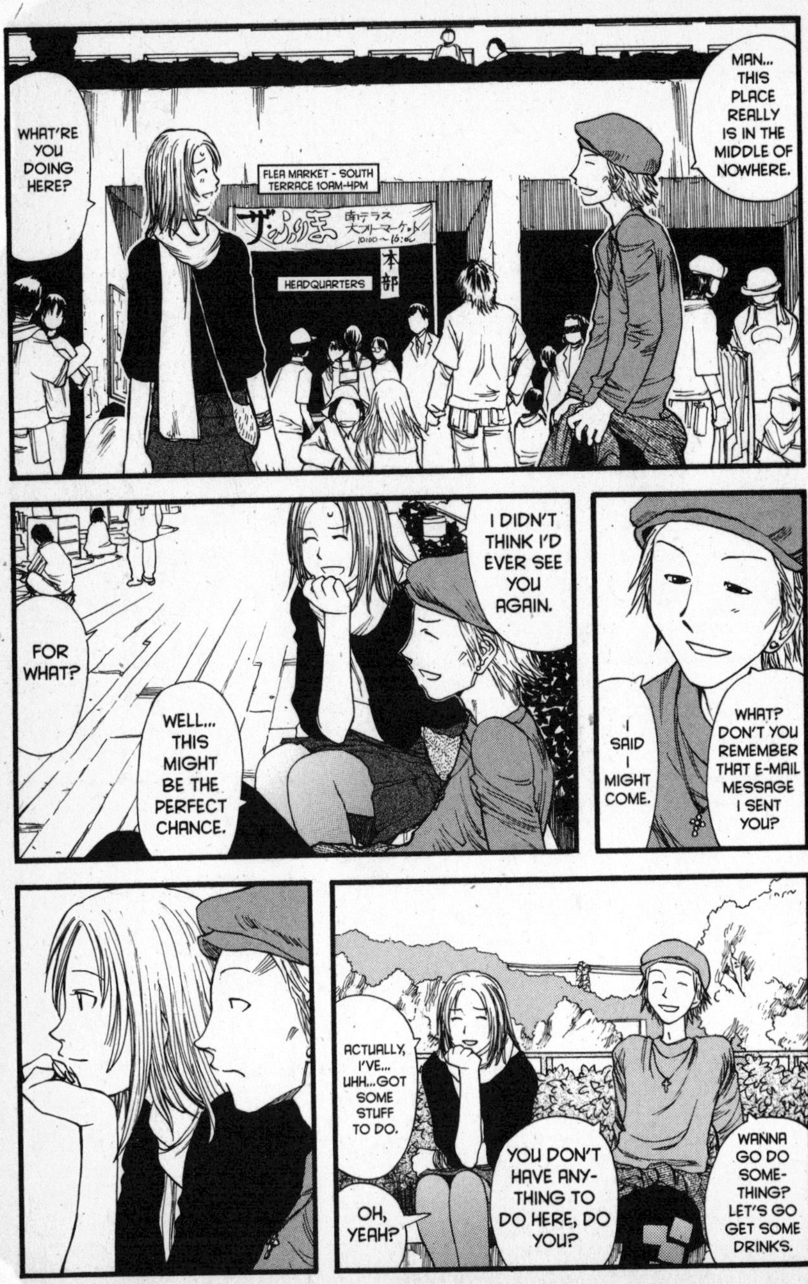
MAN... THIS PLACE REALLY IS IN THE MIDDLE OF NOWHERE.
FLEA MARKET - SOUTH TERRACE 10AM-4PM
南テラス 大フリーマーケット 10:00～16:00
HEADQUARTERS
本部
WHAT'RE YOU DOING HERE?
WHAT? DON'T YOU REMEMBER THAT E-MAIL MESSAGE I SENT YOU?
I SAID I MIGHT COME.
I DIDN'T THINK I'D EVER SEE YOU AGAIN.
FOR WHAT?
WELL... THIS MIGHT BE THE PERFECT CHANCE.
WANNA GO DO SOME-THING? LET'S GO GET SOME DRINKS.
ACTUALLY, I'VE... UHH...GOT SOME STUFF TO DO.
YOU DON'T HAVE ANY-THING TO DO HERE, DO YOU?
OH, YEAH?

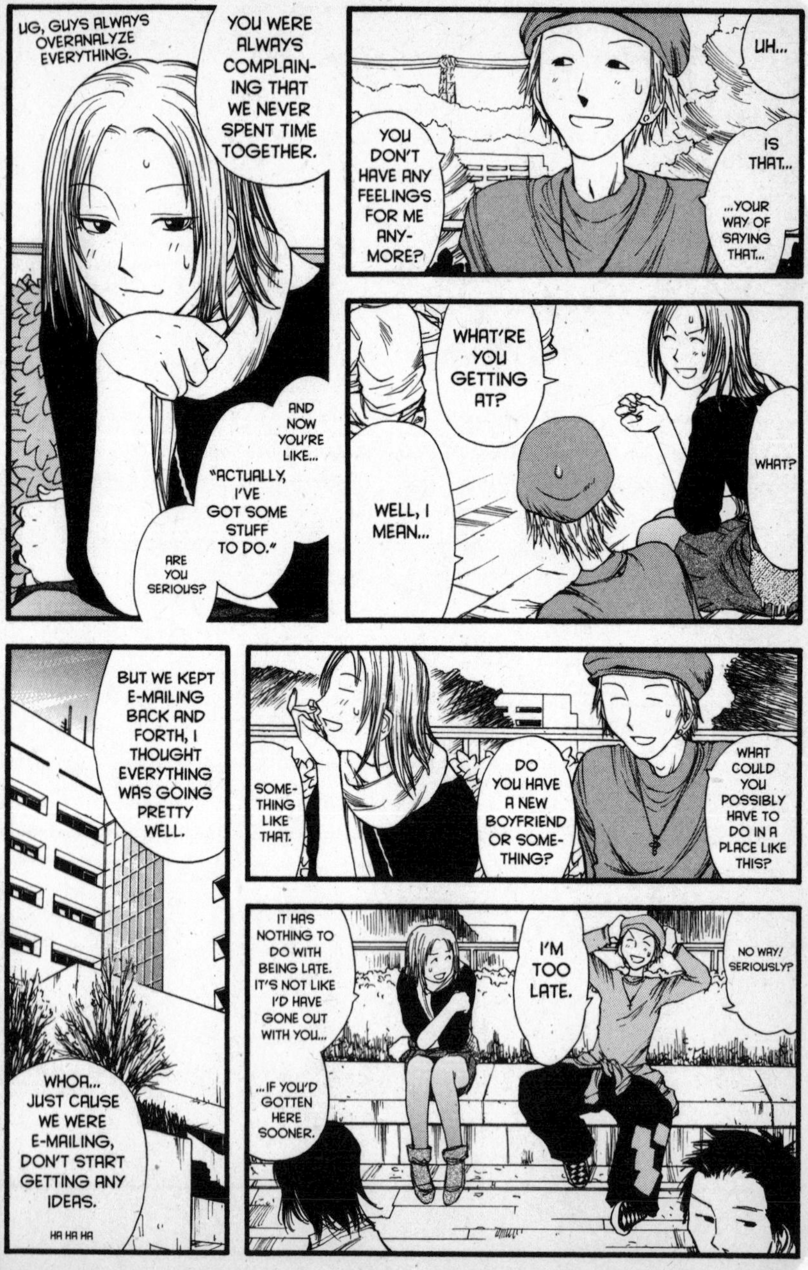
UH...
IS THAT...
...YOUR WAY OF SAYING THAT...
YOU DON'T HAVE ANY FEELINGS FOR ME ANY-MORE?
WHAT?
WHAT'RE YOU GETTING AT?
WELL, I MEAN...
YOU WERE ALWAYS COMPLAIN-ING THAT WE NEVER SPENT TIME TOGETHER.
UG, GUYS ALWAYS OVERANALYZE EVERYTHING.
AND NOW YOU'RE LIKE... "ACTUALLY, I'VE GOT SOME STUFF TO DO."
ARE YOU SERIOUS?
WHAT COULD YOU POSSIBLY HAVE TO DO IN A PLACE LIKE THIS?
DO YOU HAVE A NEW BOYFRIEND OR SOME-THING?
SOME-THING LIKE THAT.
NO WAY! SERIOUSLY?
I'M TOO LATE.
IT HAS NOTHING TO DO WITH BEING LATE. IT'S NOT LIKE I'D HAVE GONE OUT WITH YOU...
...IF YOU'D GOTTEN HERE SOONER.
BUT WE KEPT E-MAILING BACK AND FORTH, I THOUGHT EVERYTHING WAS GOING PRETTY WELL.
WHOA... JUST CAUSE WE WERE E-MAILING, DON'T START GETTING ANY IDEAS.
HA HA HA

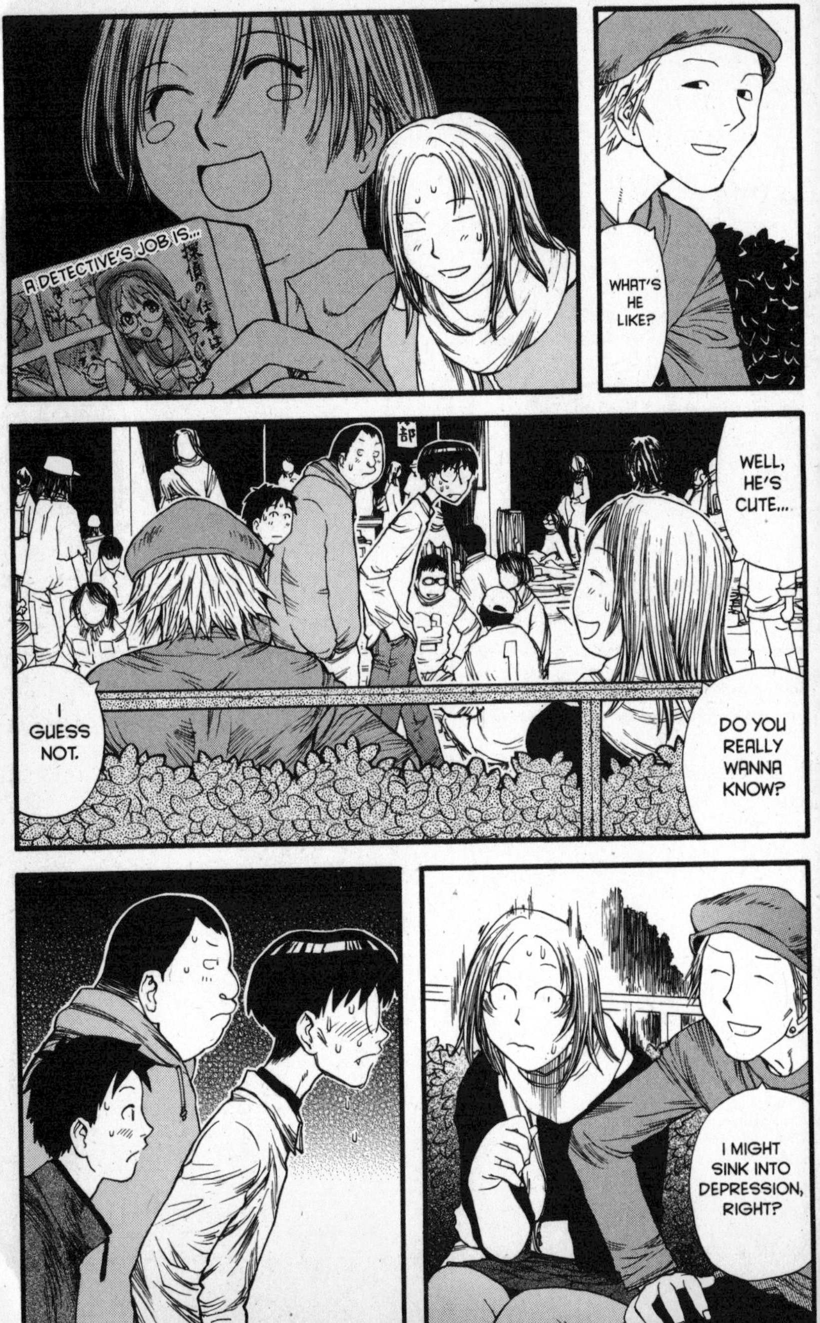
WHAT'S HE LIKE?
A DETECTIVE'S JOB IS...
探偵の仕事は
WELL, HE'S CUTE...
DO YOU REALLY WANNA KNOW?
I GUESS NOT.
I MIGHT SINK INTO DEPRESSION, RIGHT?

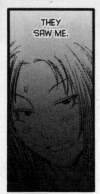

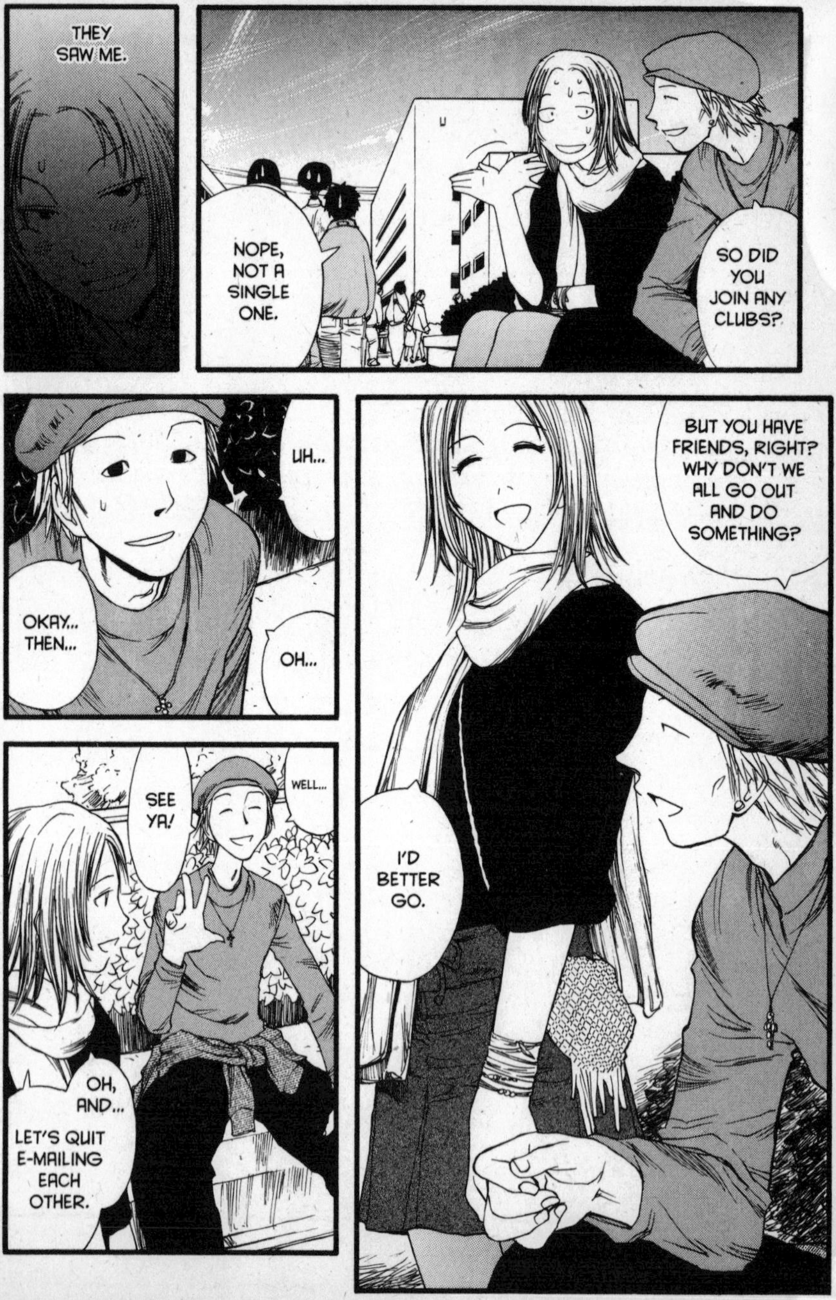
SO DID YOU JOIN ANY CLUBS?
NOPE, NOT A SINGLE ONE.
THEY SAW ME.
BUT YOU HAVE FRIENDS, RIGHT? WHY DON'T WE ALL GO OUT AND DO SOMETHING?
I'D BETTER GO.
UH...
OH...
OKAY... THEN...
WELL...
SEE YA!
OH, AND...
LET'S QUIT E-MAILING EACH OTHER.

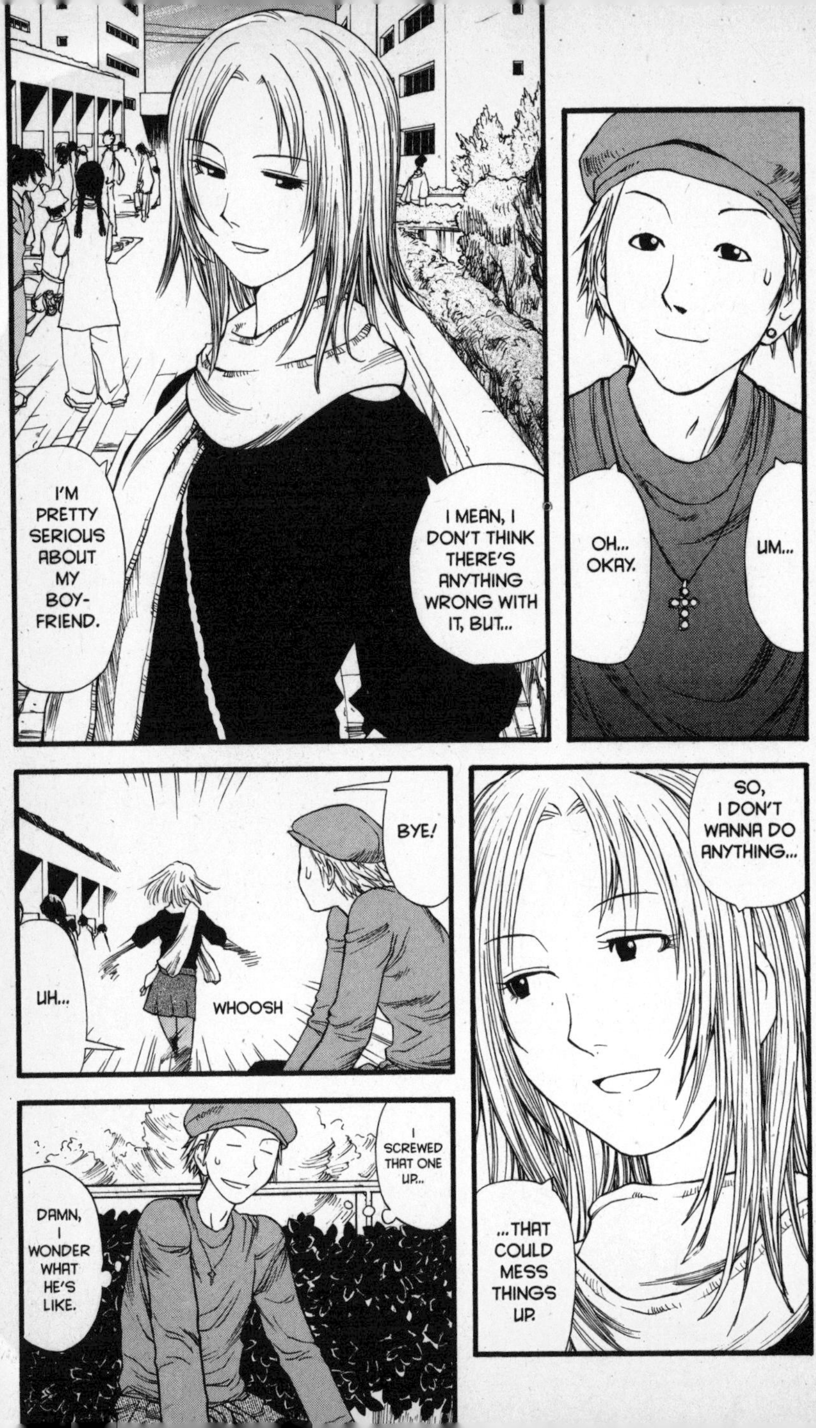
UM...
OH... OKAY.
I MEAN, I DON'T THINK THERE'S ANYTHING WRONG WITH IT, BUT...
I'M PRETTY SERIOUS ABOUT MY BOY-FRIEND.
SO, I DON'T WANNA DO ANYTHING...
...THAT COULD MESS THINGS UP.
BYE!
WHOOSH
UH...
I SCREWED THAT ONE UP...
DAMN, I WONDER WHAT HE'S LIKE.

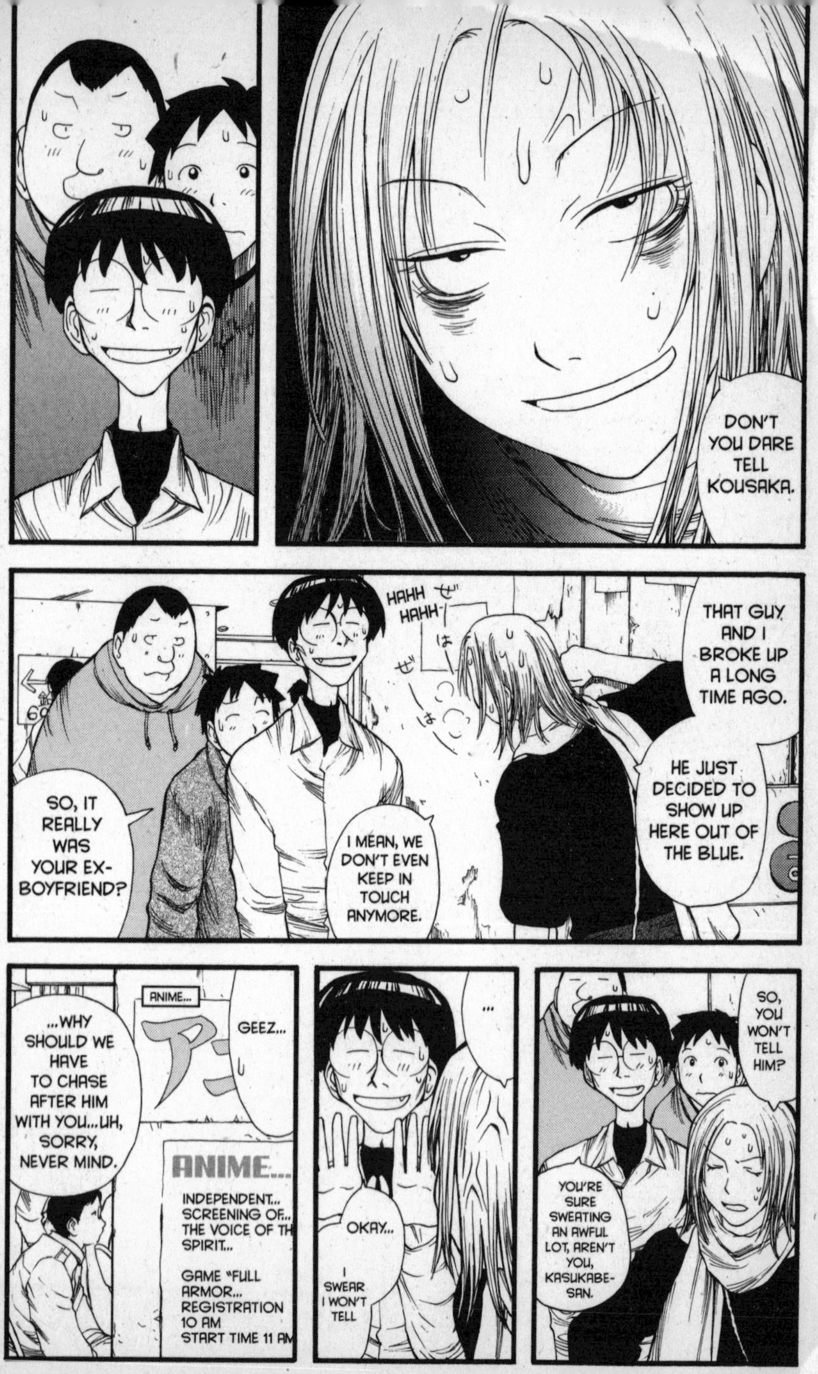
DON'T YOU DARE TELL KOUSAKA.
THAT GUY AND I BROKE UP A LONG TIME AGO.
HE JUST DECIDED TO SHOW UP HERE OUT OF THE BLUE.
HAHH ぜ HAHH
は
ぜ
は
I MEAN, WE DON'T EVEN KEEP IN TOUCH ANYMORE.
SO, IT REALLY WAS YOUR EX-BOYFRIEND?
SO, YOU WON'T TELL HIM?
YOU'RE SURE SWEATING AN AWFUL LOT, AREN'T YOU, KASUKABE-SAN.
...
OKAY...
I SWEAR I WON'T TELL
GEEZ...
...WHY SHOULD WE HAVE TO CHASE AFTER HIM WITH YOU...UH, SORRY, NEVER MIND.
ANIME...
ANIME...
INDEPENDENT... SCREENING OF... THE VOICE OF TH SPIRIT...
GAME "FULL ARMOR... REGISTRATION 10 AM START TIME 11 AM

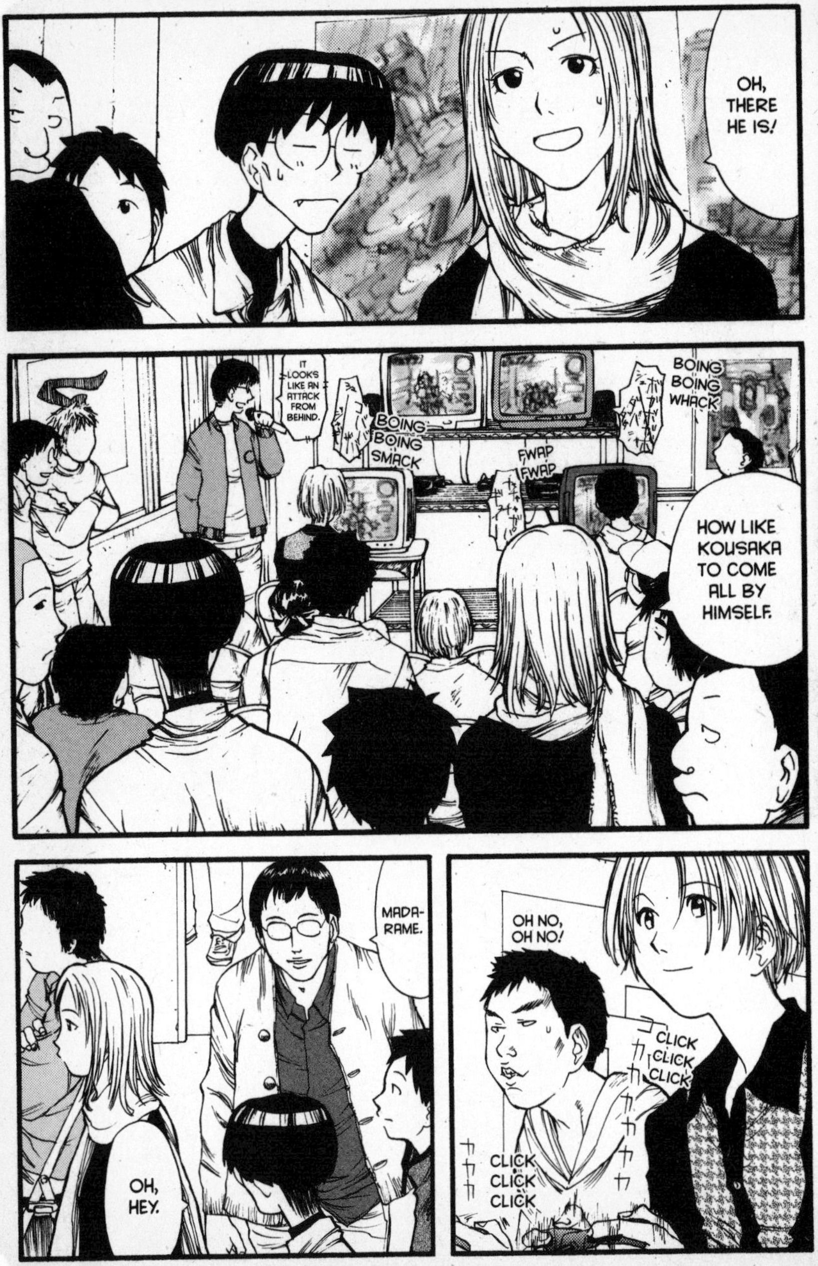
OH, THERE HE IS!
BOING BOING WHACK
HOW LIKE KOUSAKA TO COME ALL BY HIMSELF.
FWAP FWAP
BOING BOING SMACK
IT LOOKS LIKE AN ATTACK FROM BEHIND.
OH NO, OH NO!
CLICK CLICK CLICK
CLICK CLICK CLICK
MADARAME.
OH, HEY.

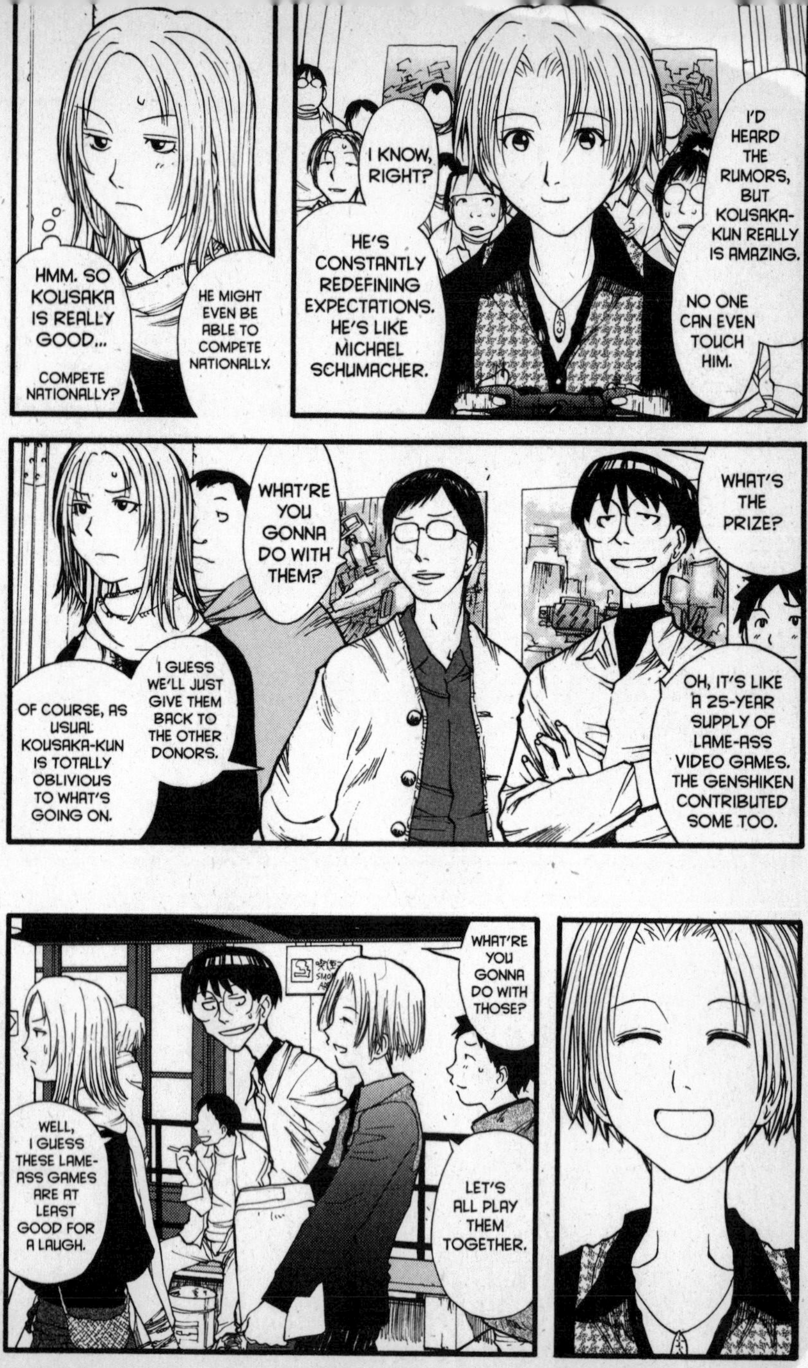
I'D HEARD THE RUMORS, BUT KOUSAKA-KUN REALLY IS AMAZING.
NO ONE CAN EVEN TOUCH HIM.
I KNOW, RIGHT?
HE'S CONSTANTLY REDEFINING EXPECTATIONS. HE'S LIKE MICHAEL SCHUMACHER.
HE MIGHT EVEN BE ABLE TO COMPETE NATIONALLY.
HMM. SO KOUSAKA IS REALLY GOOD...
COMPETE NATIONALLY?
WHAT'S THE PRIZE?
OH, IT'S LIKE A 25-YEAR SUPPLY OF LAME-ASS VIDEO GAMES. THE GENSHIKEN CONTRIBUTED SOME TOO.
WHAT'RE YOU GONNA DO WITH THEM?
I GUESS WE'LL JUST GIVE THEM BACK TO THE OTHER DONORS.
OF COURSE, AS USUAL KOUSAKA-KUN IS TOTALLY OBLIVIOUS TO WHAT'S GOING ON.
WHAT'RE YOU GONNA DO WITH THOSE?
LET'S ALL PLAY THEM TOGETHER.
WELL, I GUESS THESE LAME-ASS GAMES ARE AT LEAST GOOD FOR A LAUGH.

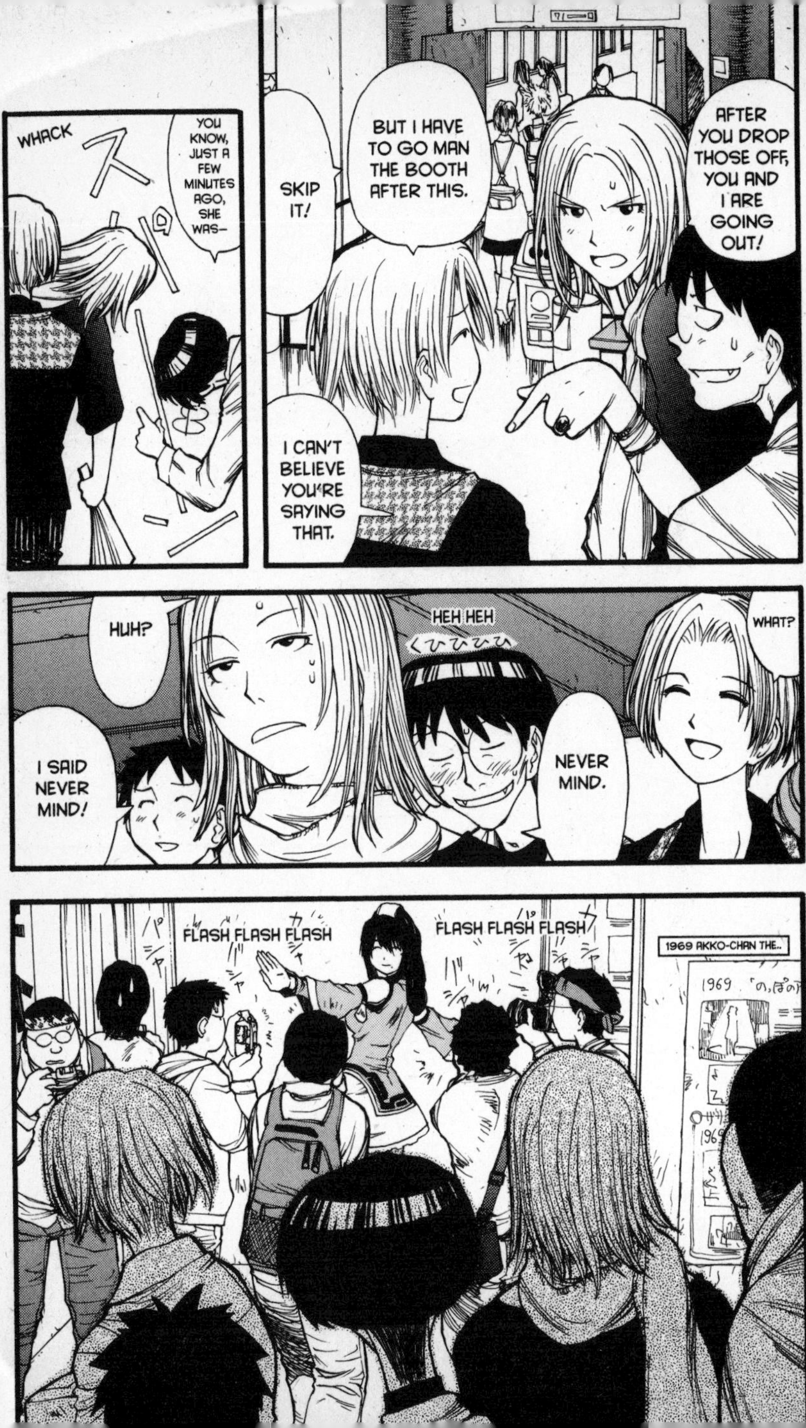
AFTER YOU DROP THOSE OFF, YOU AND I ARE GOING OUT!
BUT I HAVE TO GO MAN THE BOOTH AFTER THIS.
SKIP IT!
I CAN'T BELIEVE YOU'RE SAYING THAT.
YOU KNOW, JUST A FEW MINUTES AGO, SHE WAS—
WHACK
WHAT?
HEH HEH
くひひひひ
NEVER MIND.
HUH?
I SAID NEVER MIND!
1969 AKKO-CHAN THE..
FLASH FLASH FLASH
FLASH FLASH FLASH

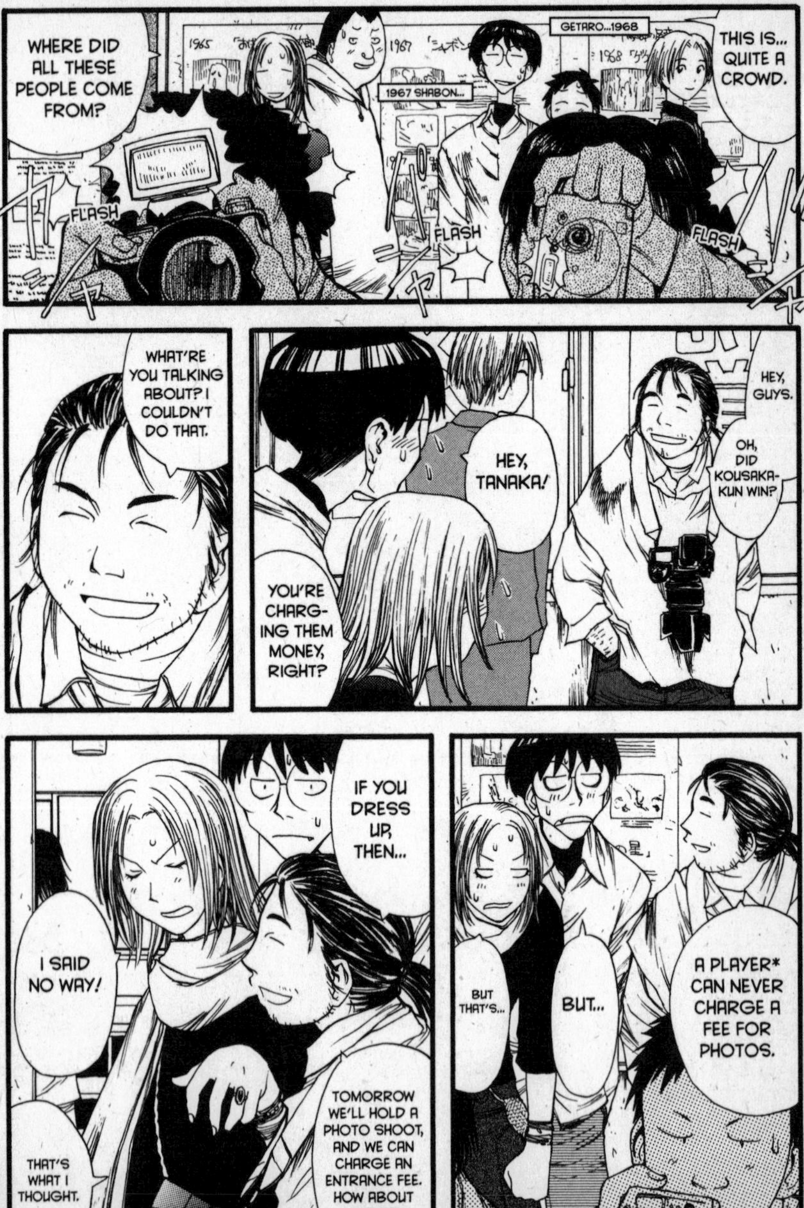
THIS IS... QUITE A CROWD.
GETARO...1968
1967 SHABON...
WHERE DID ALL THESE PEOPLE COME FROM?
FLASH
FLASH
FLASH
HEY, GUYS.
OH, DID KOUSAKA-KUN WIN?
HEY, TANAKA!
YOU'RE CHARGING THEM MONEY, RIGHT?
WHAT'RE YOU TALKING ABOUT? I COULDN'T DO THAT.
A PLAYER* CAN NEVER CHARGE A FEE FOR PHOTOS.
BUT...
BUT THAT'S...
IF YOU DRESS UP, THEN...
TOMORROW WE'LL HOLD A PHOTO SHOOT, AND WE CAN CHARGE AN ENTRANCE FEE. HOW ABOUT THAT?
I SAID NO WAY!
THAT'S WHAT I THOUGHT.

*A COSPLAYER

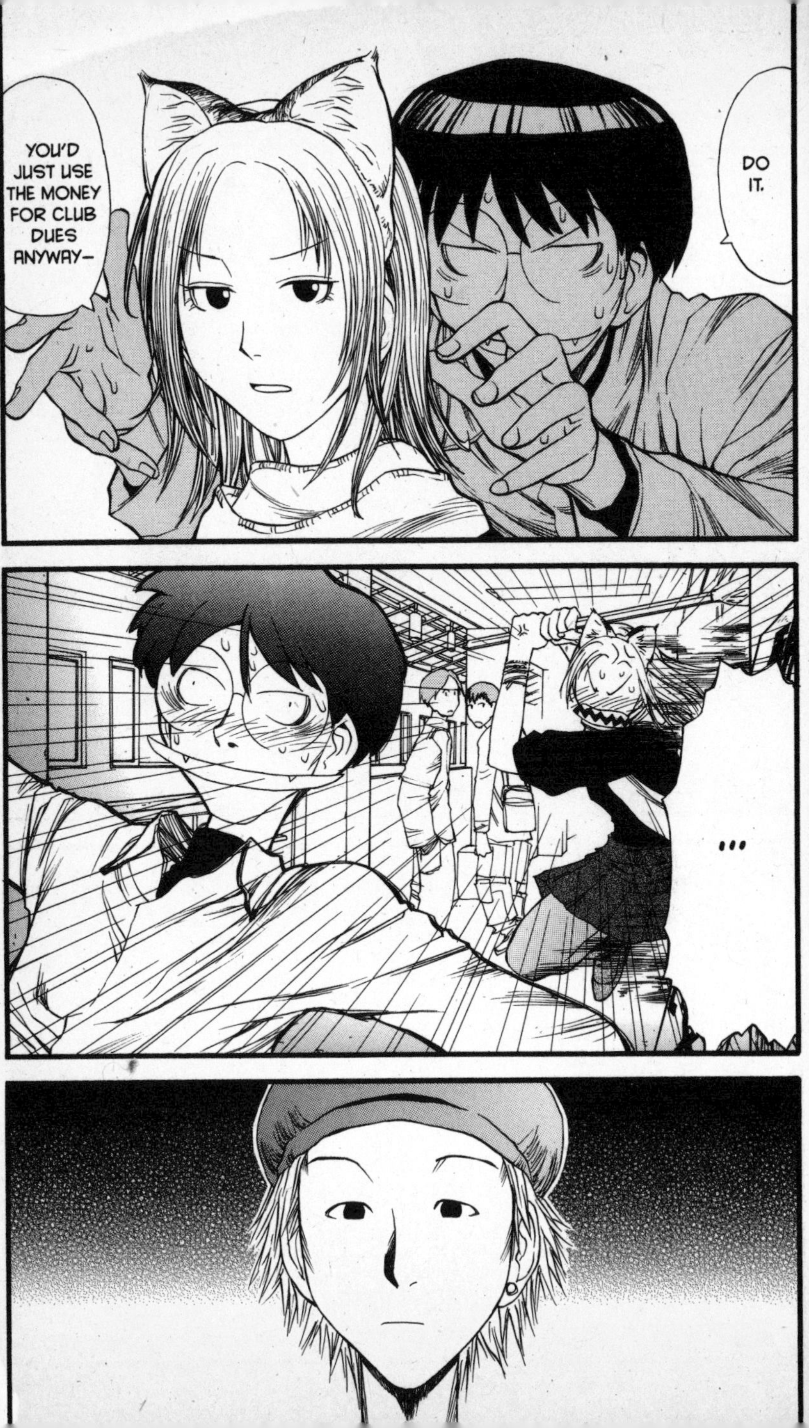
DO IT.
YOU'D JUST USE THE MONEY FOR CLUB DUES ANYWAY—
...

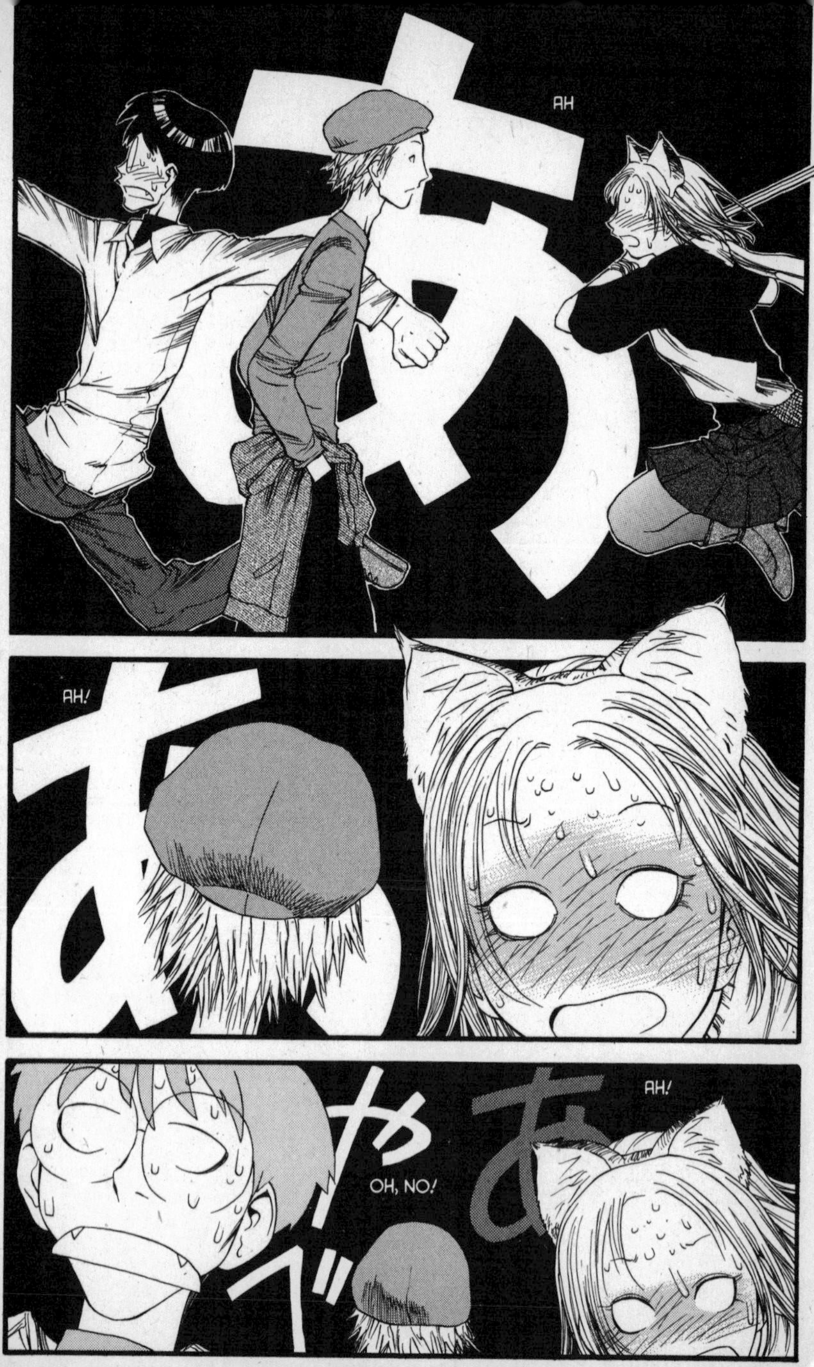
AH
AH!
AH!
OH, NO!

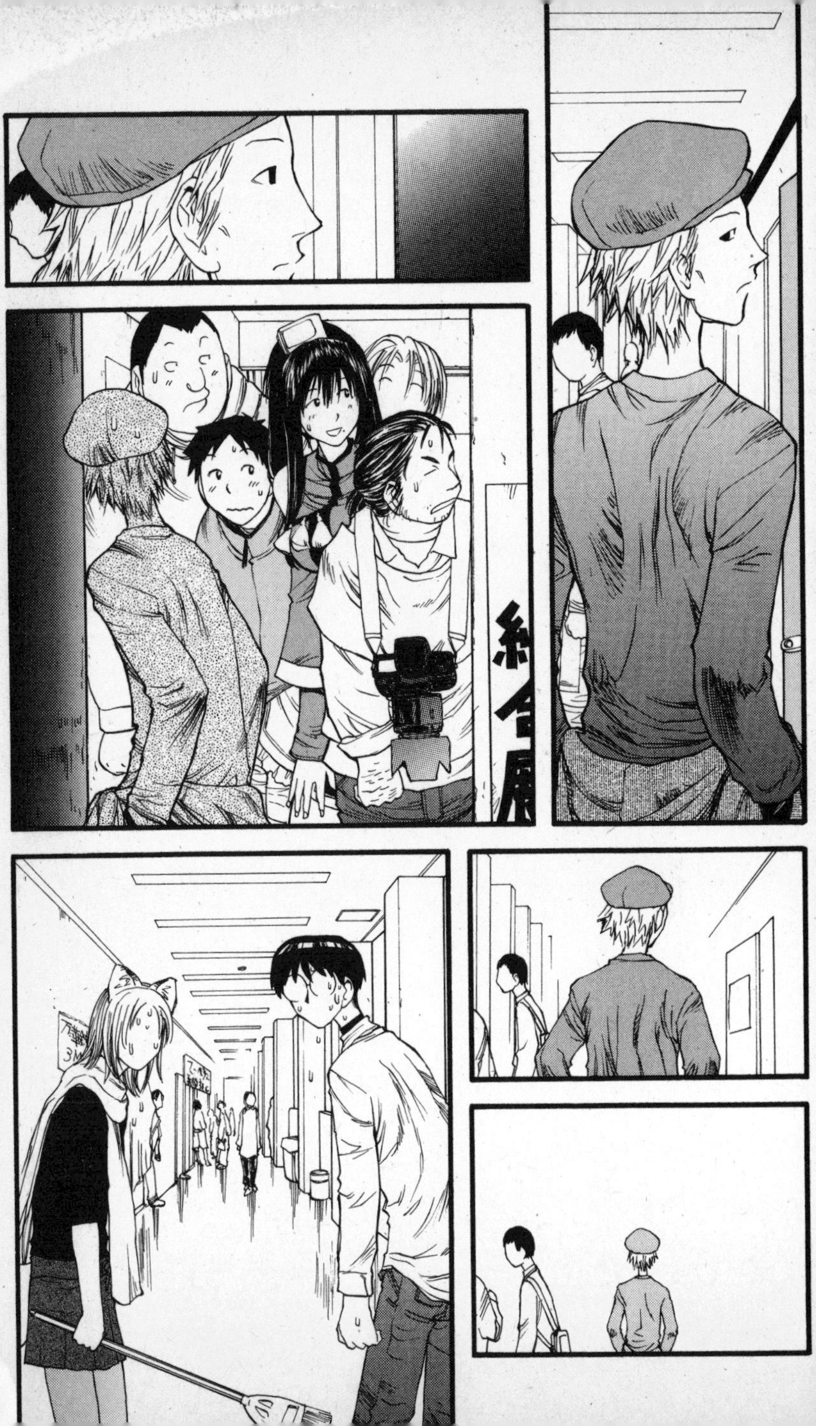

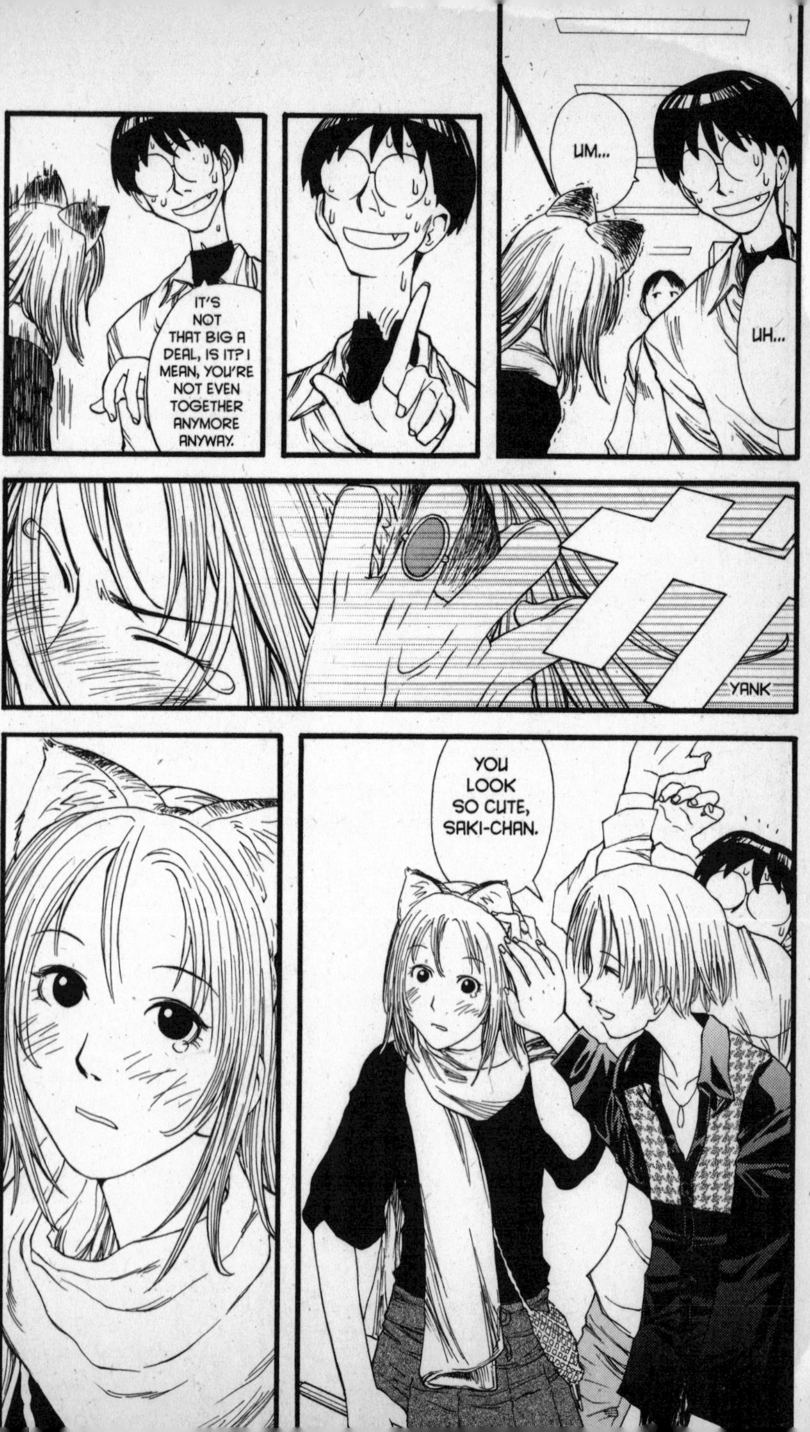
UM...
UH...
IT'S NOT THAT BIG A DEAL, IS IT? I MEAN, YOU'RE NOT EVEN TOGETHER ANYMORE ANYWAY.
YANK
YOU LOOK SO CUTE, SAKI-CHAN.

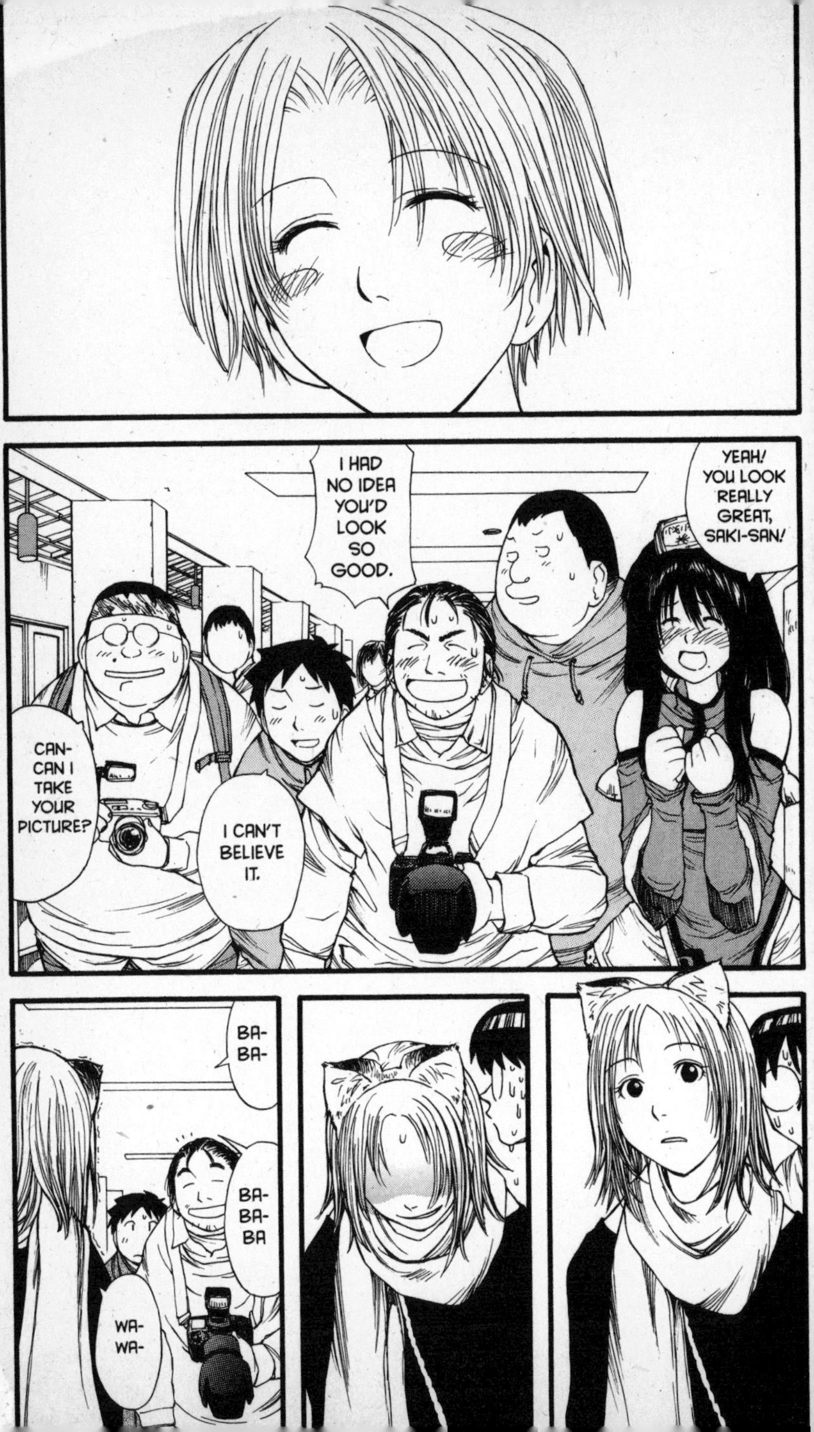
YEAH! YOU LOOK REALLY GREAT, SAKI-SAN!
I HAD NO IDEA YOU'D LOOK SO GOOD.
I CAN'T BELIEVE IT.
CAN- CAN I TAKE YOUR PICTURE?
BA- BA-
BA- BA- BA
WA- WA-

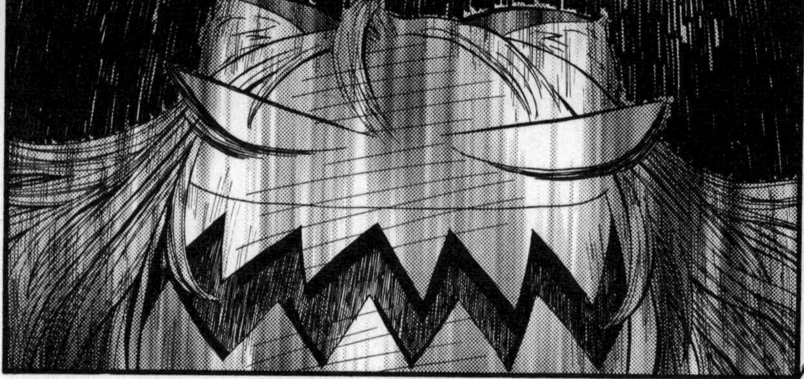

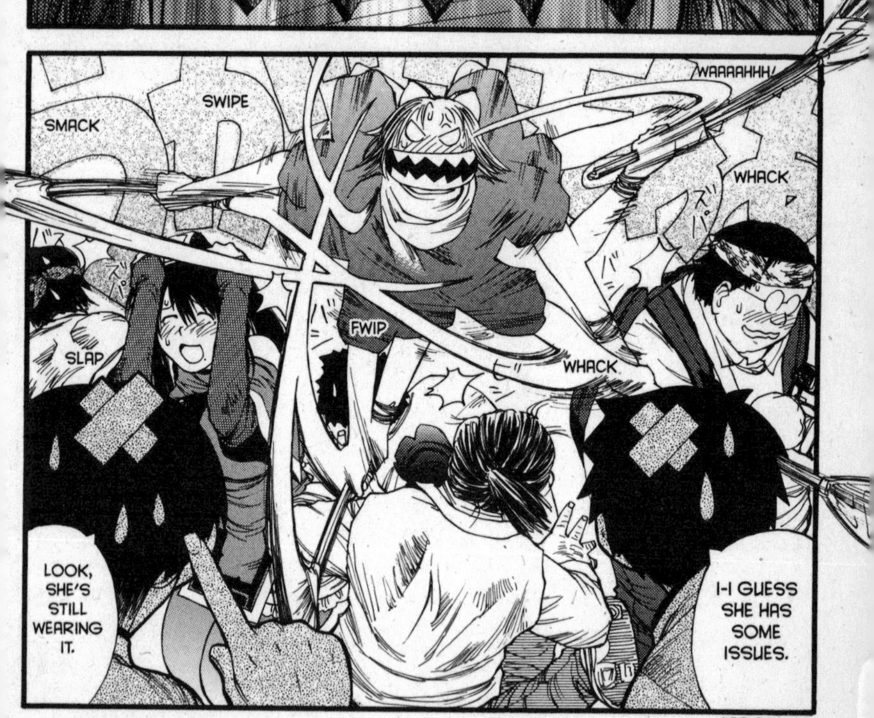
WAAAAHHH!
WHACK
SWIPE
SMACK
FWIP
WHACK
SLAP
I-I GUESS SHE HAS SOME ISSUES.
LOOK, SHE'S STILL WEARING IT.

*ABOUT $2

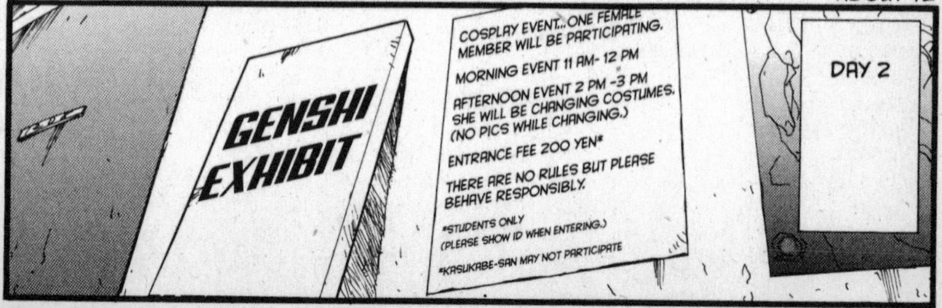
DAY 2
COSPLAY EVENT...ONE FEMALE MEMBER WILL BE PARTICIPATING.
MORNING EVENT 11 AM- 12 PM
AFTERNOON EVENT 2 PM -3 PM
SHE WILL BE CHANGING COSTUMES.
(NO PICS WHILE CHANGING.)
ENTRANCE FEE 200 YEN*
THERE ARE NO RULES BUT PLEASE BEHAVE RESPONSIBLY.
*STUDENTS ONLY
(PLEASE SHOW ID WHEN ENTERING.)
*KASUKABE-SAN MAY NOT PARTICIPATE
GENSHI EXHIBIT

END OF CHAPTER 7

THE GENSHIKEN MEMBERS PICK...

# KUJI-UN

**...THE MOST NOTABLE SCENES**

TAKEN FROM THE GENSHIKEN'S SPORADICALLY PUBLISHED ZINE "MEBAETAME"

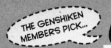

## MY FAVORITE SCENE FROM *KUJI-UN* PART 1 BY "72-YEAR-OLD PIT VIPER"

FROM PAGE 56 OF TANKOBON VOL. 4

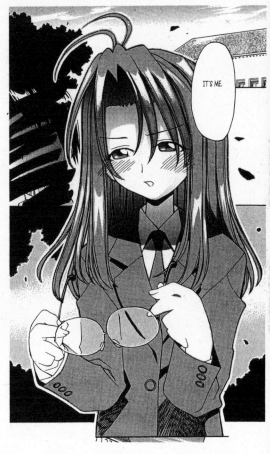

IT'S ME.

IT'S ME. STARTING TODAY, WE'LL BE DOING A SERIES CALLED "MY FAVORITE SCENE FROM KUJI-UN." WE GET TO USE COPIES OF THE ORIGINAL ART BECAUSE THIS ZINE IS JUST FOR US. WE MAY HAVE ALTERED SOME PARTS TO SUIT OUR TASTES.

SO, FOR MY FAVORITE SCENE, I'VE CHOSEN THIS SCENE WITH SHINOBU-SENSEI. EVERY TIME I SEE SHINOBU-SENSEI I GET ALL EXCITED. SO FOR ME, EVERY SHINOBU SCENE IS MY FAVORITE SCENE...HEH. THE WAY THAT HER PERSONALITY CHANGES WHEN SHE TAKES HER GLASSES OFF IS SORT OF LIKE A TUG OF WAR BETWEEN INSTINCT AND REASON. IT'S ALSO A SIGN OF HER OWN REPRESSION. IN A WAY, SHE'S ALMOST DECEIVING HERSELF. WHAT MAKES HER CHARACTER REALLY COMPLEX IS THE FACT THAT SHE DOESN'T EXACTLY BECOME A DOMINATRIX WHEN HER GLASSES ARE OFF.

I THOUGHT SHE WOULD REMOVE HER GLASSES IN ORDER TO REVEAL HER TRUE DOMINATRIX SELF TO KABURAKI, AND SAY, "LOOK AT THE REAL ME." BUT THAT DIDN'T HAPPEN. INSTEAD, SHE APPEARED AS A SLIGHTLY MORE RELAXED, MATURE VERSION OF HER USUALLY SPACEY SELF. FROM THAT POINT ON, SHE STOPPED CHANGING PERSONALITIES WHENEVER SHE REMOVED HER GLASSES, AND SHE SETTLED ON ONE PERSONALITY. I GUESS THE REAL QUESTION WASN'T WHETHER HER PERSONALITY WAS THAT OF THE DOMINATRIX OR THE SPACEY GIRL. THE GLASSES WERE NOT A SYMBOL OF HER REPRESSION, THEY WERE MERELY A TOOL USED TO INITIATE A PERSONALITY SWITCH. THE SWITCH WAS SIMPLY A WAY TO SHOW THAT HER MENTAL STATE WAS NOT YET FULLY DEVELOPED. I'M ACTUALLY NOT TOTALLY SATISFIED WITH THIS USE OF THE GLASSES (LAUGHS). I THINK THE GLASSES SHOULD BE A REPRESENTATION OF HER REPRESSION AND OF HER RESISTANCE TO THE OUTSIDE WORLD...THAT'S HOW I FEEL, BUT THEN AGAIN, IF THE DOMINATRIX VERSION WERE HER TRUE SELF, IT WOULD TOTALLY CHANGE HER CHARACTER...AND THE MANGA (BITTER LAUGHS). SHE CAN'T BE A FULL-TIME DOMINATRIX. LATELY HER FACIAL EXPRESSIONS AND HER LOOK, WHETHER IT'S HER GIRLISH LOOK WHEN HER GLASSES ARE ON, OR HER MATURE LOOK WHEN HER GLASSES ARE OFF, HAVE GOTTEN 50% MORE EVIL (LAUGHS). ANYWAY, SOMETIMES WHEN I CATCH SIGHT OF HER, I GET SO EXCITED I JUST BURST INTO TEARS. I FEEL LIKE I'M GONNA FALL APART (TEARS)...TEE HEE. ANYWAY, I HOPE WE GET TO HEAR ETSUKO SAKURA DO HER VOICE. THAT'S ALL! NEXT, IT'S BENJAMIN TAKEYO'S TURN. [PIT VIPER]

## CHAPTER 7- MOMENTS LATER

### LET'S PLAY

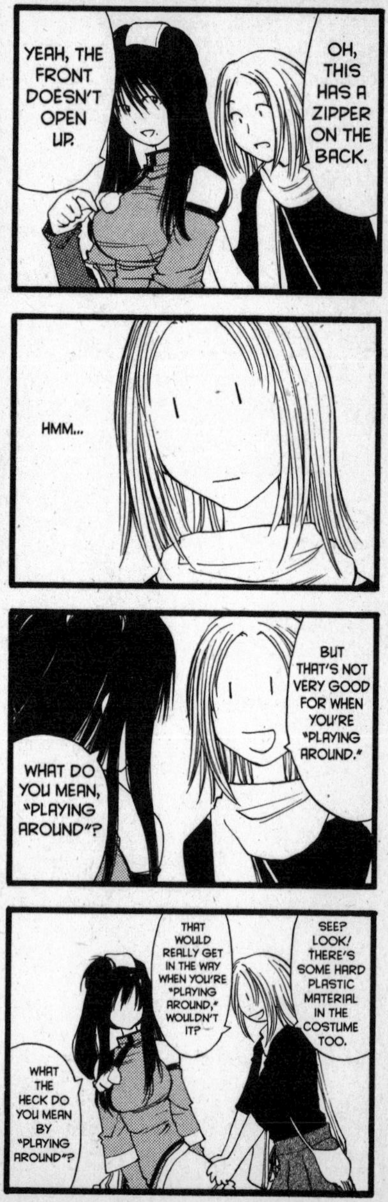
OH, THIS HAS A ZIPPER ON THE BACK.
YEAH, THE FRONT DOESN'T OPEN UP.
HMM...
BUT THAT'S NOT VERY GOOD FOR WHEN YOU'RE "PLAYING AROUND."
WHAT DO YOU MEAN, "PLAYING AROUND"?
SEE? LOOK! THERE'S SOME HARD PLASTIC MATERIAL IN THE COSTUME TOO.
THAT WOULD REALLY GET IN THE WAY WHEN YOU'RE "PLAYING AROUND," WOULDN'T IT?
WHAT THE HECK DO YOU MEAN BY "PLAYING AROUND"?

### CRAFTSMEN

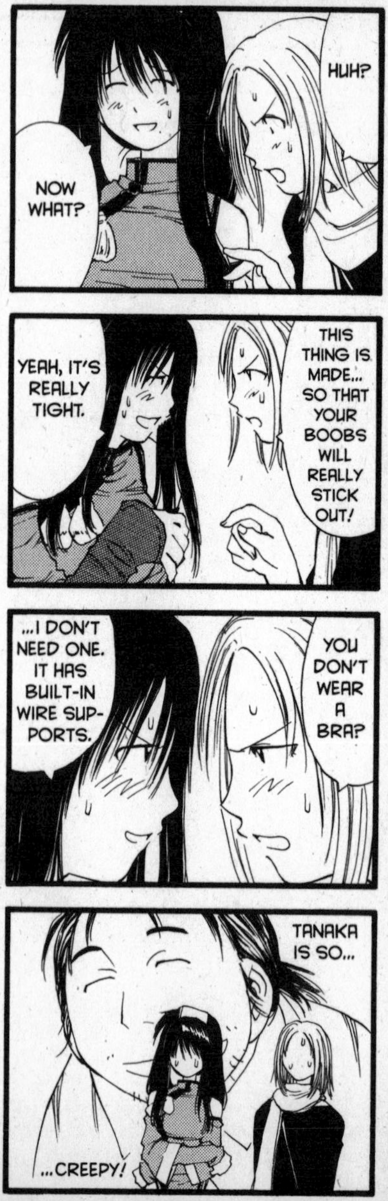
HUH?
NOW WHAT?
THIS THING IS MADE... SO THAT YOUR BOOBS WILL REALLY STICK OUT!
YEAH, IT'S REALLY TIGHT.
YOU DON'T WEAR A BRA?
...I DON'T NEED ONE. IT HAS BUILT-IN WIRE SUPPORTS.
TANAKA IS SO...
...CREEPY!

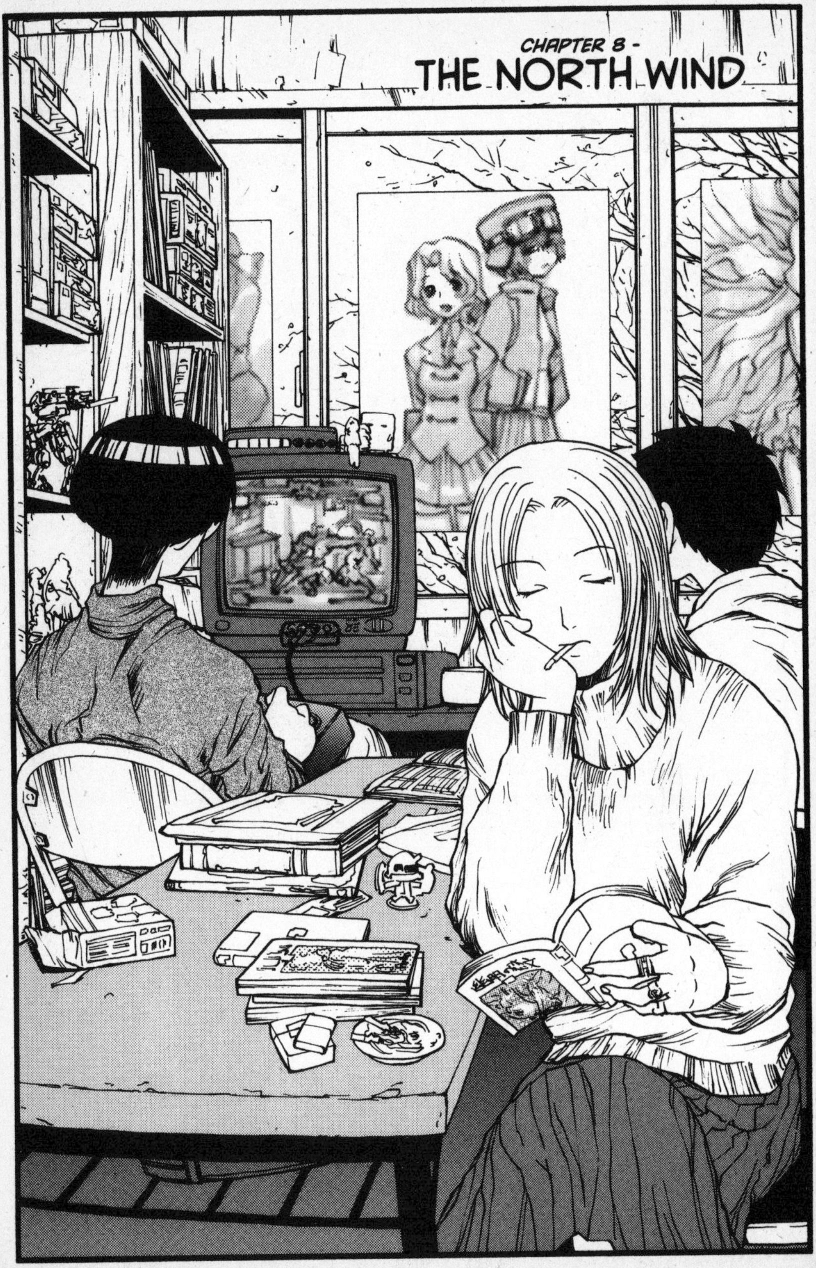
CHAPTER 8 -
THE NORTH WIND

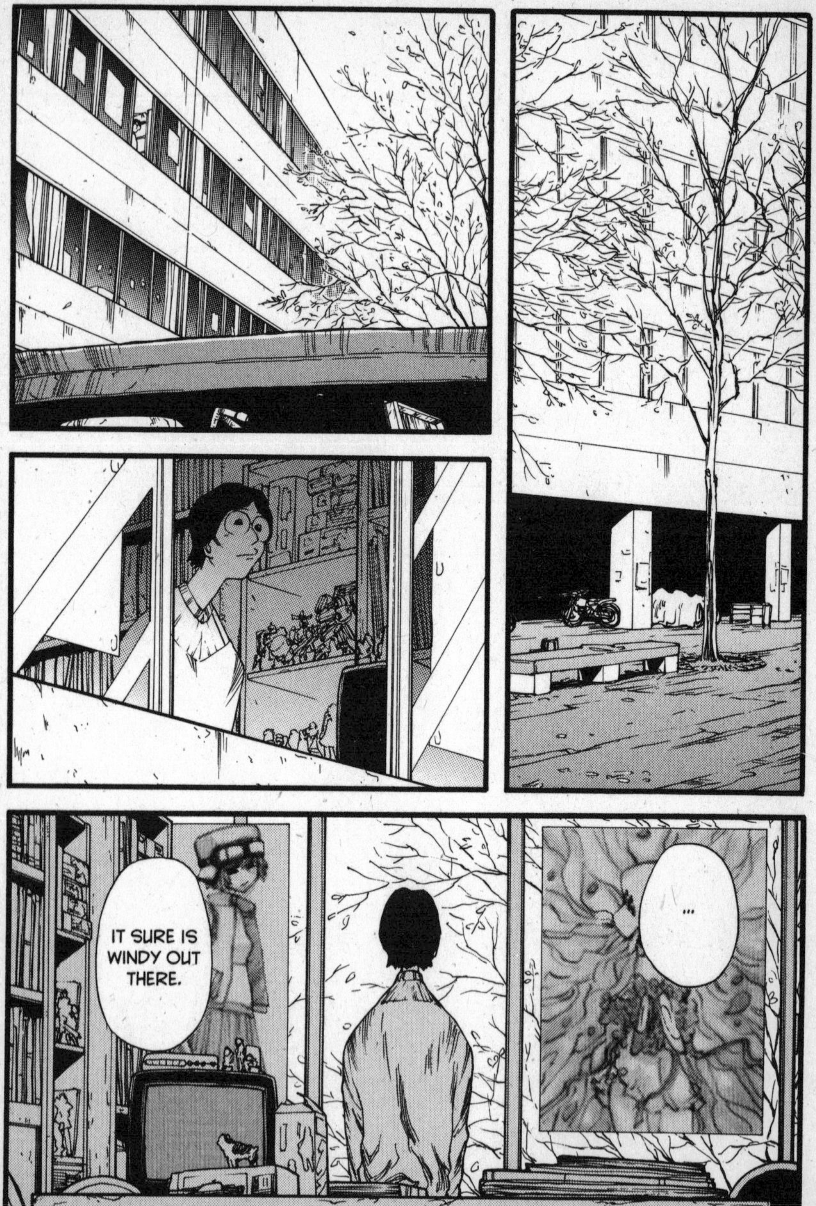
...
IT SURE IS WINDY OUT THERE.

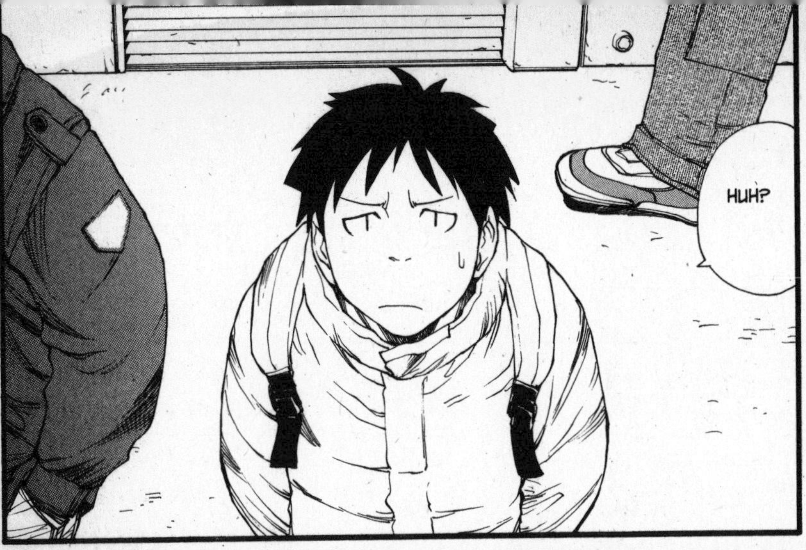
HUH?

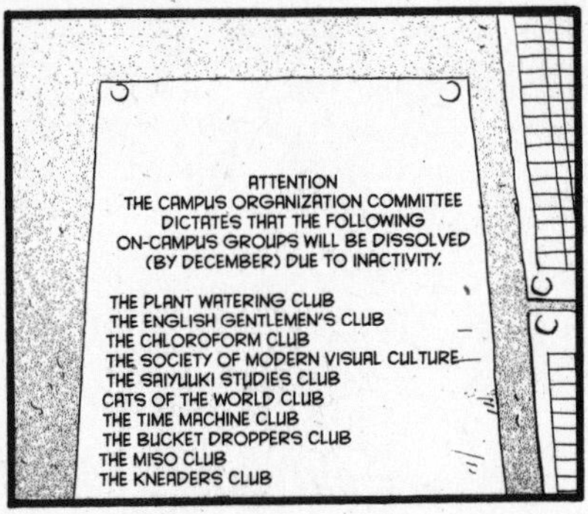
ATTENTION
THE CAMPUS ORGANIZATION COMMITTEE DICTATES THAT THE FOLLOWING ON-CAMPUS GROUPS WILL BE DISSOLVED (BY DECEMBER) DUE TO INACTIVITY.
THE PLANT WATERING CLUB
THE ENGLISH GENTLEMEN'S CLUB
THE CHLOROFORM CLUB
THE SOCIETY OF MODERN VISUAL CULTURE
THE SAIYUUKI STUDIES CLUB
CATS OF THE WORLD CLUB
THE TIME MACHINE CLUB
THE BUCKET DROPPERS CLUB
THE MISO CLUB
THE KNEADERS CLUB

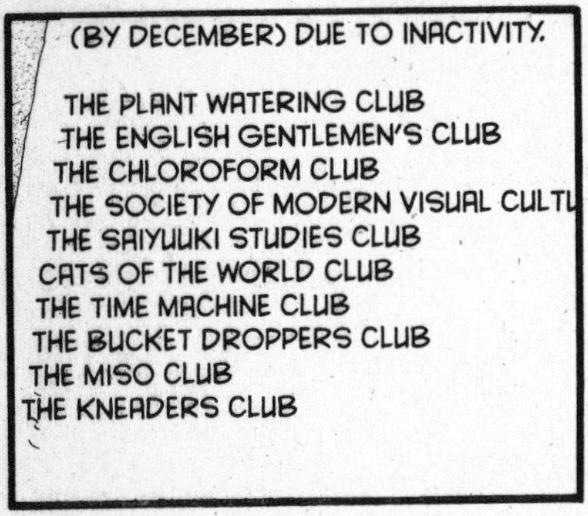
(BY DECEMBER) DUE TO INACTIVITY.
THE PLANT WATERING CLUB
THE ENGLISH GENTLEMEN'S CLUB
THE CHLOROFORM CLUB
THE SOCIETY OF MODERN VISUAL CULTU
THE SAIYUUKI STUDIES CLUB
CATS OF THE WORLD CLUB
THE TIME MACHINE CLUB
THE BUCKET DROPPERS CLUB
THE MISO CLUB
THE KNEADERS CLUB

# THE SOCIETY OF MODERN VISUAL CULTURE

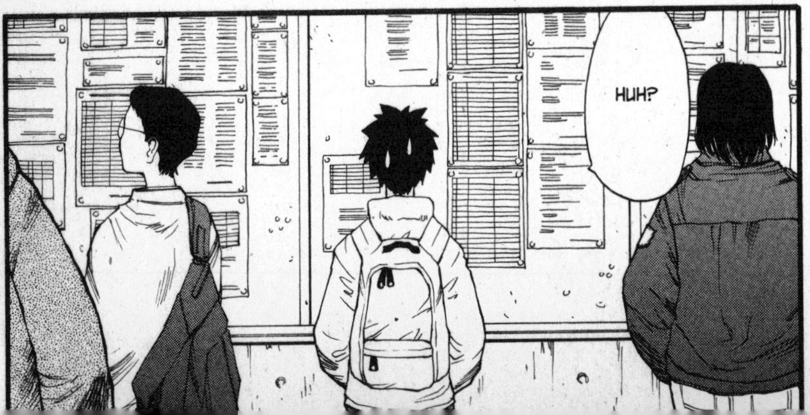
HUH?

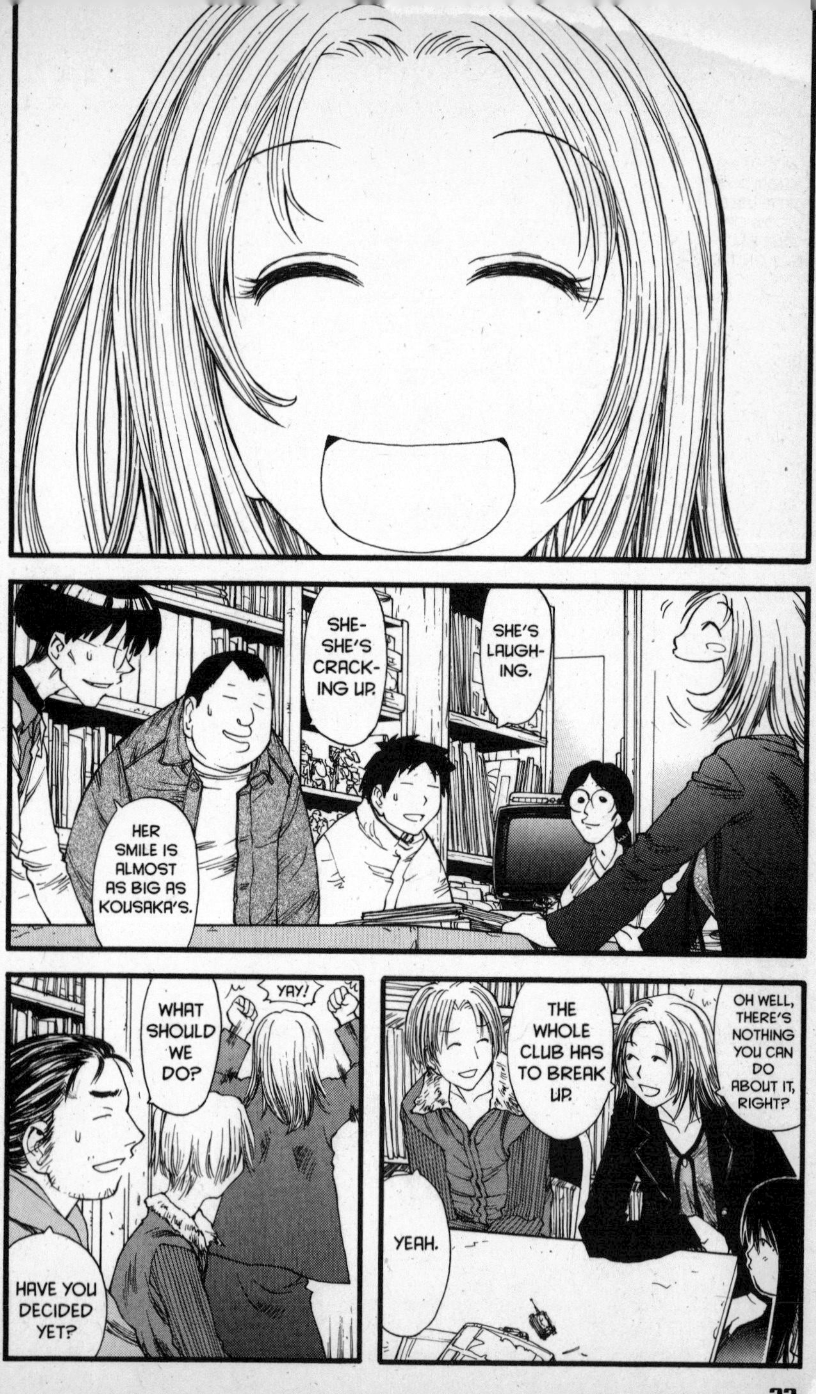
SHE'S LAUGH-ING.
SHE-SHE'S CRACK-ING UP.
HER SMILE IS ALMOST AS BIG AS KOUSAKA'S.
OH WELL, THERE'S NOTHING YOU CAN DO ABOUT IT, RIGHT?
THE WHOLE CLUB HAS TO BREAK UP.
YEAH.
YAY!
WHAT SHOULD WE DO?
HAVE YOU DECIDED YET?

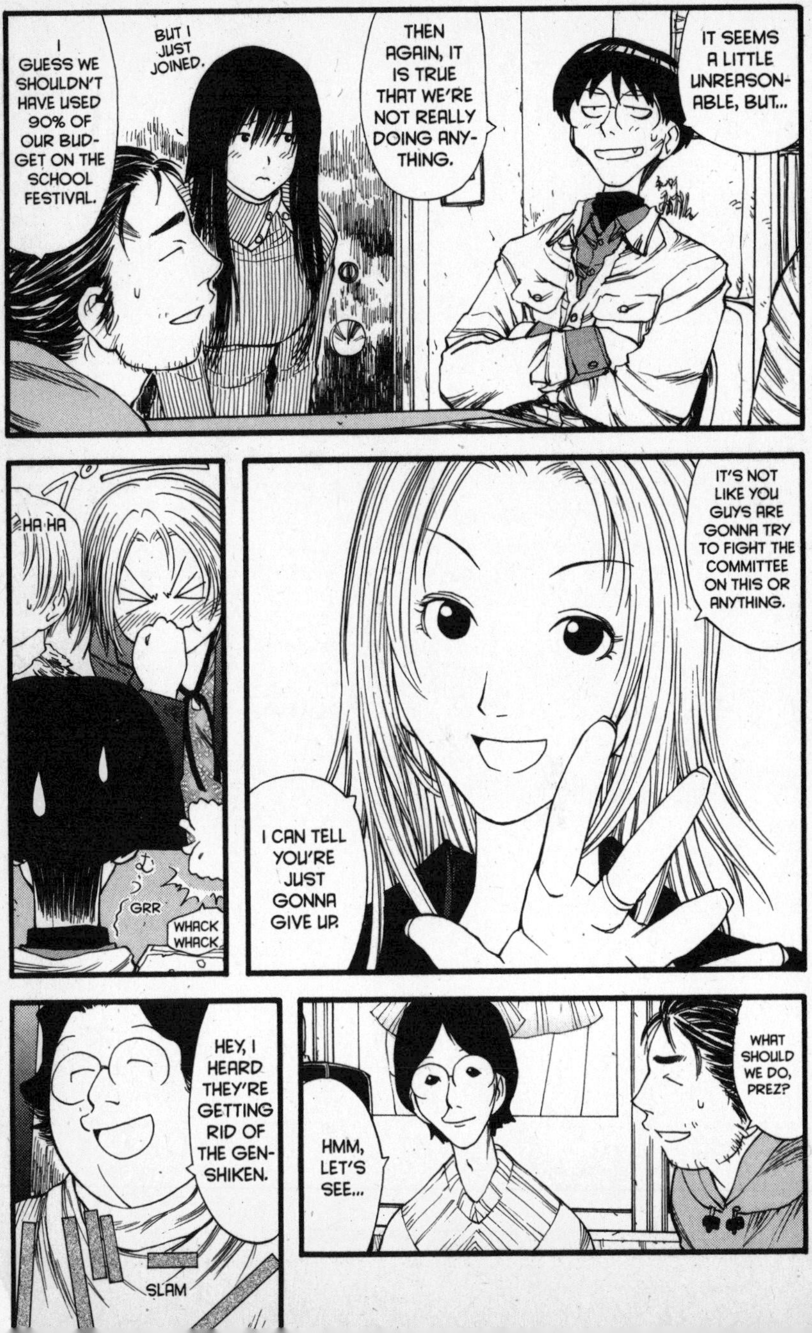
IT SEEMS A LITTLE UNREASONABLE, BUT...
THEN AGAIN, IT IS TRUE THAT WE'RE NOT REALLY DOING ANYTHING.
BUT I JUST JOINED.
I GUESS WE SHOULDN'T HAVE USED 90% OF OUR BUDGET ON THE SCHOOL FESTIVAL.
IT'S NOT LIKE YOU GUYS ARE GONNA TRY TO FIGHT THE COMMITTEE ON THIS OR ANYTHING.
I CAN TELL YOU'RE JUST GONNA GIVE UP.
HA HA
GRR
WHACK WHACK
WHAT SHOULD WE DO, PREZ?
HMM, LET'S SEE...
HEY, I HEARD THEY'RE GETTING RID OF THE GENSHIKEN.
SLAM

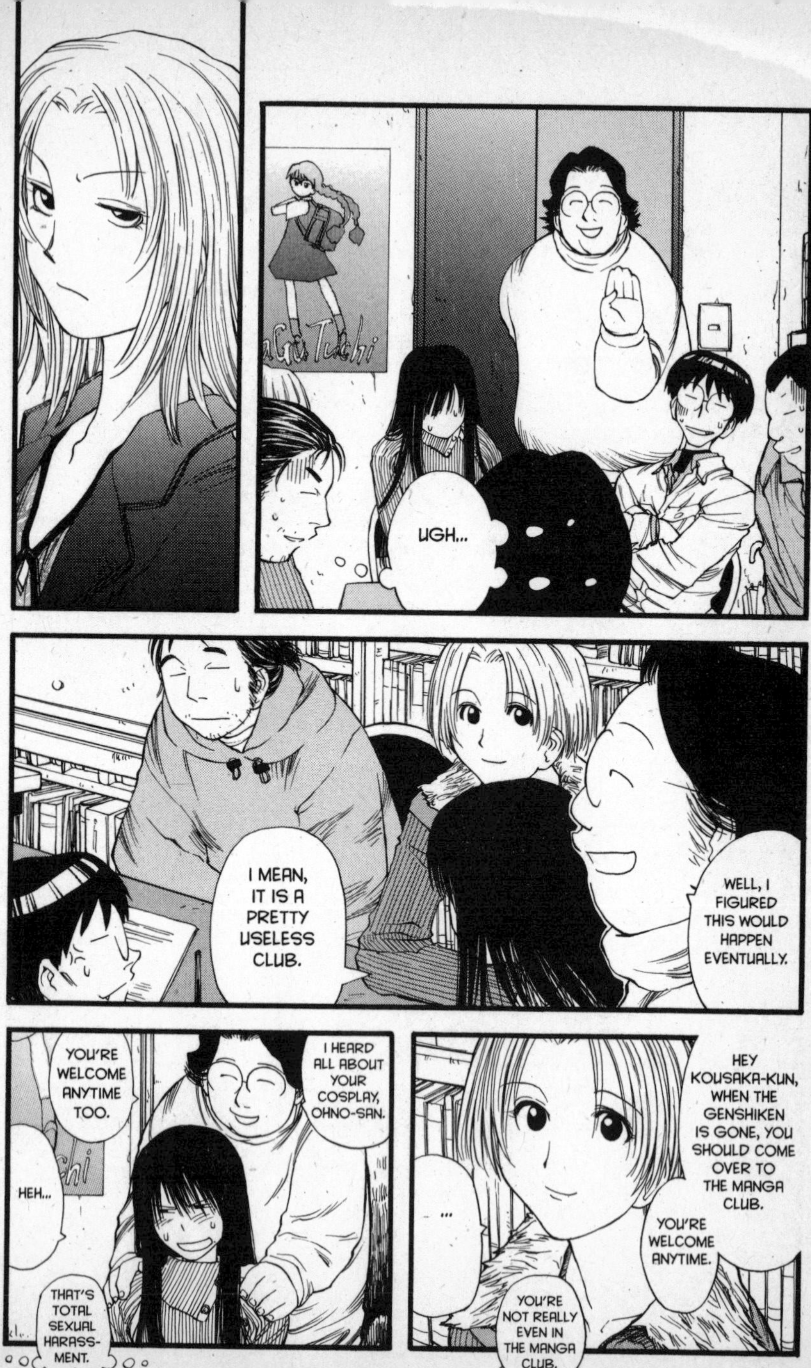
UGH...
WELL, I FIGURED THIS WOULD HAPPEN EVENTUALLY.
...
I MEAN, IT IS A PRETTY USELESS CLUB.
HEY KOUSAKA-KUN, WHEN THE GENSHIKEN IS GONE, YOU SHOULD COME OVER TO THE MANGA CLUB.
YOU'RE WELCOME ANYTIME.
...
YOU'RE NOT REALLY EVEN IN THE MANGA CLUB.
I HEARD ALL ABOUT YOUR COSPLAY, OHNO-SAN.
YOU'RE WELCOME ANYTIME TOO.
HEH...
THAT'S TOTAL SEXUAL HARASSMENT.

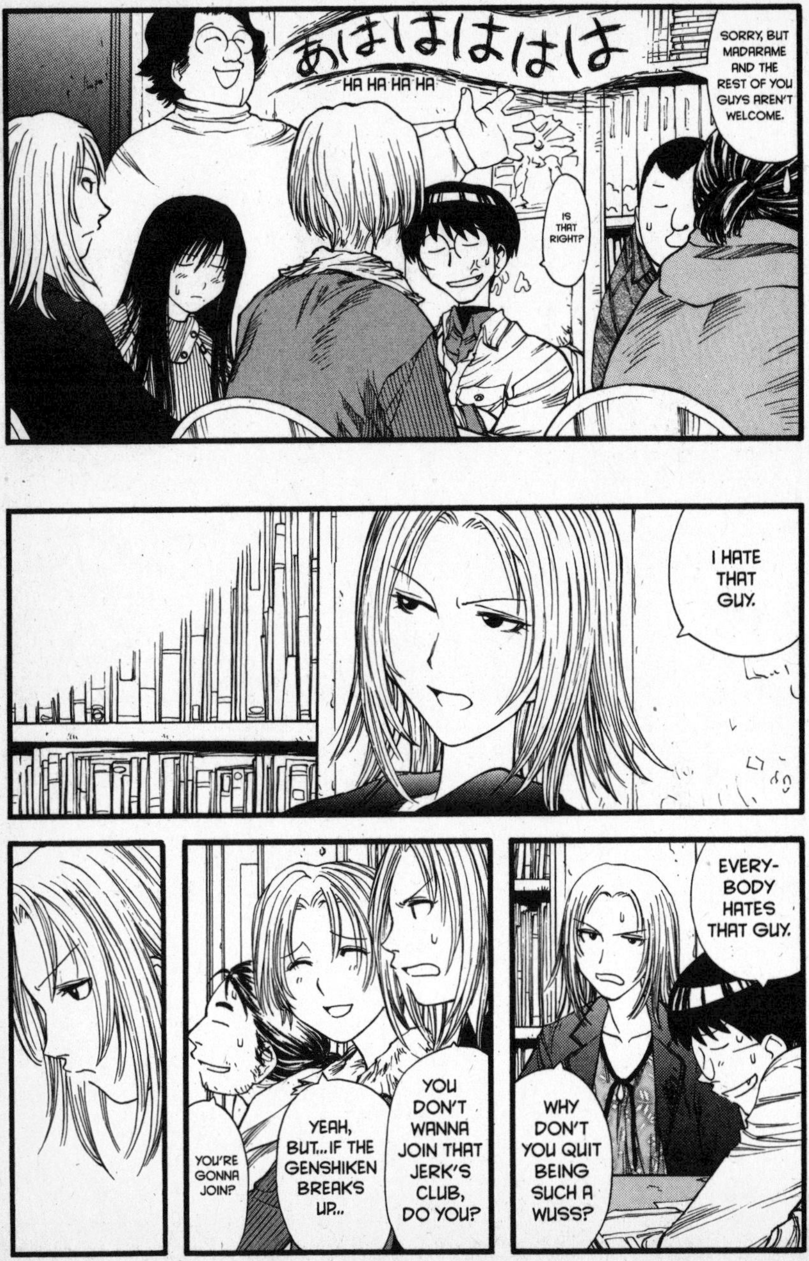
SORRY, BUT MADARAME AND THE REST OF YOU GUYS AREN'T WELCOME.
あははははは
HA HA HA HA
IS THAT RIGHT?
I HATE THAT GUY.
EVERY-BODY HATES THAT GUY.
WHY DON'T YOU QUIT BEING SUCH A WUSS?
YOU DON'T WANNA JOIN THAT JERK'S CLUB, DO YOU?
YEAH, BUT...IF THE GENSHIKEN BREAKS UP...
YOU'RE GONNA JOIN?

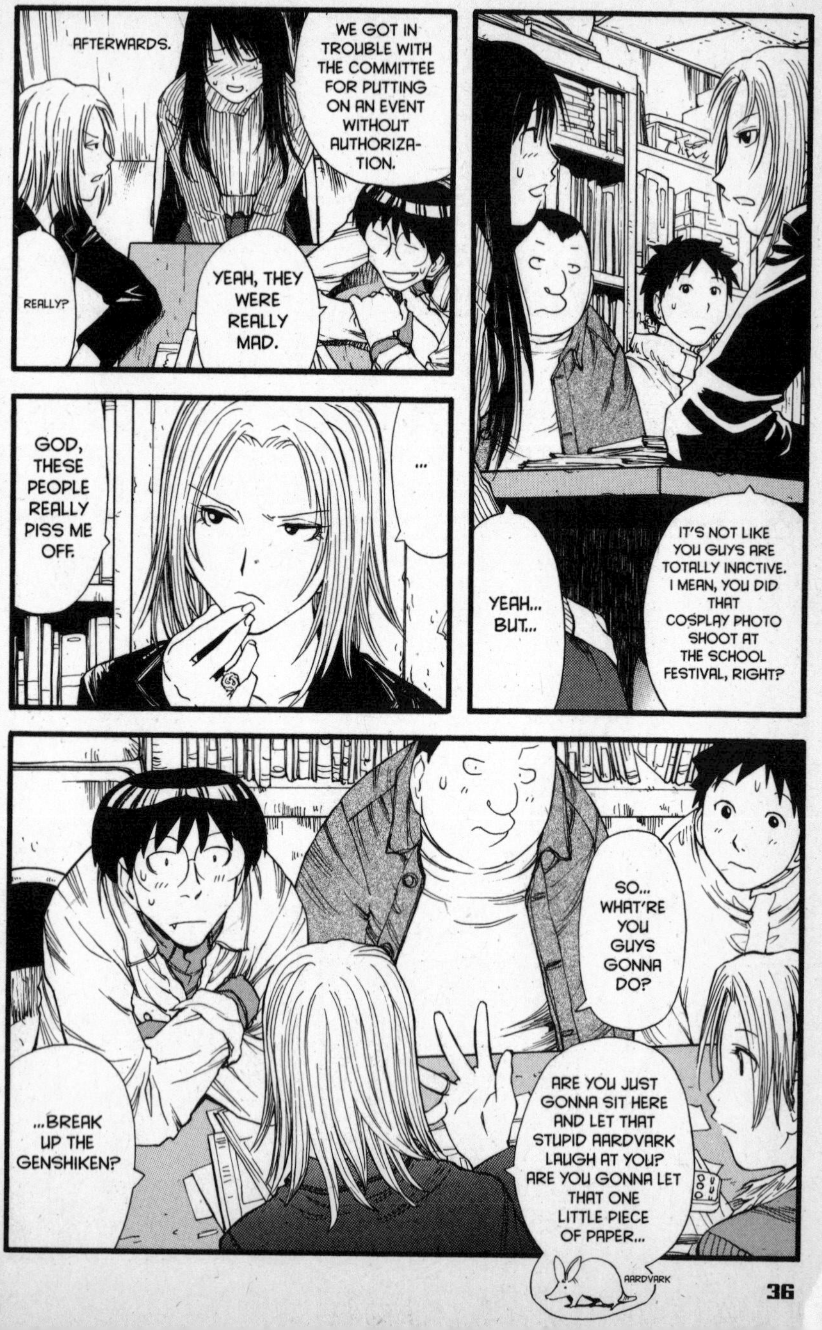
IT'S NOT LIKE YOU GUYS ARE TOTALLY INACTIVE. I MEAN, YOU DID THAT COSPLAY PHOTO SHOOT AT THE SCHOOL FESTIVAL, RIGHT?
YEAH... BUT...
WE GOT IN TROUBLE WITH THE COMMITTEE FOR PUTTING ON AN EVENT WITHOUT AUTHORIZATION.
AFTERWARDS.
YEAH, THEY WERE REALLY MAD.
REALLY?
...
GOD, THESE PEOPLE REALLY PISS ME OFF.
SO... WHAT'RE YOU GUYS GONNA DO?
ARE YOU JUST GONNA SIT HERE AND LET THAT STUPID AARDVARK LAUGH AT YOU? ARE YOU GONNA LET THAT ONE LITTLE PIECE OF PAPER...
...BREAK UP THE GENSHIKEN?
AARDVARK

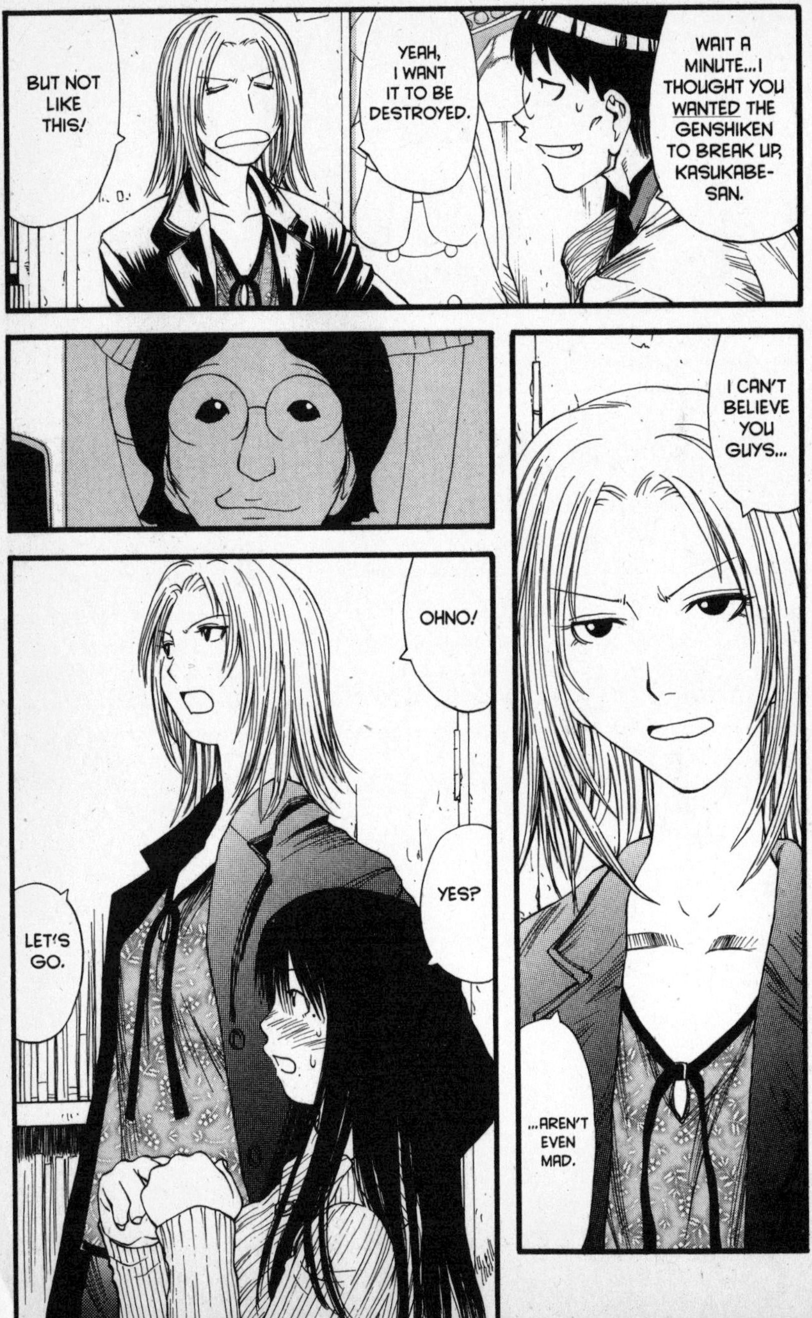
WAIT A MINUTE...I THOUGHT YOU WANTED THE GENSHIKEN TO BREAK UP, KASUKABE-SAN.
YEAH, I WANT IT TO BE DESTROYED.
BUT NOT LIKE THIS!
I CAN'T BELIEVE YOU GUYS...
...AREN'T EVEN MAD.
OHNO!
YES?
LET'S GO.

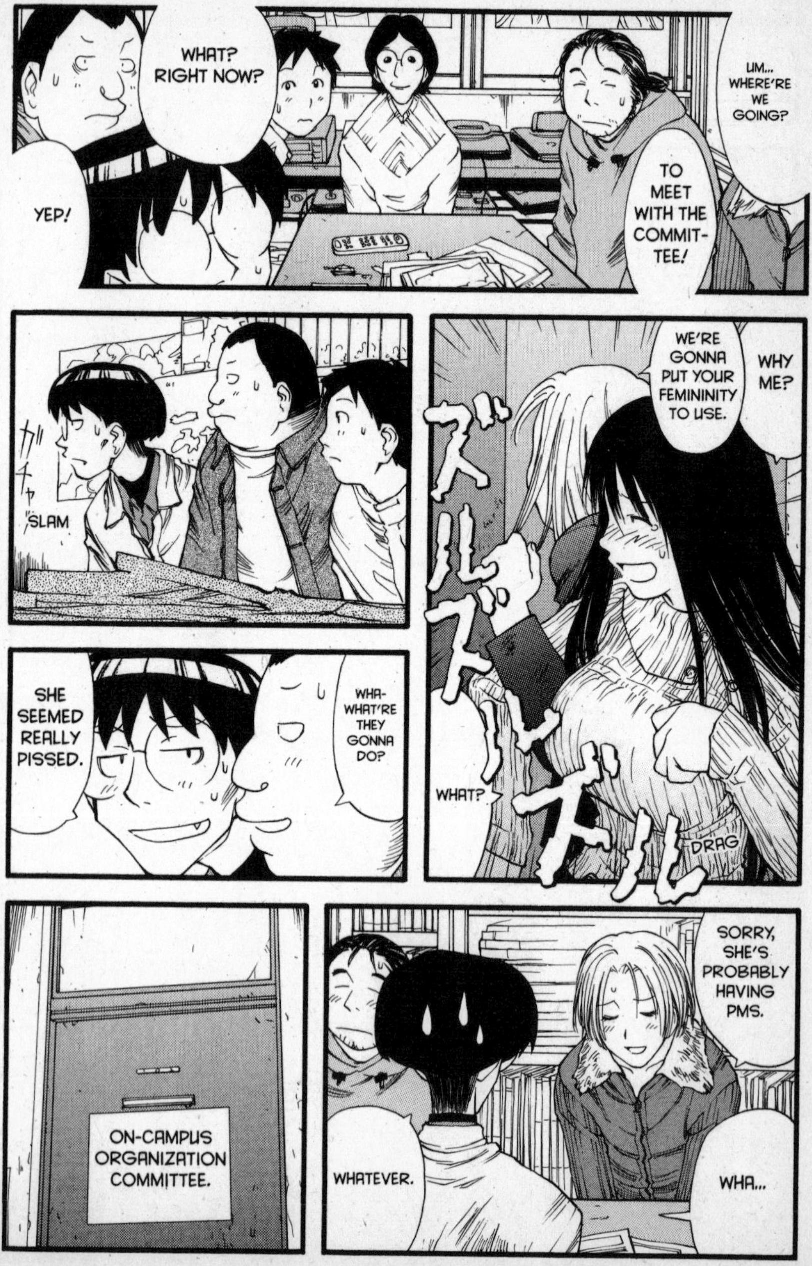
UM... WHERE'RE WE GOING?
TO MEET WITH THE COMMIT-TEE!
WHAT? RIGHT NOW?
YEP!
WHY ME?
WE'RE GONNA PUT YOUR FEMININITY TO USE.
WHAT?
DRAG
ガチャ
SLAM
WHA-WHAT'RE THEY GONNA DO?
SHE SEEMED REALLY PISSED.
SORRY, SHE'S PROBABLY HAVING PMS.
WHA...
WHATEVER.
ON-CAMPUS ORGANIZATION COMMITTEE.

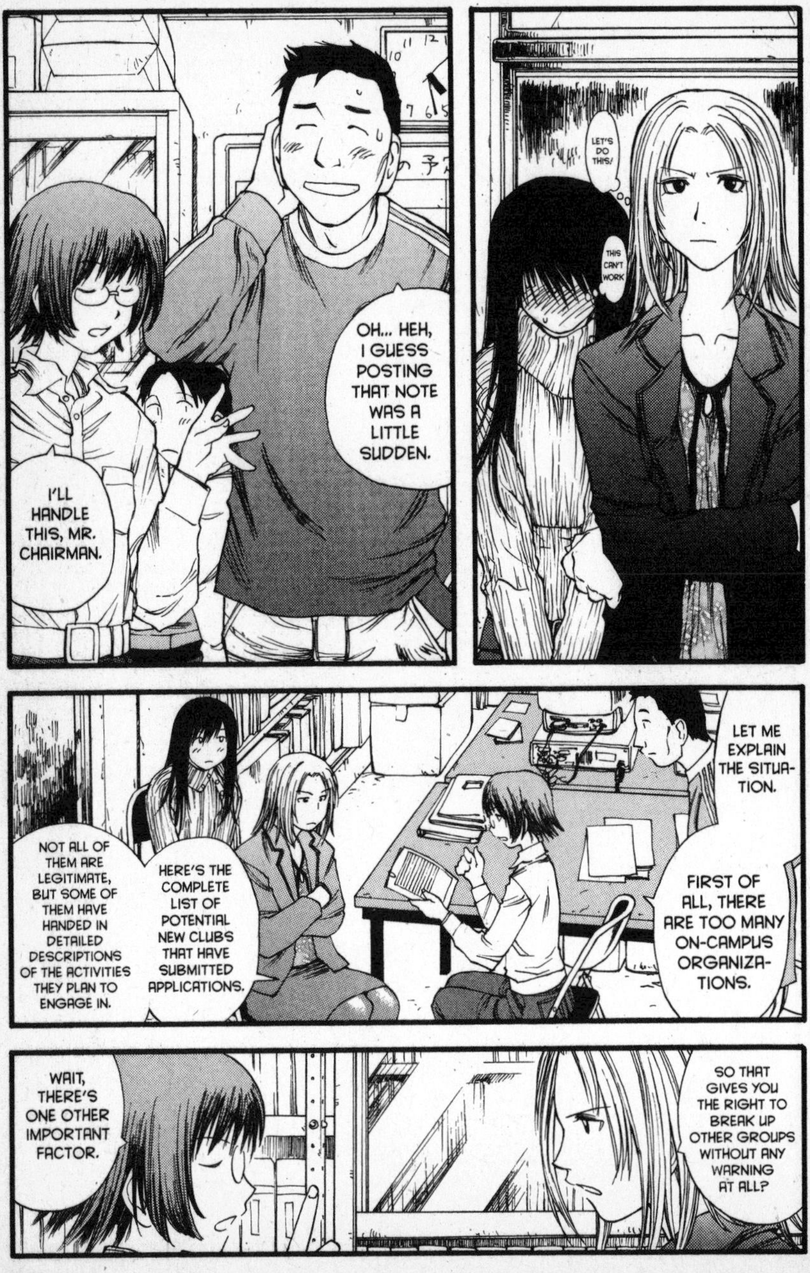
LET'S DO THIS!
THIS CAN'T WORK
OH... HEH, I GUESS POSTING THAT NOTE WAS A LITTLE SUDDEN.
I'LL HANDLE THIS, MR. CHAIRMAN.
LET ME EXPLAIN THE SITUATION.
FIRST OF ALL, THERE ARE TOO MANY ON-CAMPUS ORGANIZATIONS.
HERE'S THE COMPLETE LIST OF POTENTIAL NEW CLUBS THAT HAVE SUBMITTED APPLICATIONS.
NOT ALL OF THEM ARE LEGITIMATE, BUT SOME OF THEM HAVE HANDED IN DETAILED DESCRIPTIONS OF THE ACTIVITIES THEY PLAN TO ENGAGE IN.
SO THAT GIVES YOU THE RIGHT TO BREAK UP OTHER GROUPS WITHOUT ANY WARNING AT ALL?
WAIT, THERE'S ONE OTHER IMPORTANT FACTOR.

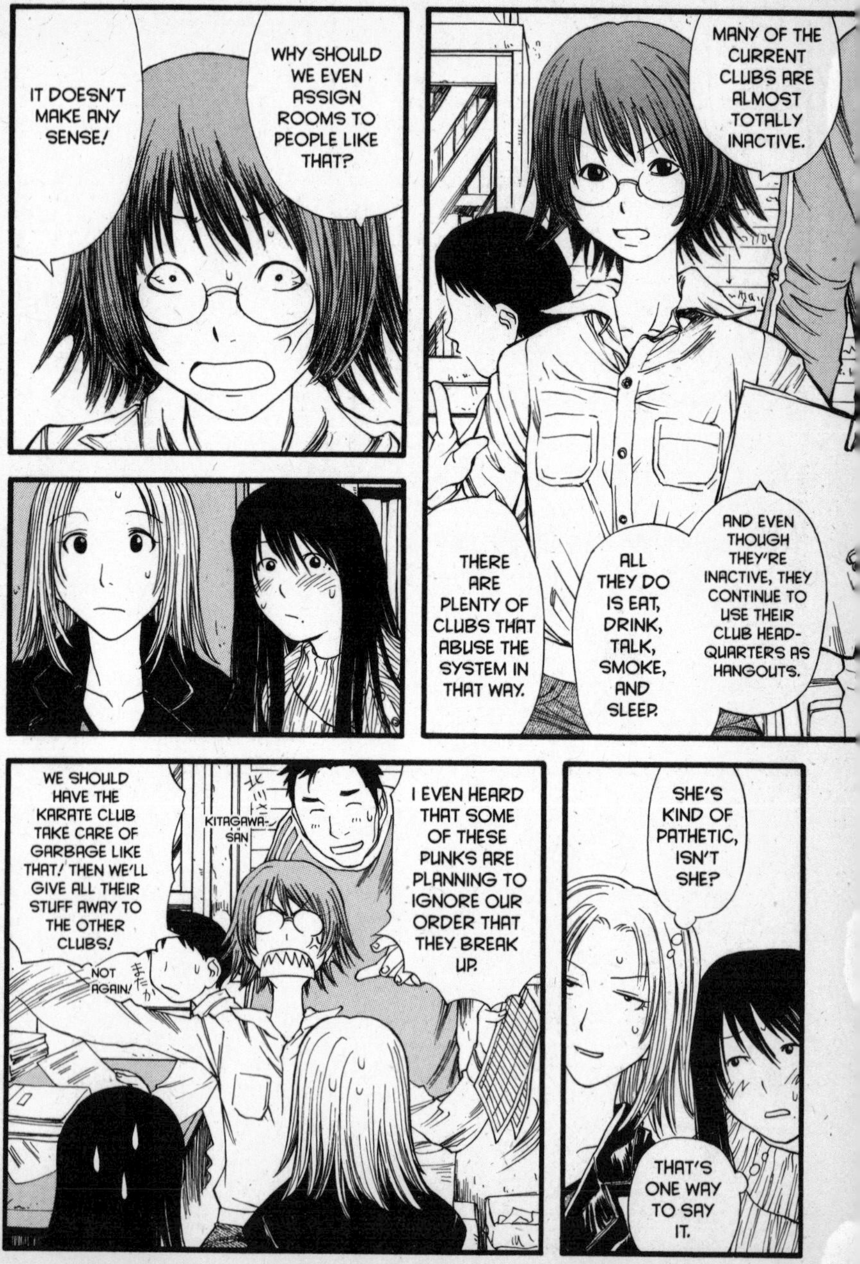

MANY OF THE CURRENT CLUBS ARE ALMOST TOTALLY INACTIVE.
AND EVEN THOUGH THEY'RE INACTIVE, THEY CONTINUE TO USE THEIR CLUB HEAD-QUARTERS AS HANGOUTS.
ALL THEY DO IS EAT, DRINK, TALK, SMOKE, AND SLEEP.
THERE ARE PLENTY OF CLUBS THAT ABUSE THE SYSTEM IN THAT WAY.
WHY SHOULD WE EVEN ASSIGN ROOMS TO PEOPLE LIKE THAT?
IT DOESN'T MAKE ANY SENSE!
SHE'S KIND OF PATHETIC, ISN'T SHE?
THAT'S ONE WAY TO SAY IT.
I EVEN HEARD THAT SOME OF THESE PUNKS ARE PLANNING TO IGNORE OUR ORDER THAT THEY BREAK UP.
KITAGAWA-SAN
WE SHOULD HAVE THE KARATE CLUB TAKE CARE OF GARBAGE LIKE THAT! THEN WE'LL GIVE ALL THEIR STUFF AWAY TO THE OTHER CLUBS!
NOT AGAIN!
またか

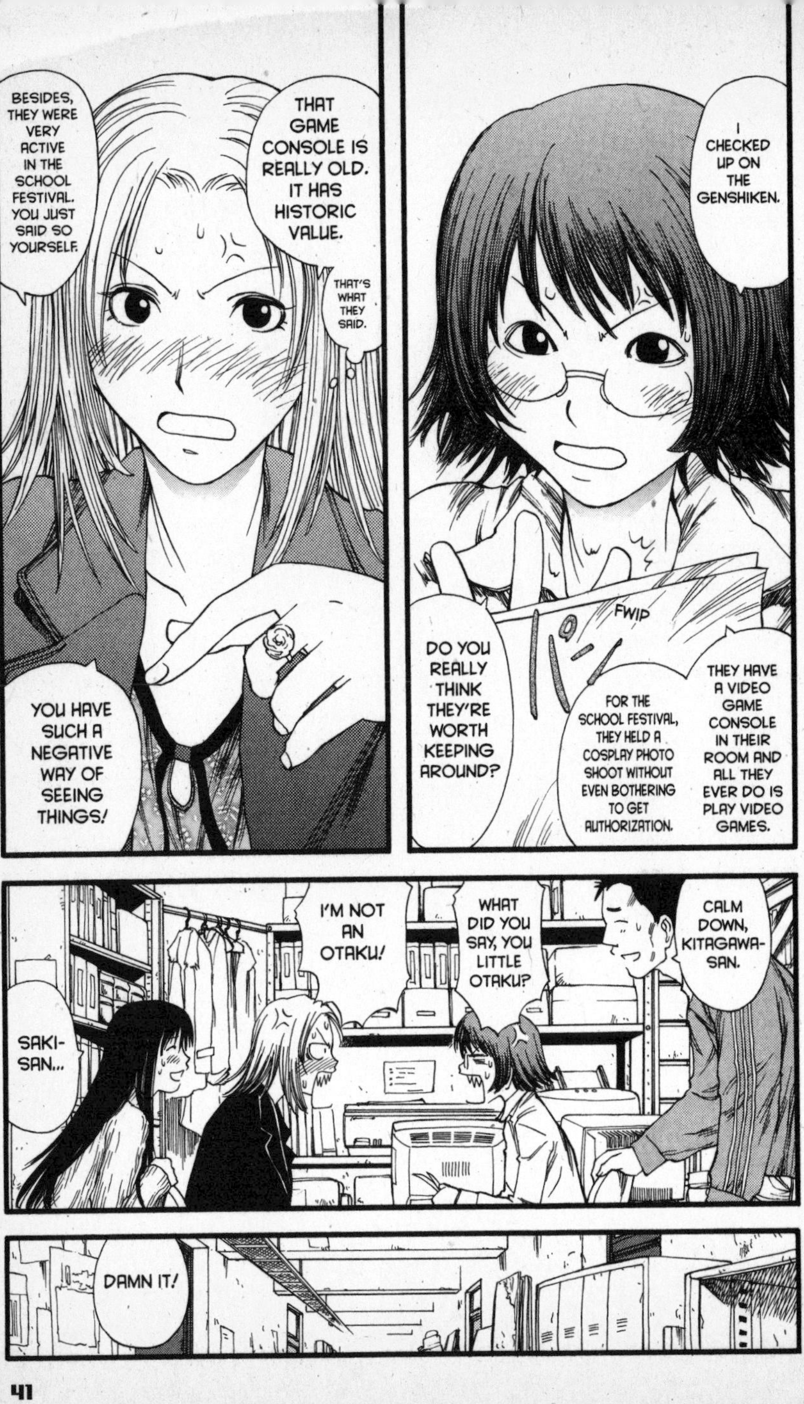
I CHECKED UP ON THE GENSHIKEN.
THEY HAVE A VIDEO GAME CONSOLE IN THEIR ROOM AND ALL THEY EVER DO IS PLAY VIDEO GAMES.
FWIP
FOR THE SCHOOL FESTIVAL, THEY HELD A COSPLAY PHOTO SHOOT WITHOUT EVEN BOTHERING TO GET AUTHORIZATION.
DO YOU REALLY THINK THEY'RE WORTH KEEPING AROUND?
THAT GAME CONSOLE IS REALLY OLD. IT HAS HISTORIC VALUE.
BESIDES, THEY WERE VERY ACTIVE IN THE SCHOOL FESTIVAL. YOU JUST SAID SO YOURSELF.
THAT'S WHAT THEY SAID.
YOU HAVE SUCH A NEGATIVE WAY OF SEEING THINGS!
CALM DOWN, KITAGAWA-SAN.
WHAT DID YOU SAY, YOU LITTLE OTAKU?
I'M NOT AN OTAKU!
SAKI-SAN...
DAMN IT!

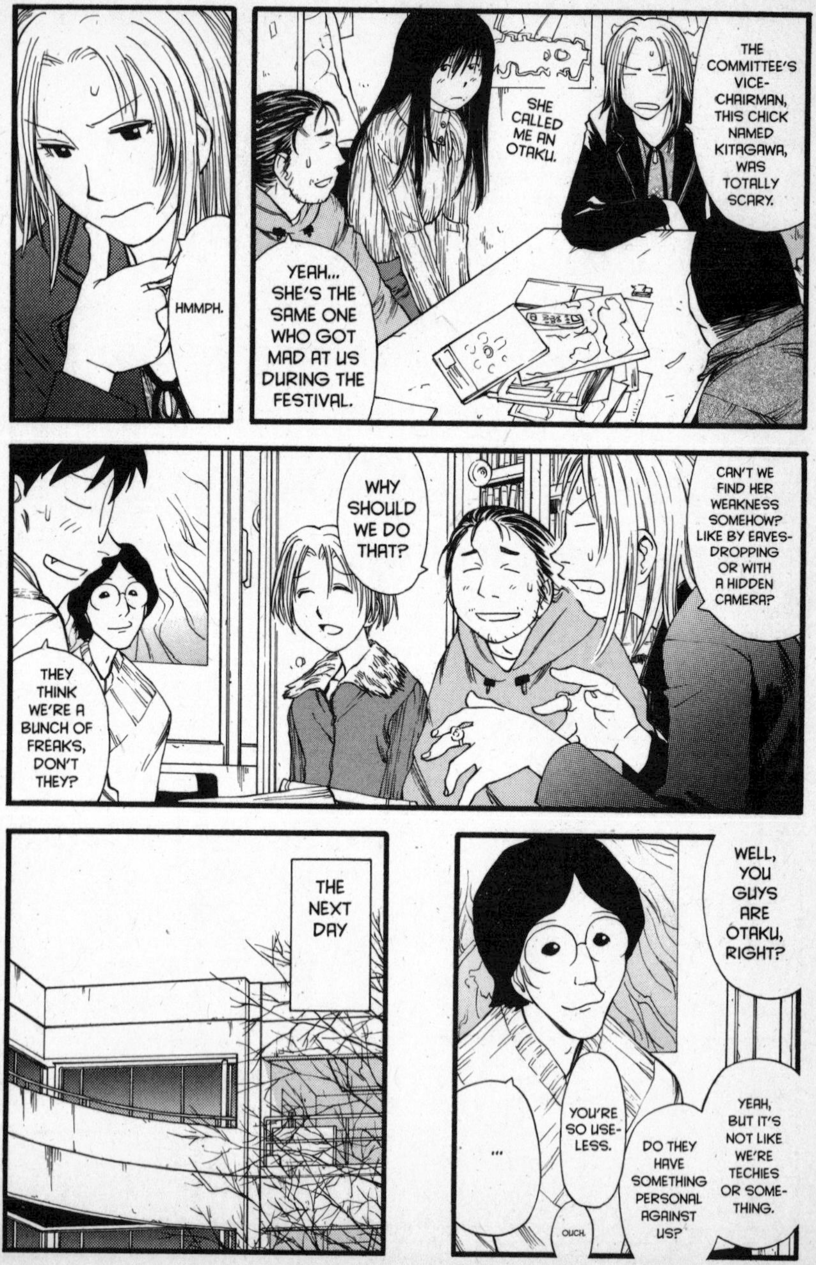
THE COMMITTEE'S VICE-CHAIRMAN, THIS CHICK NAMED KITAGAWA, WAS TOTALLY SCARY.
SHE CALLED ME AN OTAKU.
YEAH... SHE'S THE SAME ONE WHO GOT MAD AT US DURING THE FESTIVAL.
HMMPH.
CAN'T WE FIND HER WEAKNESS SOMEHOW? LIKE BY EAVES-DROPPING OR WITH A HIDDEN CAMERA?
WHY SHOULD WE DO THAT?
THEY THINK WE'RE A BUNCH OF FREAKS, DON'T THEY?
WELL, YOU GUYS ARE OTAKU, RIGHT?
YEAH, BUT IT'S NOT LIKE WE'RE TECHIES OR SOME-THING.
DO THEY HAVE SOMETHING PERSONAL AGAINST US?
YOU'RE SO USE-LESS.
...
OUCH.
THE NEXT DAY

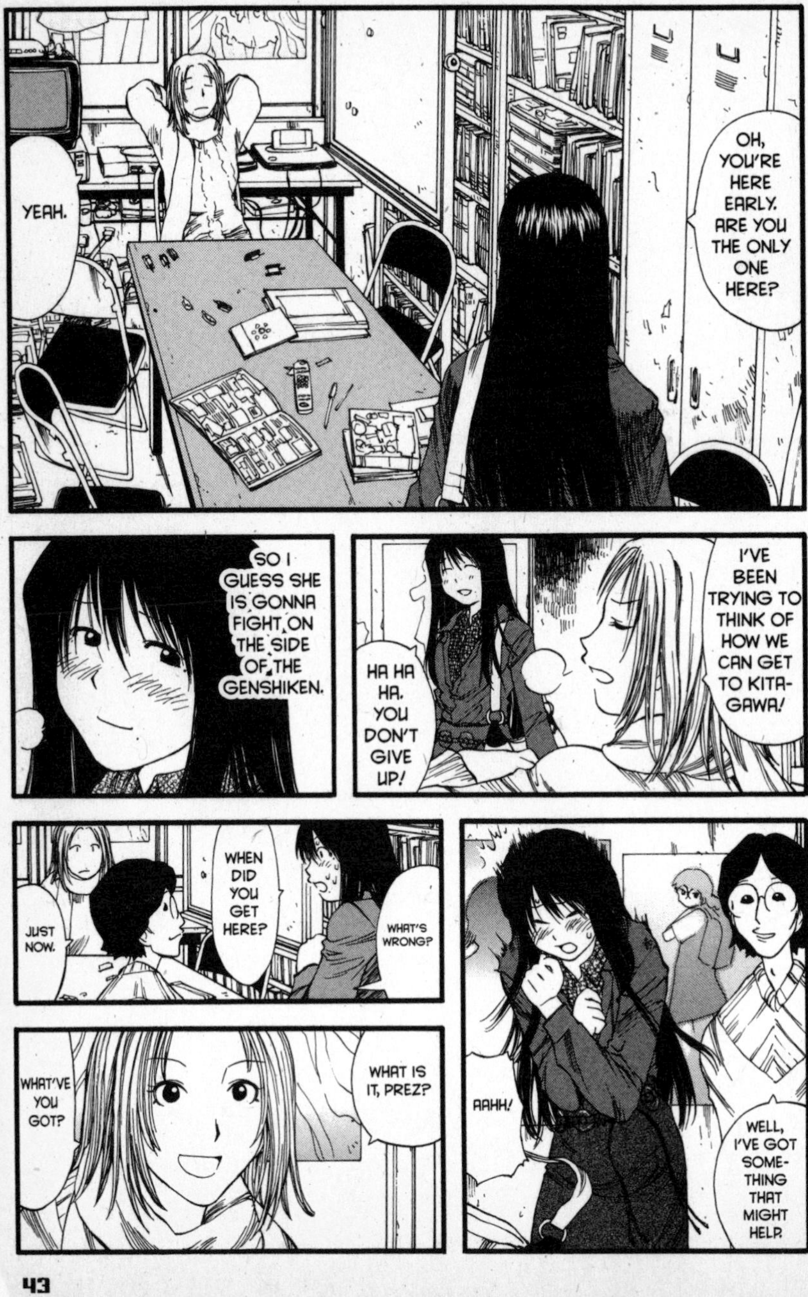
OH, YOU'RE HERE EARLY. ARE YOU THE ONLY ONE HERE?
YEAH.
I'VE BEEN TRYING TO THINK OF HOW WE CAN GET TO KITA-GAWA!
HA HA HA. YOU DON'T GIVE UP!
SO I GUESS SHE IS GONNA FIGHT ON THE SIDE OF THE GENSHIKEN.
AAHH!
WELL, I'VE GOT SOME-THING THAT MIGHT HELP.
WHAT'S WRONG?
WHEN DID YOU GET HERE?
JUST NOW.
WHAT IS IT, PREZ?
WHAT'VE YOU GOT?

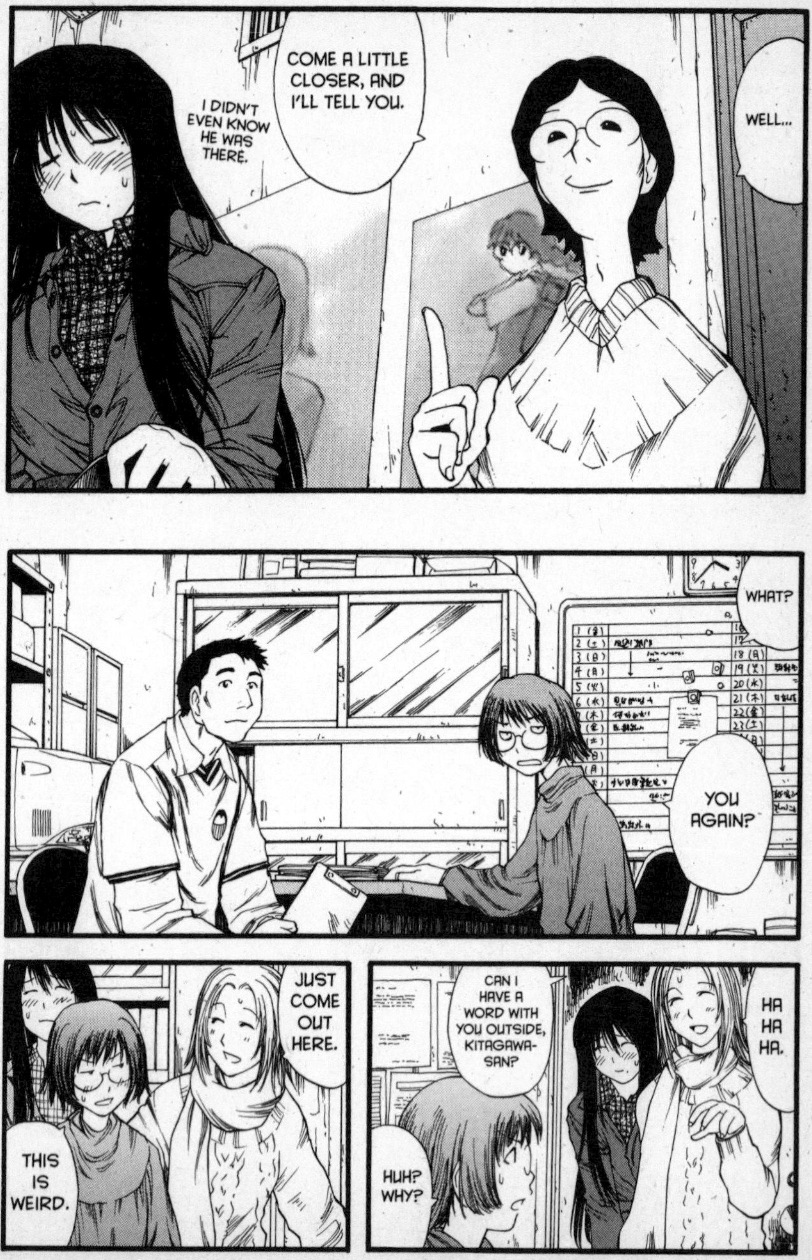
WELL...
COME A LITTLE CLOSER, AND I'LL TELL YOU.
I DIDN'T EVEN KNOW HE WAS THERE.
WHAT?
YOU AGAIN?
HA HA HA.
CAN I HAVE A WORD WITH YOU OUTSIDE, KITAGAWA-SAN?
HUH? WHY?
JUST COME OUT HERE.
THIS IS WEIRD.

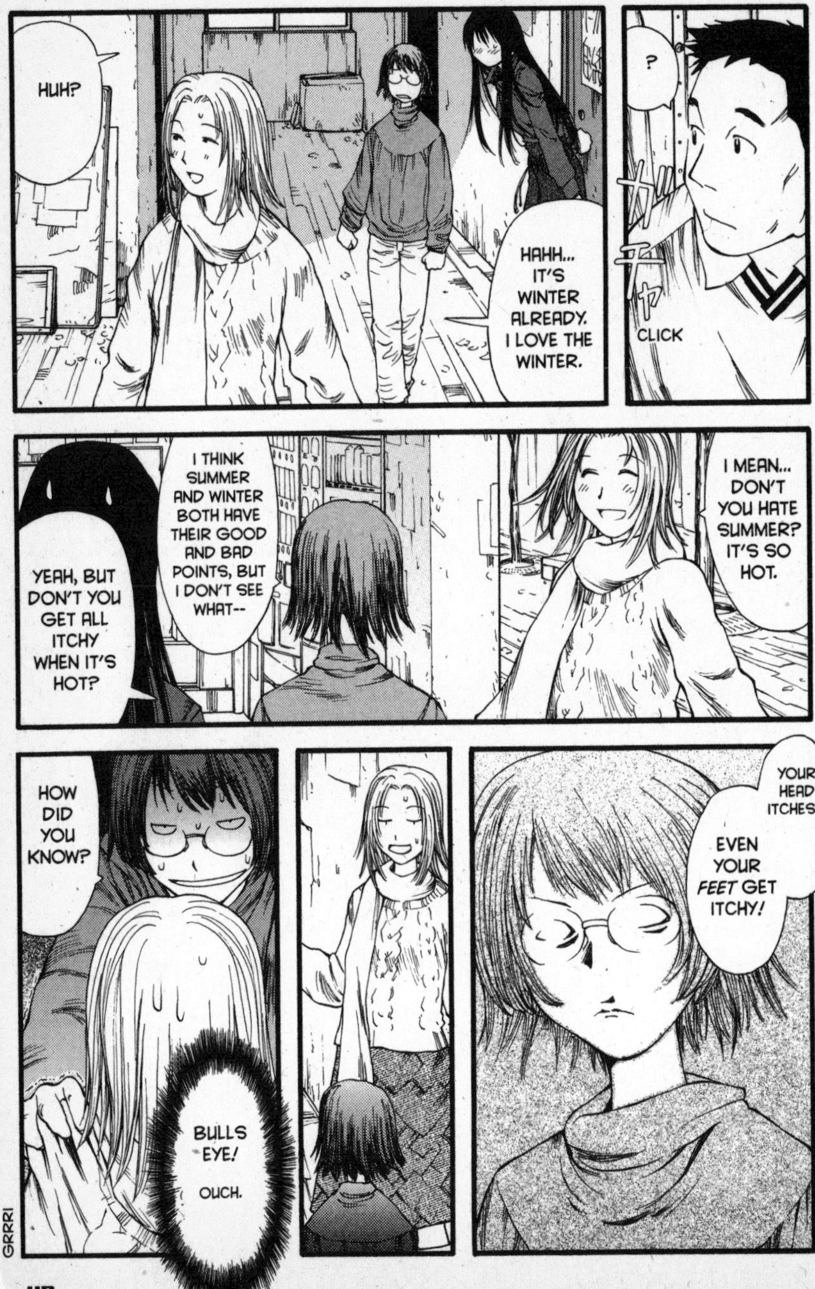
?
CLICK
HUH?
HAHH... IT'S WINTER ALREADY. I LOVE THE WINTER.
I MEAN... DON'T YOU HATE SUMMER? IT'S SO HOT.
I THINK SUMMER AND WINTER BOTH HAVE THEIR GOOD AND BAD POINTS, BUT I DON'T SEE WHAT--
YEAH, BUT DON'T YOU GET ALL ITCHY WHEN IT'S HOT?
YOUR HEAD ITCHES...
EVEN YOUR *FEET* GET ITCHY!
HOW DID YOU KNOW?
BULLS EYE!
OUCH.
GRRRI

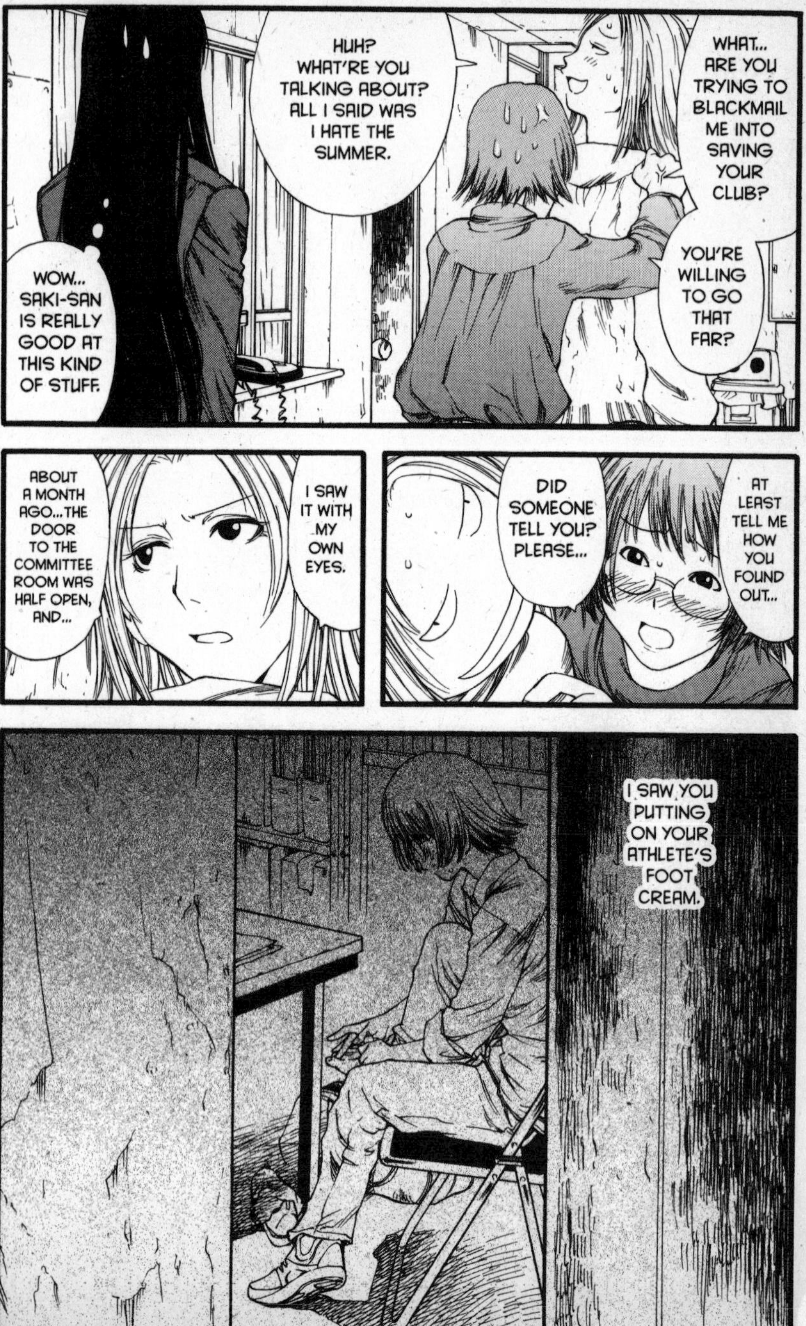
WHAT... ARE YOU TRYING TO BLACKMAIL ME INTO SAVING YOUR CLUB?
YOU'RE WILLING TO GO THAT FAR?
HUH? WHAT'RE YOU TALKING ABOUT? ALL I SAID WAS I HATE THE SUMMER.
WOW... SAKI-SAN IS REALLY GOOD AT THIS KIND OF STUFF.
AT LEAST TELL ME HOW YOU FOUND OUT...
DID SOMEONE TELL YOU? PLEASE...
I SAW IT WITH MY OWN EYES.
ABOUT A MONTH AGO...THE DOOR TO THE COMMITTEE ROOM WAS HALF OPEN, AND...
I SAW YOU PUTTING ON YOUR ATHLETE'S FOOT CREAM.

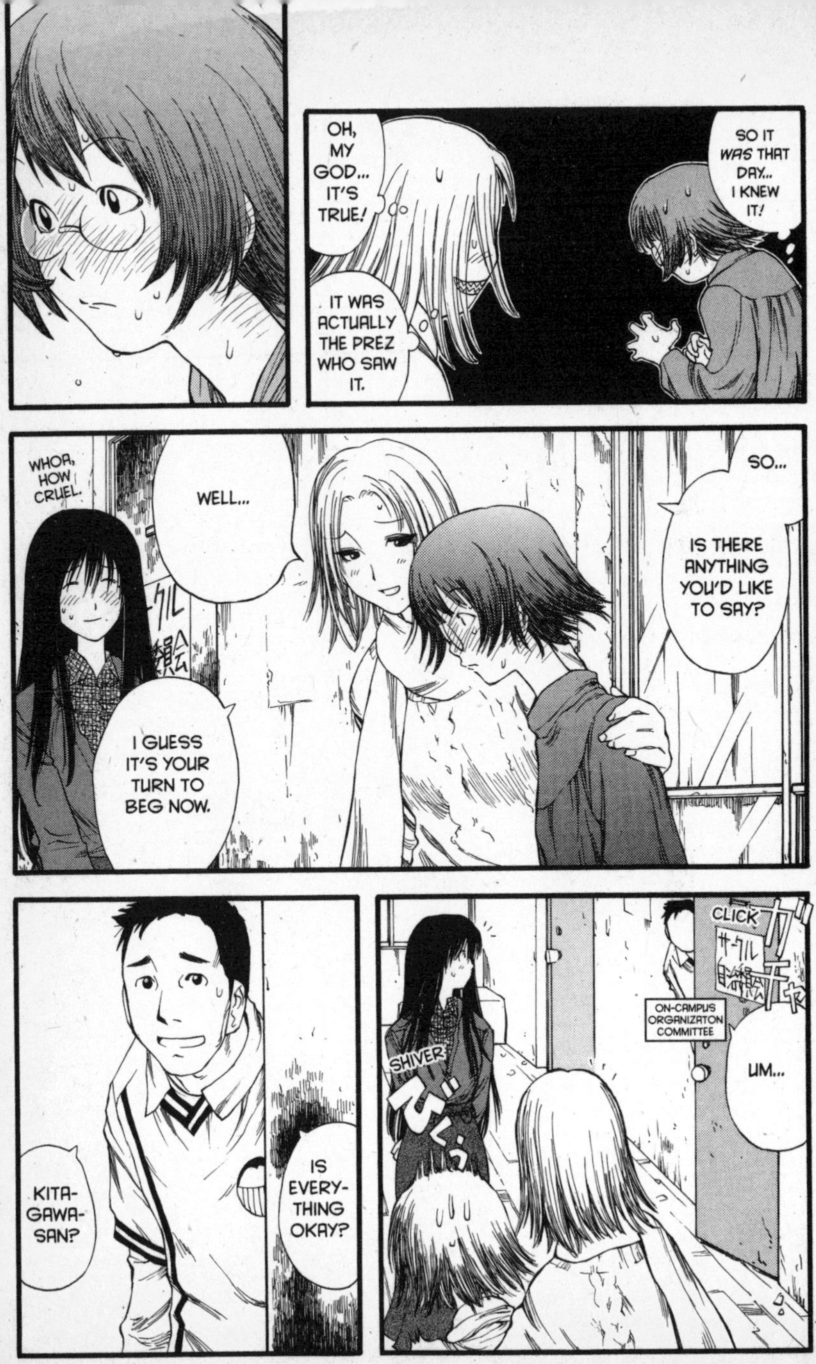
SO IT WAS THAT DAY... I KNEW IT!
OH, MY GOD... IT'S TRUE!
IT WAS ACTUALLY THE PREZ WHO SAW IT.
SO...
IS THERE ANYTHING YOU'D LIKE TO SAY?
WELL...
WHOA, HOW CRUEL.
I GUESS IT'S YOUR TURN TO BEG NOW.
CLICK
ON-CAMPUS ORGANIZATON COMMITTEE
UM...
SHIVER
IS EVERYTHING OKAY?
KITAGAWA-SAN?

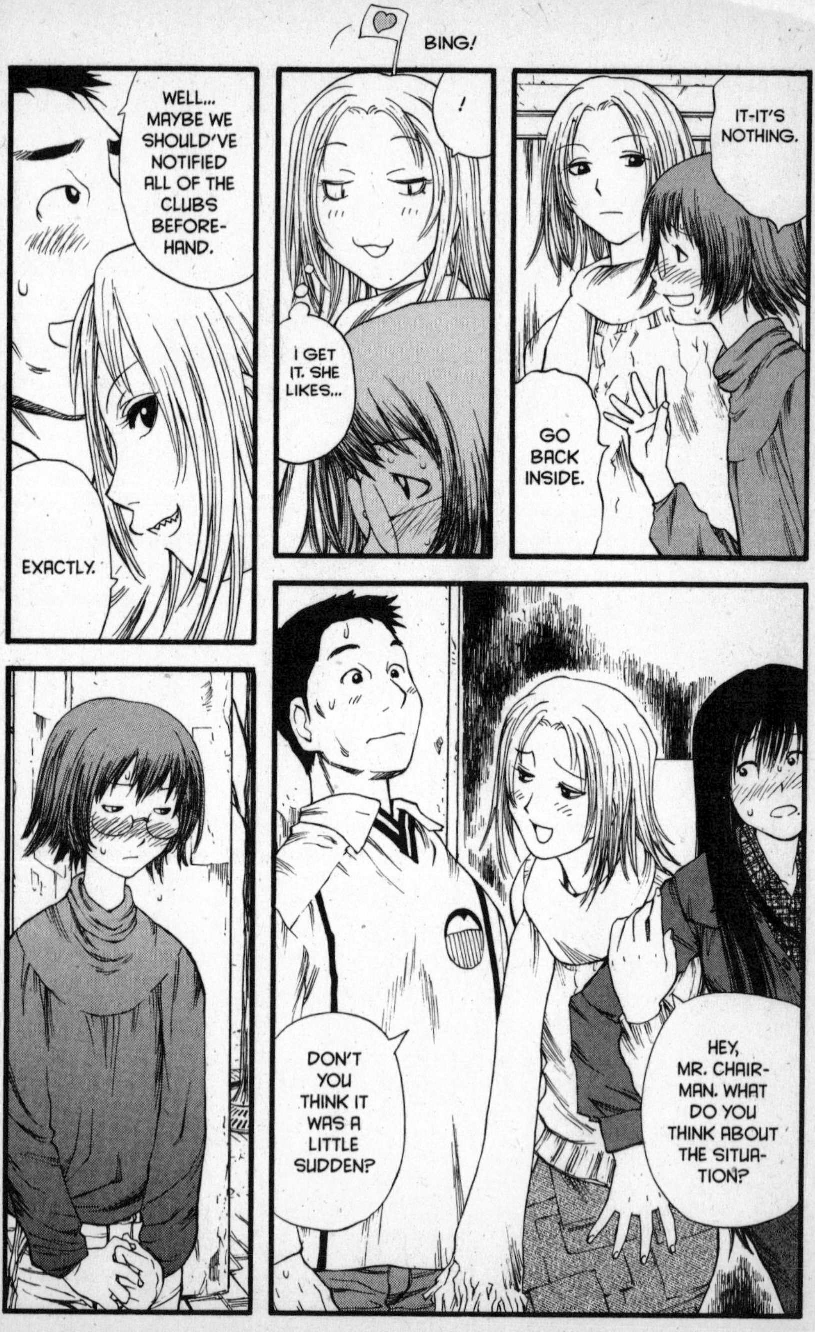
IT-IT'S NOTHING.
GO BACK INSIDE.
BING!
!
I GET IT. SHE LIKES...
WELL... MAYBE WE SHOULD'VE NOTIFIED ALL OF THE CLUBS BEFORE-HAND.
EXACTLY.
HEY, MR. CHAIR-MAN. WHAT DO YOU THINK ABOUT THE SITUA-TION?
DON'T YOU THINK IT WAS A LITTLE SUDDEN?

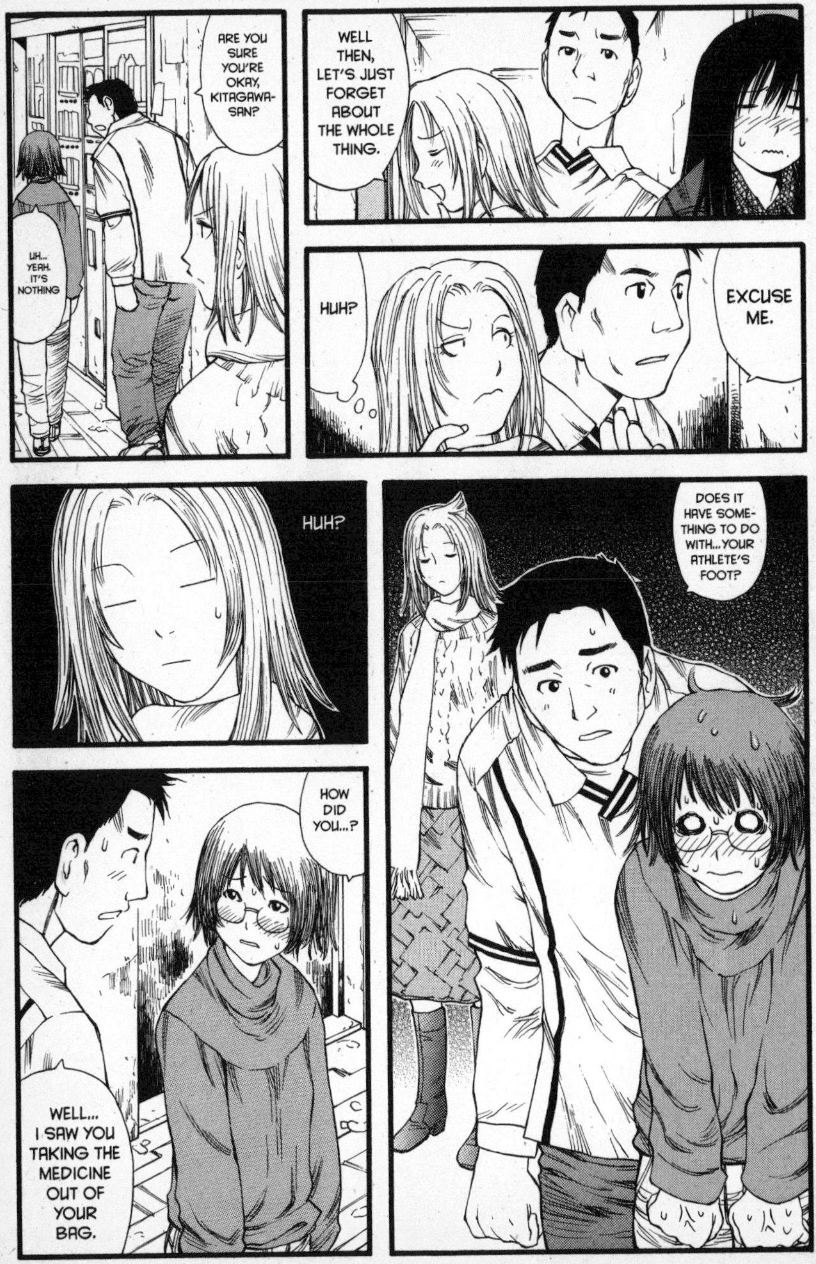
WELL THEN, LET'S JUST FORGET ABOUT THE WHOLE THING.
EXCUSE ME.
HUH?
ARE YOU SURE YOU'RE OKAY, KITAGAWA-SAN?
UH... YEAH. IT'S NOTHING
DOES IT HAVE SOME-THING TO DO WITH... YOUR ATHLETE'S FOOT?
HUH?
HOW DID YOU...?
WELL... I SAW YOU TAKING THE MEDICINE OUT OF YOUR BAG.

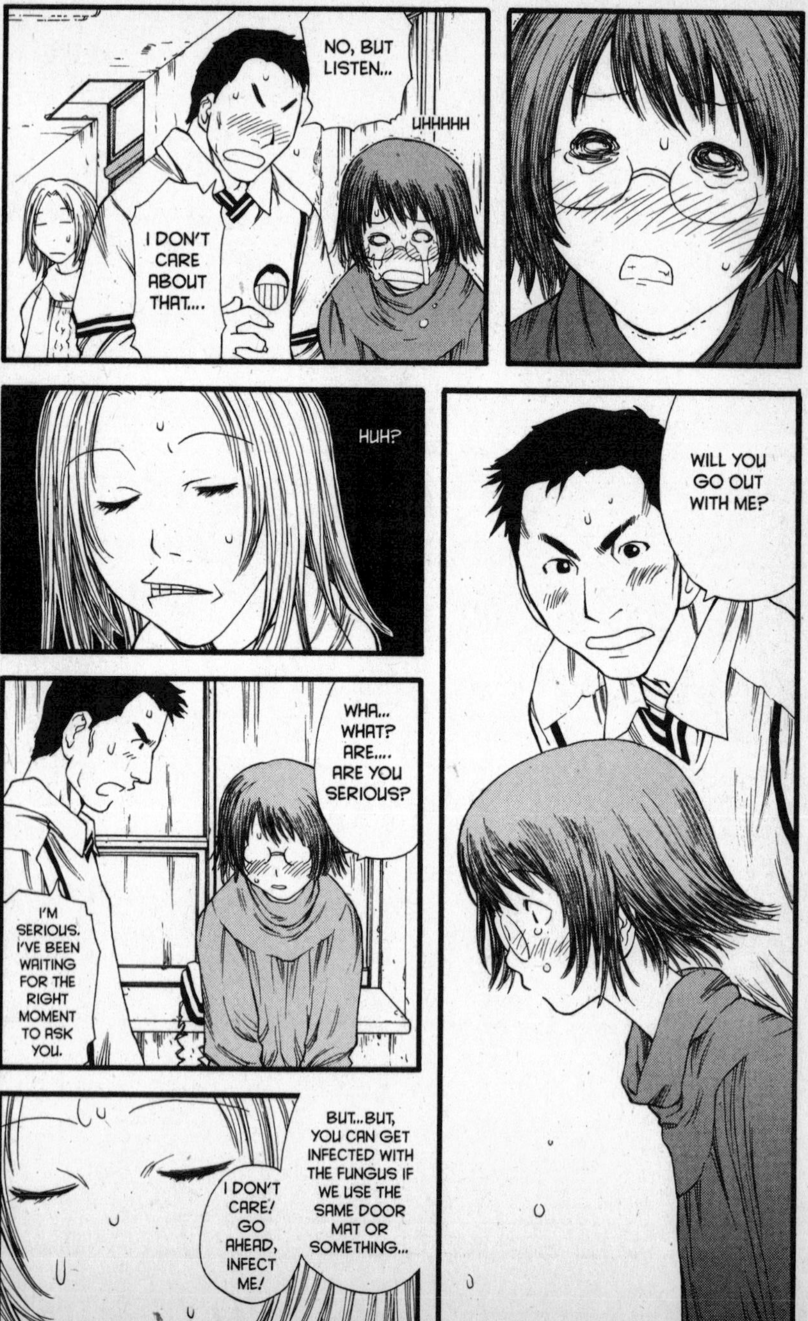
NO, BUT LISTEN...
UHHHHH
I DON'T CARE ABOUT THAT....
WILL YOU GO OUT WITH ME?
HUH?
WHA... WHAT? ARE.... ARE YOU SERIOUS?
I'M SERIOUS. I'VE BEEN WAITING FOR THE RIGHT MOMENT TO ASK YOU.
BUT...BUT, YOU CAN GET INFECTED WITH THE FUNGUS IF WE USE THE SAME DOOR MAT OR SOMETHING...
I DON'T CARE! GO AHEAD, INFECT ME!

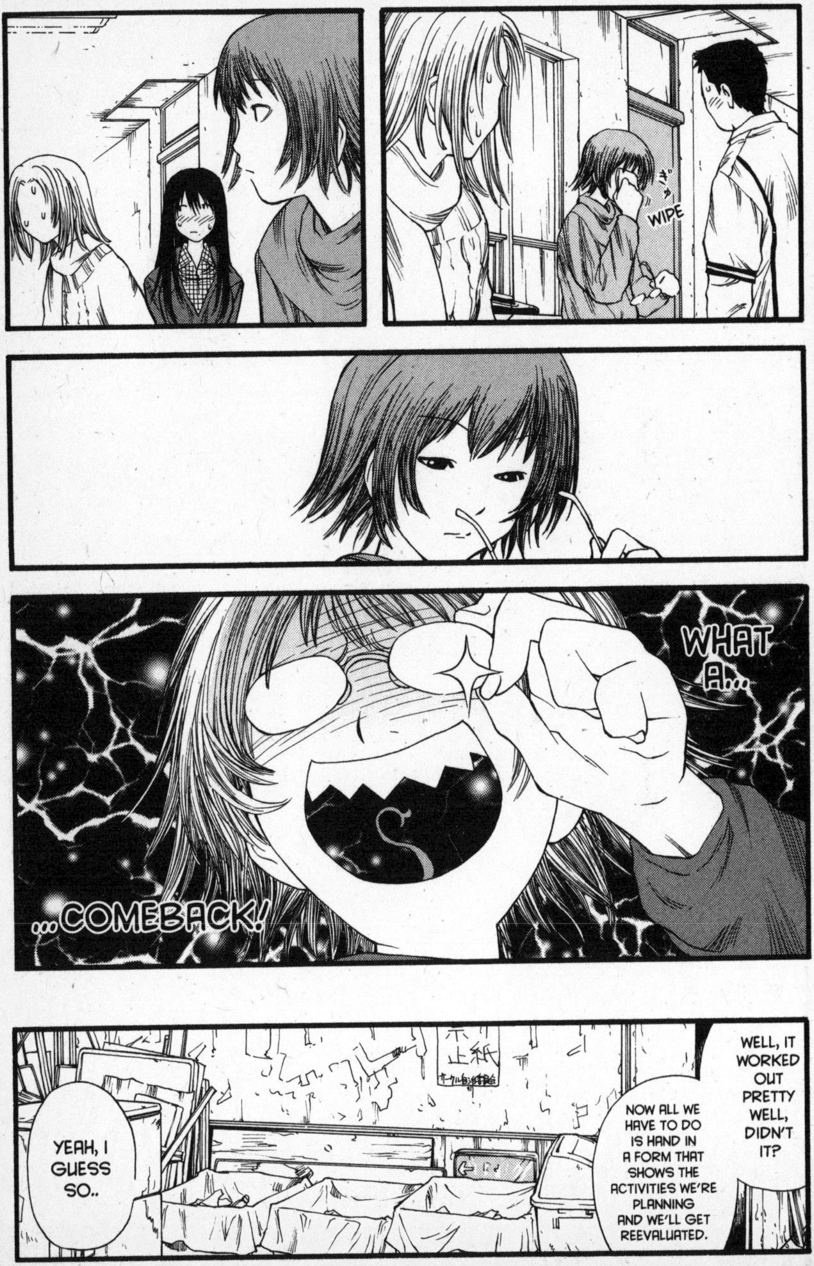
ぎゅ
WIPE
WHAT A...
...COMEBACK!
WELL, IT WORKED OUT PRETTY WELL, DIDN'T IT?
NOW ALL WE HAVE TO DO IS HAND IN A FORM THAT SHOWS THE ACTIVITIES WE'RE PLANNING AND WE'LL GET REEVALUATED.
YEAH, I GUESS SO..

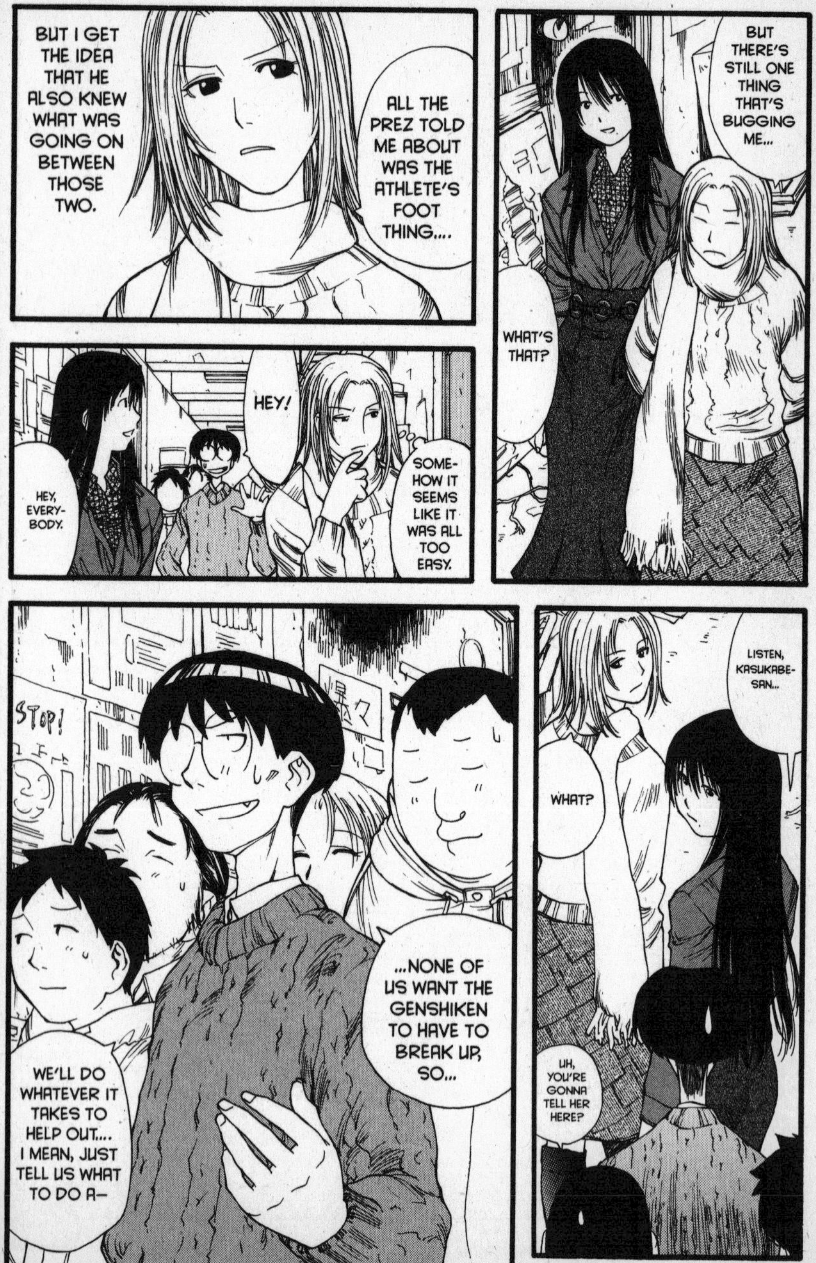
BUT THERE'S STILL ONE THING THAT'S BUGGING ME...
WHAT'S THAT?
ALL THE PREZ TOLD ME ABOUT WAS THE ATHLETE'S FOOT THING....
BUT I GET THE IDEA THAT HE ALSO KNEW WHAT WAS GOING ON BETWEEN THOSE TWO.
SOME-HOW IT SEEMS LIKE IT WAS ALL TOO EASY.
HEY!
HEY, EVERY-BODY.
LISTEN, KASUKABE-SAN...
WHAT?
UH, YOU'RE GONNA TELL HER HERE?
...NONE OF US WANT THE GENSHIKEN TO HAVE TO BREAK UP, SO...
WE'LL DO WHATEVER IT TAKES TO HELP OUT.... I MEAN, JUST TELL US WHAT TO DO A—
STOP!

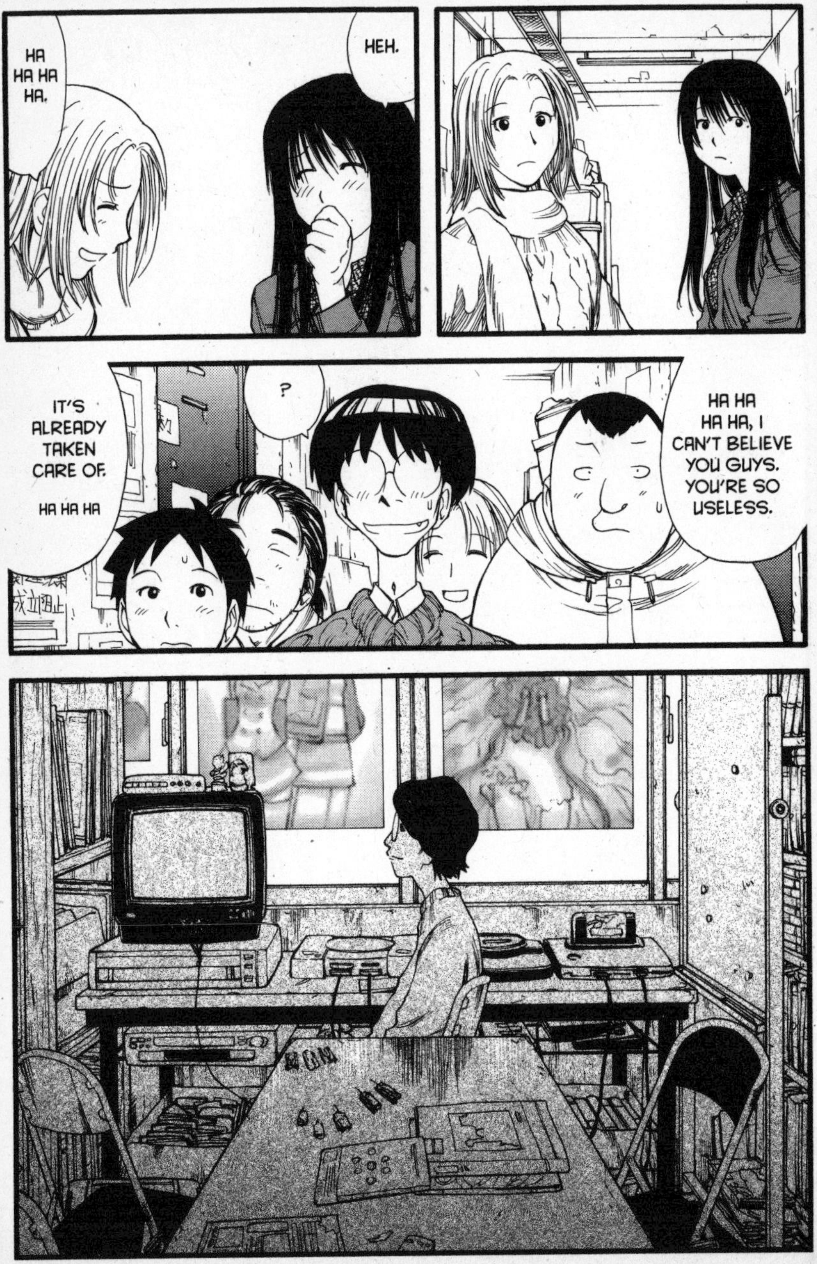
HEH.
HA HA HA HA.
HA HA HA HA, I CAN'T BELIEVE YOU GUYS. YOU'RE SO USELESS.
?
IT'S ALREADY TAKEN CARE OF.
HA HA HA

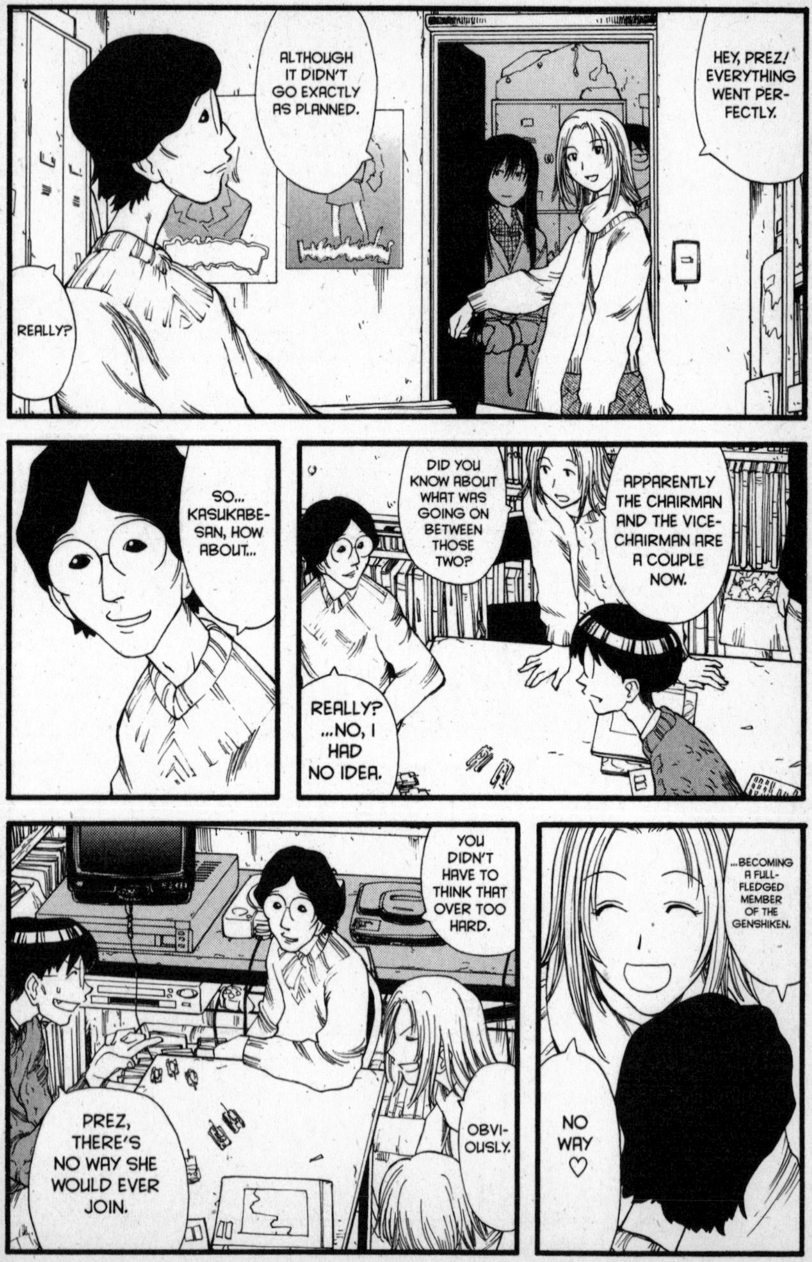
HEY, PREZ! EVERYTHING WENT PERFECTLY.
ALTHOUGH IT DIDN'T GO EXACTLY AS PLANNED.
REALLY?
APPARENTLY THE CHAIRMAN AND THE VICE-CHAIRMAN ARE A COUPLE NOW.
DID YOU KNOW ABOUT WHAT WAS GOING ON BETWEEN THOSE TWO?
REALLY? ...NO, I HAD NO IDEA.
SO... KASUKABE-SAN, HOW ABOUT...
...BECOMING A FULL-FLEDGED MEMBER OF THE GENSHIKEN.
NO WAY ♡
YOU DIDN'T HAVE TO THINK THAT OVER TOO HARD.
OBVI-OUSLY.
PREZ, THERE'S NO WAY SHE WOULD EVER JOIN.

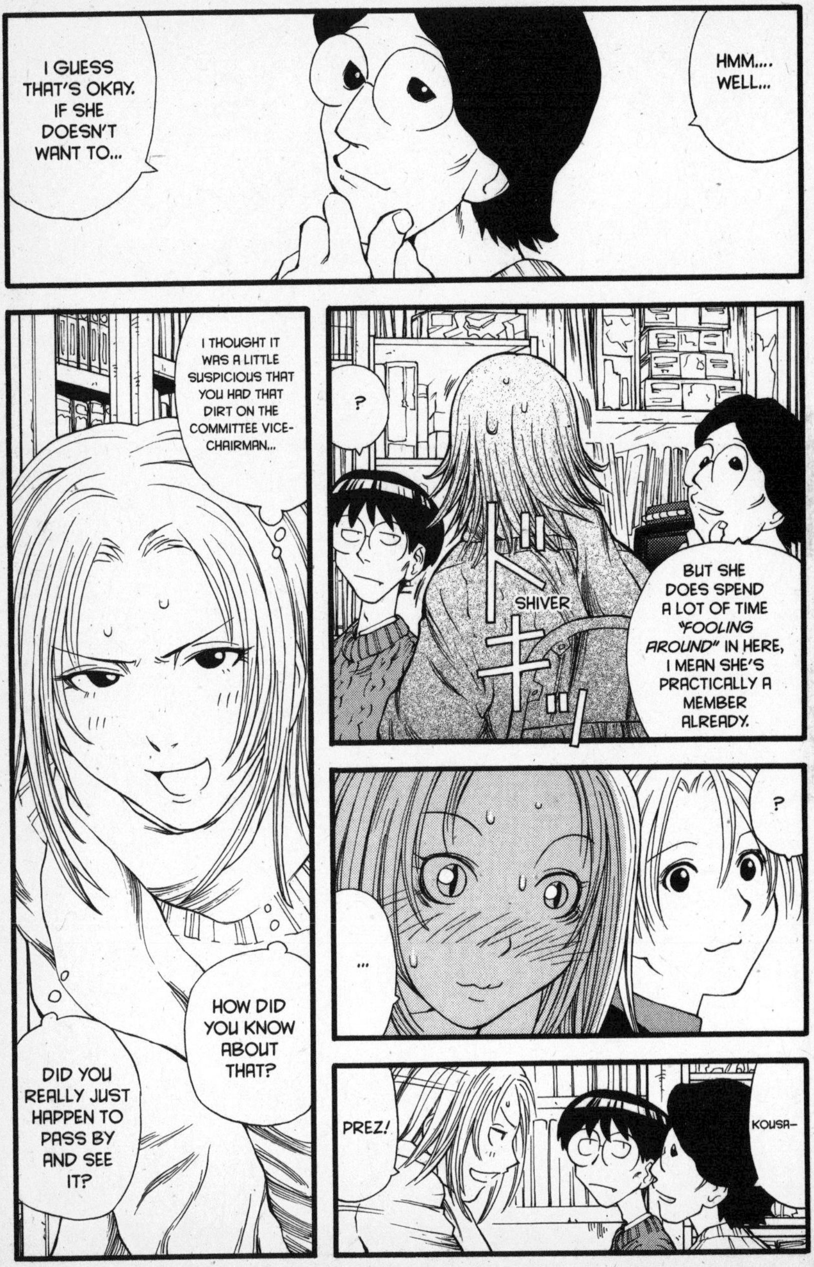
HMM.... WELL...
I GUESS THAT'S OKAY. IF SHE DOESN'T WANT TO...
BUT SHE DOES SPEND A LOT OF TIME "FOOLING AROUND" IN HERE, I MEAN SHE'S PRACTICALLY A MEMBER ALREADY.
SHIVER
?
?
...
KOUSA–
PREZ!
I THOUGHT IT WAS A LITTLE SUSPICIOUS THAT YOU HAD THAT DIRT ON THE COMMITTEE VICE-CHAIRMAN...
HOW DID YOU KNOW ABOUT THAT?
DID YOU REALLY JUST HAPPEN TO PASS BY AND SEE IT?

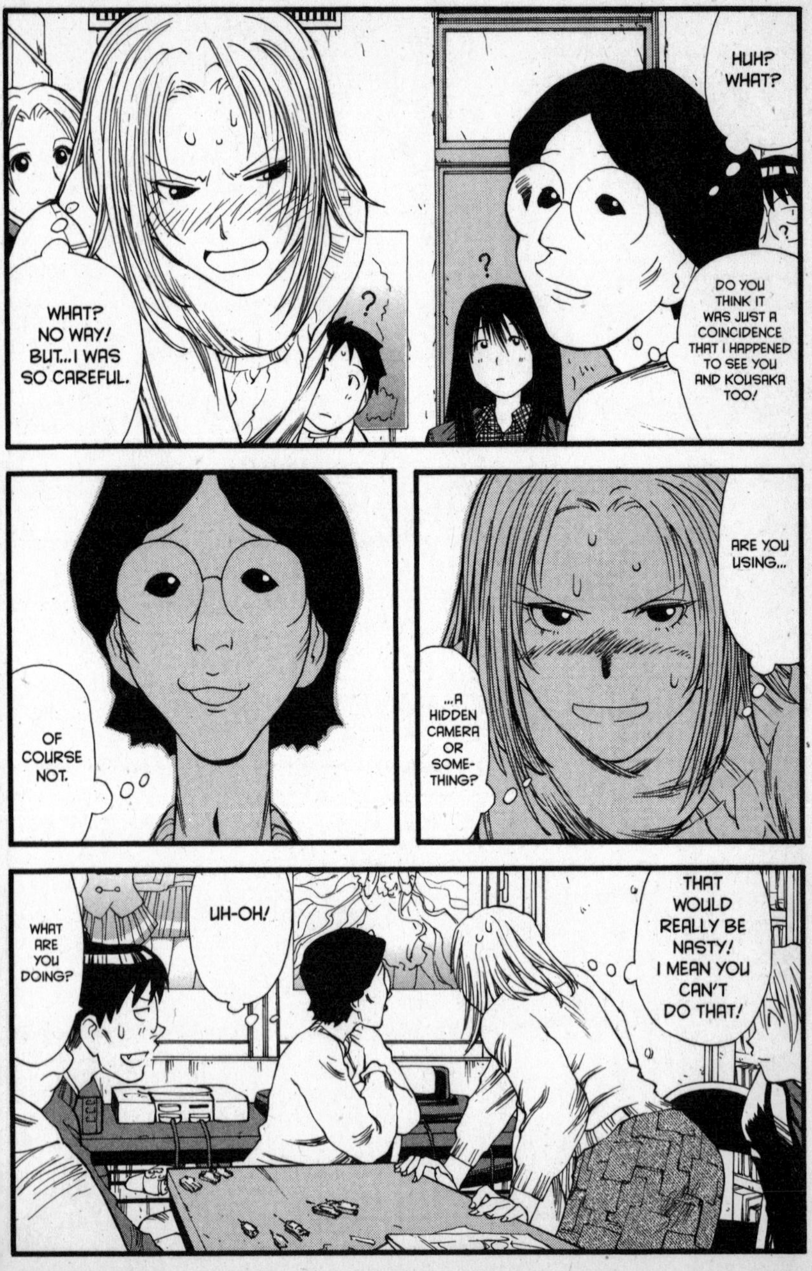
HUH? WHAT?
DO YOU THINK IT WAS JUST A COINCIDENCE THAT I HAPPENED TO SEE YOU AND KOUSAKA TOO!
WHAT? NO WAY! BUT...I WAS SO CAREFUL.
ARE YOU USING...
...A HIDDEN CAMERA OR SOME-THING?
OF COURSE NOT.
THAT WOULD REALLY BE NASTY! I MEAN YOU CAN'T DO THAT!
UH-OH!
WHAT ARE YOU DOING?

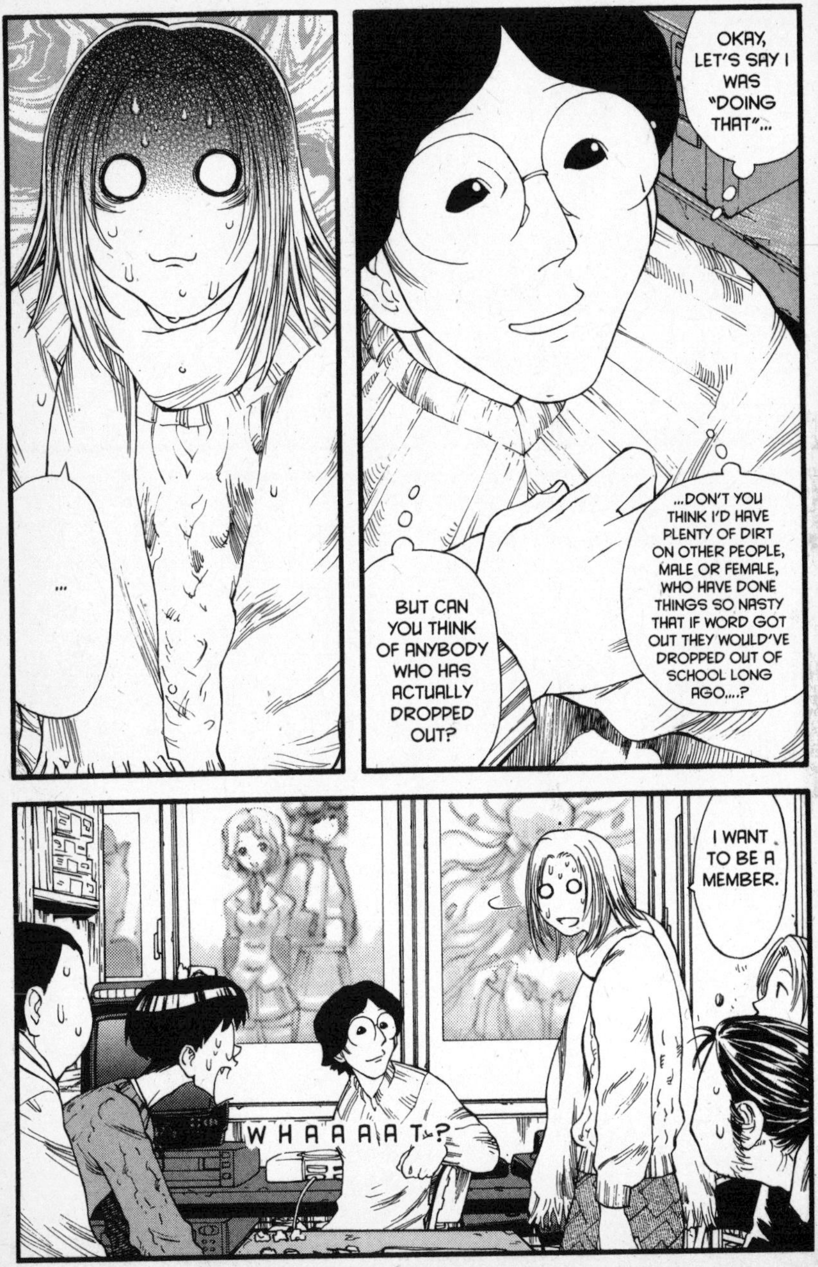
OKAY, LET'S SAY I WAS "DOING THAT"...
...DON'T YOU THINK I'D HAVE PLENTY OF DIRT ON OTHER PEOPLE, MALE OR FEMALE, WHO HAVE DONE THINGS SO NASTY THAT IF WORD GOT OUT THEY WOULD'VE DROPPED OUT OF SCHOOL LONG AGO....?
BUT CAN YOU THINK OF ANYBODY WHO HAS ACTUALLY DROPPED OUT?
...
I WANT TO BE A MEMBER.
WHAAAAAT?

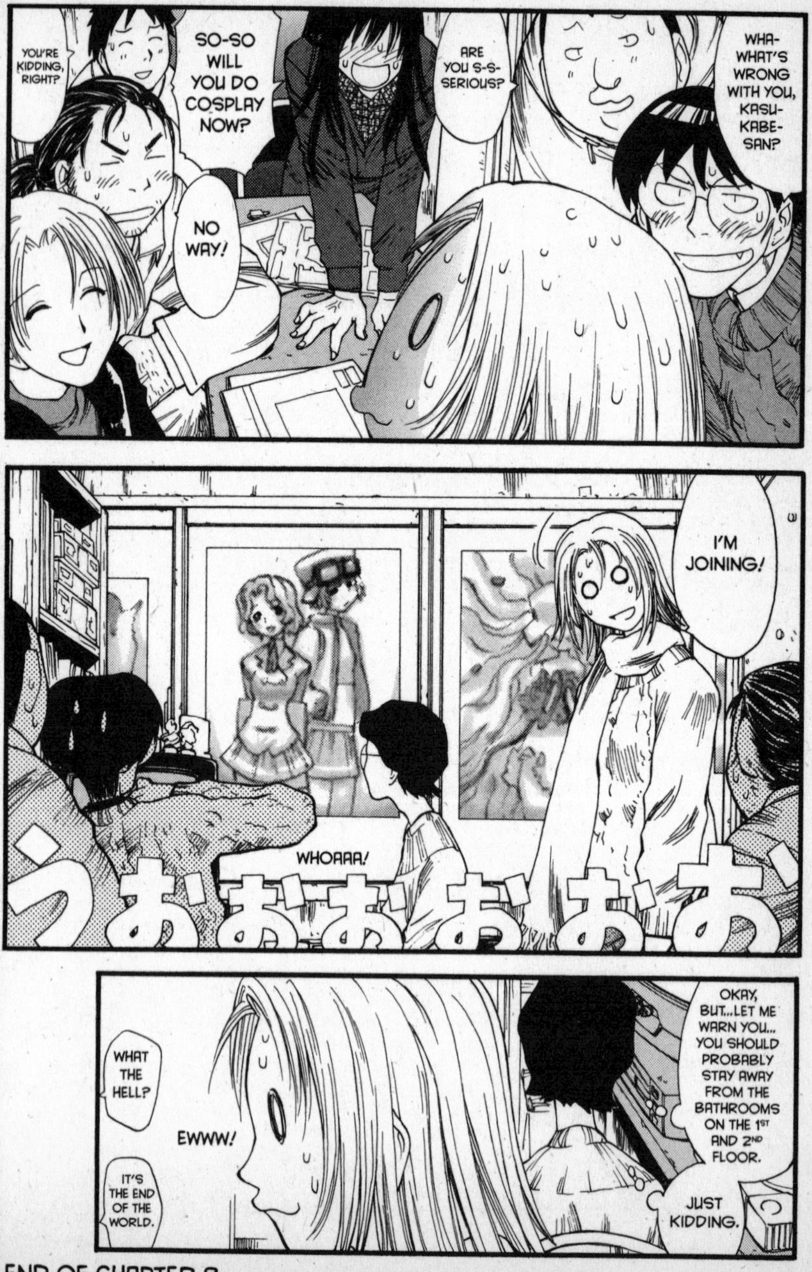
WHA-WHAT'S WRONG WITH YOU, KASU-KABE-SAN?
ARE YOU S-S-SERIOUS?
SO-SO WILL YOU DO COSPLAY NOW?
NO WAY!
YOU'RE KIDDING, RIGHT?
I'M JOINING!
WHOAAA!
OKAY, BUT...LET ME WARN YOU... YOU SHOULD PROBABLY STAY AWAY FROM THE BATHROOMS ON THE 1ST AND 2ND FLOOR.
JUST KIDDING.
EWWW!
WHAT THE HELL?
IT'S THE END OF THE WORLD.

END OF CHAPTER 8

THE GENSHIKEN MEMBERS PICK...

# KUJI-UN ...THE MOST NOTABLE SCENES

TAKEN FROM THE GENSHIKEN'S SPORADICALLY PUBLISHED ZINE "MEBAETAME"

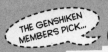

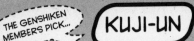

## MY FAVORITE SCENE FROM *KUJI-UN* PART 2 BY BENJAMIN TAKEYO

TANKOBON VOL. 3 PAGE 14

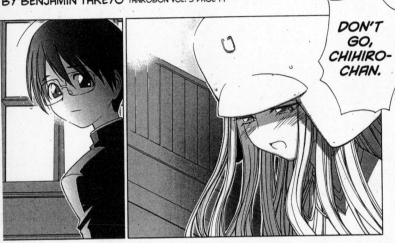

DON'T GO, CHIHIRO-CHAN.

WOW, PIT VIPER REALLY WENT ALL OUT (LAUGHS). I'M GOING TO PICK A MORE NORMAL SCENE. WOMEN ALWAYS SEEM TO SET UP TRAPS, BUT THEN BACK AWAY AT THE LAST MINUTE. THIS IS A SCENE THAT SHOWS THE PRESIDENT'S WEAKNESS AS WELL AS SOME OF HER LESS VIRTUOUS TRAITS. I THINK SHE USES THOSE CHARACTERISTICS IN ORDER TO GET WHAT SHE WANTS. THIS IS ALSO THE ONLY SCENE WHERE SHE REFERS TO CHIHIRO AS CHIHIRO-CHAN. EVEN WHEN THEY'RE ALONE TOGETHER, SHE ALWAYS CALLS HIM CHIHIRO-KUN. SHE NEVER CALLED HIM CHIHIRO-CHAN AGAIN AFTER THIS SCENE (AT LEAST SHE HASN'T SO FAR).

BUT I THINK THAT, PARADOXICALLY, THIS ACTUALLY SHOWS WHAT A STRONG CHARACTER SHE IS. IT JUST SHOWS HOW MUCH RESTRAINT SHE USES IN EVERYDAY LIFE...SUCH RESTRAINT (LAUGHS).

I REALLY...TRULY HOPE THAT SHE LIVES HAPPILY EVER AFTER. BUT...I THINK THAT MIGHT BE TOUGH. IF THIS BECOMES A VIDEOGAME, I WOULD MAKE IT SO THAT SHE WAS ALWAYS IN "LOVEY DOVEY MODE," AND SHE WOULD CALL PEOPLE "CHAN" ALL THE TIME...WHAT I'M TRYING TO SAY IS...HURRY UP, AND MAKE THIS INTO A VIDEOGAME. I WORK UP AN APPETITE JUST IMAGINING HOW SHE'D LOOK. I COULD PROBABLY EAT NINE BOWLS OF RICE. [BENJAMIN]

WELL, I THINK YOU WENT "ALL OUT" YOURSELF. THE PRESIDENT REALLY IS POPULAR, ISN'T SHE? I WONDER IF SHE'S THE MOST POPULAR KUJI-UN CHARACTER. DOES EVERYBODY REALLY LOVE HELMETS THAT MUCH? ACTUALLY, I THINK IT'S HER UNDENIABLE "GIRL NEXT DOOR" PERSONALITY THAT MAKES HER A TRULY POWERFUL HEROINE. PERSONALLY, I LIKE THE FACT THAT SHE'S SHORT, BUT...SHE'S STILL TOO TALL FOR ME. SORRY. I HAD A FEELING THAT THIS WOULD HAPPEN, BUT...IT LOOKS LIKE THIS HAS JUST BECOME A CHARACTER POPULARITY CONTEST (LAUGHS). NEXT, WE'LL HEAR FROM THE OWL. [PIT VIPER].

## CHAPTER 8- MOMENTS LATER

### CANDID CAMERA

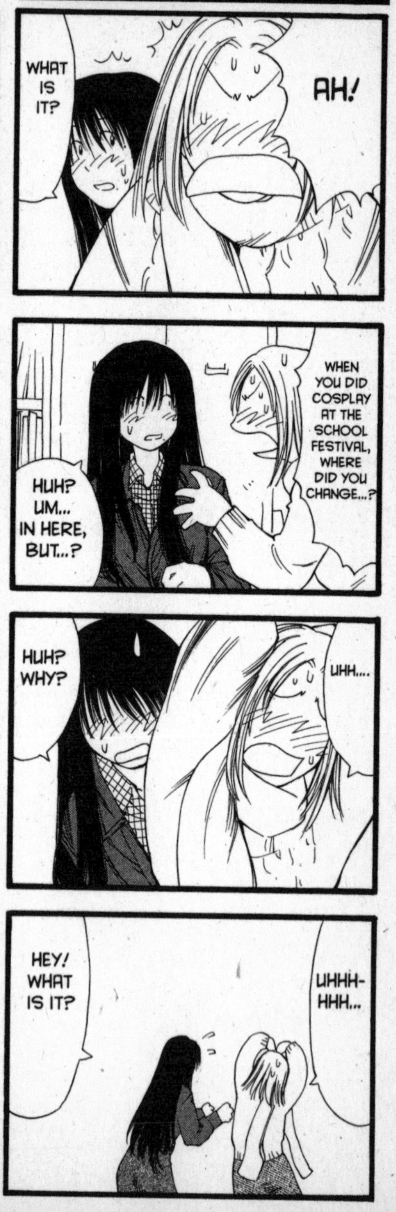
AH!
WHAT IS IT?
WHEN YOU DID COSPLAY AT THE SCHOOL FESTIVAL, WHERE DID YOU CHANGE...?
HUH? UM... IN HERE, BUT...?
UHH....
HUH? WHY?
UHHH-HHH...
HEY! WHAT IS IT?

### KASUKABE'S BRAIN

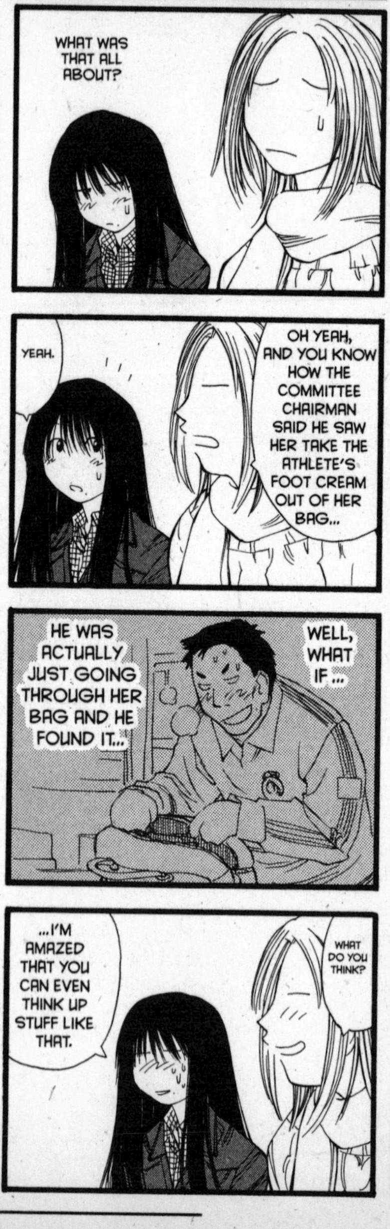
WHAT WAS THAT ALL ABOUT?
OH YEAH, AND YOU KNOW HOW THE COMMITTEE CHAIRMAN SAID HE SAW HER TAKE THE ATHLETE'S FOOT CREAM OUT OF HER BAG...
YEAH.
WELL, WHAT IF ...
HE WAS ACTUALLY JUST GOING THROUGH HER BAG AND HE FOUND IT...
WHAT DO YOU THINK?
...I'M AMAZED THAT YOU CAN EVEN THINK UP STUFF LIKE THAT.

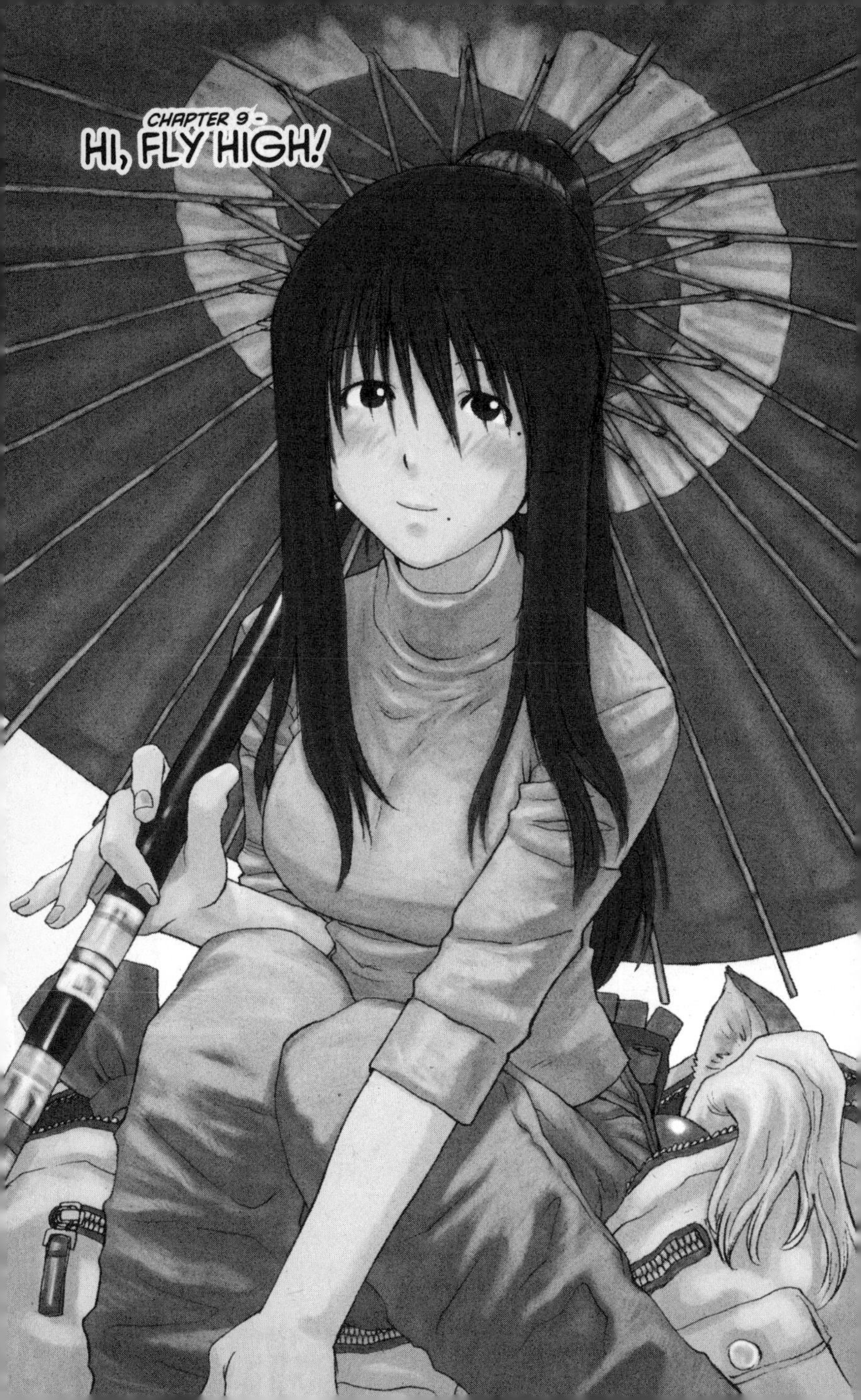
CHAPTER 9 -
HI, FLY HIGH!

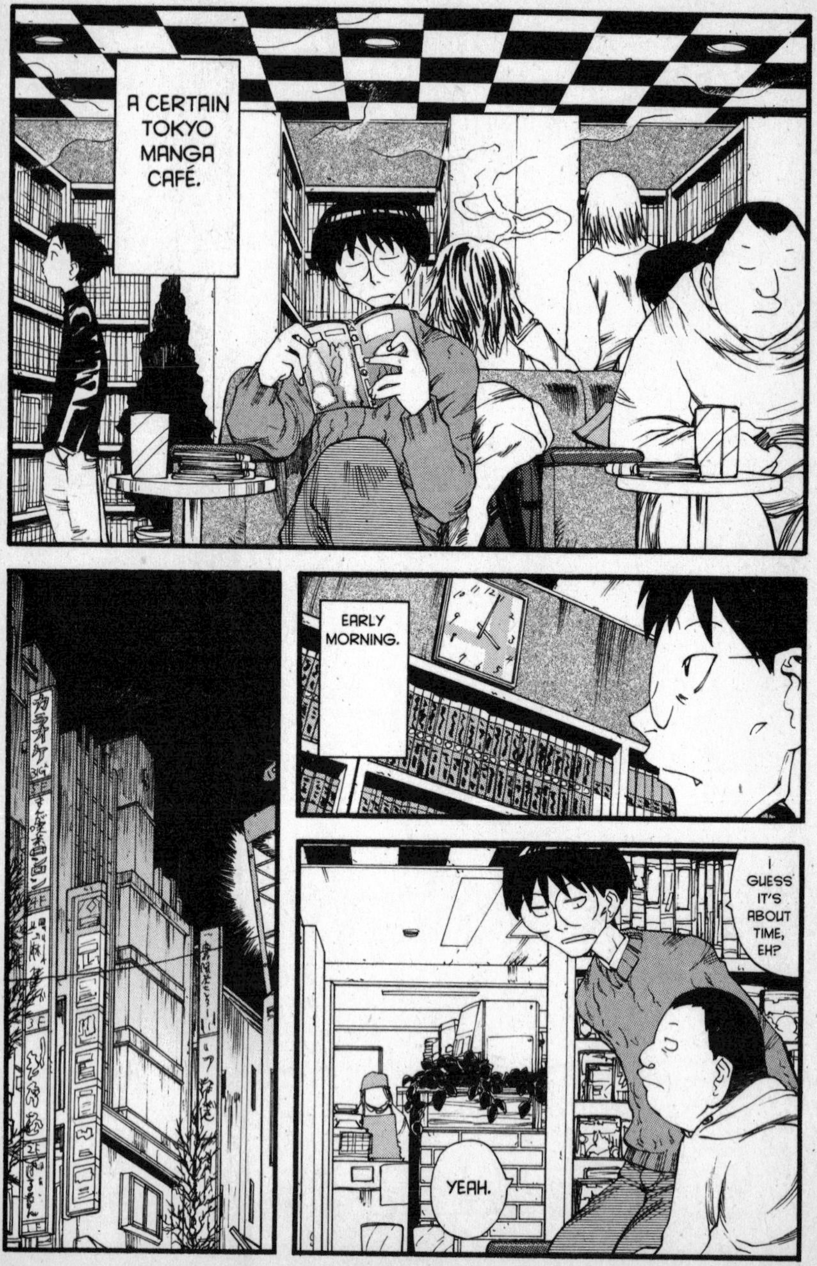
A CERTAIN TOKYO MANGA CAFÉ.
EARLY MORNING.
I GUESS IT'S ABOUT TIME, EH?
YEAH.

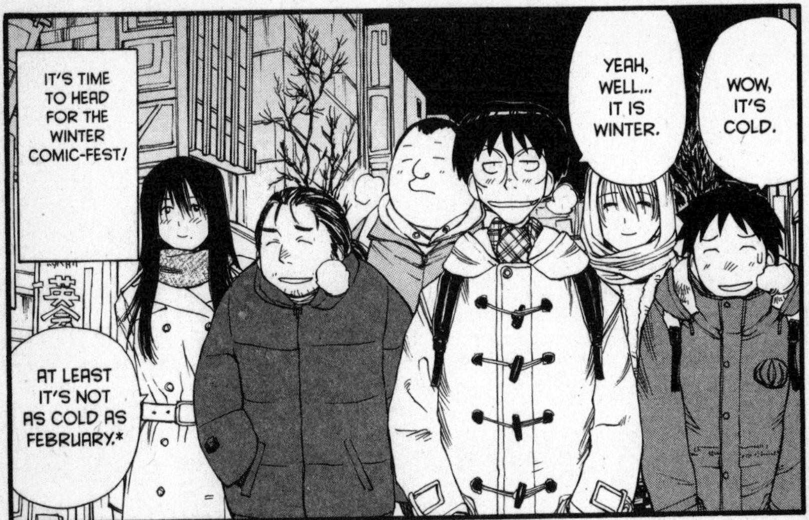
WOW, IT'S COLD.
YEAH, WELL... IT IS WINTER.
IT'S TIME TO HEAD FOR THE WINTER COMIC-FEST!
AT LEAST IT'S NOT AS COLD AS FEBRUARY.*

*TANAKA GOES TO A GARAGE KIT MODEL CONVENTION EVERY FEBRUARY.

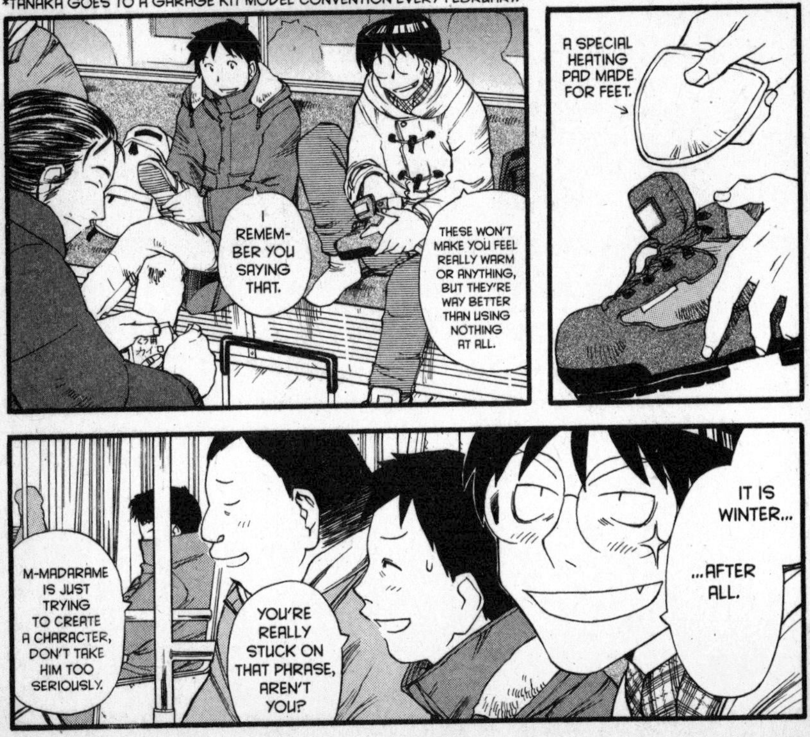
A SPECIAL HEATING PAD MADE FOR FEET.
THESE WON'T MAKE YOU FEEL REALLY WARM OR ANYTHING, BUT THEY'RE WAY BETTER THAN USING NOTHING AT ALL.
I REMEMBER YOU SAYING THAT.
IT IS WINTER...
...AFTER ALL.
YOU'RE REALLY STUCK ON THAT PHRASE, AREN'T YOU?
M-MADARAME IS JUST TRYING TO CREATE A CHARACTER, DON'T TAKE HIM TOO SERIOUSLY.

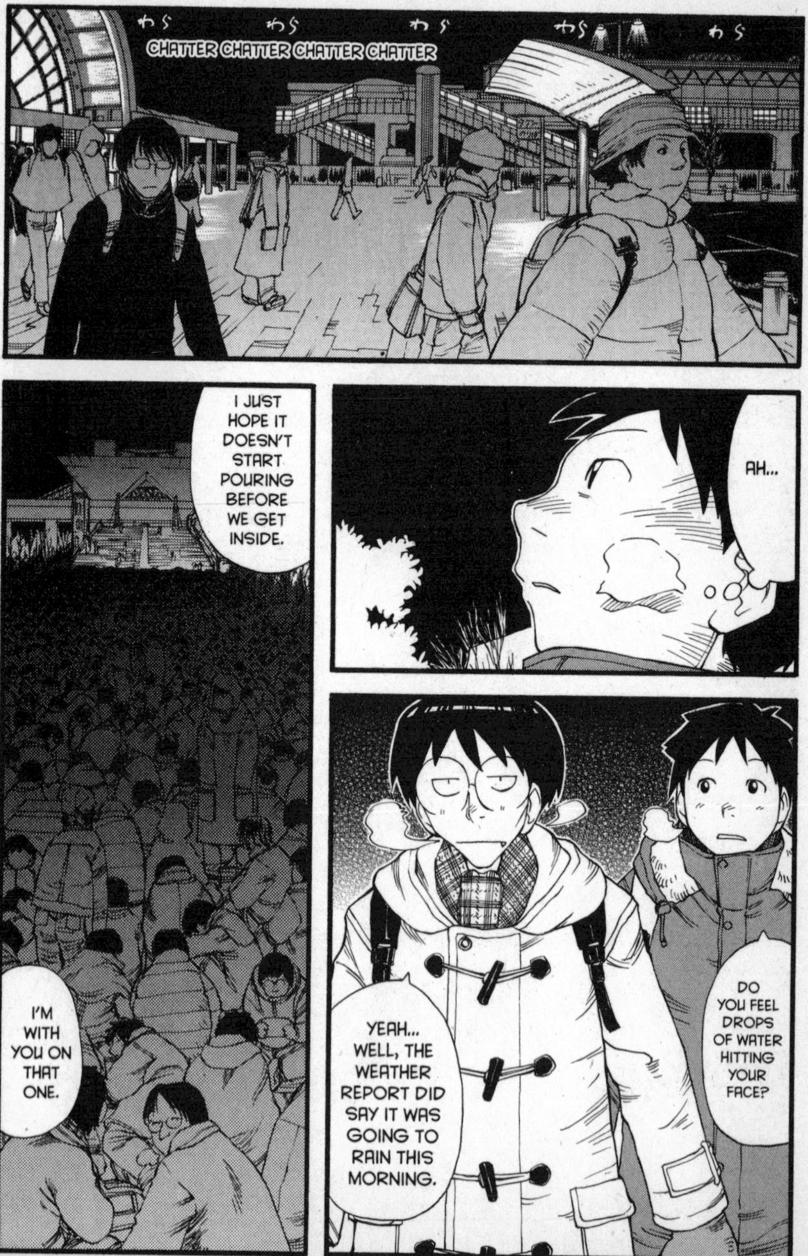
わら わら わら わら わら
CHATTER CHATTER CHATTER CHATTER
AH...
DO YOU FEEL DROPS OF WATER HITTING YOUR FACE?
YEAH... WELL, THE WEATHER REPORT DID SAY IT WAS GOING TO RAIN THIS MORNING.
I JUST HOPE IT DOESN'T START POURING BEFORE WE GET INSIDE.
I'M WITH YOU ON THAT ONE.

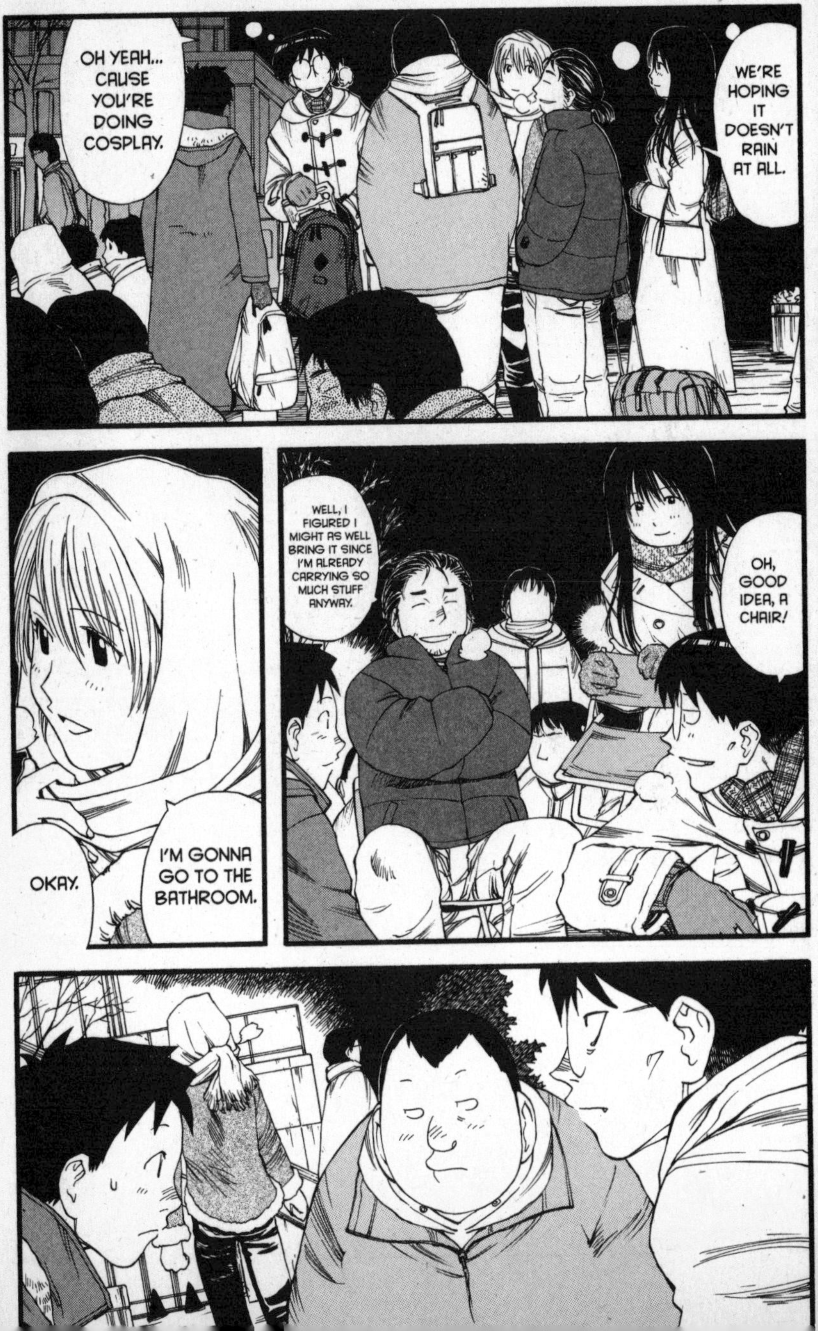
WE'RE HOPING IT DOESN'T RAIN AT ALL.
OH YEAH... CAUSE YOU'RE DOING COSPLAY.
OH, GOOD IDEA, A CHAIR!
WELL, I FIGURED I MIGHT AS WELL BRING IT SINCE I'M ALREADY CARRYING SO MUCH STUFF ANYWAY.
I'M GONNA GO TO THE BATHROOM.
OKAY.

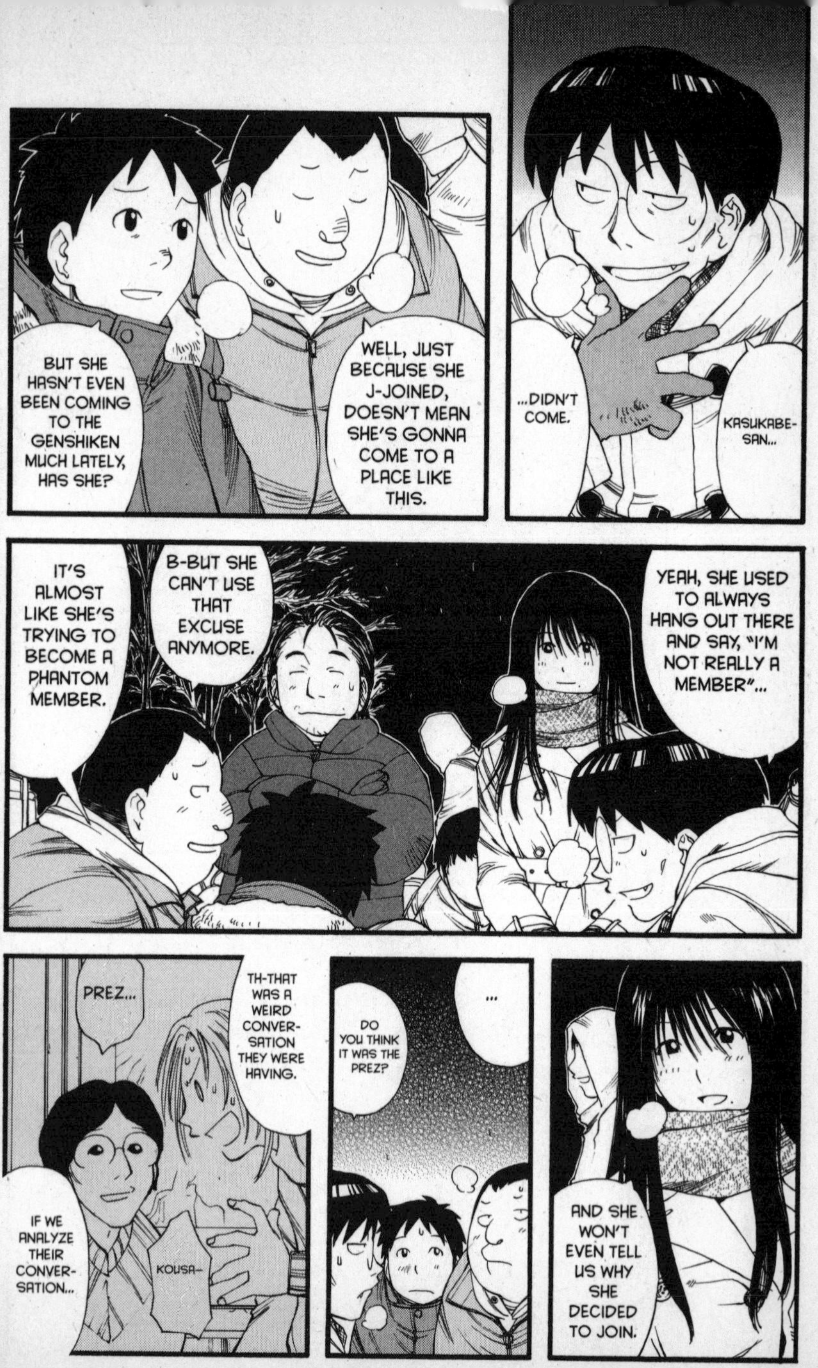
KASUKABE-SAN...
...DIDN'T COME.
WELL, JUST BECAUSE SHE J-JOINED, DOESN'T MEAN SHE'S GONNA COME TO A PLACE LIKE THIS.
BUT SHE HASN'T EVEN BEEN COMING TO THE GENSHIKEN MUCH LATELY, HAS SHE?
YEAH, SHE USED TO ALWAYS HANG OUT THERE AND SAY, "I'M NOT REALLY A MEMBER"...
B-BUT SHE CAN'T USE THAT EXCUSE ANYMORE.
IT'S ALMOST LIKE SHE'S TRYING TO BECOME A PHANTOM MEMBER.
AND SHE WON'T EVEN TELL US WHY SHE DECIDED TO JOIN.
...
DO YOU THINK IT WAS THE PREZ?
TH-THAT WAS A WEIRD CONVERSATION THEY WERE HAVING.
PREZ...
IF WE ANALYZE THEIR CONVERSATION...
KOUSA-

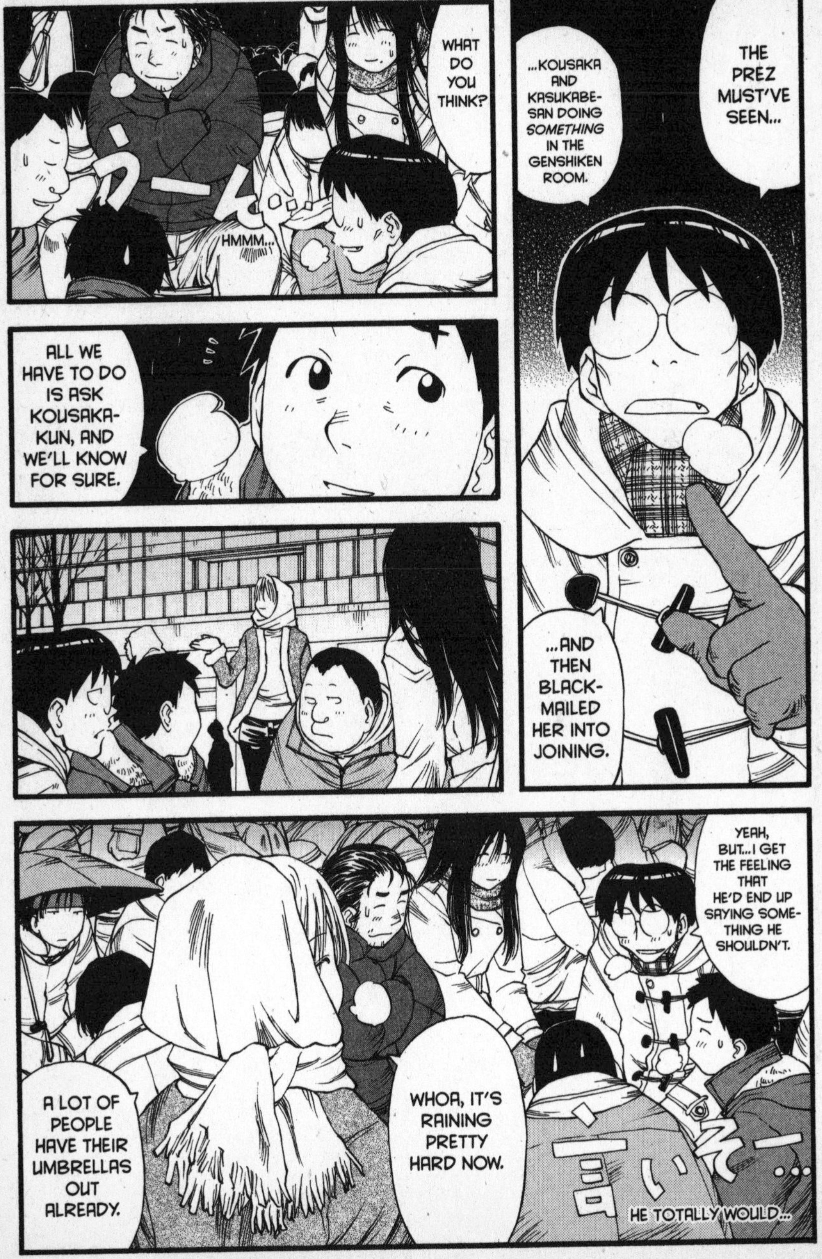
THE PREZ MUST'VE SEEN...
...KOUSAKA AND KASUKABE-SAN DOING *SOMETHING* IN THE GENSHIKEN ROOM.
...AND THEN BLACK-MAILED HER INTO JOINING.
WHAT DO YOU THINK?
HMMM...
ALL WE HAVE TO DO IS ASK KOUSAKA-KUN, AND WE'LL KNOW FOR SURE.
YEAH, BUT...I GET THE FEELING THAT HE'D END UP SAYING SOME-THING HE SHOULDN'T.
HE TOTALLY WOULD...
WHOA, IT'S RAINING PRETTY HARD NOW.
A LOT OF PEOPLE HAVE THEIR UMBRELLAS OUT ALREADY.

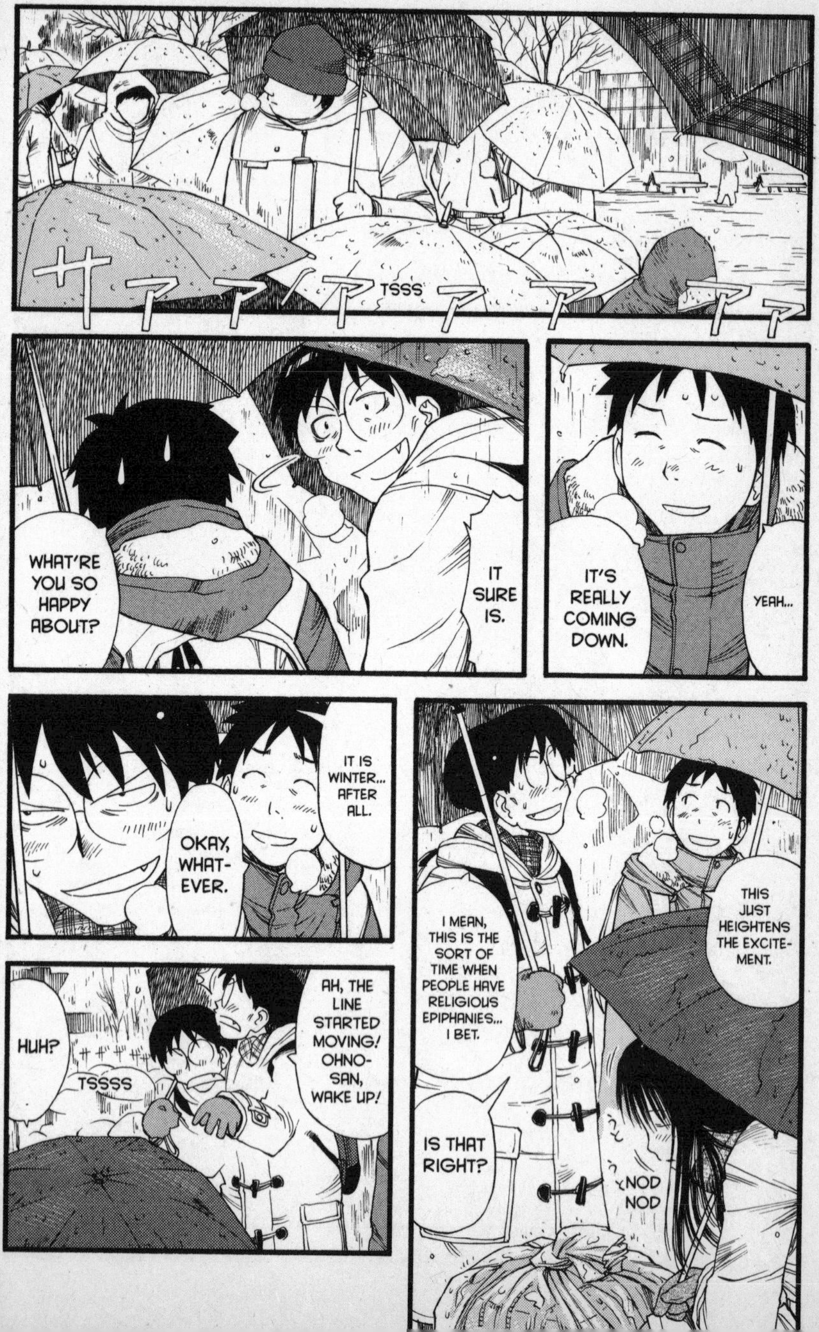
サアアアアアア
TSSS
IT'S REALLY COMING DOWN.
YEAH...
IT SURE IS.
WHAT'RE YOU SO HAPPY ABOUT?
THIS JUST HEIGHTENS THE EXCITEMENT.
I MEAN, THIS IS THE SORT OF TIME WHEN PEOPLE HAVE RELIGIOUS EPIPHANIES... I BET.
IS THAT RIGHT?
うとうと
NOD NOD
IT IS WINTER... AFTER ALL.
OKAY, WHATEVER.
AH, THE LINE STARTED MOVING! OHNO-SAN, WAKE UP!
HUH?
TSSSS

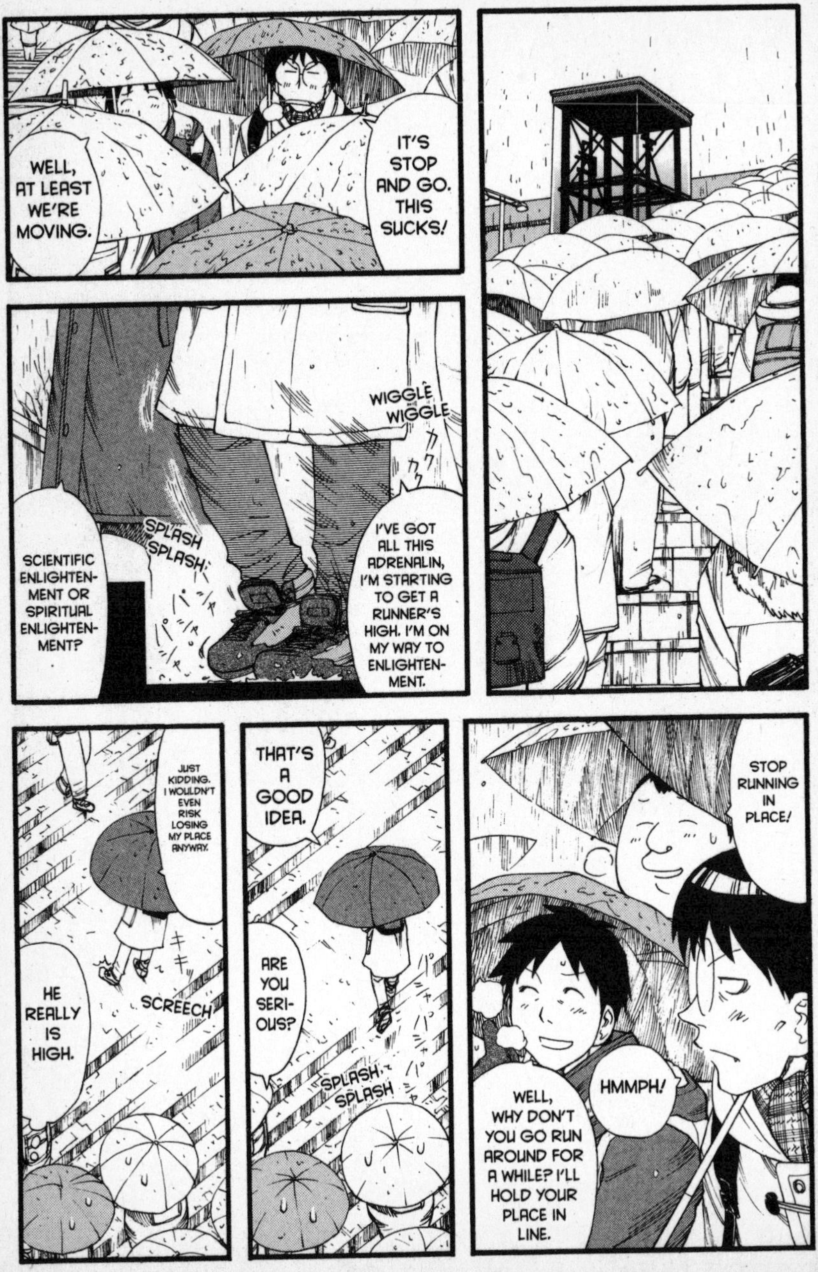
IT'S STOP AND GO. THIS SUCKS!
WELL, AT LEAST WE'RE MOVING.
WIGGLE WIGGLE
I'VE GOT ALL THIS ADRENALIN, I'M STARTING TO GET A RUNNER'S HIGH. I'M ON MY WAY TO ENLIGHTENMENT.
SPLASH SPLASH
SCIENTIFIC ENLIGHTENMENT OR SPIRITUAL ENLIGHTENMENT?
STOP RUNNING IN PLACE!
HMMPH!
WELL, WHY DON'T YOU GO RUN AROUND FOR A WHILE? I'LL HOLD YOUR PLACE IN LINE.
THAT'S A GOOD IDEA.
ARE YOU SERIOUS?
SPLASH, SPLASH
JUST KIDDING. I WOULDN'T EVEN RISK LOSING MY PLACE ANYWAY.
SCREECH
HE REALLY IS HIGH.

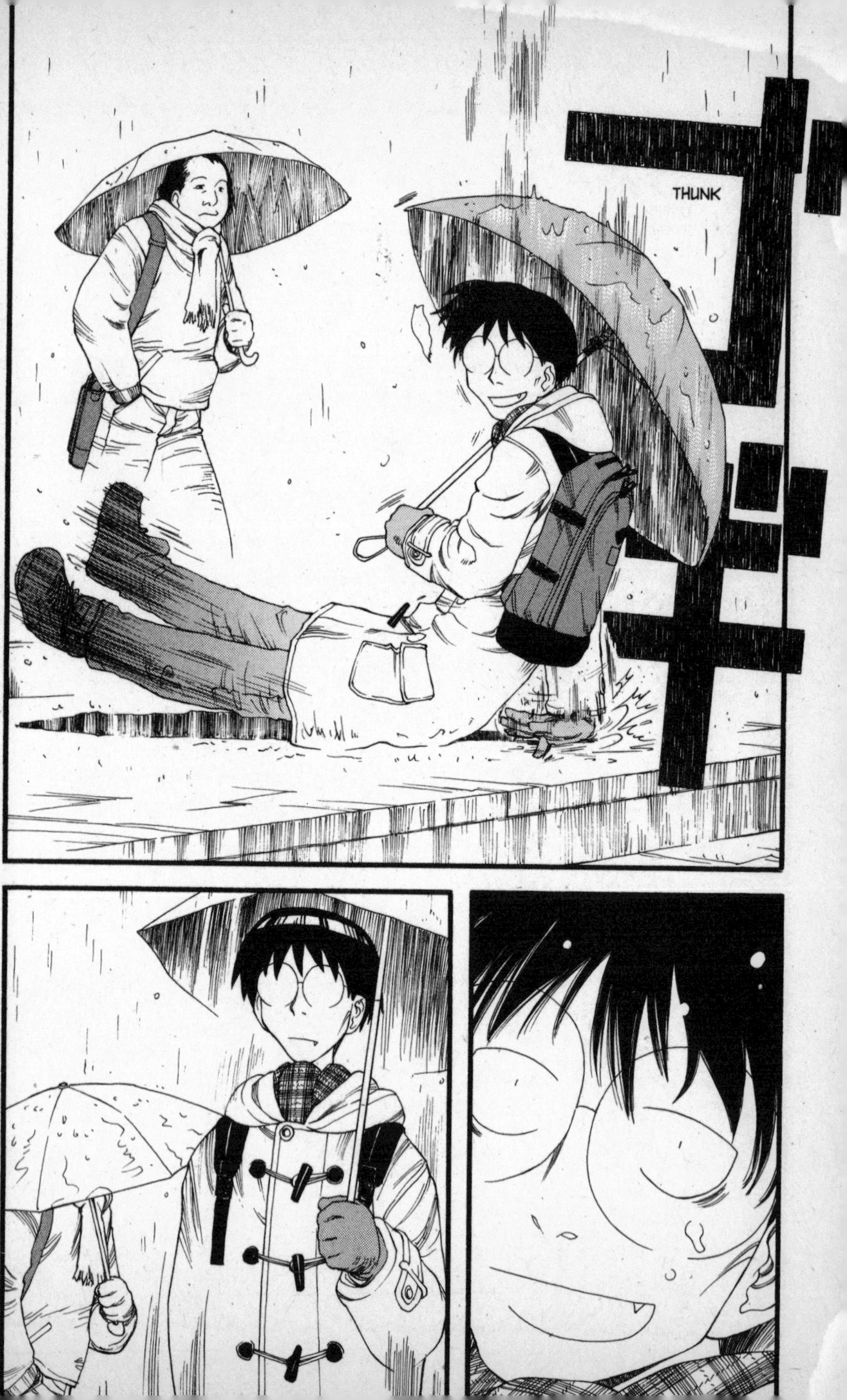
THUNK

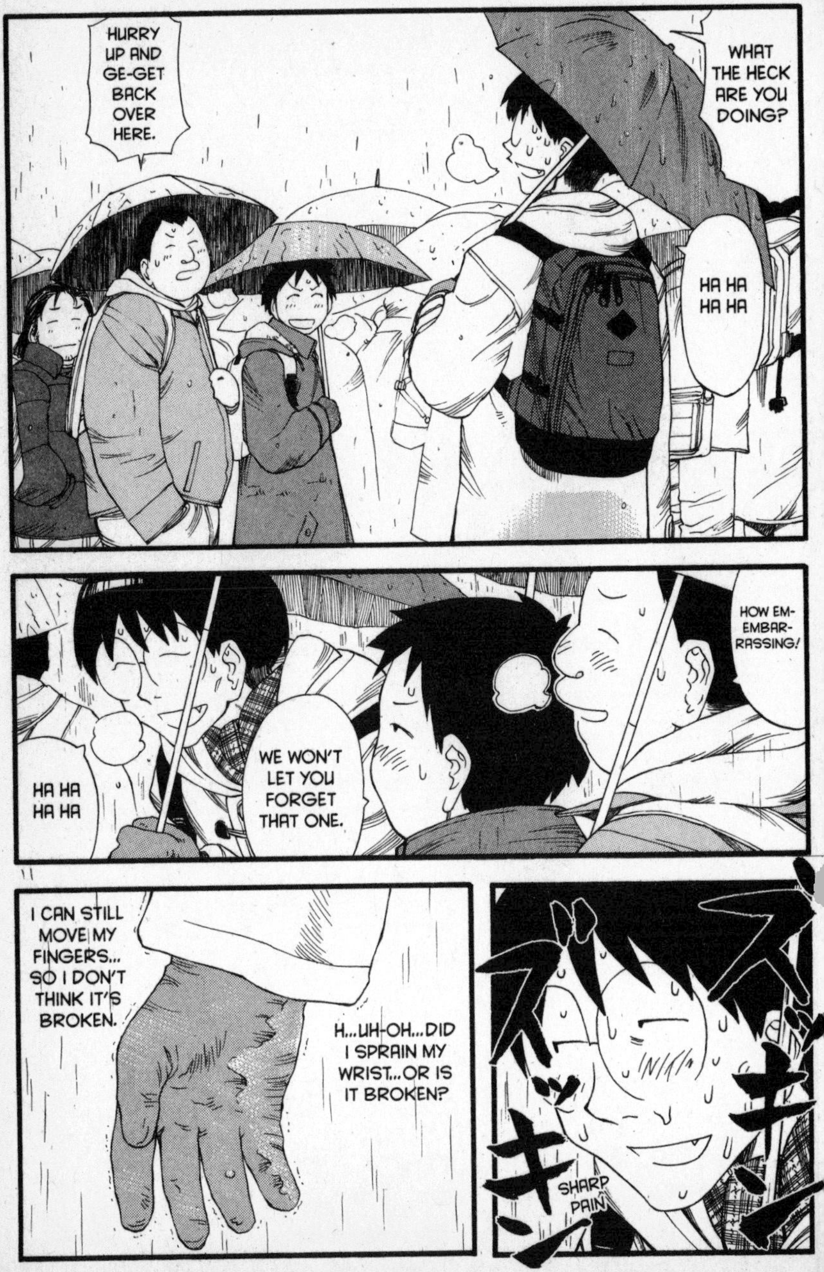
WHAT THE HECK ARE YOU DOING?
HA HA HA HA
HURRY UP AND GE-GET BACK OVER HERE.
HOW EM-EMBARRASSING!
WE WON'T LET YOU FORGET THAT ONE.
HA HA HA HA
SHARP PAIN
H...UH-OH...DID I SPRAIN MY WRIST...OR IS IT BROKEN?
I CAN STILL MOVE MY FINGERS... SO I DON'T THINK IT'S BROKEN.

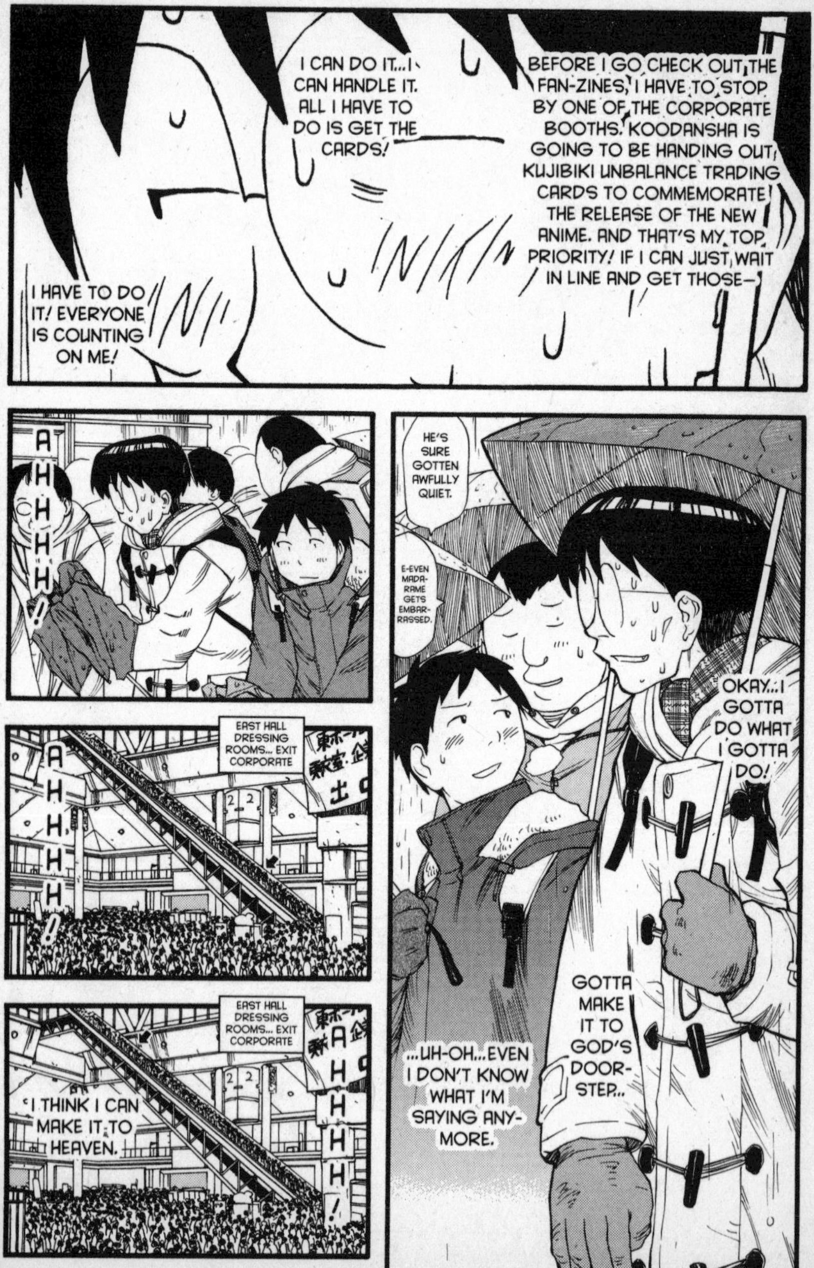
BEFORE I GO CHECK OUT THE FAN-ZINES, I HAVE TO STOP BY ONE OF THE CORPORATE BOOTHS. KOODANSHA IS GOING TO BE HANDING OUT KUJIBIKI UNBALANCE TRADING CARDS TO COMMEMORATE THE RELEASE OF THE NEW ANIME. AND THAT'S MY TOP PRIORITY! IF I CAN JUST WAIT IN LINE AND GET THOSE—
I CAN DO IT...I CAN HANDLE IT. ALL I HAVE TO DO IS GET THE CARDS!
I HAVE TO DO IT! EVERYONE IS COUNTING ON ME!
HE'S SURE GOTTEN AWFULLY QUIET.
E-EVEN MADARAME GETS EMBARRASSED.
OKAY...I GOTTA DO WHAT I GOTTA DO!
GOTTA MAKE IT TO GOD'S DOORSTEP...
...UH-OH...EVEN I DON'T KNOW WHAT I'M SAYING ANYMORE.
AHHHHH!
EAST HALL DRESSING ROOMS... EXIT CORPORATE
AHHHHHH!
EAST HALL DRESSING ROOMS... EXIT CORPORATE
I THINK I CAN MAKE IT TO HEAVEN.
AHHHHHH!

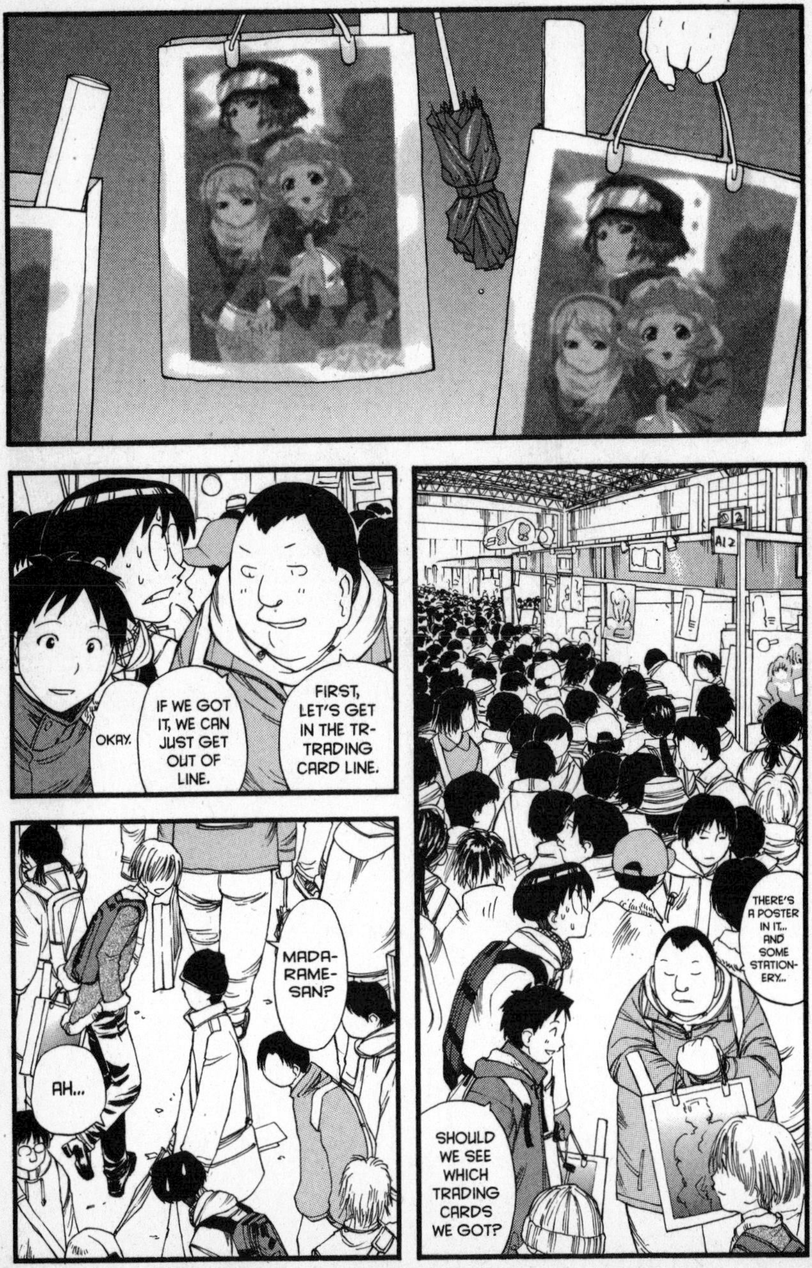
THERE'S A POSTER IN IT... AND SOME STATIONERY...
SHOULD WE SEE WHICH TRADING CARDS WE GOT?
FIRST, LET'S GET IN THE TR- TRADING CARD LINE.
IF WE GOT IT, WE CAN JUST GET OUT OF LINE.
OKAY.
MADA-RAME-SAN?
AH...

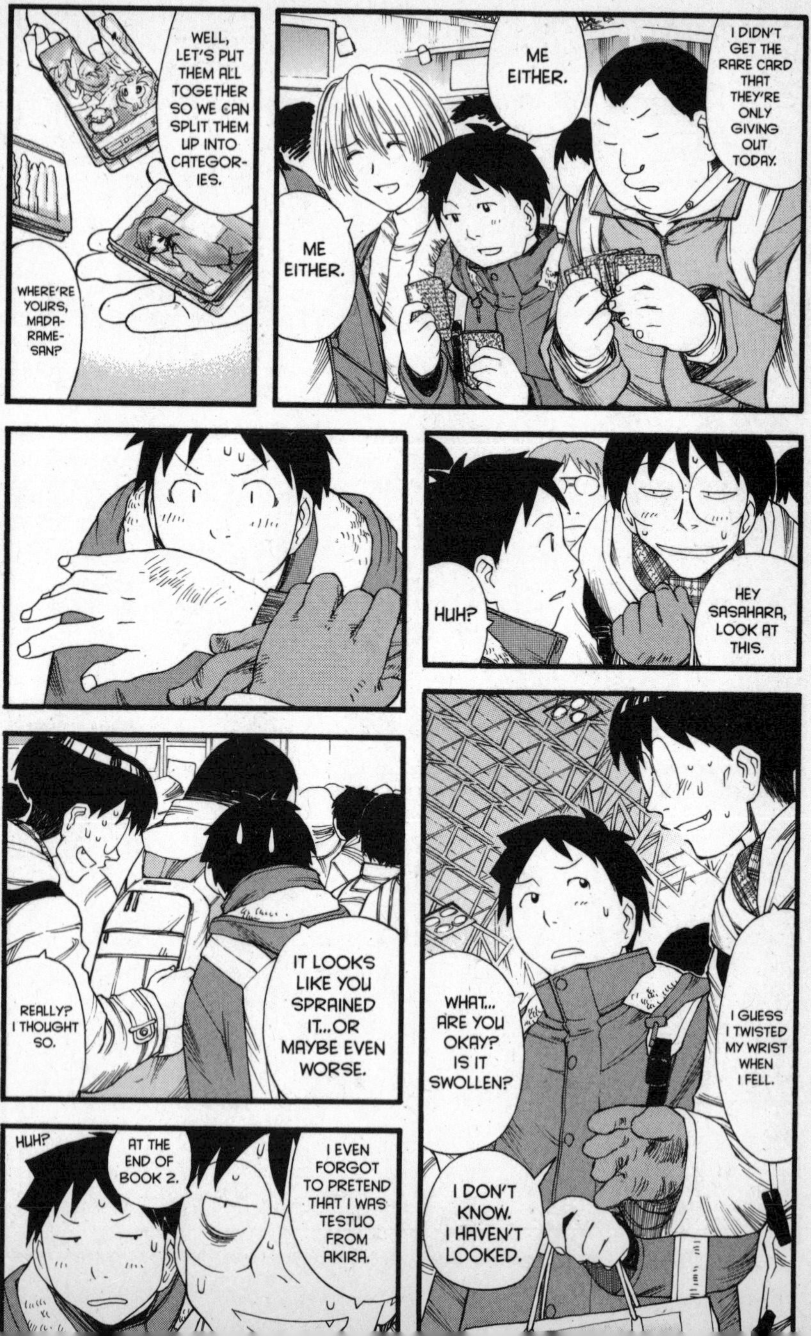
I DIDN'T GET THE RARE CARD THAT THEY'RE ONLY GIVING OUT TODAY.
ME EITHER.
ME EITHER.
WELL, LET'S PUT THEM ALL TOGETHER SO WE CAN SPLIT THEM UP INTO CATEGOR-IES.
WHERE'RE YOURS, MADA-RAME-SAN?
HEY SASAHARA, LOOK AT THIS.
HUH?
I GUESS I TWISTED MY WRIST WHEN I FELL.
WHAT... ARE YOU OKAY? IS IT SWOLLEN?
I DON'T KNOW. I HAVEN'T LOOKED.
IT LOOKS LIKE YOU SPRAINED IT...OR MAYBE EVEN WORSE.
REALLY? I THOUGHT SO.
I EVEN FORGOT TO PRETEND THAT I WAS TESTUO FROM AKIRA.
AT THE END OF BOOK 2.
HUH?

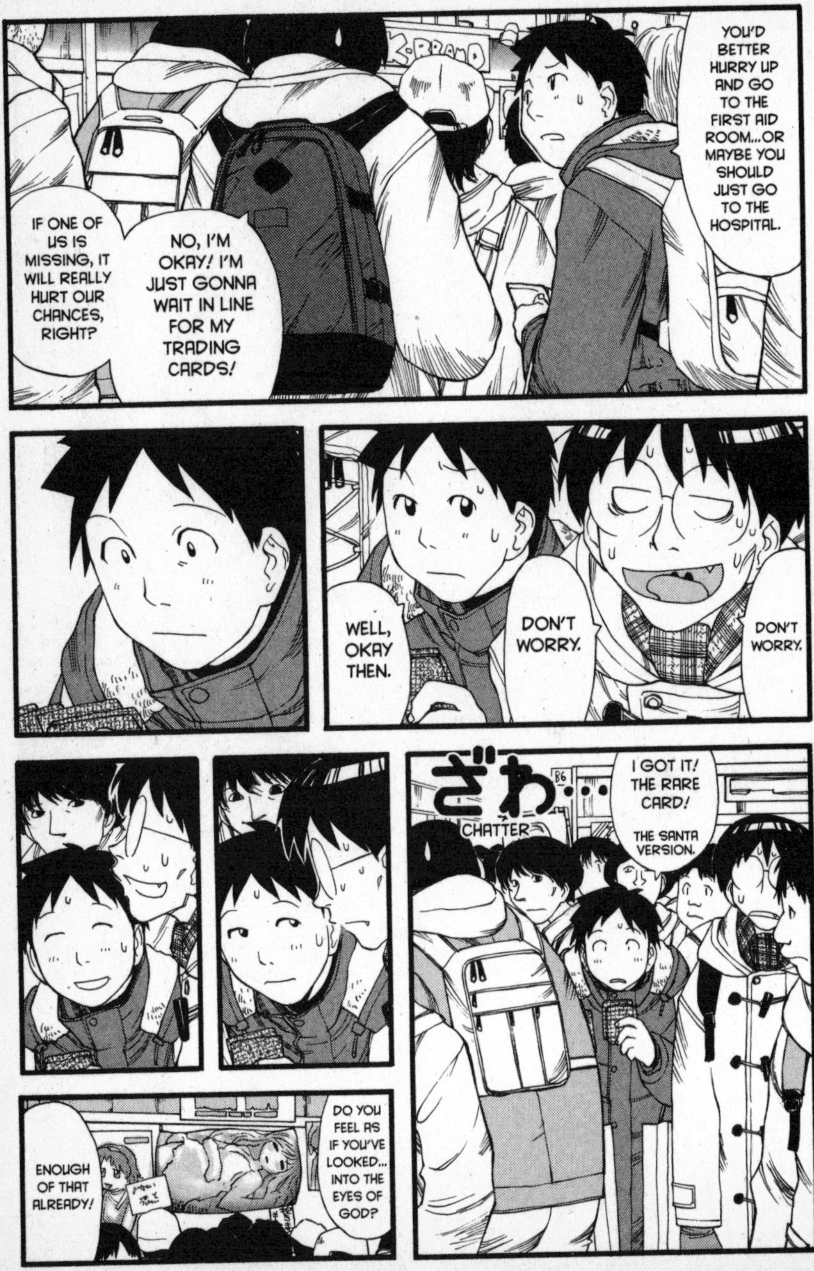
YOU'D BETTER HURRY UP AND GO TO THE FIRST AID ROOM...OR MAYBE YOU SHOULD JUST GO TO THE HOSPITAL.
NO, I'M OKAY! I'M JUST GONNA WAIT IN LINE FOR MY TRADING CARDS!
IF ONE OF US IS MISSING, IT WILL REALLY HURT OUR CHANCES, RIGHT?
DON'T WORRY.
DON'T WORRY.
WELL, OKAY THEN.
ざわ…
CHATTER
I GOT IT! THE RARE CARD!
THE SANTA VERSION.
DO YOU FEEL AS IF YOU'VE LOOKED... INTO THE EYES OF GOD?
ENOUGH OF THAT ALREADY!

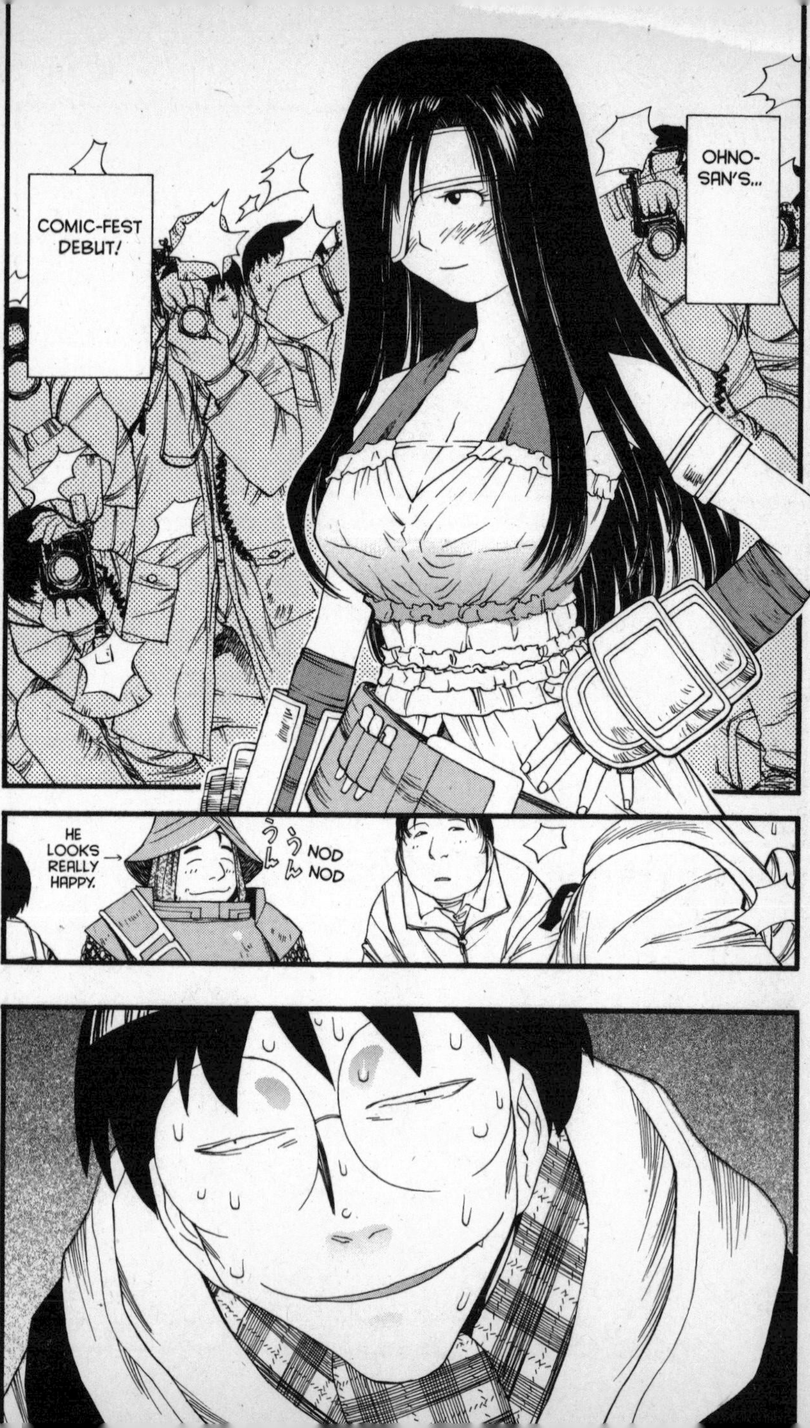
OHNO-SAN'S...
COMIC-FEST DEBUT!
うんうん
NOD NOD
HE LOOKS REALLY HAPPY.

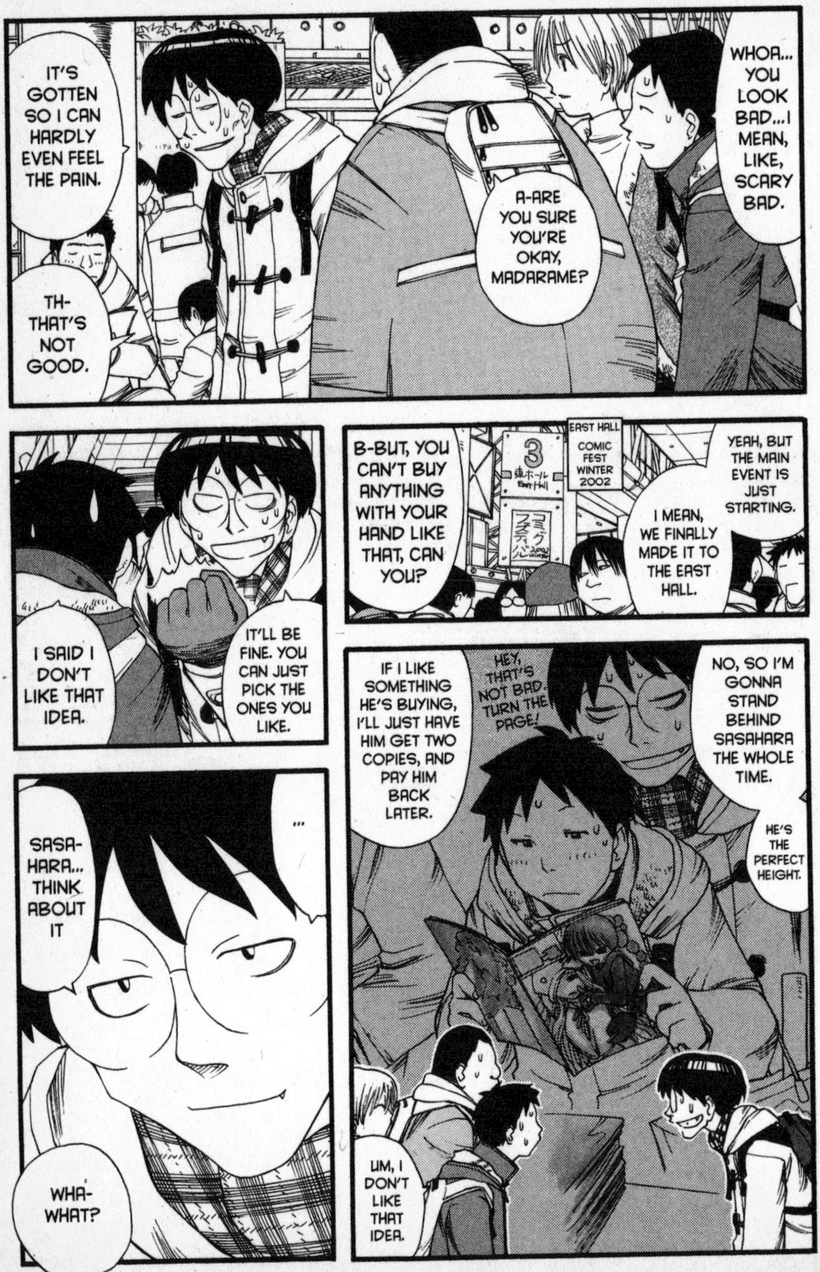
WHOA... YOU LOOK BAD...I MEAN, LIKE, SCARY BAD.
A-ARE YOU SURE YOU'RE OKAY, MADARAME?
IT'S GOTTEN SO I CAN HARDLY EVEN FEEL THE PAIN.
TH-THAT'S NOT GOOD.
EAST HALL
COMIC FEST WINTER 2002
3
YEAH, BUT THE MAIN EVENT IS JUST STARTING.
I MEAN, WE FINALLY MADE IT TO THE EAST HALL.
B-BUT, YOU CAN'T BUY ANYTHING WITH YOUR HAND LIKE THAT, CAN YOU?
IT'LL BE FINE. YOU CAN JUST PICK THE ONES YOU LIKE.
I SAID I DON'T LIKE THAT IDEA.
NO, SO I'M GONNA STAND BEHIND SASAHARA THE WHOLE TIME.
HE'S THE PERFECT HEIGHT.
HEY, THAT'S NOT BAD. TURN THE PAGE!
IF I LIKE SOMETHING HE'S BUYING, I'LL JUST HAVE HIM GET TWO COPIES, AND PAY HIM BACK LATER.
UM, I DON'T LIKE THAT IDEA.
...
SASA-HARA... THINK ABOUT IT
WHA-WHAT?

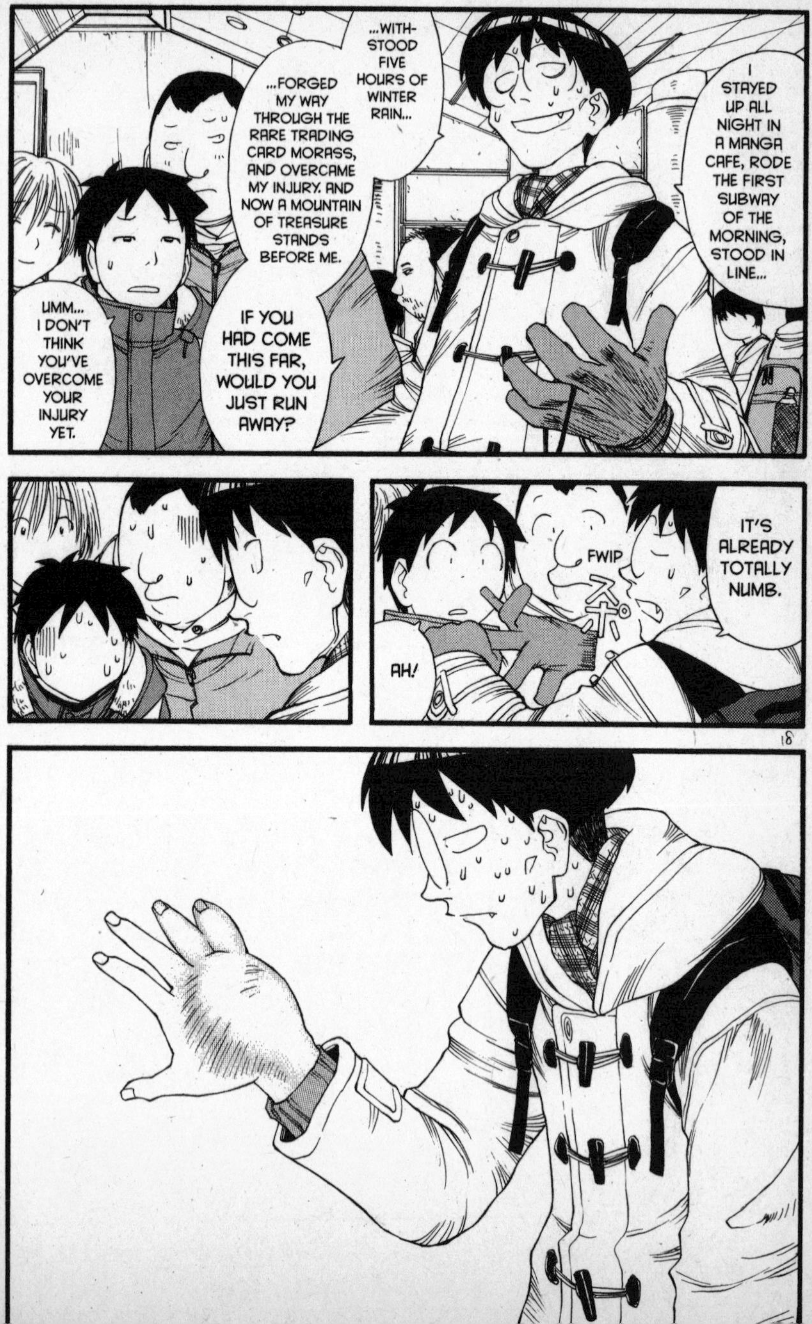
I STAYED UP ALL NIGHT IN A MANGA CAFE, RODE THE FIRST SUBWAY OF THE MORNING, STOOD IN LINE...
...WITH-STOOD FIVE HOURS OF WINTER RAIN...
...FORGED MY WAY THROUGH THE RARE TRADING CARD MORASS, AND OVERCAME MY INJURY. AND NOW A MOUNTAIN OF TREASURE STANDS BEFORE ME.
IF YOU HAD COME THIS FAR, WOULD YOU JUST RUN AWAY?
UMM... I DON'T THINK YOU'VE OVERCOME YOUR INJURY YET.
IT'S ALREADY TOTALLY NUMB.
FWIP
スポ
AH!
18

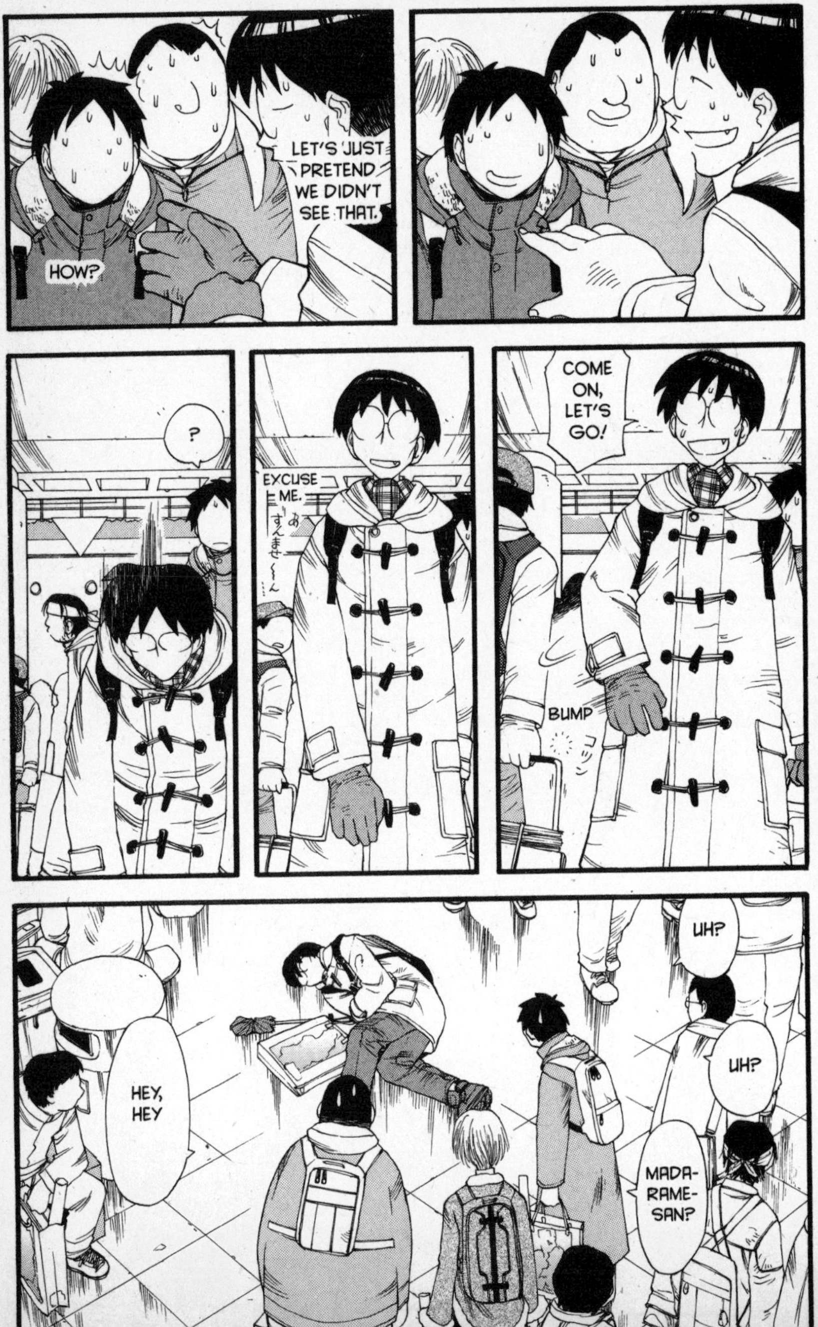
LET'S JUST PRETEND WE DIDN'T SEE THAT.
HOW?
COME ON, LET'S GO!
BUMP
EXCUSE ME.
?
UH?
UH?
MADARAME-SAN?
HEY, HEY

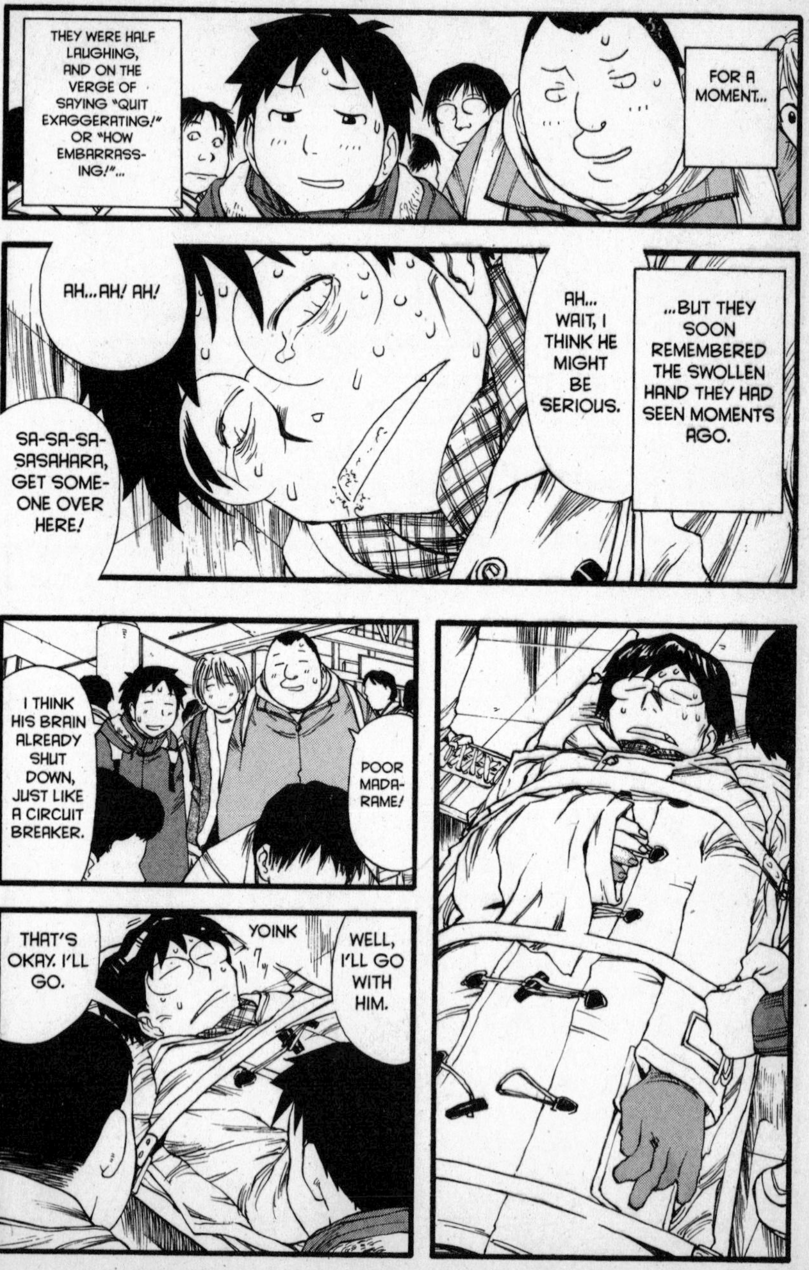
FOR A MOMENT...
THEY WERE HALF LAUGHING, AND ON THE VERGE OF SAYING "QUIT EXAGGERATING!" OR "HOW EMBARRASSING!"...
...BUT THEY SOON REMEMBERED THE SWOLLEN HAND THEY HAD SEEN MOMENTS AGO.
AH... WAIT, I THINK HE MIGHT BE SERIOUS.
AH...AH! AH!
SA-SA-SA-SASAHARA, GET SOMEONE OVER HERE!
POOR MADARAME!
I THINK HIS BRAIN ALREADY SHUT DOWN, JUST LIKE A CIRCUIT BREAKER.
WELL, I'LL GO WITH HIM.
YOINK
THAT'S OKAY. I'LL GO.

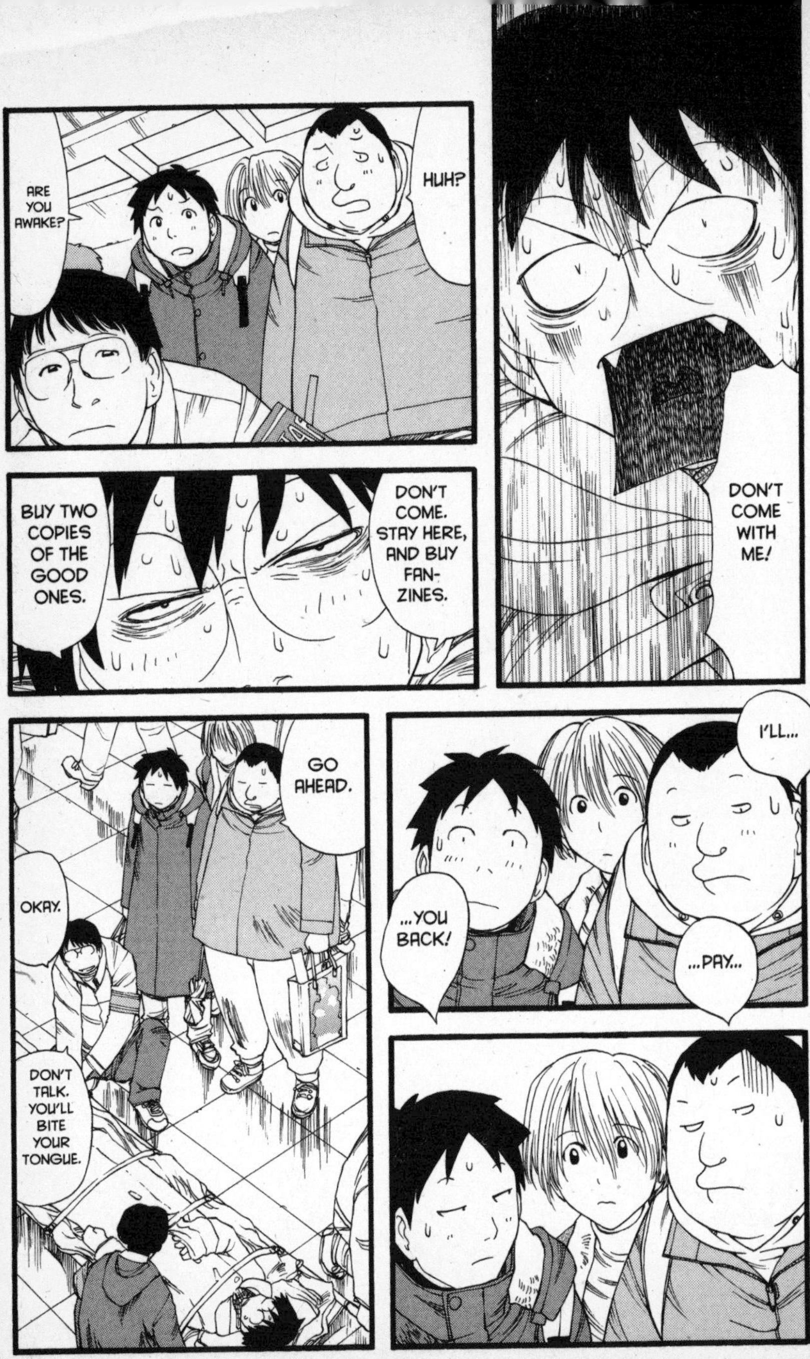

DON'T COME WITH ME!
HUH?
ARE YOU AWAKE?
DON'T COME. STAY HERE, AND BUY FAN-ZINES.
BUY TWO COPIES OF THE GOOD ONES.
I'LL...
...PAY...
...YOU BACK!
GO AHEAD.
OKAY.
DON'T TALK. YOU'LL BITE YOUR TONGUE.

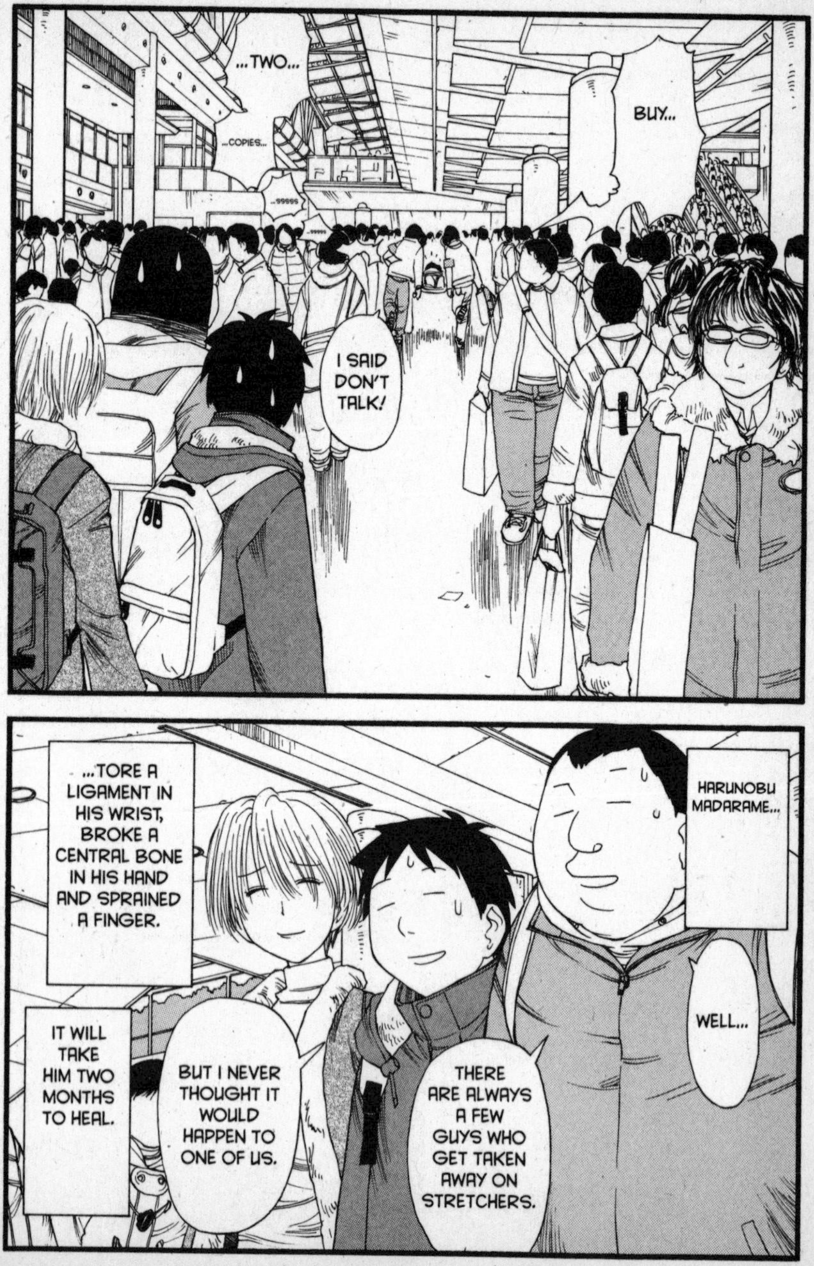
BUY...
...TWO...
...COPIES...
I SAID DON'T TALK!
HARUNOBU MADARAME...
...TORE A LIGAMENT IN HIS WRIST, BROKE A CENTRAL BONE IN HIS HAND AND SPRAINED A FINGER.
WELL...
THERE ARE ALWAYS A FEW GUYS WHO GET TAKEN AWAY ON STRETCHERS.
BUT I NEVER THOUGHT IT WOULD HAPPEN TO ONE OF US.
IT WILL TAKE HIM TWO MONTHS TO HEAL.

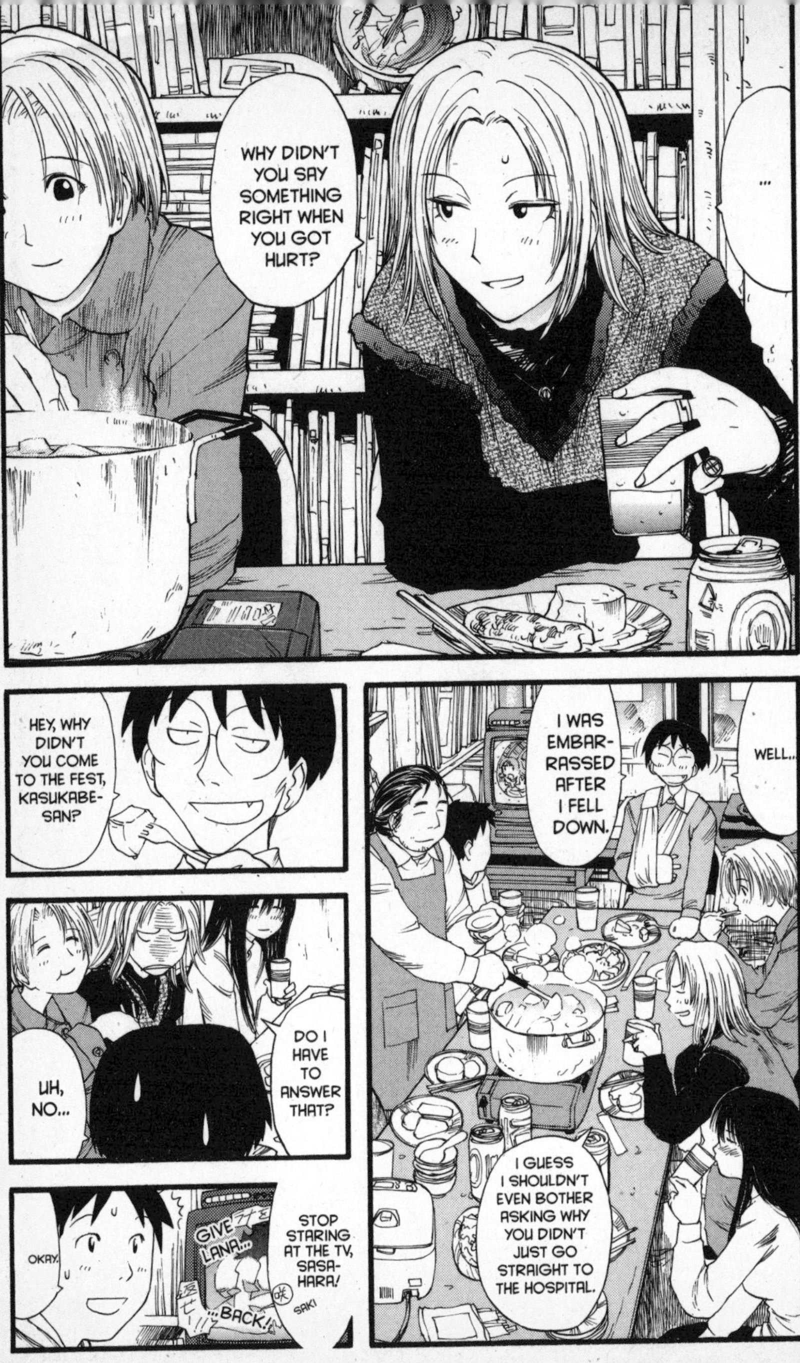
...
WHY DIDN'T YOU SAY SOMETHING RIGHT WHEN YOU GOT HURT?
WELL...
I WAS EMBARRASSED AFTER I FELL DOWN.
I GUESS I SHOULDN'T EVEN BOTHER ASKING WHY YOU DIDN'T JUST GO STRAIGHT TO THE HOSPITAL.
HEY, WHY DIDN'T YOU COME TO THE FEST, KASUKABE-SAN?
DO I HAVE TO ANSWER THAT?
UH, NO...
STOP STARING AT THE TV, SASAHARA!
SAKI
GIVE LANA...
...BACK!
OKAY.

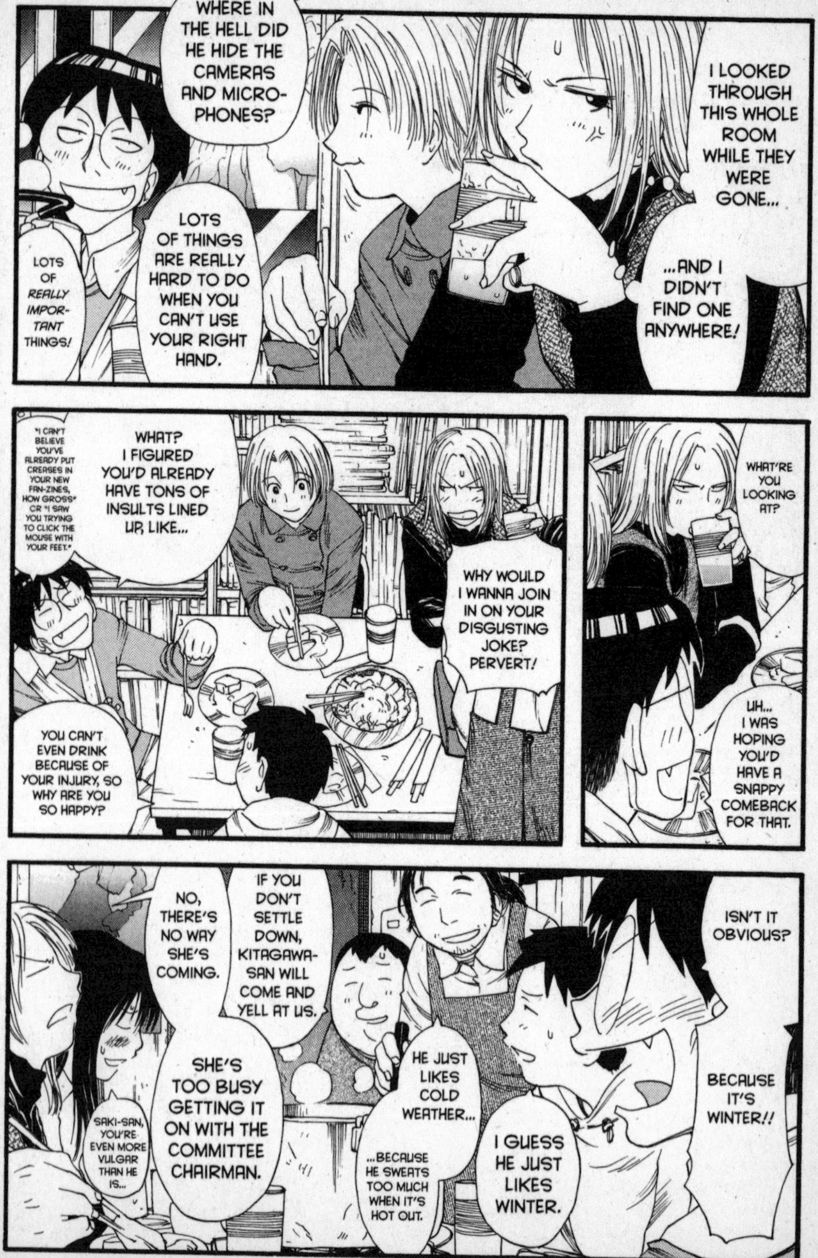
I LOOKED THROUGH THIS WHOLE ROOM WHILE THEY WERE GONE...
...AND I DIDN'T FIND ONE ANYWHERE!
WHERE IN THE HELL DID HE HIDE THE CAMERAS AND MICRO-PHONES?
LOTS OF THINGS ARE REALLY HARD TO DO WHEN YOU CAN'T USE YOUR RIGHT HAND.
LOTS OF *REALLY IMPOR-TANT* THINGS!
WHAT'RE YOU LOOKING AT?
UH... I WAS HOPING YOU'D HAVE A SNAPPY COMEBACK FOR THAT.
YOU CAN'T EVEN DRINK BECAUSE OF YOUR INJURY, SO WHY ARE YOU SO HAPPY?
WHAT? I FIGURED YOU'D ALREADY HAVE TONS OF INSULTS LINED UP, LIKE...
"I CAN'T BELIEVE YOU'VE ALREADY PUT CREASES IN YOUR NEW FAN-ZINES, HOW GROSS" OR "I SAW YOU TRYING TO CLICK THE MOUSE WITH YOUR FEET."
WHY WOULD I WANNA JOIN IN ON YOUR DISGUSTING JOKE? PERVERT!
ISN'T IT OBVIOUS?
BECAUSE IT'S WINTER!!
I GUESS HE JUST LIKES WINTER.
HE JUST LIKES COLD WEATHER...
...BECAUSE HE SWEATS TOO MUCH WHEN IT'S HOT OUT.
IF YOU DON'T SETTLE DOWN, KITAGAWA-SAN WILL COME AND YELL AT US.
NO, THERE'S NO WAY SHE'S COMING.
SHE'S TOO BUSY GETTING IT ON WITH THE COMMITTEE CHAIRMAN.
SAKI-SAN, YOU'RE EVEN MORE VULGAR THAN HE IS...

END OF CHAPTER 9

THE GENSHIKEN MEMBERS PICK...

# KUJI-UN

**...THE MOST NOTABLE SCENES**

TAKEN FROM THE GENSHIKEN'S SPORADICALLY PUBLISHED ZINE "MEBAETAME"

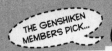

## MY FAVORITE SCENE FROM *KUJI-UN* PART 3 BY "THE OWL" FROM TANKOBON BOOK 4 PG 103

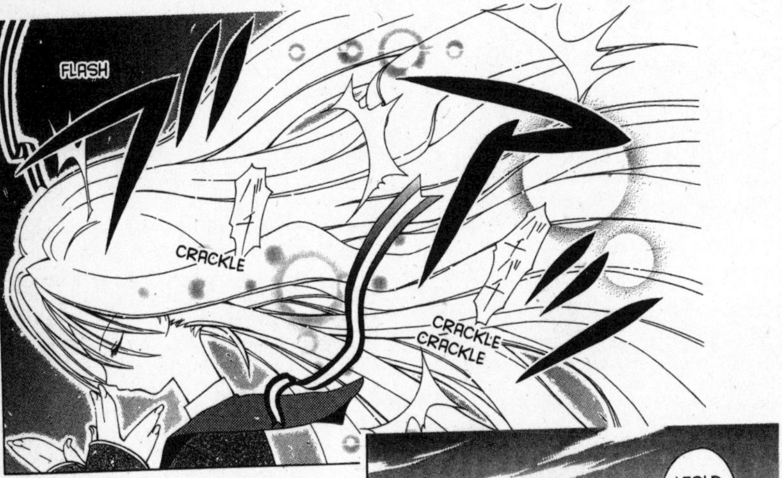
FLASH
CRACKLE
CRACKLE CRACKLE

*SORRY, BUT I DIDN'T PICK A REGULAR CHARACTER (LAUGHS). I CHOSE MAORI-SAN. SHE'S WILD AND CAREFREE, AND SHE'S ALWAYS VERY ACTIVE IN THE FESTIVAL TWICE A YEAR. SHE'S USING MAGIC IN THE ABOVE PANEL, AND WHEN YOU COMBINE IT WITH THE PANEL TO THE RIGHT, YOU'RE LEFT WITH AN UNFORGETTABLE SCENE. IT'S ESPECIALLY MEMORABLE BECAUSE SHE LETS DOWN HER HAIR (LAUGHS). SHINOBU'S GLASSES SYMBOLIZE HER ATTEMPT TO CUT HERSELF OFF FROM THE OUTSIDE WORLD, AND WHEN SHE REMOVES THEM HER PERSONALITY CHANGES. SIMILARLY, WHEN MAORI-SAN TAKES OUT HER BRAIDS, IT SYMBOLIZES THE RELEASE OF A REPRESSED PART OF HER PERSONALITY. SHINOBU EVEN WEARS HER GLASSES WHEN SHE'S DOING IT, BUT WHAT ABOUT MAORI'S BRAIDS? DOES SHE TAKE THEM OUT? I BET SHE LEAVES THEM IN (LAUGHS). [THE OWL]*

*...INSTEAD OF A POPULARITY CONTEST, NOW THIS IS TURNING INTO AN EXAMINATION OF THE MOST MINUTE AND MEANINGLESS DETAILS. I MEAN, I REALLY DON'T THINK HER BRAIDS SYMBOLIZE ANYTHING. ...THAT REMINDS ME, A WHILE AGO, YOU KEPT GOING ON AND ON ABOUT HOW THE BRAIDS LOOKED ON THE MAORI-SAN ACTION FIGURE. ...YOU REALLY LOVE THOSE BRAIDS, DON'T YOU ♡? NEXT, IT'S KODAMA'S TURN. [PIT VIPER]*

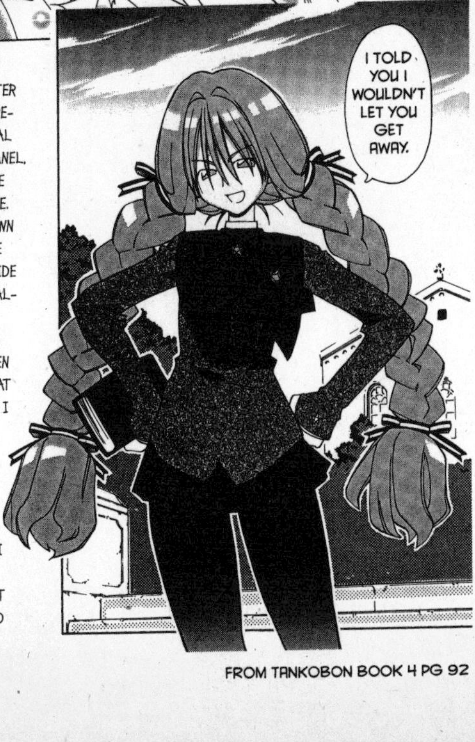
I TOLD YOU I WOULDN'T LET YOU GET AWAY.

FROM TANKOBON BOOK 4 PG 92

CHAPTER 9- MOMENTS LATER

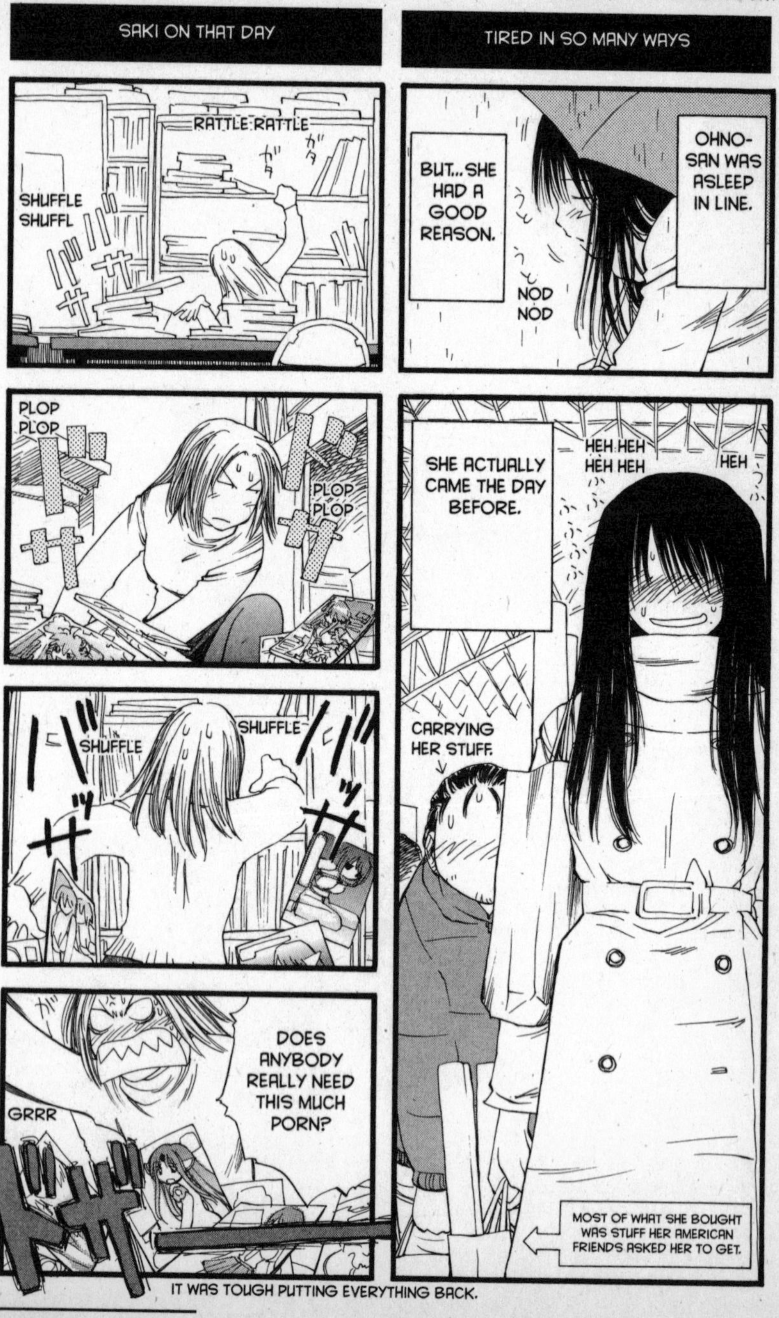
TIRED IN SO MANY WAYS
OHNO-SAN WAS ASLEEP IN LINE.
BUT...SHE HAD A GOOD REASON.
NOD NOD
HEH HEH HEH HEH
HEH
SHE ACTUALLY CAME THE DAY BEFORE.
CARRYING HER STUFF.
MOST OF WHAT SHE BOUGHT WAS STUFF HER AMERICAN FRIENDS ASKED HER TO GET.
SAKI ON THAT DAY
RATTLE RATTLE
SHUFFLE SHUFFL
PLOP PLOP
PLOP PLOP
SHUFFLE
SHUFFLE
DOES ANYBODY REALLY NEED THIS MUCH PORN?
GRRR
IT WAS TOUGH PUTTING EVERYTHING BACK.

# CHAPTER 10 - SADOMASOCHISM

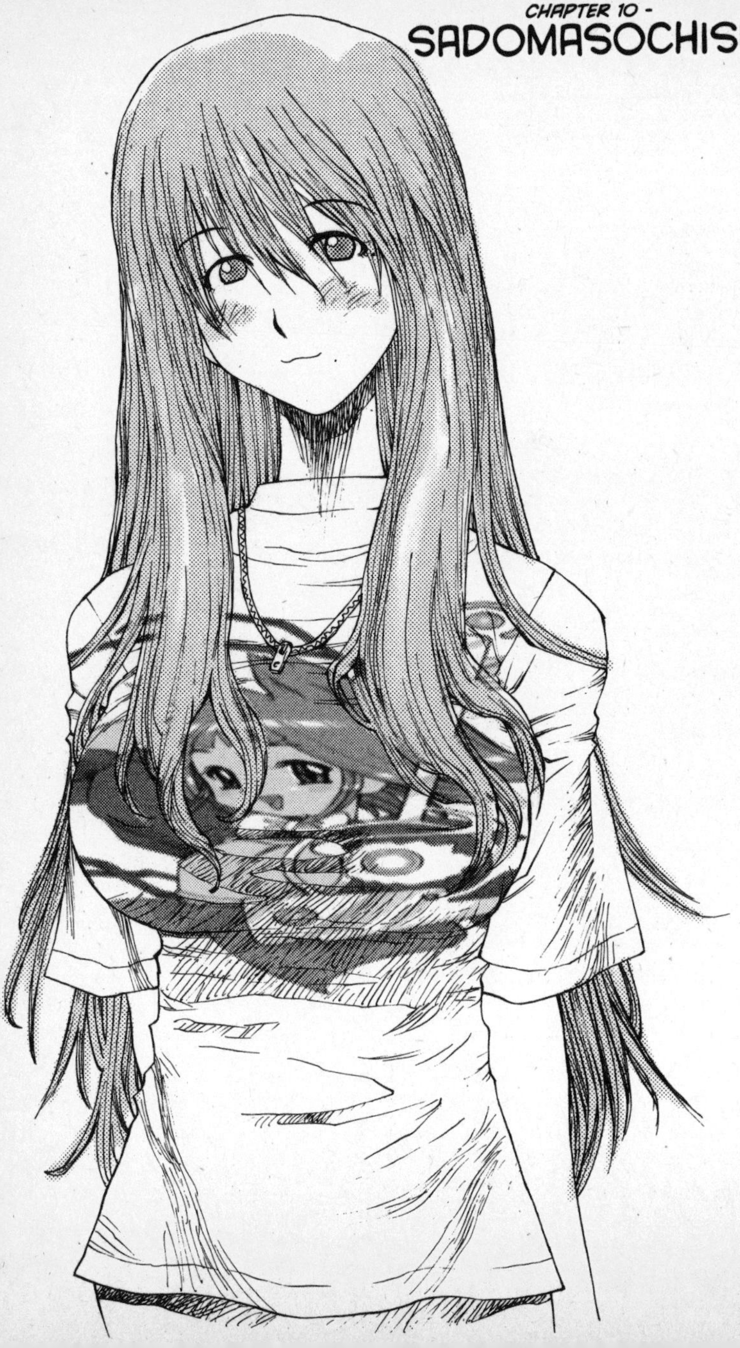

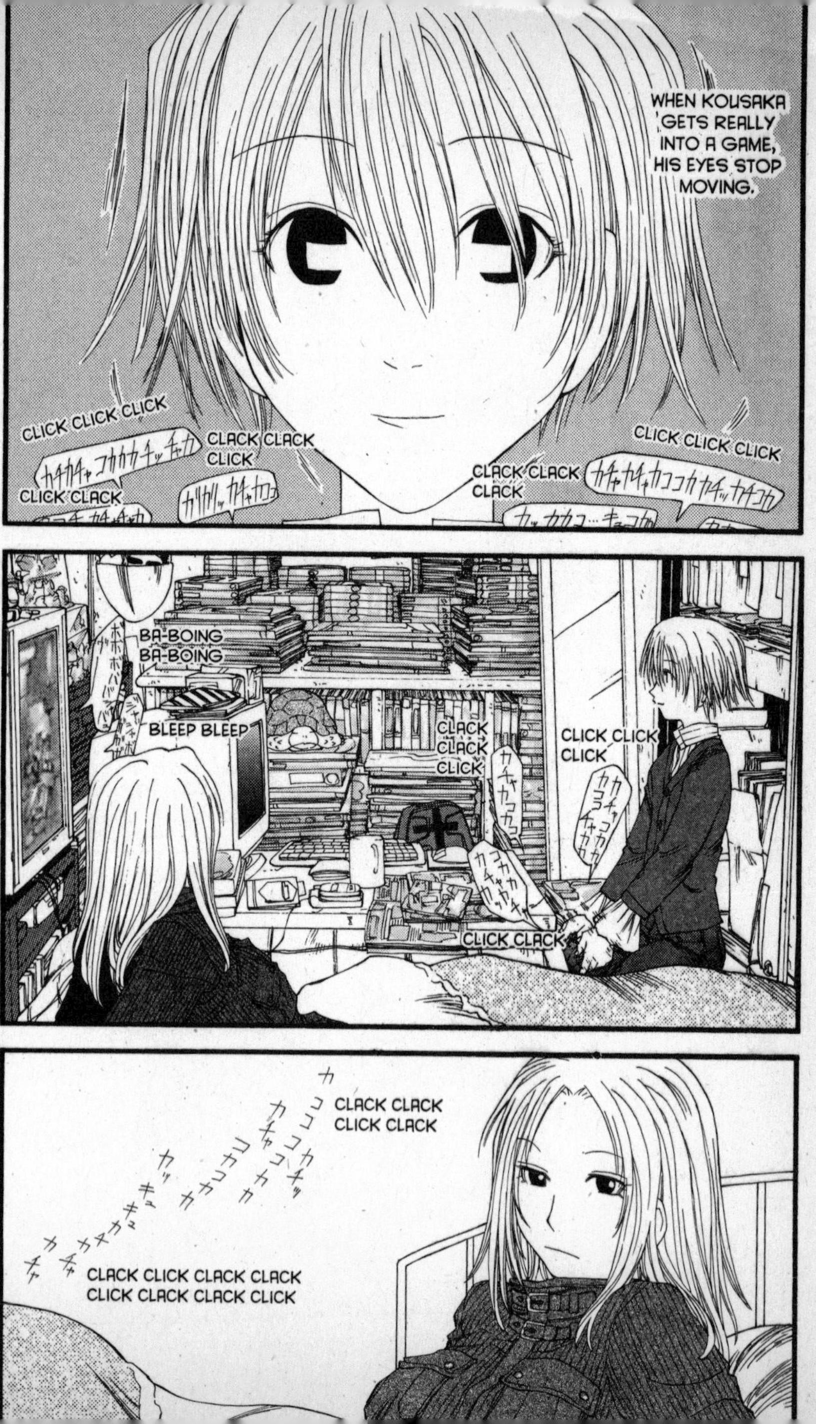
WHEN KOUSAKA GETS REALLY INTO A GAME, HIS EYES STOP MOVING.
CLICK CLICK CLICK
CLACK CLACK CLACK
CLACK CLACK CLICK
CLICK CLICK CLICK
CLICK CLACK
CLICK CLICK CLICK
CLACK CLACK CLICK
CLICK CLACK
BLEEP BLEEP
BA-BOING BA-BOING
CLACK CLACK CLICK CLACK
CLACK CLICK CLACK CLACK CLICK CLACK CLACK CLICK

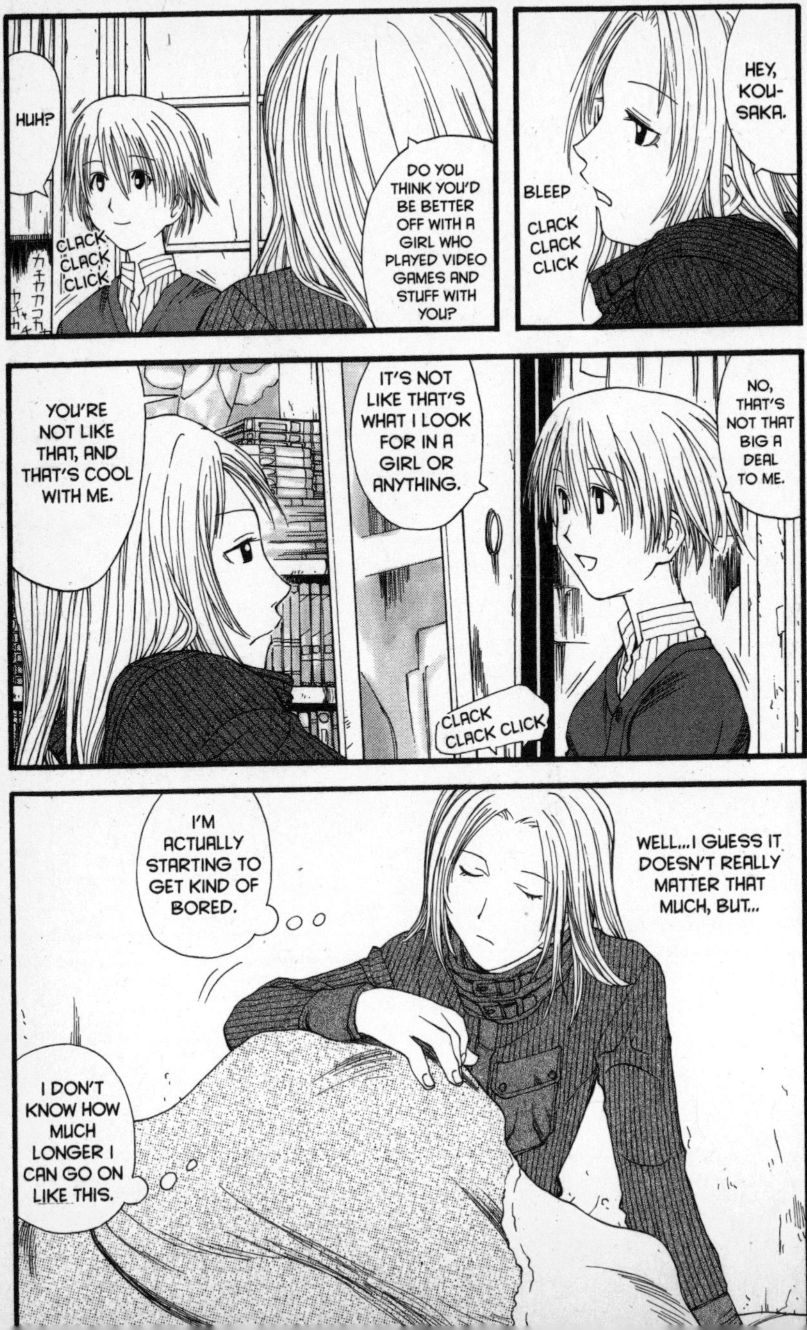
HEY, KOU-SAKA.
BLEEP
CLACK CLACK CLICK
DO YOU THINK YOU'D BE BETTER OFF WITH A GIRL WHO PLAYED VIDEO GAMES AND STUFF WITH YOU?
HUH?
CLACK CLACK CLICK
NO, THAT'S NOT THAT BIG A DEAL TO ME.
CLACK CLACK CLICK
IT'S NOT LIKE THAT'S WHAT I LOOK FOR IN A GIRL OR ANYTHING.
YOU'RE NOT LIKE THAT, AND THAT'S COOL WITH ME.
WELL...I GUESS IT DOESN'T REALLY MATTER THAT MUCH, BUT...
I'M ACTUALLY STARTING TO GET KIND OF BORED.
I DON'T KNOW HOW MUCH LONGER I CAN GO ON LIKE THIS.

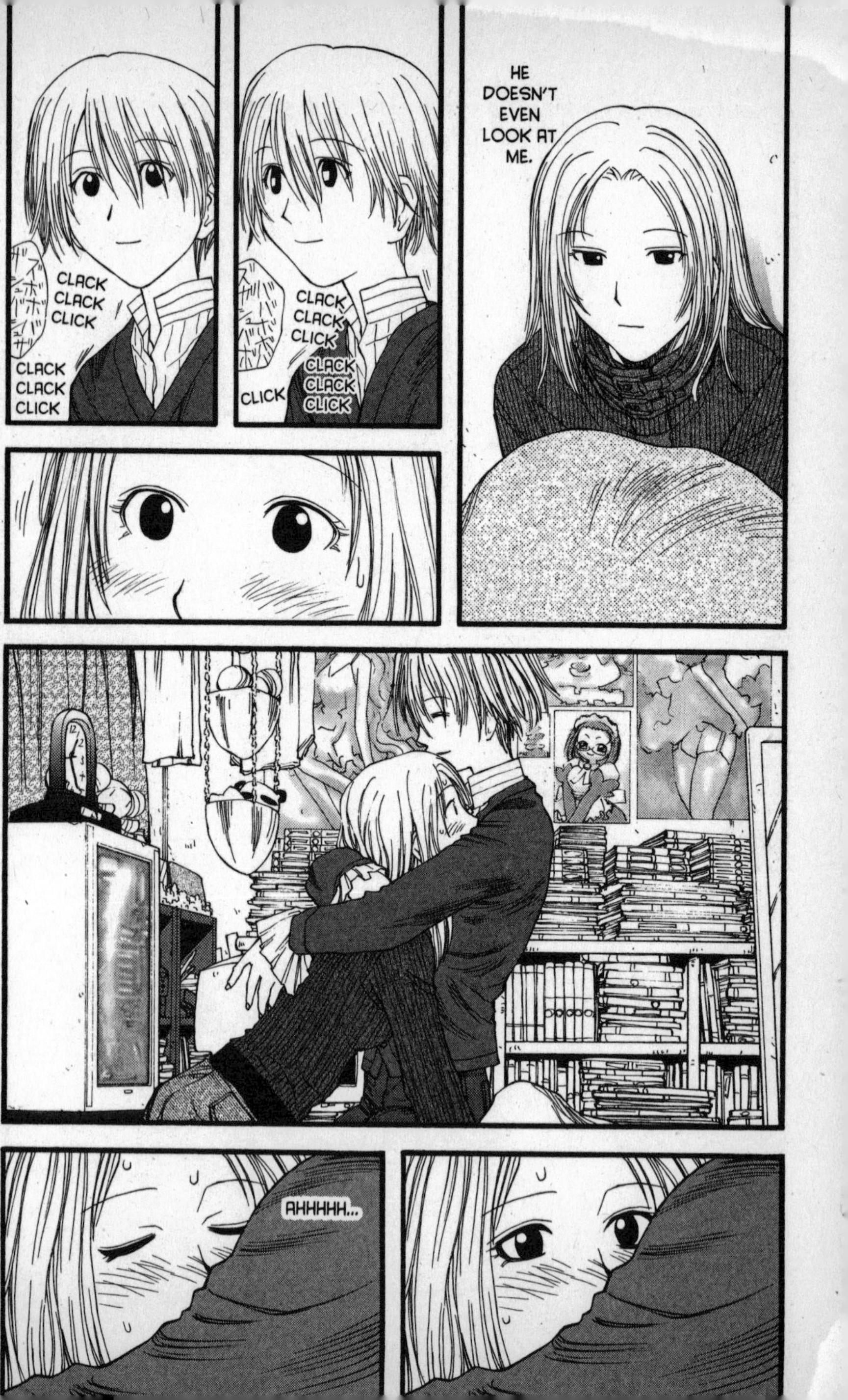
HE DOESN'T EVEN LOOK AT ME.
CLACK CLACK CLICK
CLACK CLACK CLICK
CLICK
CLACK CLACK CLICK
CLACK CLACK CLICK
AHHHHH...

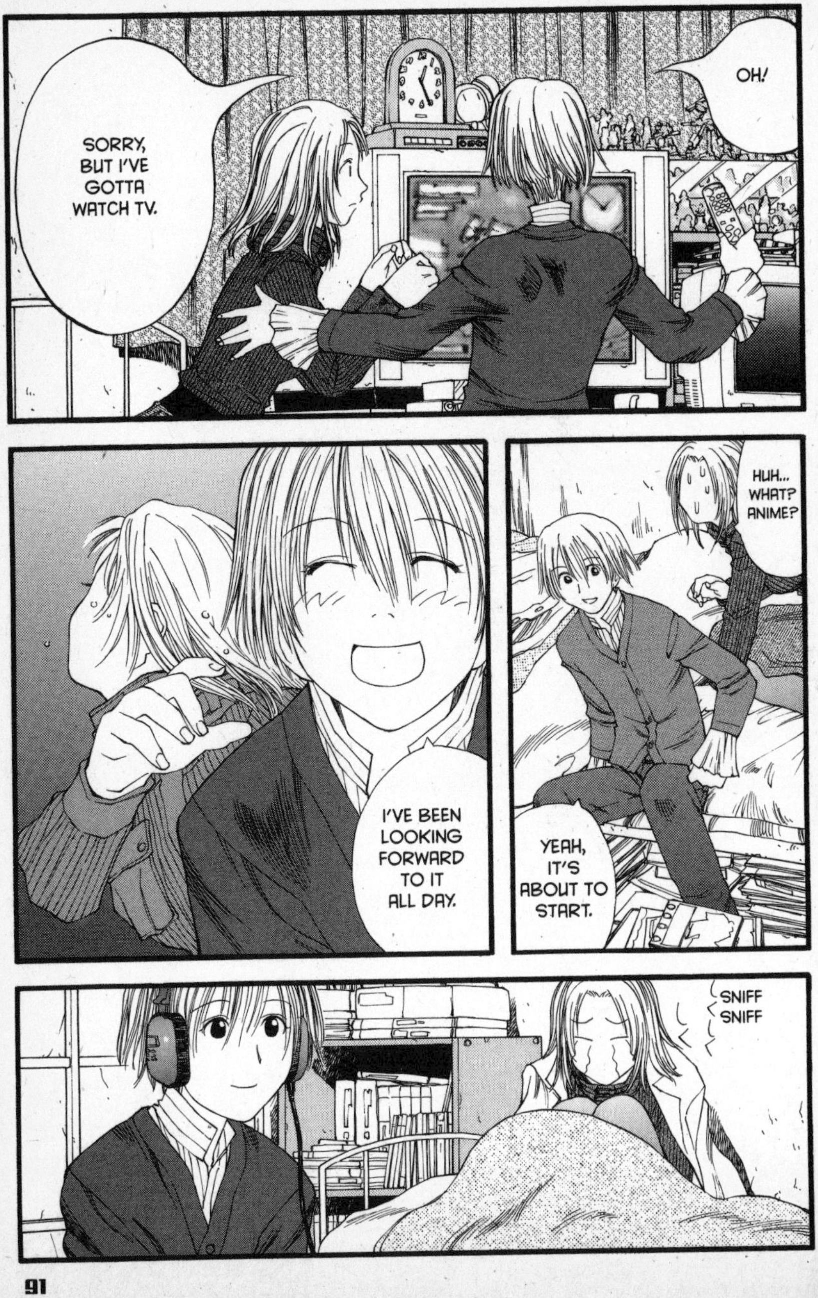
OH!
SORRY, BUT I'VE GOTTA WATCH TV.
HUH... WHAT? ANIME?
YEAH, IT'S ABOUT TO START.
I'VE BEEN LOOKING FORWARD TO IT ALL DAY.
SNIFF SNIFF

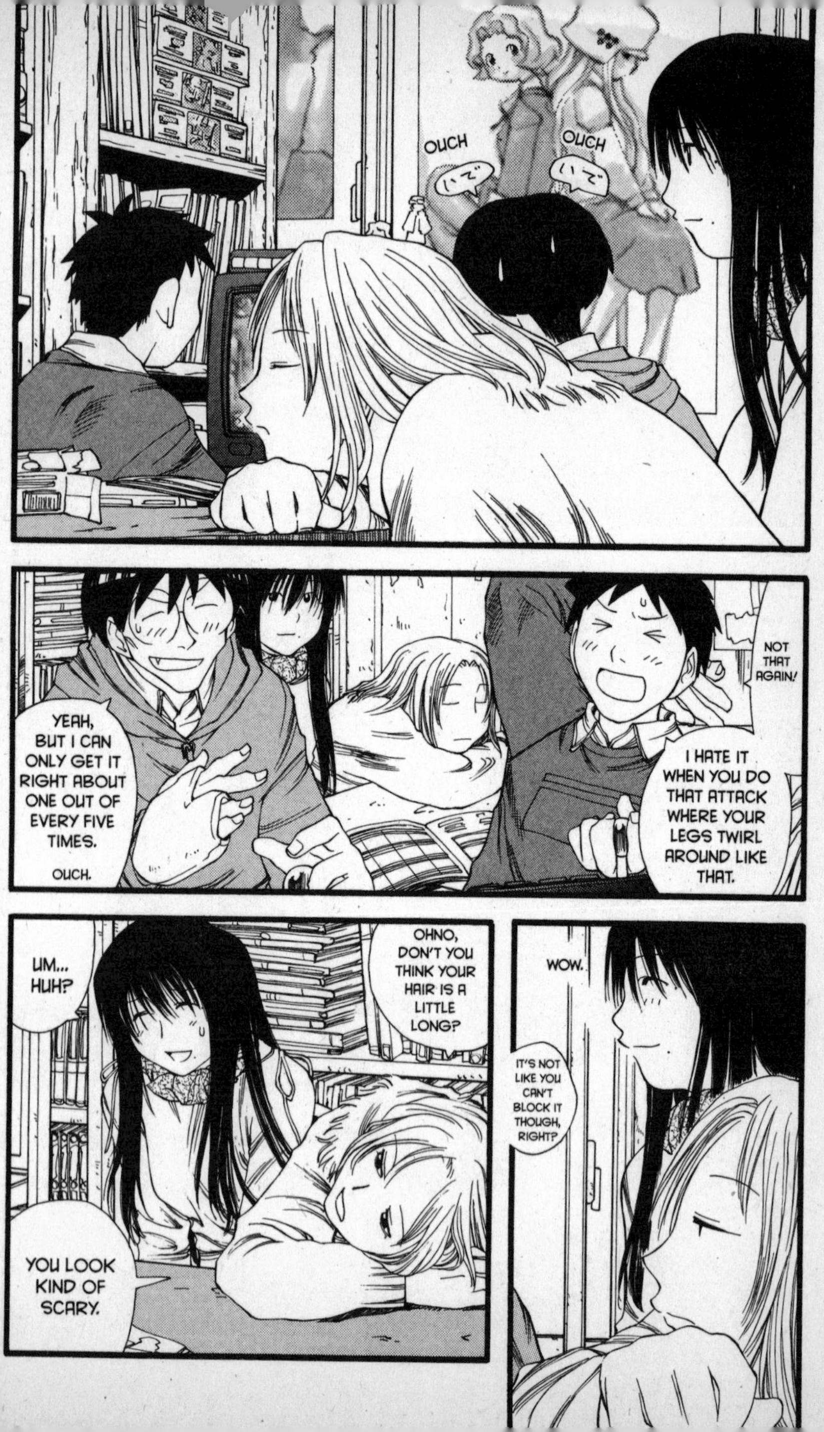
OUCH
いで
OUCH
いで
NOT THAT AGAIN!
I HATE IT WHEN YOU DO THAT ATTACK WHERE YOUR LEGS TWIRL AROUND LIKE THAT.
YEAH, BUT I CAN ONLY GET IT RIGHT ABOUT ONE OUT OF EVERY FIVE TIMES.
OUCH.
WOW.
IT'S NOT LIKE YOU CAN'T BLOCK IT THOUGH, RIGHT?
OHNO, DON'T YOU THINK YOUR HAIR IS A LITTLE LONG?
UM... HUH?
YOU LOOK KIND OF SCARY.

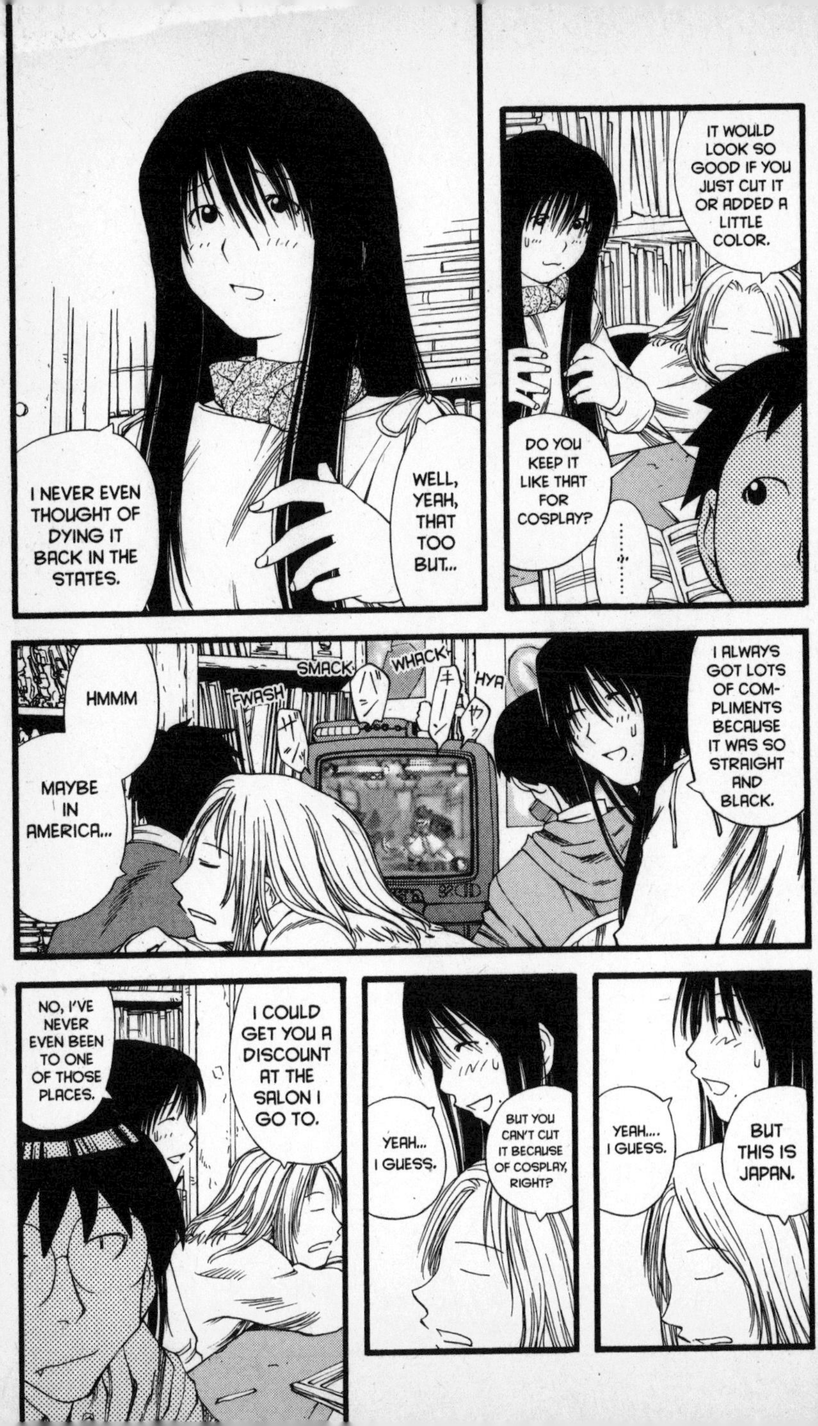
IT WOULD LOOK SO GOOD IF YOU JUST CUT IT OR ADDED A LITTLE COLOR.
DO YOU KEEP IT LIKE THAT FOR COSPLAY?
……
WELL, YEAH, THAT TOO BUT...
I NEVER EVEN THOUGHT OF DYING IT BACK IN THE STATES.
I ALWAYS GOT LOTS OF COM-PLIMENTS BECAUSE IT WAS SO STRAIGHT AND BLACK.
HYA
WHACK
SMACK
FWASH
HMMM
MAYBE IN AMERICA...
BUT THIS IS JAPAN.
YEAH.... I GUESS.
BUT YOU CAN'T CUT IT BECAUSE OF COSPLAY, RIGHT?
YEAH... I GUESS.
I COULD GET YOU A DISCOUNT AT THE SALON I GO TO.
NO, I'VE NEVER EVEN BEEN TO ONE OF THOSE PLACES.

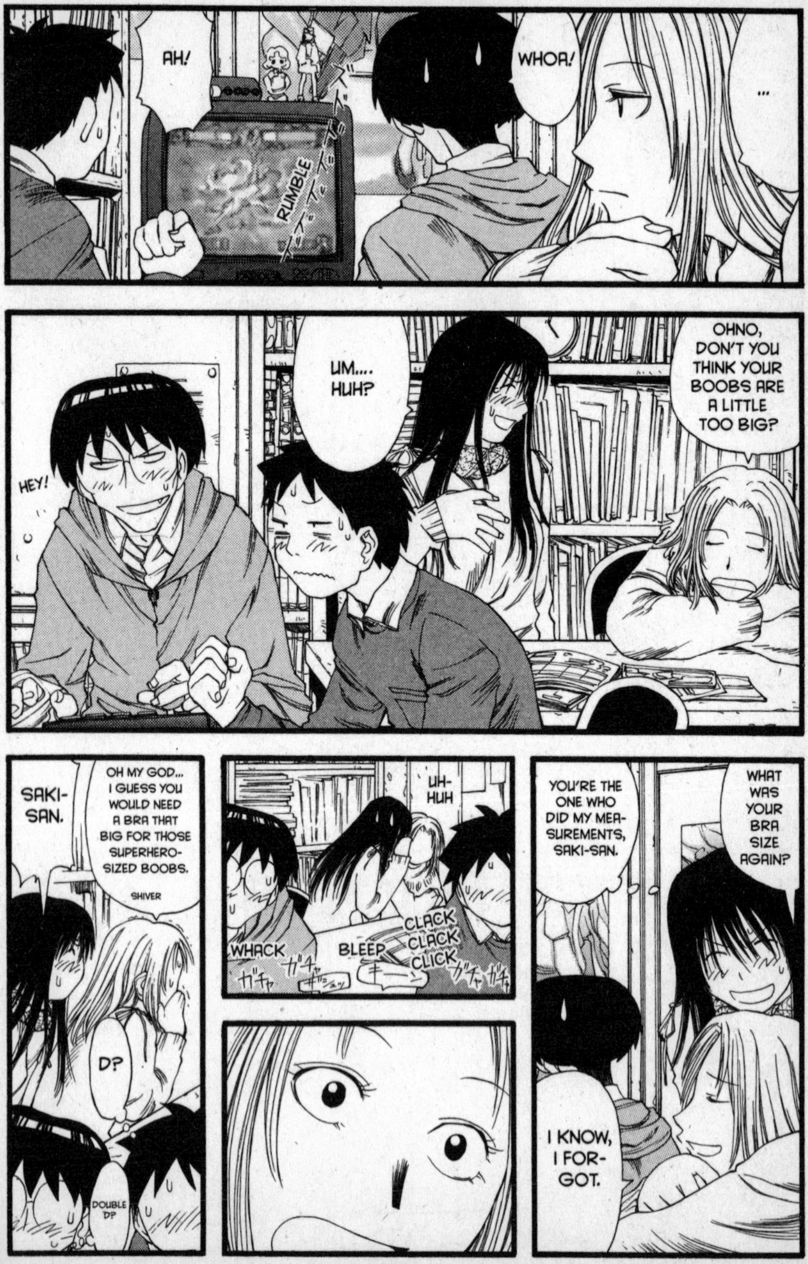
...
WHOA!
RUMBLE
AH!
OHNO, DON'T YOU THINK YOUR BOOBS ARE A LITTLE TOO BIG?
UM.... HUH?
HEY!
WHAT WAS YOUR BRA SIZE AGAIN?
YOU'RE THE ONE WHO DID MY MEA-SUREMENTS, SAKI-SAN.
I KNOW, I FOR-GOT.
UH-HUH
CLACK CLACK CLICK
BLEEP
WHACK
OH MY GOD... I GUESS YOU WOULD NEED A BRA THAT BIG FOR THOSE SUPERHERO-SIZED BOOBS.
SAKI-SAN.
SHIVER
D?
DOUBLE D?

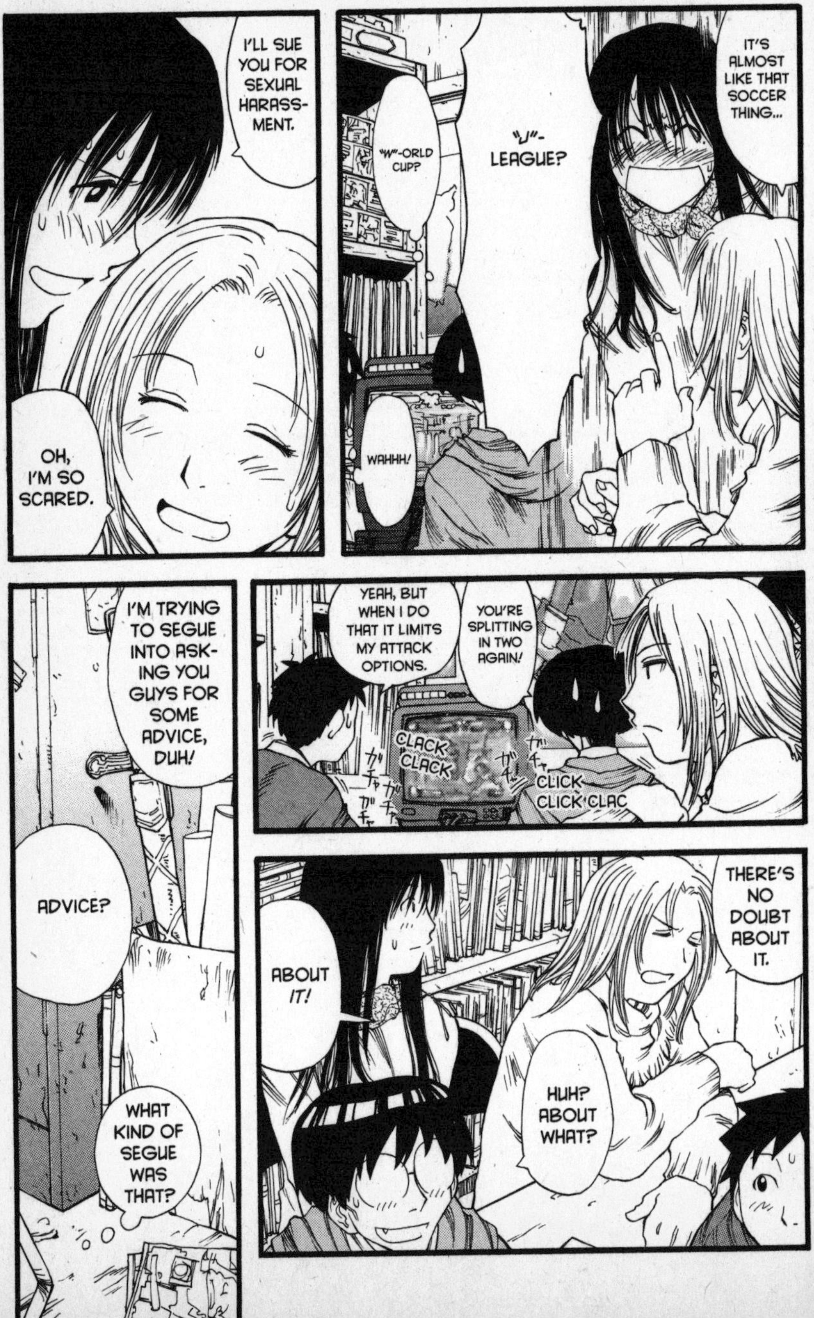
IT'S ALMOST LIKE THAT SOCCER THING...
"J"-LEAGUE?
"W"-ORLD CUP?
WAHHH!
I'LL SUE YOU FOR SEXUAL HARASS-MENT.
OH, I'M SO SCARED.
YOU'RE SPLITTING IN TWO AGAIN!
YEAH, BUT WHEN I DO THAT IT LIMITS MY ATTACK OPTIONS.
CLACK CLACK
CLICK CLICK CLAC
THERE'S NO DOUBT ABOUT IT.
ABOUT IT!
HUH? ABOUT WHAT?
I'M TRYING TO SEGUE INTO ASK-ING YOU GUYS FOR SOME ADVICE, DUH!
ADVICE?
WHAT KIND OF SEGUE WAS THAT?

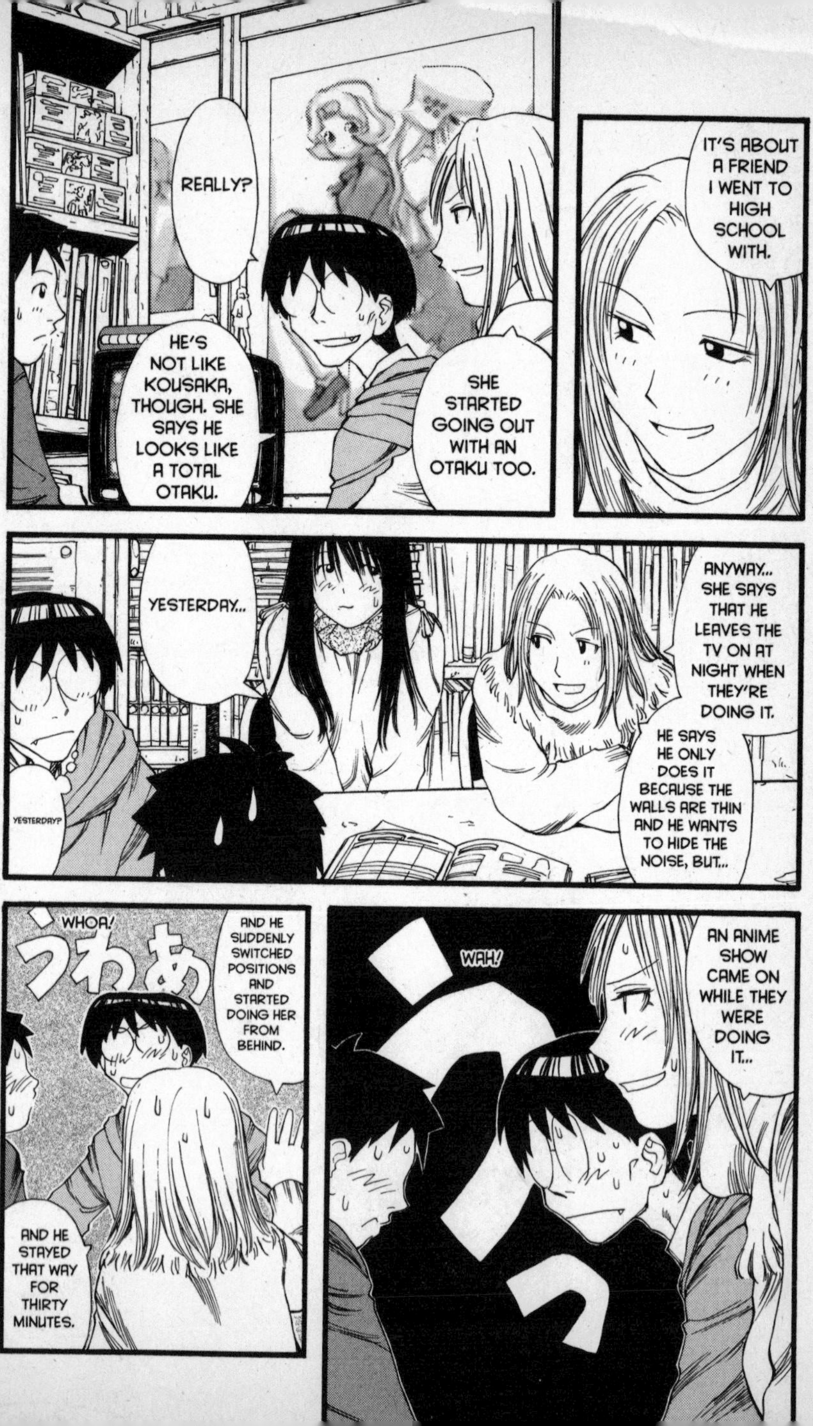
IT'S ABOUT A FRIEND I WENT TO HIGH SCHOOL WITH.
SHE STARTED GOING OUT WITH AN OTAKU TOO.
REALLY?
HE'S NOT LIKE KOUSAKA, THOUGH. SHE SAYS HE LOOKS LIKE A TOTAL OTAKU.
ANYWAY... SHE SAYS THAT HE LEAVES THE TV ON AT NIGHT WHEN THEY'RE DOING IT.
HE SAYS HE ONLY DOES IT BECAUSE THE WALLS ARE THIN AND HE WANTS TO HIDE THE NOISE, BUT...
YESTERDAY...
YESTERDAY?
AN ANIME SHOW CAME ON WHILE THEY WERE DOING IT...
WAH!
AND HE SUDDENLY SWITCHED POSITIONS AND STARTED DOING HER FROM BEHIND.
WHOA!
うわあ
AND HE STAYED THAT WAY FOR THIRTY MINUTES.

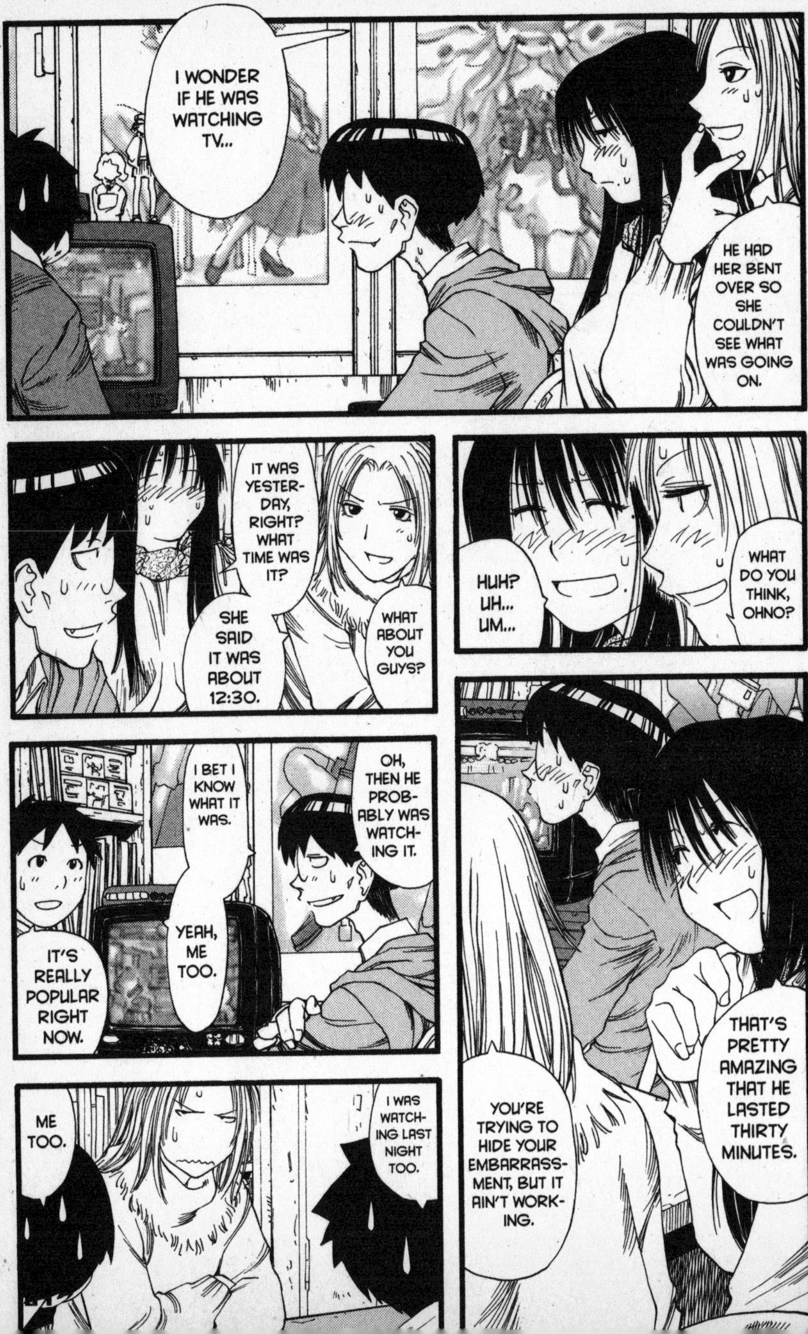
HE HAD HER BENT OVER SO SHE COULDN'T SEE WHAT WAS GOING ON.
I WONDER IF HE WAS WATCHING TV...
WHAT DO YOU THINK, OHNO?
HUH? UH... UM...
IT WAS YESTER-DAY, RIGHT? WHAT TIME WAS IT?
SHE SAID IT WAS ABOUT 12:30.
WHAT ABOUT YOU GUYS?
THAT'S PRETTY AMAZING THAT HE LASTED THIRTY MINUTES.
YOU'RE TRYING TO HIDE YOUR EMBARRASS-MENT, BUT IT AIN'T WORK-ING.
OH, THEN HE PROB-ABLY WAS WATCH-ING IT.
I BET I KNOW WHAT IT WAS.
YEAH, ME TOO.
IT'S REALLY POPULAR RIGHT NOW.
I WAS WATCH-ING LAST NIGHT TOO.
ME TOO.

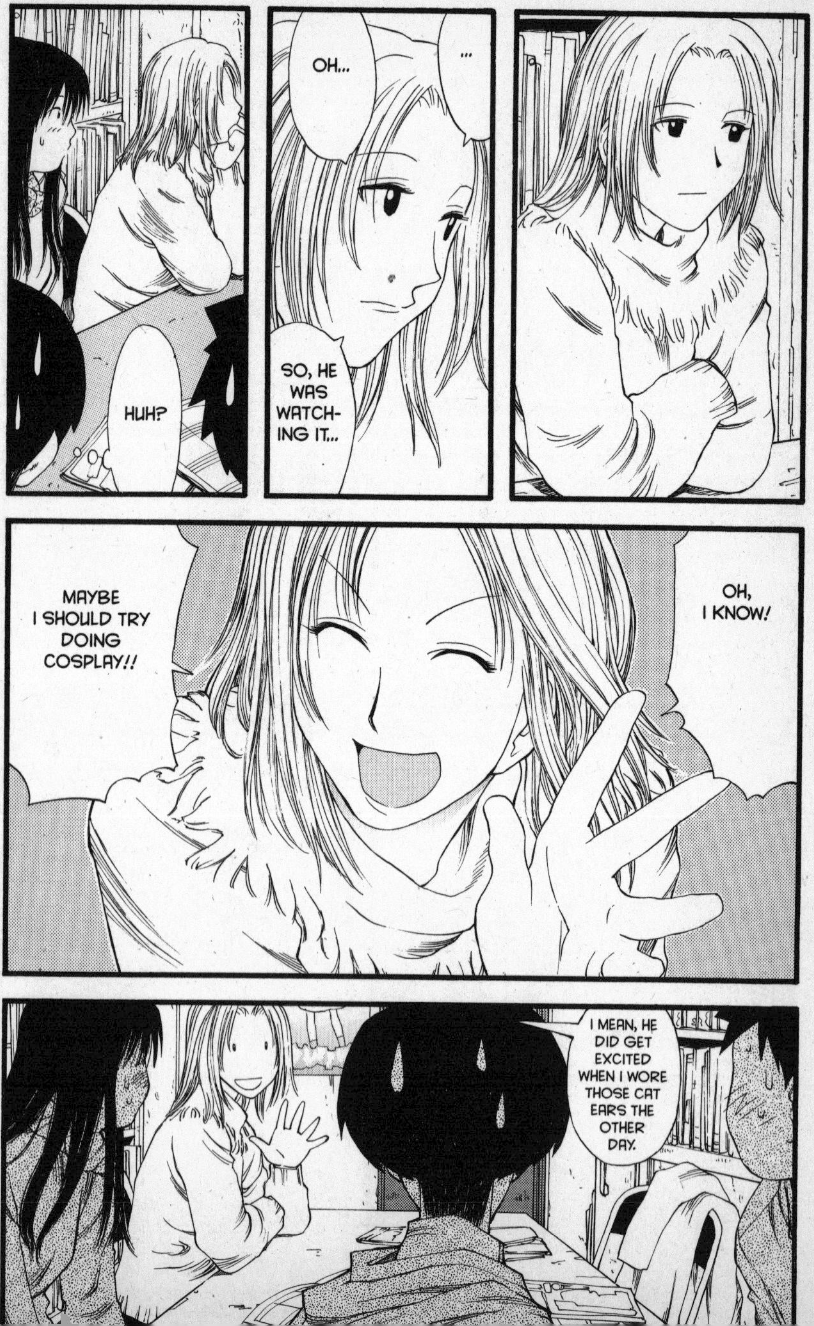
...
OH...
SO, HE WAS WATCHING IT...
HUH?
OH, I KNOW!
MAYBE I SHOULD TRY DOING COSPLAY!!
I MEAN, HE DID GET EXCITED WHEN I WORE THOSE CAT EARS THE OTHER DAY.

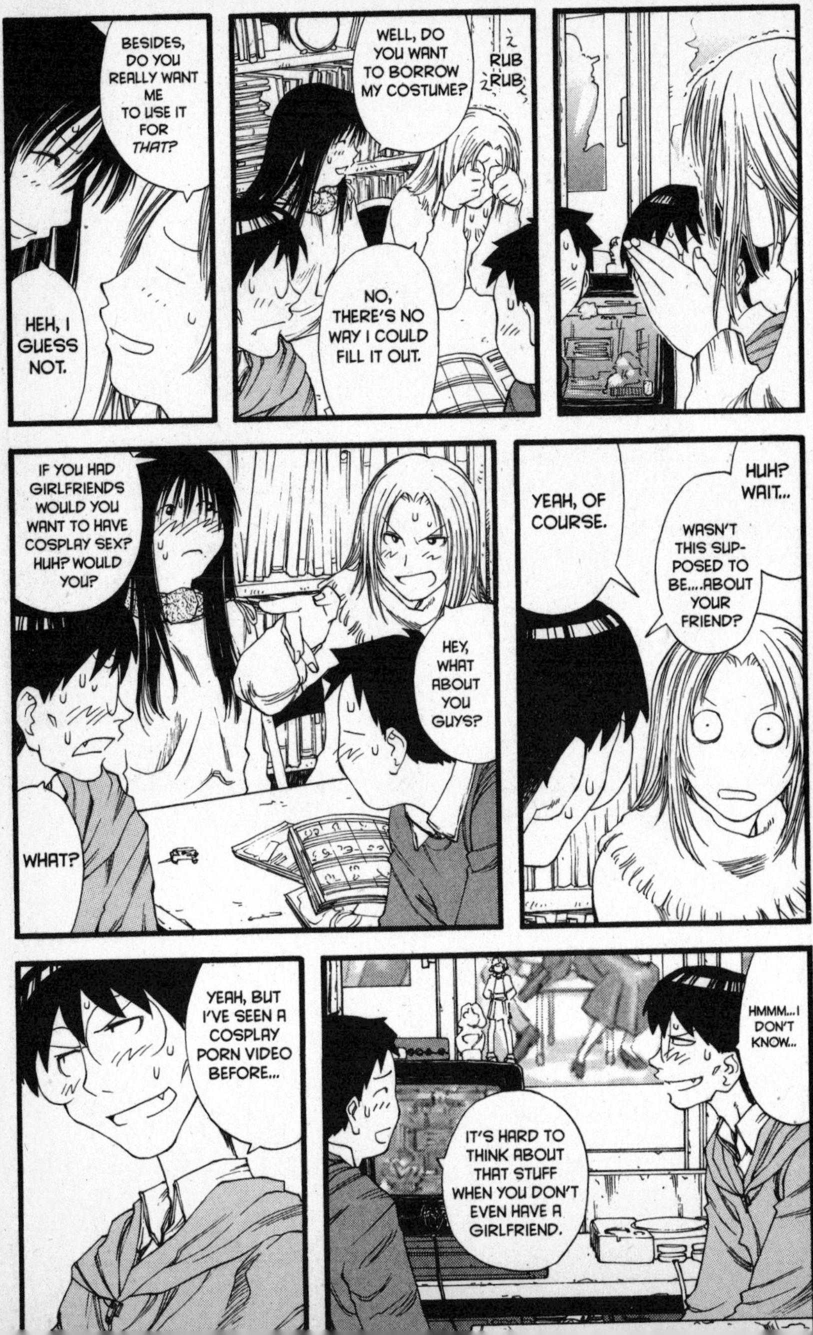
WELL, DO YOU WANT TO BORROW MY COSTUME?
RUB RUB
NO, THERE'S NO WAY I COULD FILL IT OUT.
BESIDES, DO YOU REALLY WANT ME TO USE IT FOR *THAT?*
HEH, I GUESS NOT.
HUH? WAIT...
WASN'T THIS SUP-POSED TO BE....ABOUT YOUR FRIEND?
YEAH, OF COURSE.
IF YOU HAD GIRLFRIENDS WOULD YOU WANT TO HAVE COSPLAY SEX? HUH? WOULD YOU?
HEY, WHAT ABOUT YOU GUYS?
WHAT?
HMMM...I DON'T KNOW...
IT'S HARD TO THINK ABOUT THAT STUFF WHEN YOU DON'T EVEN HAVE A GIRLFRIEND.
YEAH, BUT I'VE SEEN A COSPLAY PORN VIDEO BEFORE...

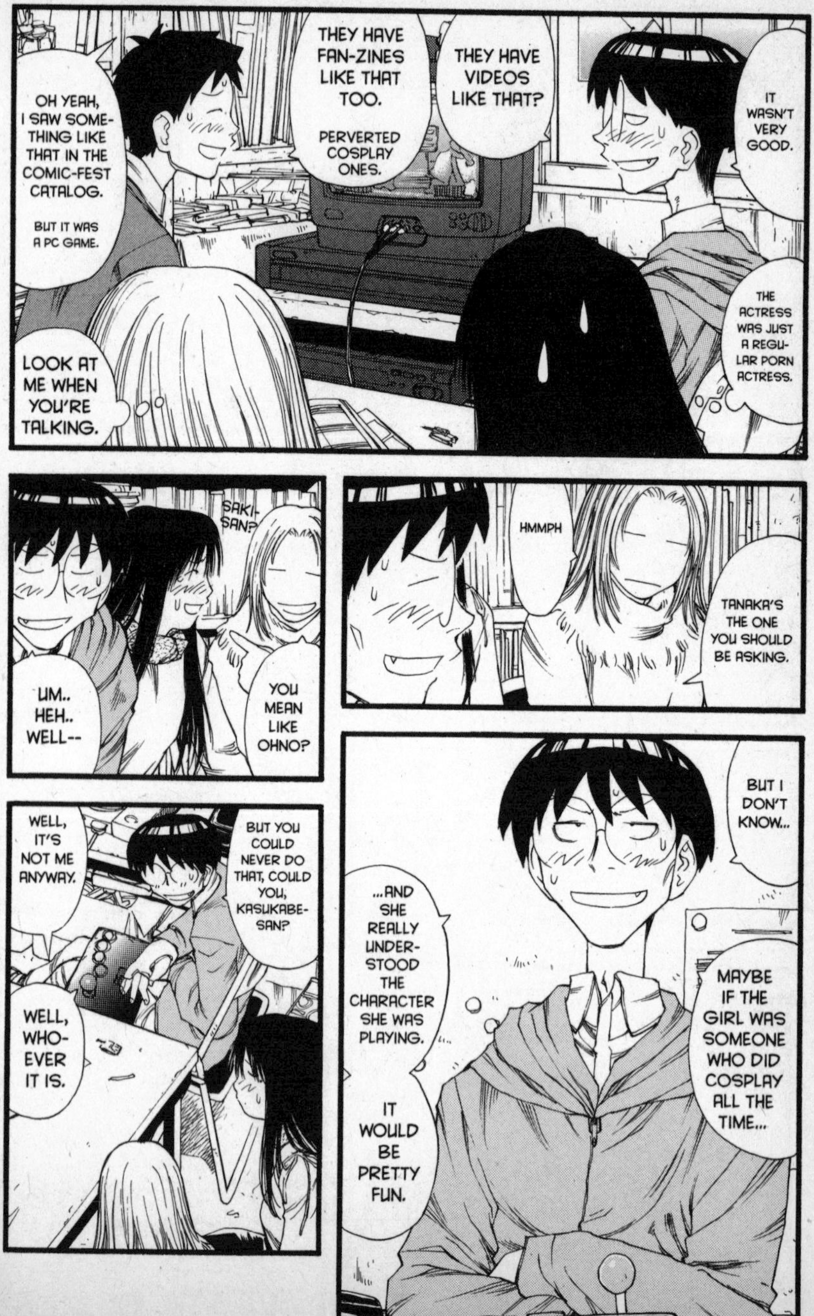
IT WASN'T VERY GOOD.
THE ACTRESS WAS JUST A REGULAR PORN ACTRESS.
THEY HAVE VIDEOS LIKE THAT?
THEY HAVE FAN-ZINES LIKE THAT TOO.
PERVERTED COSPLAY ONES.
OH YEAH, I SAW SOMETHING LIKE THAT IN THE COMIC-FEST CATALOG.
BUT IT WAS A PC GAME.
LOOK AT ME WHEN YOU'RE TALKING.
TANAKA'S THE ONE YOU SHOULD BE ASKING.
HMMPH
SAKI-SAN?
YOU MEAN LIKE OHNO?
UM.. HEH.. WELL--
BUT I DON'T KNOW...
MAYBE IF THE GIRL WAS SOMEONE WHO DID COSPLAY ALL THE TIME...
...AND SHE REALLY UNDERSTOOD THE CHARACTER SHE WAS PLAYING.
IT WOULD BE PRETTY FUN.
BUT YOU COULD NEVER DO THAT, COULD YOU, KASUKABE-SAN?
WELL, IT'S NOT ME ANYWAY.
WELL, WHOEVER IT IS.

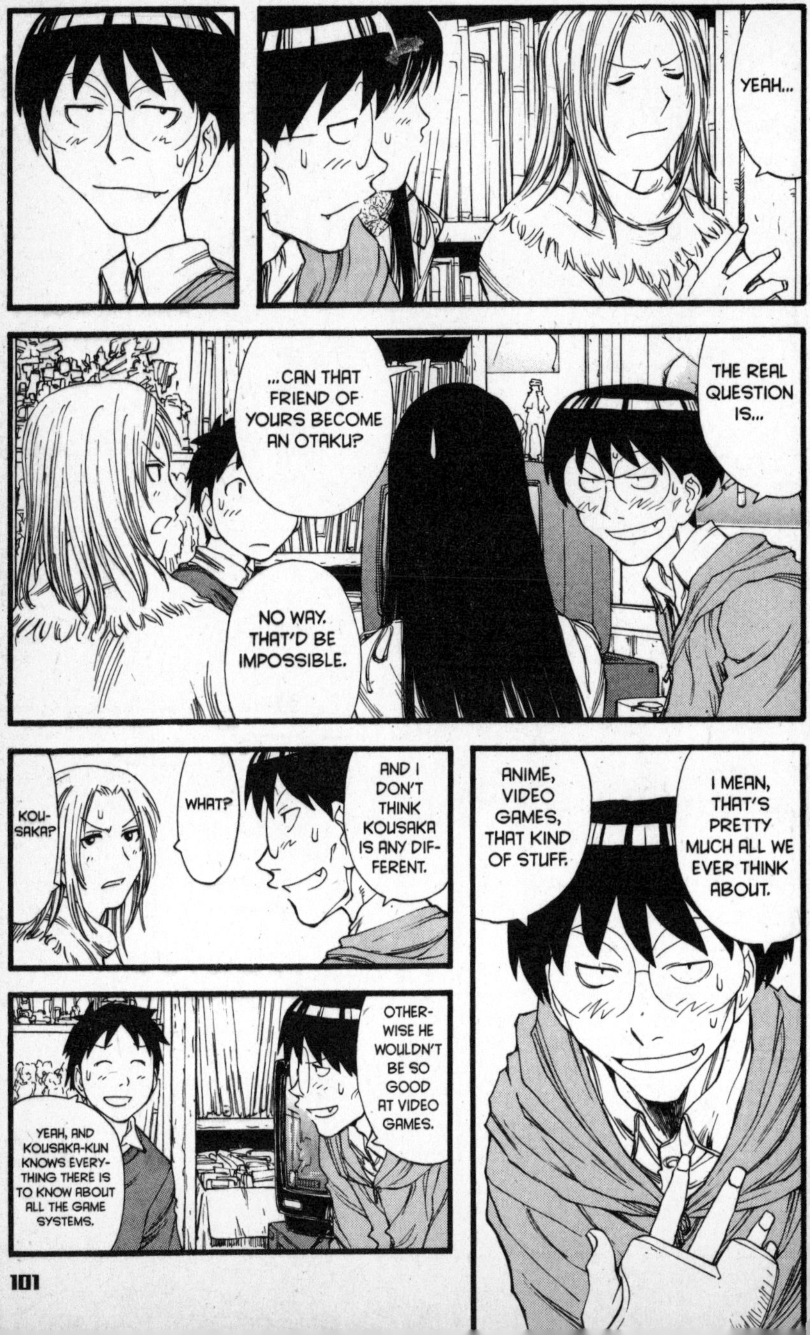
YEAH...
THE REAL QUESTION IS...
...CAN THAT FRIEND OF YOURS BECOME AN OTAKU?
NO WAY. THAT'D BE IMPOSSIBLE.
I MEAN, THAT'S PRETTY MUCH ALL WE EVER THINK ABOUT.
ANIME, VIDEO GAMES, THAT KIND OF STUFF.
AND I DON'T THINK KOUSAKA IS ANY DIFFERENT.
WHAT?
KOUSAKA?
OTHERWISE HE WOULDN'T BE SO GOOD AT VIDEO GAMES.
YEAH, AND KOUSAKA-KUN KNOWS EVERYTHING THERE IS TO KNOW ABOUT ALL THE GAME SYSTEMS.

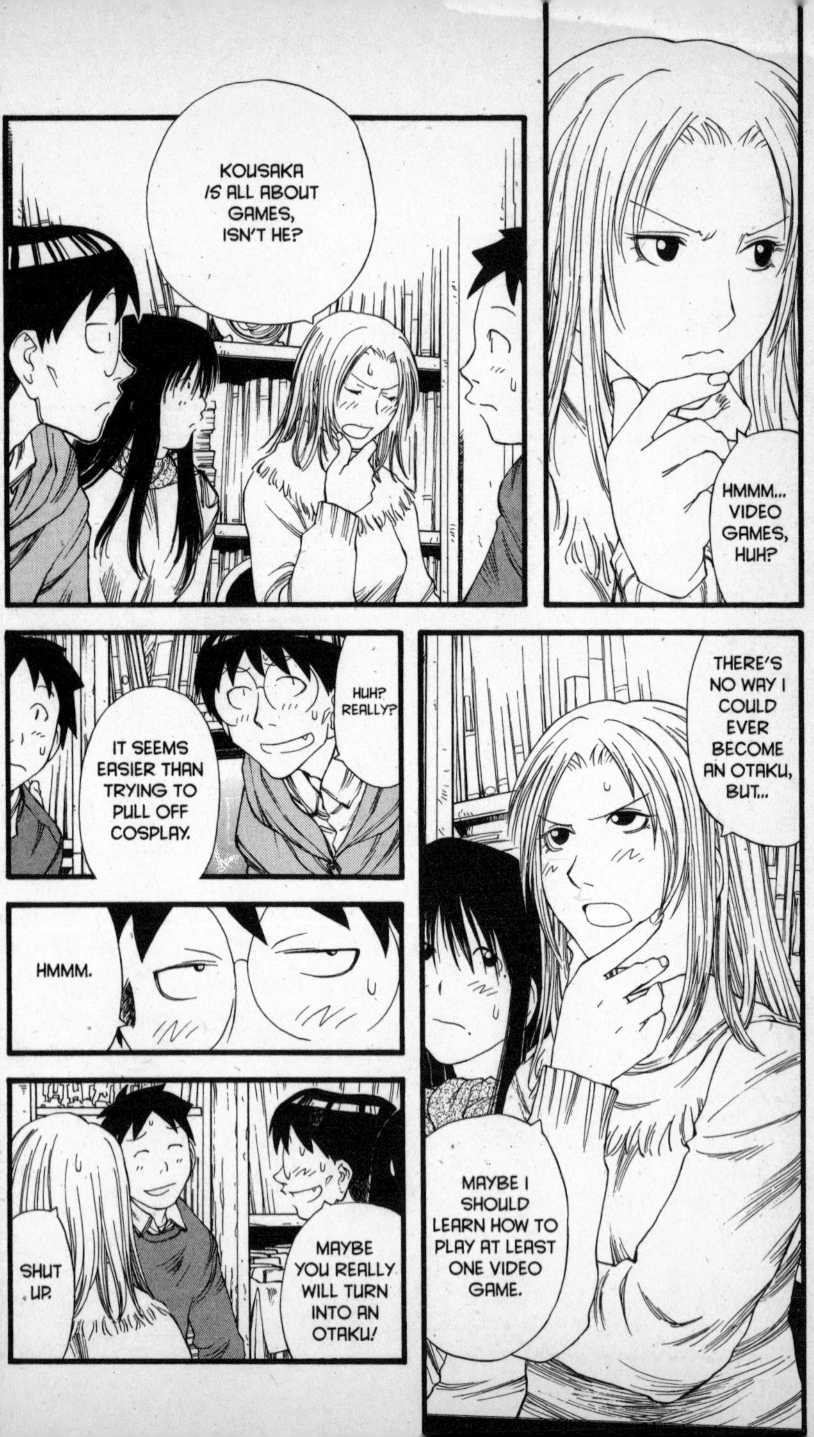
HMMM... VIDEO GAMES, HUH?
KOUSAKA IS ALL ABOUT GAMES, ISN'T HE?
THERE'S NO WAY I COULD EVER BECOME AN OTAKU, BUT...
MAYBE I SHOULD LEARN HOW TO PLAY AT LEAST ONE VIDEO GAME.
HUH? REALLY?
IT SEEMS EASIER THAN TRYING TO PULL OFF COSPLAY.
HMMM.
MAYBE YOU REALLY WILL TURN INTO AN OTAKU!
SHUT UP.

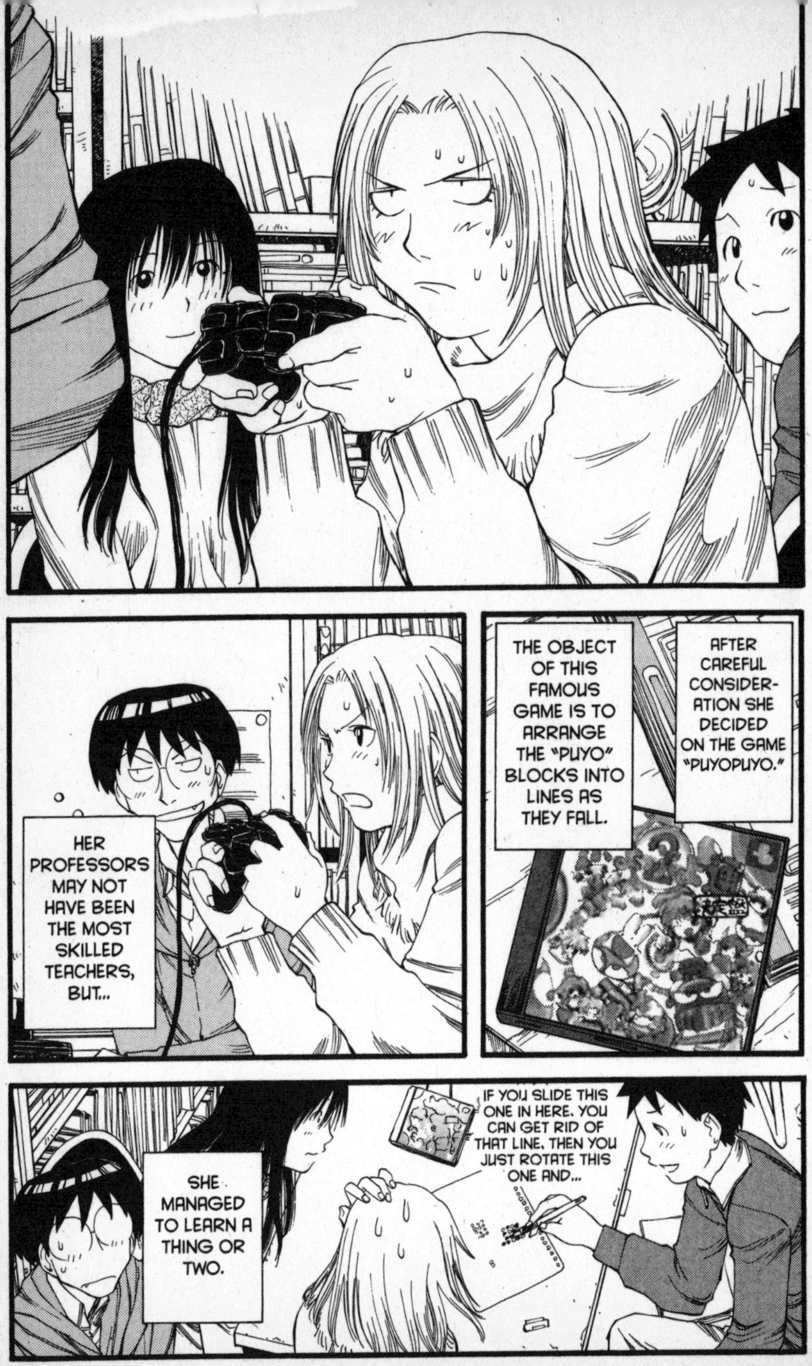
AFTER CAREFUL CONSIDERATION SHE DECIDED ON THE GAME "PUYOPUYO."
THE OBJECT OF THIS FAMOUS GAME IS TO ARRANGE THE "PUYO" BLOCKS INTO LINES AS THEY FALL.
HER PROFESSORS MAY NOT HAVE BEEN THE MOST SKILLED TEACHERS, BUT...
IF YOU SLIDE THIS ONE IN HERE, YOU CAN GET RID OF THAT LINE, THEN YOU JUST ROTATE THIS ONE AND...
SHE MANAGED TO LEARN A THING OR TWO.

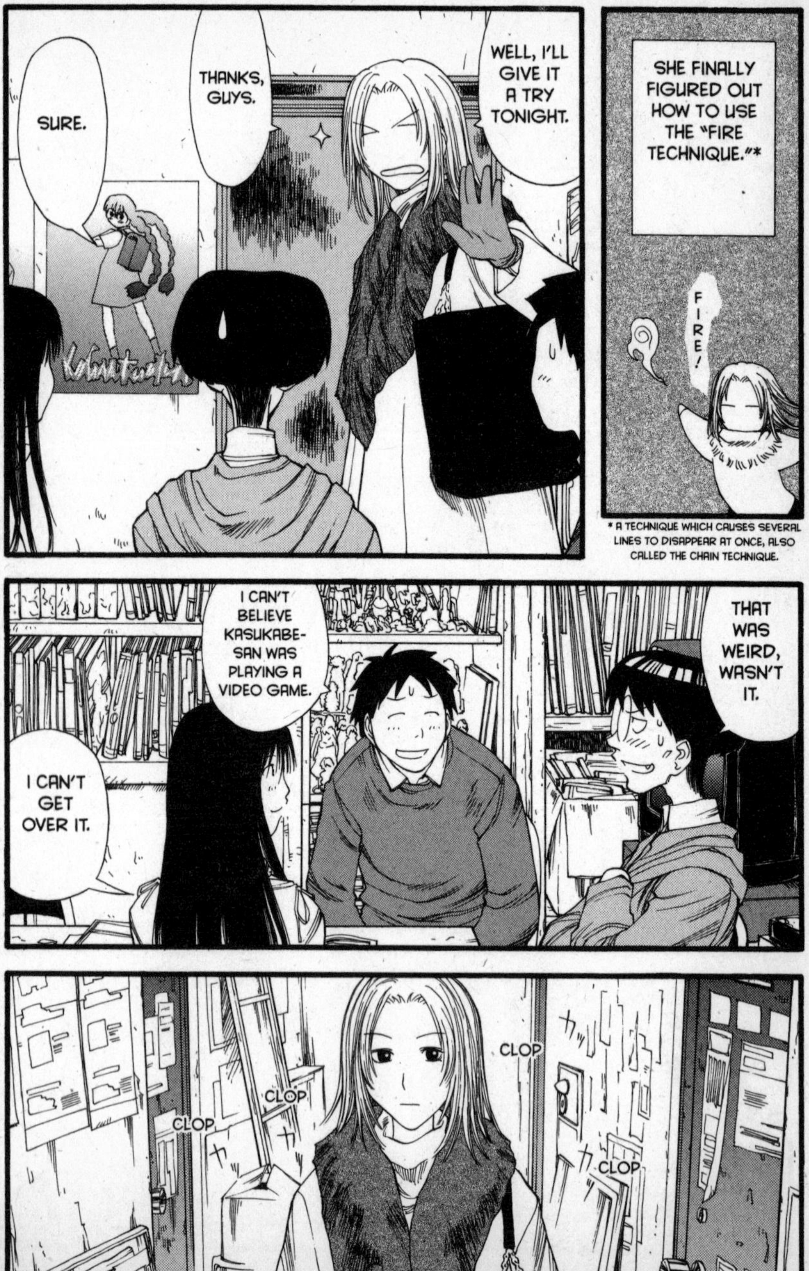
SHE FINALLY FIGURED OUT HOW TO USE THE "FIRE TECHNIQUE."*
FIRE!
WELL, I'LL GIVE IT A TRY TONIGHT.
THANKS, GUYS.
SURE.
THAT WAS WEIRD, WASN'T IT.
I CAN'T BELIEVE KASUKABE-SAN WAS PLAYING A VIDEO GAME.
I CAN'T GET OVER IT.
CLOP
CLOP
CLOP
CLOP

* A TECHNIQUE WHICH CAUSES SEVERAL LINES TO DISAPPEAR AT ONCE, ALSO CALLED THE CHAIN TECHNIQUE.

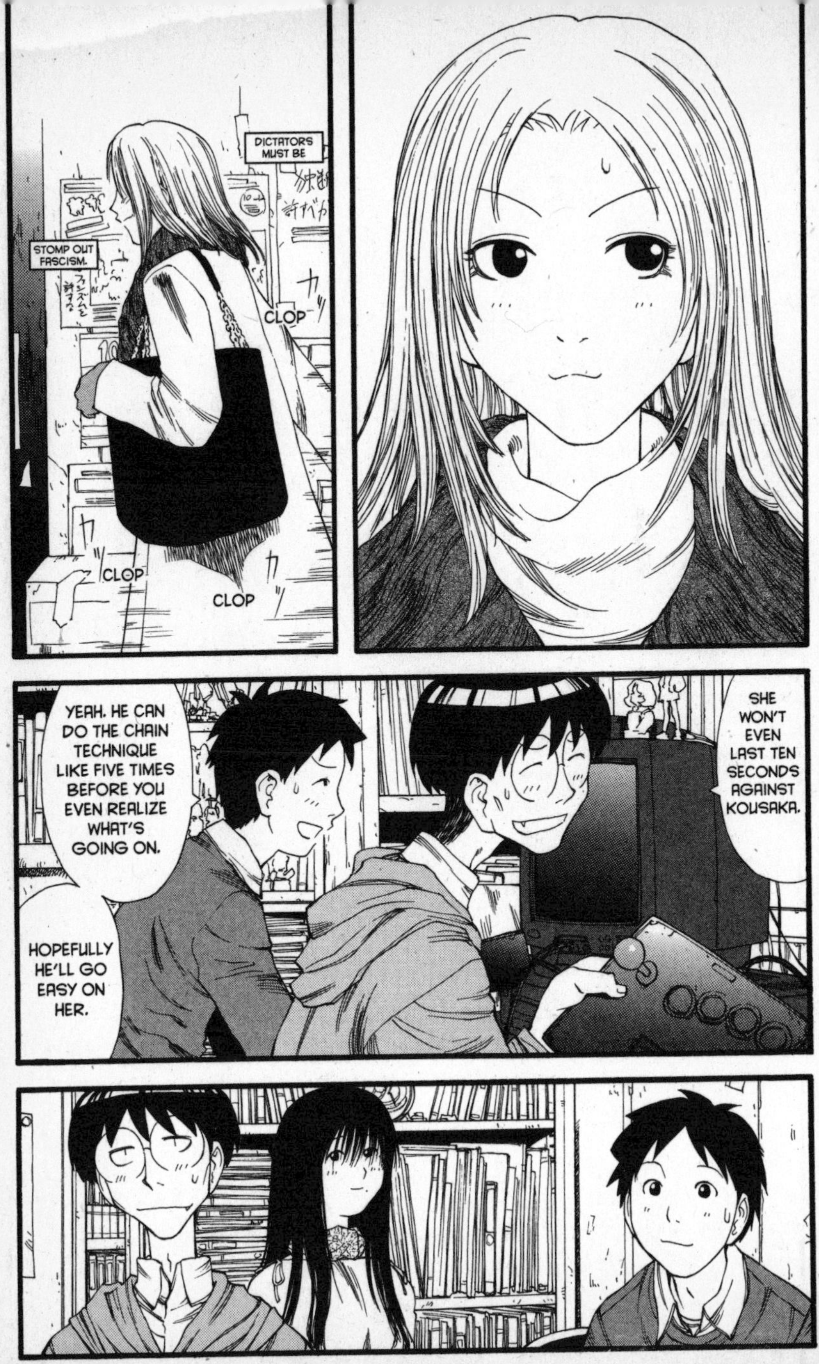
DICTATORS MUST BE
STOMP OUT FASCISM.
CLOP
CLOP
CLOP
SHE WON'T EVEN LAST TEN SECONDS AGAINST KOUSAKA.
YEAH. HE CAN DO THE CHAIN TECHNIQUE LIKE FIVE TIMES BEFORE YOU EVEN REALIZE WHAT'S GOING ON.
HOPEFULLY HE'LL GO EASY ON HER.

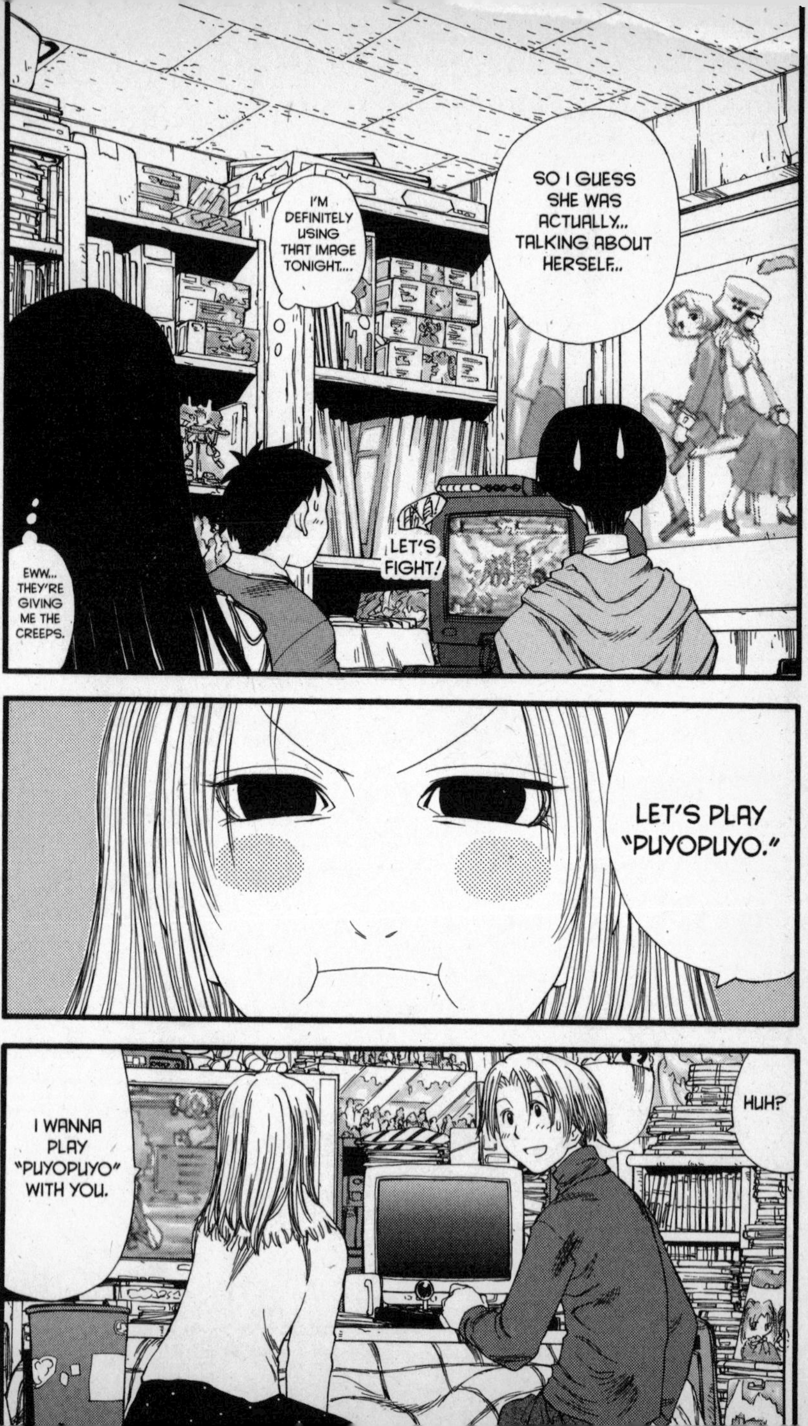
SO I GUESS SHE WAS ACTUALLY... TALKING ABOUT HERSELF...
I'M DEFINITELY USING THAT IMAGE TONIGHT....
LET'S FIGHT!
EWW... THEY'RE GIVING ME THE CREEPS.
LET'S PLAY "PUYOPUYO."
HUH?
I WANNA PLAY "PUYOPUYO" WITH YOU.

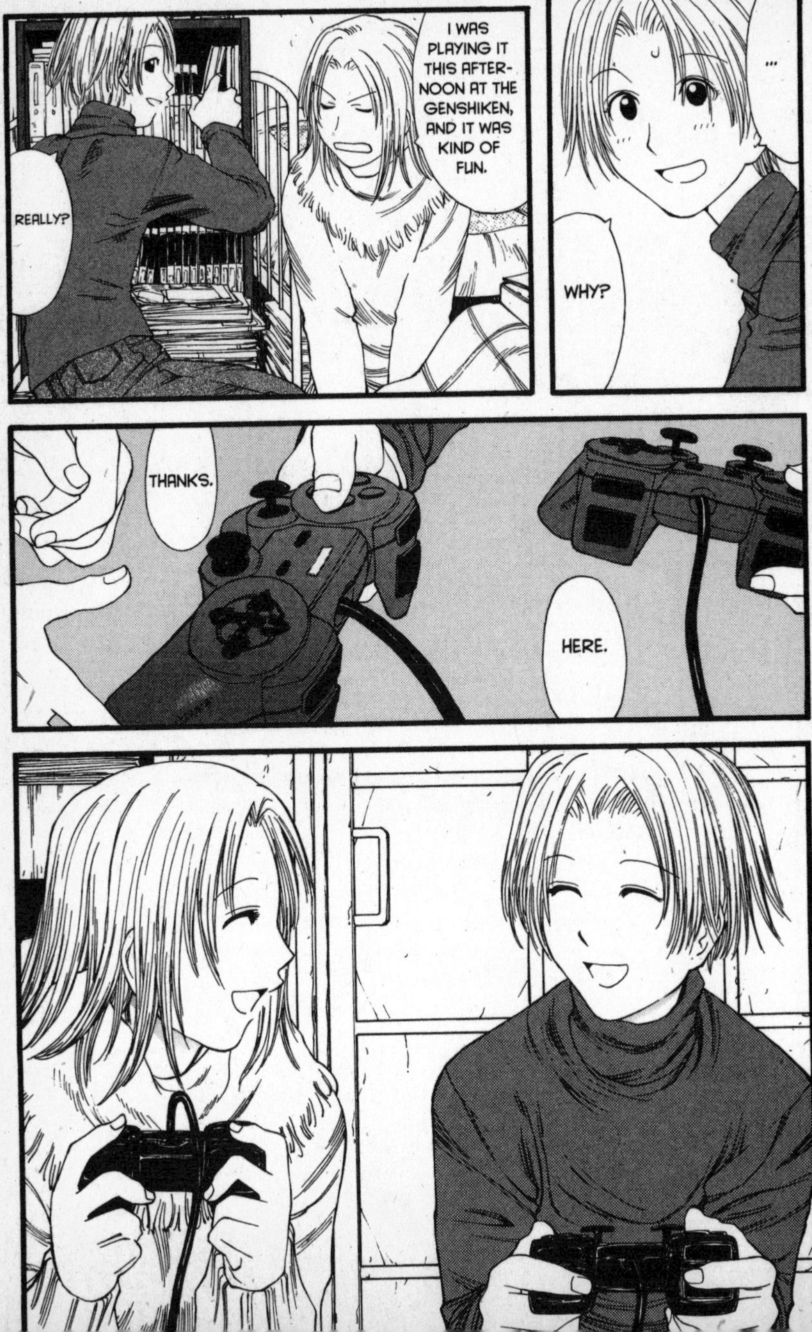
...
WHY?
I WAS PLAYING IT THIS AFTER-NOON AT THE GENSHIKEN, AND IT WAS KIND OF FUN.
REALLY?
HERE.
THANKS.

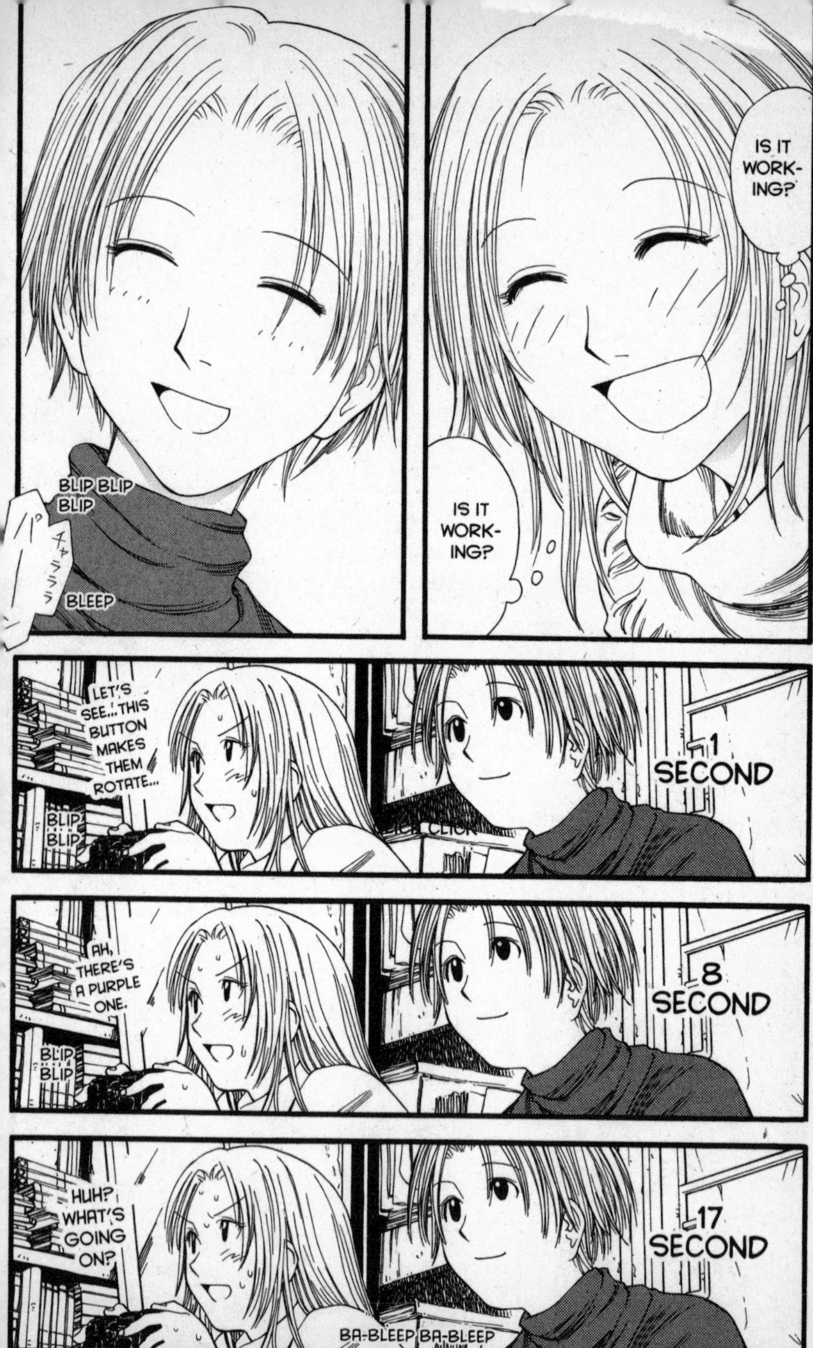
IS IT WORKING?
IS IT WORKING?
BLIP BLIP BLIP
パー
チャラララ
BLEEP
1 SECOND
LET'S SEE... THIS BUTTON MAKES THEM ROTATE...
BLIP BLIP
CLICK
8 SECOND
AH, THERE'S A PURPLE ONE.
BLIP BLIP
17 SECOND
HUH? WHAT'S GOING ON?
BA-BLEEP BA-BLEEP

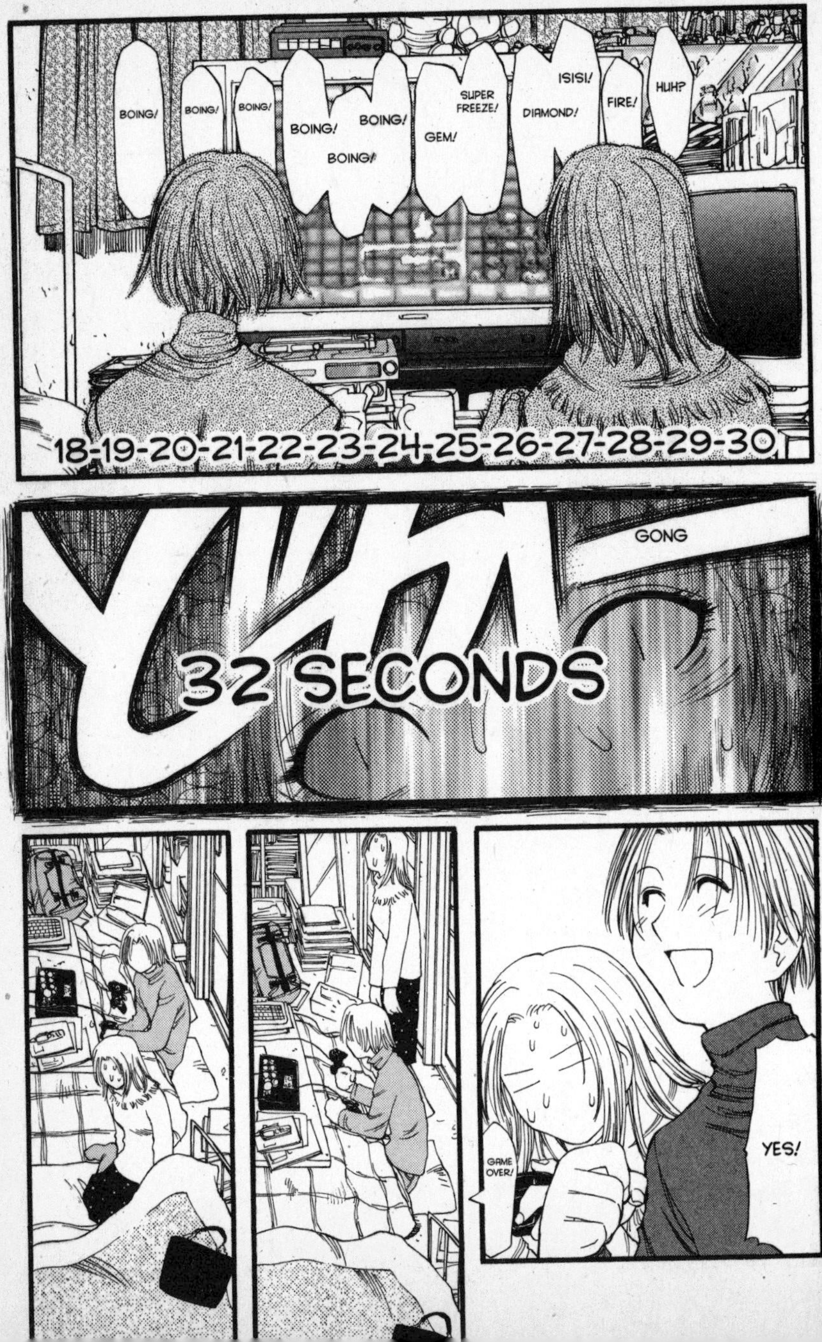
HUH?
FIRE!
ISISI!
DIAMOND!
SUPER FREEZE!
GEM!
BOING!
BOING!
BOING!
BOING!
BOING!
BOING!
18-19-20-21-22-23-24-25-26-27-28-29-30
GONG
32 SECONDS
YES!
GAME OVER!

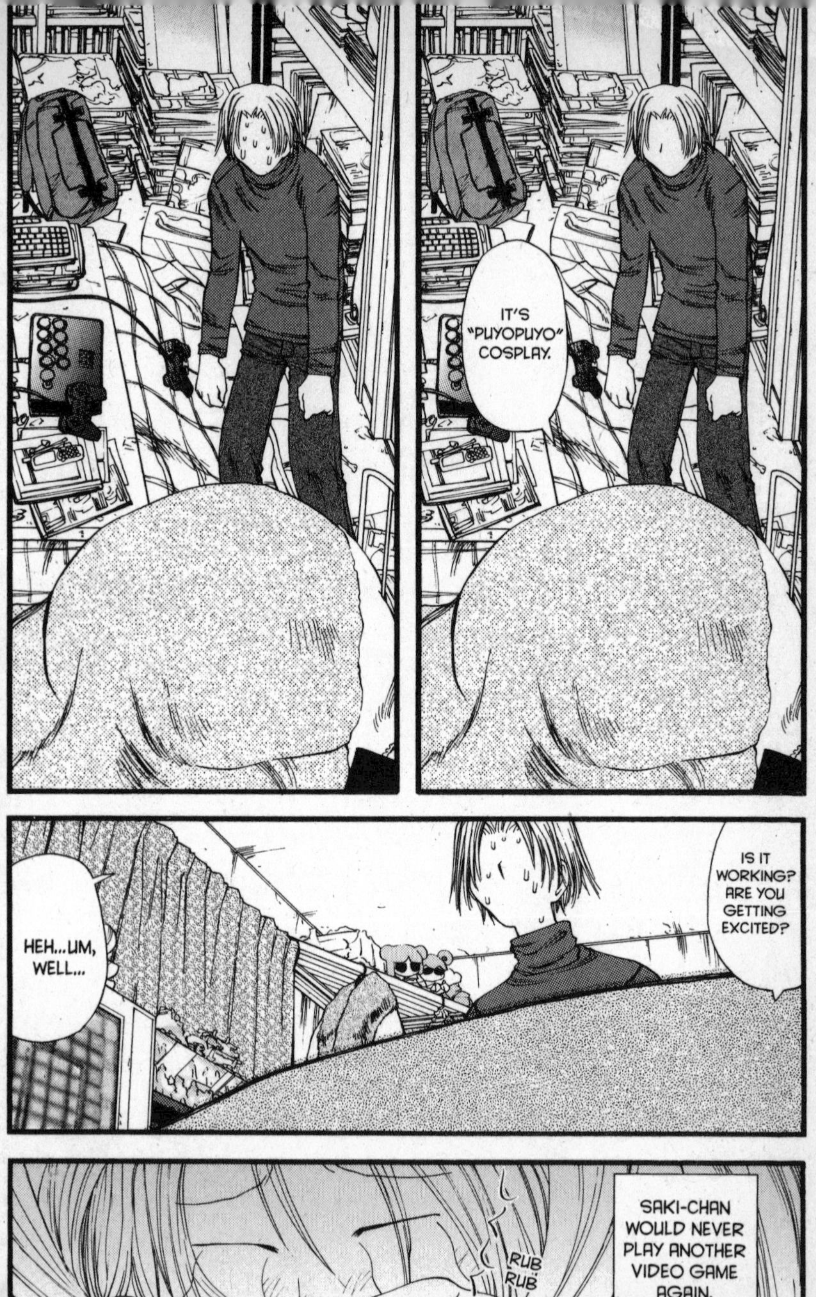
IT'S "PUYOPUYO" COSPLAY.
IS IT WORKING? ARE YOU GETTING EXCITED?
HEH...UM, WELL...
SAKI-CHAN WOULD NEVER PLAY ANOTHER VIDEO GAME AGAIN.
RUB RUB

END OF CHAPTER 10

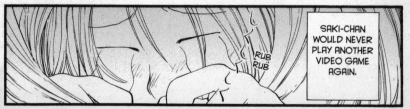

THE GENSHIKEN MEMBERS PICK...

# KUJI-UN

## ...THE MOST NOTABLE SCENES

TAKEN FROM THE GENSHIKEN'S SPORADICALLY PUBLISHED ZINE "MEBAETAME"

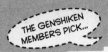

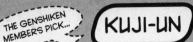

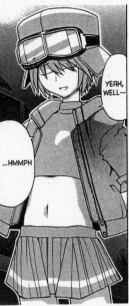

### MY FAVORITE SCENE FROM *KUJI-UN* PART 3 BY "KODAMA"

FROM PAGE 72 OF TANKOBON BOOK 5

YEAH, WELL--
...HMMPH
HEY... THAT WAS RUDE.
ALL I WANT IS FOR HIM TO BE HAPPY.
I'M PRETTY SURE EVEN YOU CAN UNDER-STAND THAT, RIGHT?


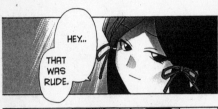

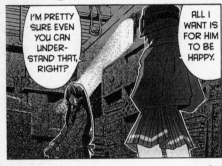

THIS IS MY SCENE. THIS SCENE REVEALS THE COMPLEXITIES OF THESE TWO ADVERSARIES, THE YAKUZA MAH-JONG PRO, AND THE DAUGHTER OF THE YAKUZA BOSS. IZUMI-SAN SOMEHOW ENDED UP PLAYING MAHJONG WITH THE VICE-PRESIDENT'S FAMILY'S CLAN. THIS STRANGE RELATIONSHIP IN WHICH TWO ENEMIES DEVELOP A BOND OF TRUST IS RARELY SEEN IN KUJI-UN. I THINK SCENES LIKE THIS ARE TRULY FASCINATING, DON'T YOU? [KODAMA]

I'M SORRY, BUT THIS IS SO TYPICAL THAT IT'S BORING (LAUGHS). I THOUGHT YOU WERE GONNA PICK SOMETHING MORE SENTIMENTAL, SO I WAS A LITTLE SURPRISED. YOU AND THE OWL WRITE ABOUT SUCH BORING STUFF. I HAVE NO IDEA WHAT TOSHIZO-KUN IS GOING TO WRITE ABOUT.

...OH, THIS IS REALLY NOTHING, BUT IN THE TOP LEFT PICTURE OF THE VICE PRESIDENT, IT LOOKS LIKE THEY FORGOT TO COLOR IN PART OF THE RIBBON ON THE LEFT. I WONDER IF THEY CORRECTED IT IN THE SECOND PRINTING. NOT THAT IT MATTERS. [PIT VIPER]

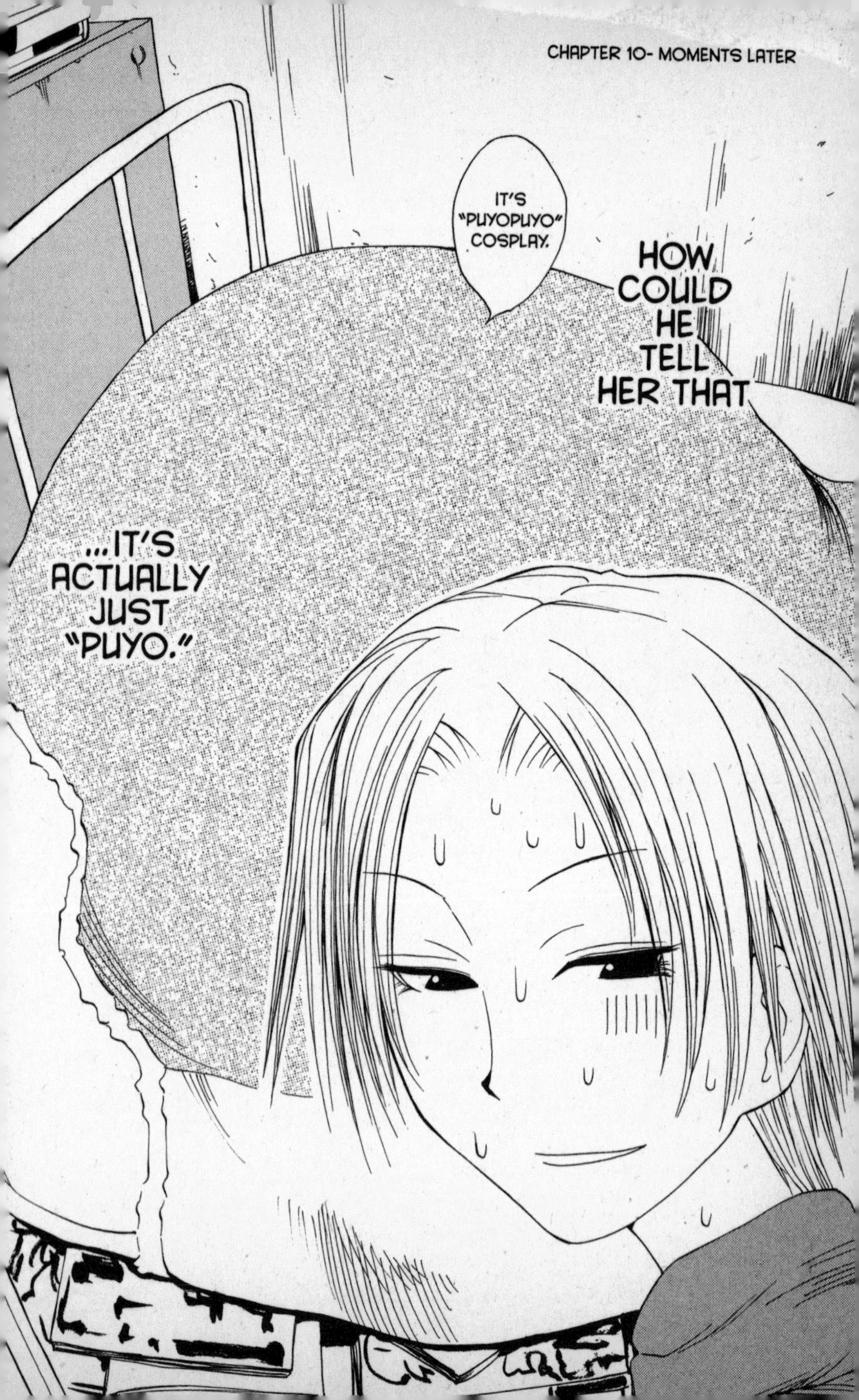
CHAPTER 10- MOMENTS LATER
IT'S "PUYOPUYO" COSPLAY.
HOW COULD HE TELL HER THAT
...IT'S ACTUALLY JUST "PUYO."

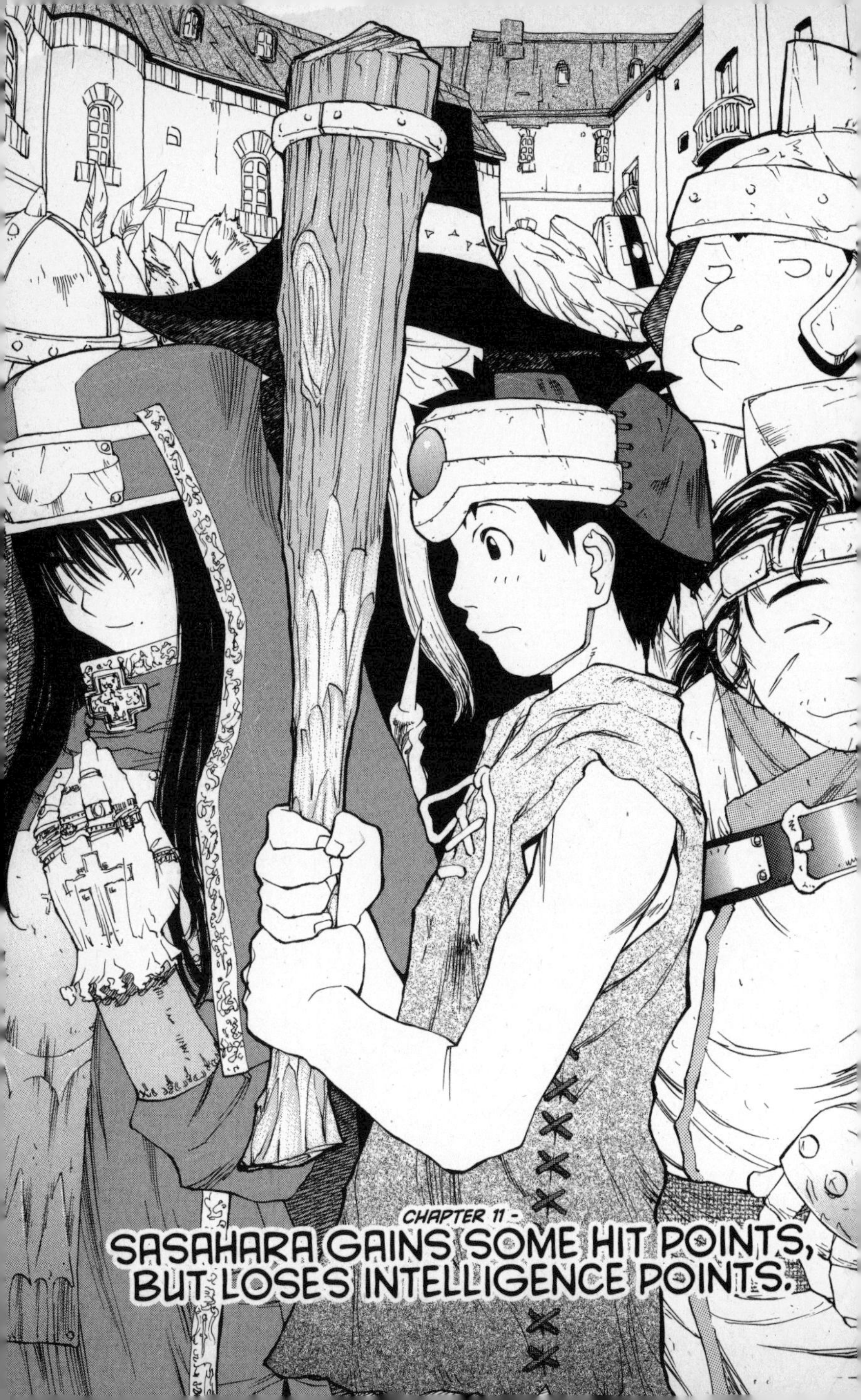
CHAPTER 11 -
SASAHARA GAINS SOME HIT POINTS, BUT LOSES INTELLIGENCE POINTS.

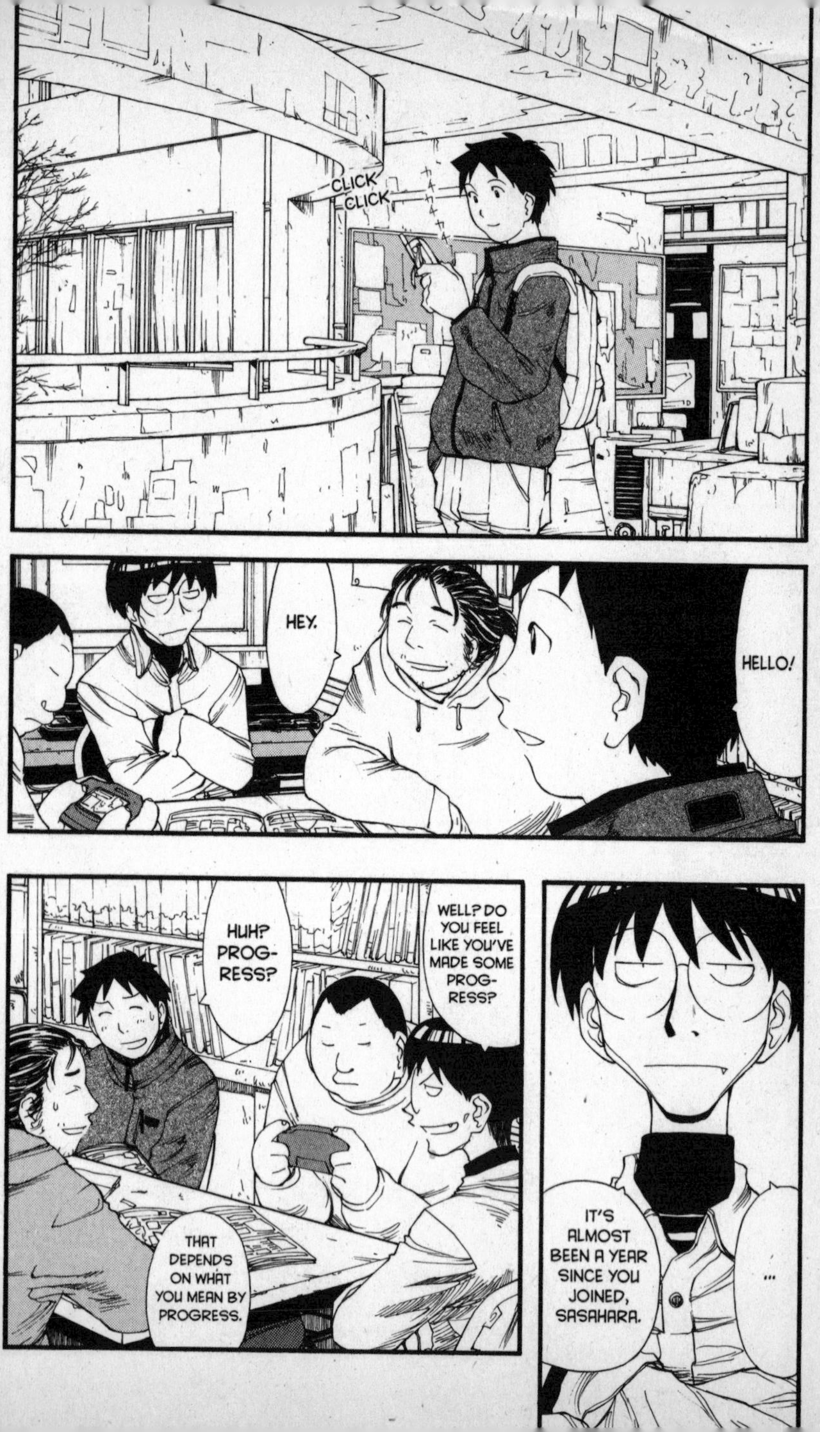
CLICK
CLICK
HELLO!
HEY.
...
IT'S ALMOST BEEN A YEAR SINCE YOU JOINED, SASAHARA.
WELL? DO YOU FEEL LIKE YOU'VE MADE SOME PROG-RESS?
HUH? PROG-RESS?
THAT DEPENDS ON WHAT YOU MEAN BY PROGRESS.

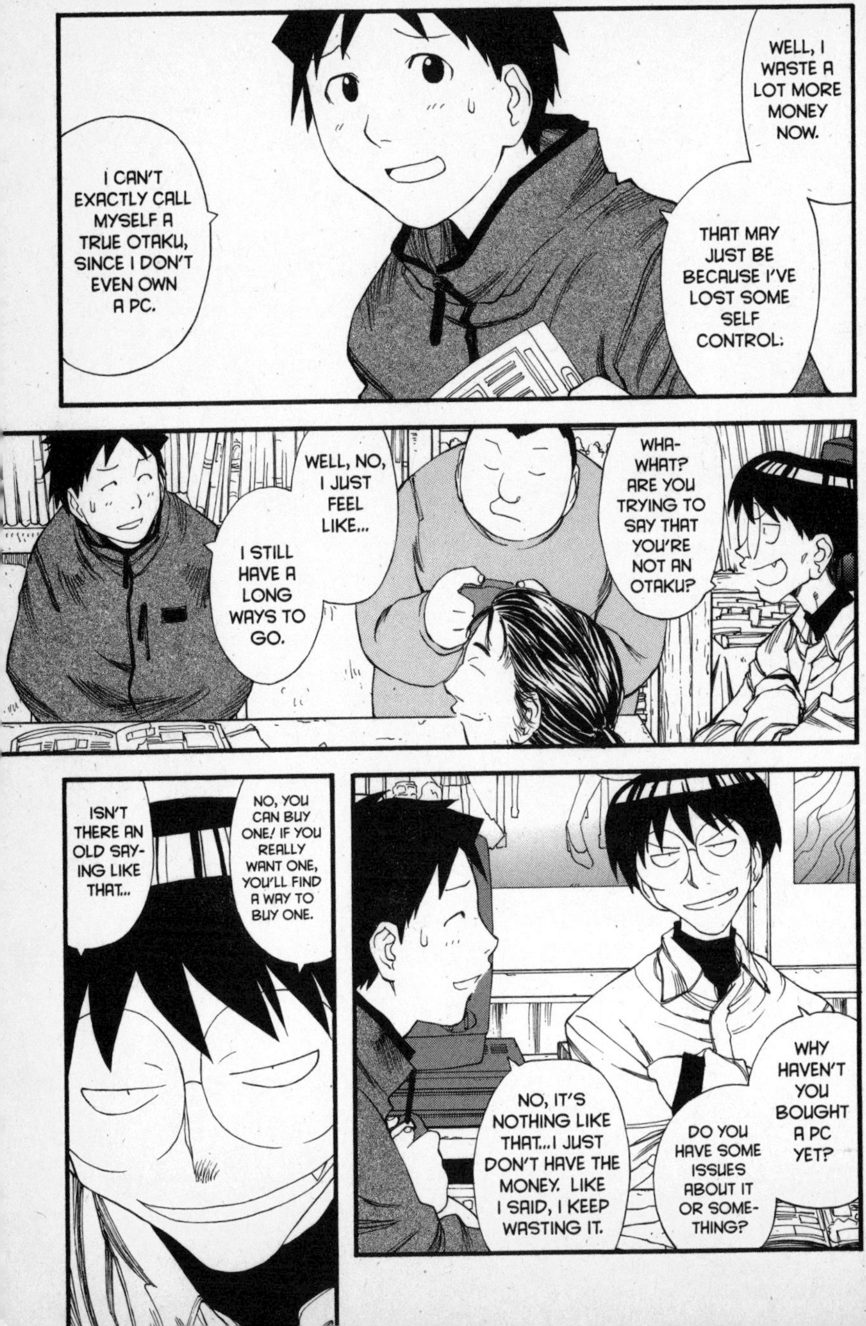
WELL, I WASTE A LOT MORE MONEY NOW.
THAT MAY JUST BE BECAUSE I'VE LOST SOME SELF CONTROL.
I CAN'T EXACTLY CALL MYSELF A TRUE OTAKU, SINCE I DON'T EVEN OWN A PC.
WHA-WHAT? ARE YOU TRYING TO SAY THAT YOU'RE NOT AN OTAKU?
WELL, NO, I JUST FEEL LIKE...
I STILL HAVE A LONG WAYS TO GO.
WHY HAVEN'T YOU BOUGHT A PC YET?
DO YOU HAVE SOME ISSUES ABOUT IT OR SOME-THING?
NO, IT'S NOTHING LIKE THAT...I JUST DON'T HAVE THE MONEY. LIKE I SAID, I KEEP WASTING IT.
NO, YOU CAN BUY ONE! IF YOU REALLY WANT ONE, YOU'LL FIND A WAY TO BUY ONE.
ISN'T THERE AN OLD SAYING LIKE THAT...

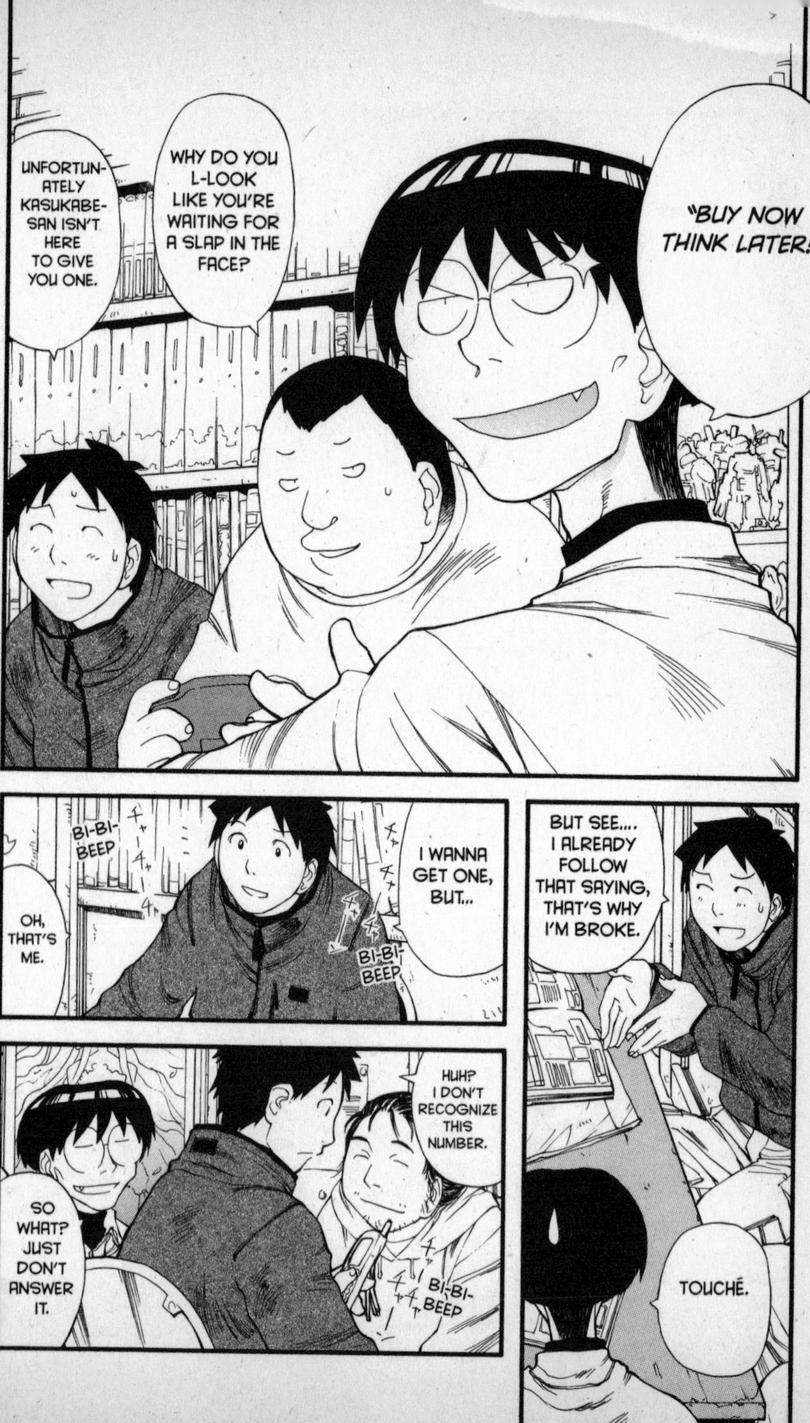
"BUY NOW THINK LATER!"
WHY DO YOU L-LOOK LIKE YOU'RE WAITING FOR A SLAP IN THE FACE?
UNFORTUN-ATELY KASUKABE-SAN ISN'T HERE TO GIVE YOU ONE.
BUT SEE.... I ALREADY FOLLOW THAT SAYING, THAT'S WHY I'M BROKE.
TOUCHÉ.
I WANNA GET ONE, BUT...
BI-BI-BEEP
BI-BI-BEEP
OH, THAT'S ME.
HUH? I DON'T RECOGNIZE THIS NUMBER.
BI-BI-BEEP
SO WHAT? JUST DON'T ANSWER IT.

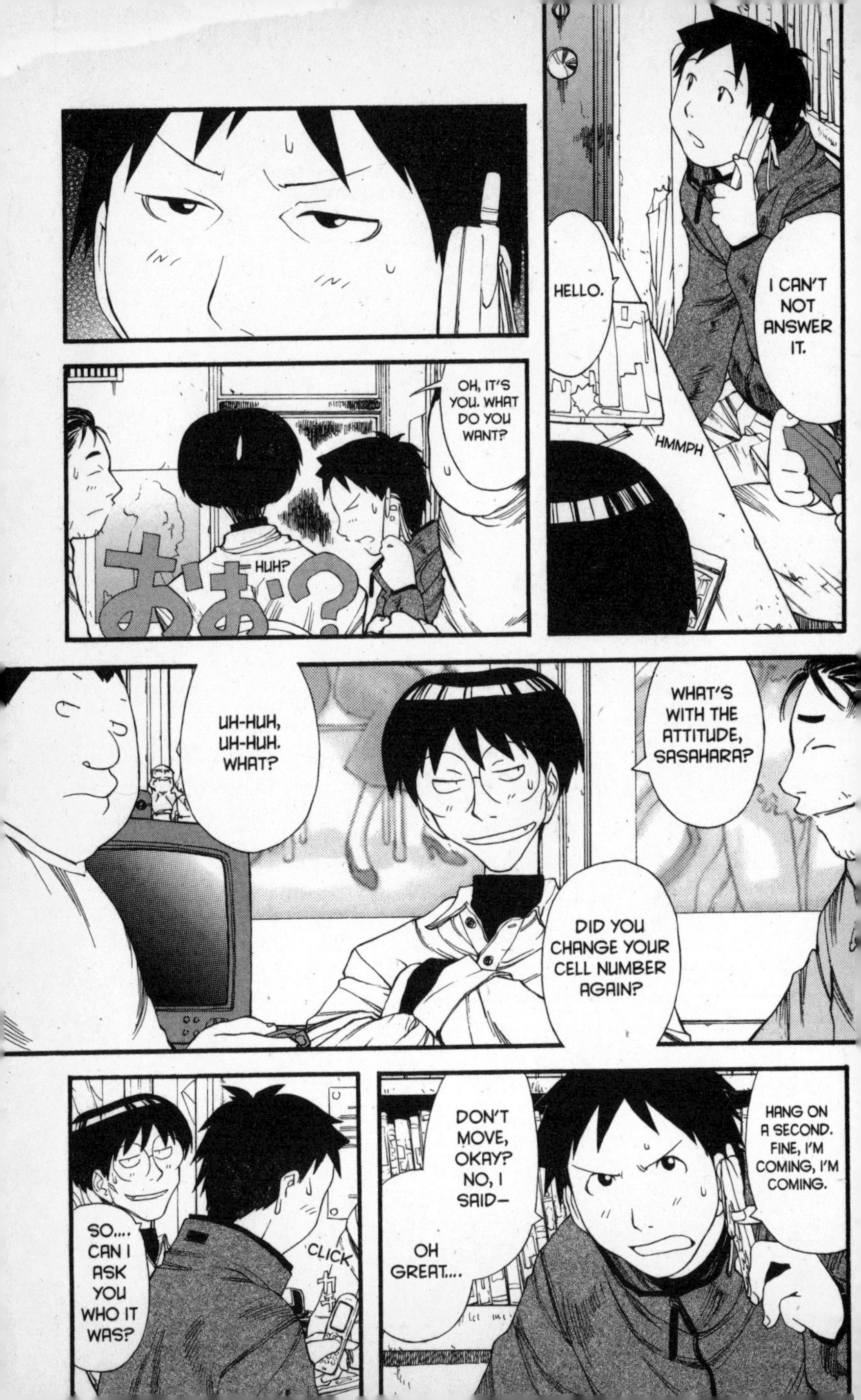
I CAN'T NOT ANSWER IT.
HELLO.
HMMPH
OH, IT'S YOU. WHAT DO YOU WANT?
HUH?
WHAT'S WITH THE ATTITUDE, SASAHARA?
DID YOU CHANGE YOUR CELL NUMBER AGAIN?
UH-HUH, UH-HUH. WHAT?
HANG ON A SECOND. FINE, I'M COMING, I'M COMING.
DON'T MOVE, OKAY? NO, I SAID—
OH GREAT....
CLICK
SO.... CAN I ASK YOU WHO IT WAS?

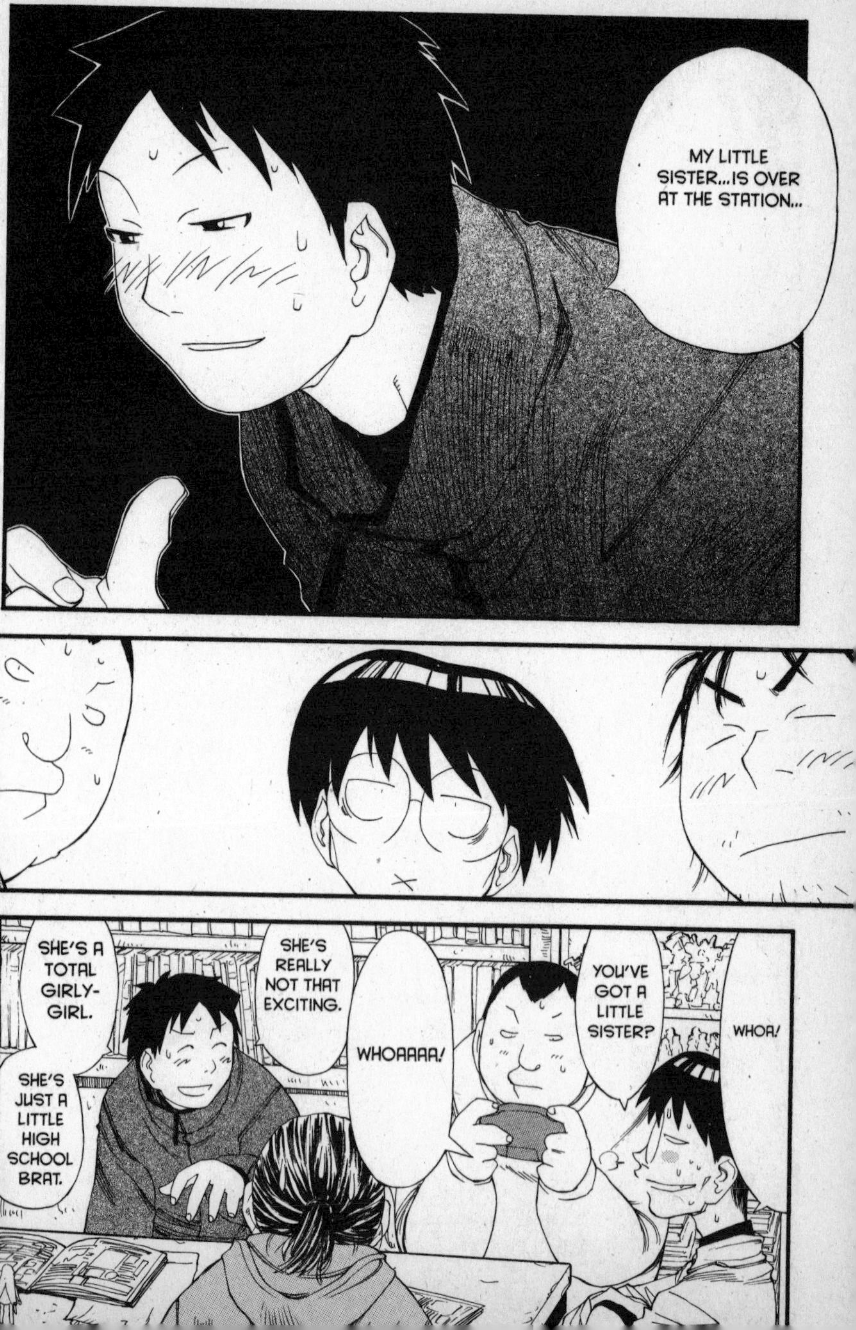
MY LITTLE SISTER...IS OVER AT THE STATION...
WHOA!
YOU'VE GOT A LITTLE SISTER?
WHOAAAA!
SHE'S REALLY NOT THAT EXCITING.
SHE'S A TOTAL GIRLY-GIRL.
SHE'S JUST A LITTLE HIGH SCHOOL BRAT.

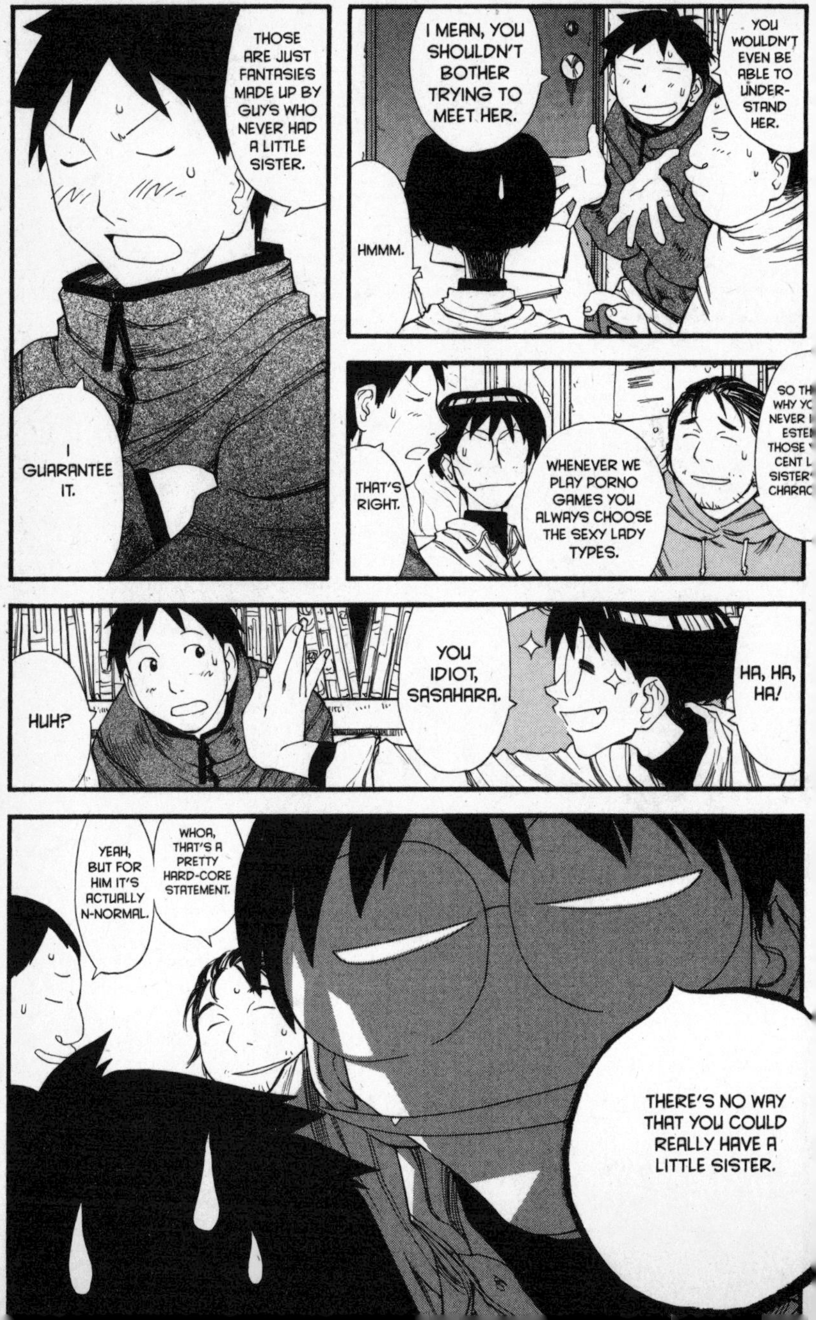
YOU WOULDN'T EVEN BE ABLE TO UNDERSTAND HER.
I MEAN, YOU SHOULDN'T BOTHER TRYING TO MEET HER.
HMMM.
WHENEVER WE PLAY PORNO GAMES YOU ALWAYS CHOOSE THE SEXY LADY TYPES.
THAT'S RIGHT.
THOSE ARE JUST FANTASIES MADE UP BY GUYS WHO NEVER HAD A LITTLE SISTER.
I GUARANTEE IT.
HA, HA, HA!
YOU IDIOT, SASAHARA.
HUH?
THERE'S NO WAY THAT YOU COULD REALLY HAVE A LITTLE SISTER.
WHOA, THAT'S A PRETTY HARD-CORE STATEMENT.
YEAH, BUT FOR HIM IT'S ACTUALLY N-NORMAL.

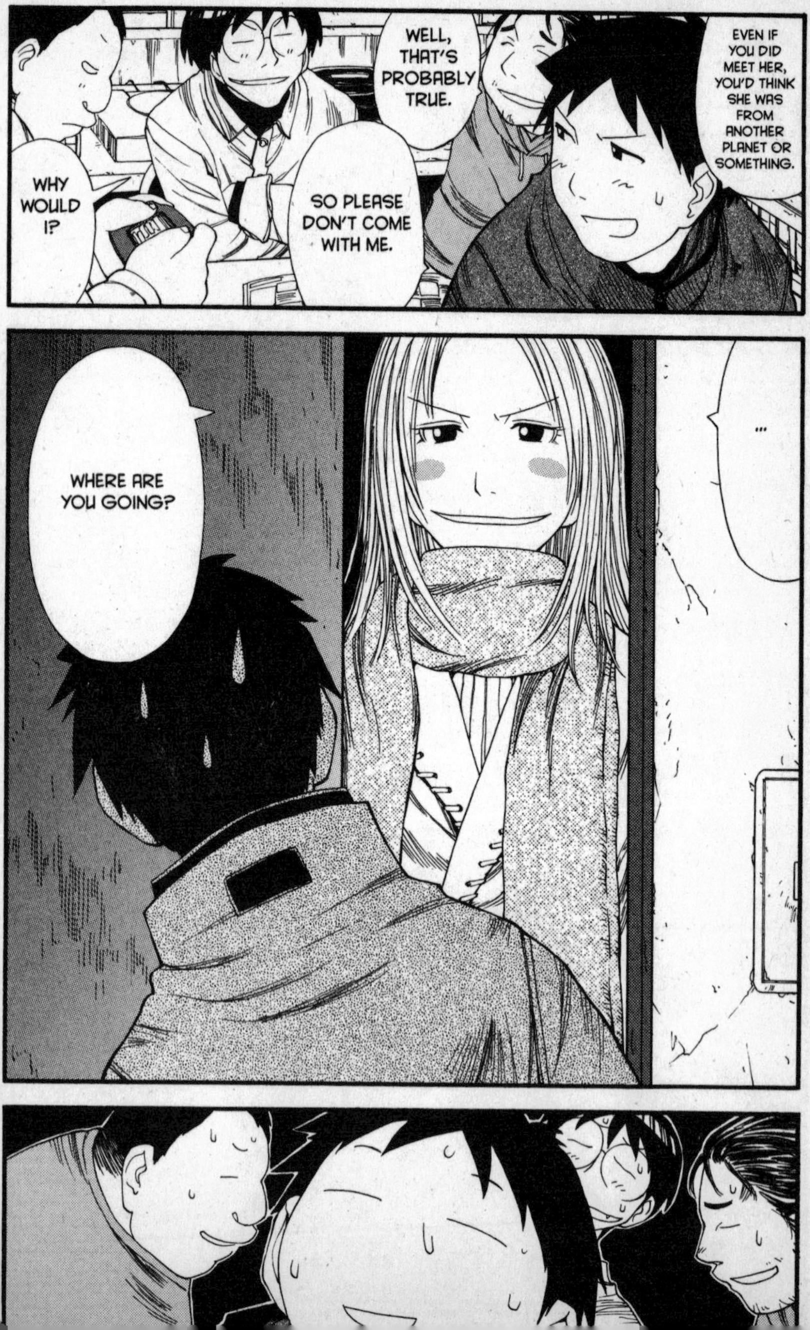
EVEN IF YOU DID MEET HER, YOU'D THINK SHE WAS FROM ANOTHER PLANET OR SOMETHING.
WELL, THAT'S PROBABLY TRUE.
SO PLEASE DON'T COME WITH ME.
WHY WOULD I?
...
WHERE ARE YOU GOING?

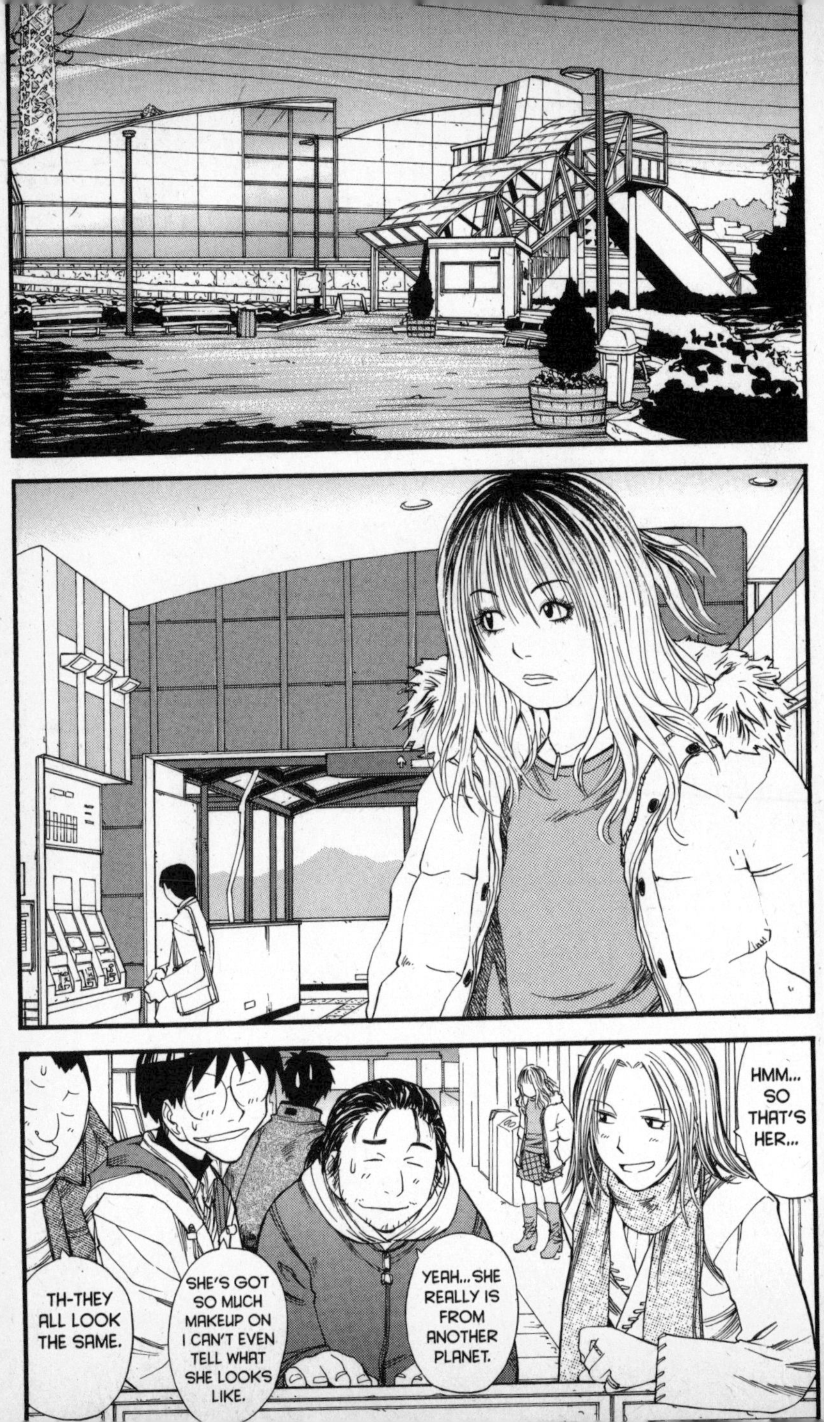
HMM... SO THAT'S HER...
YEAH...SHE REALLY IS FROM ANOTHER PLANET.
SHE'S GOT SO MUCH MAKEUP ON I CAN'T EVEN TELL WHAT SHE LOOKS LIKE.
TH-THEY ALL LOOK THE SAME.

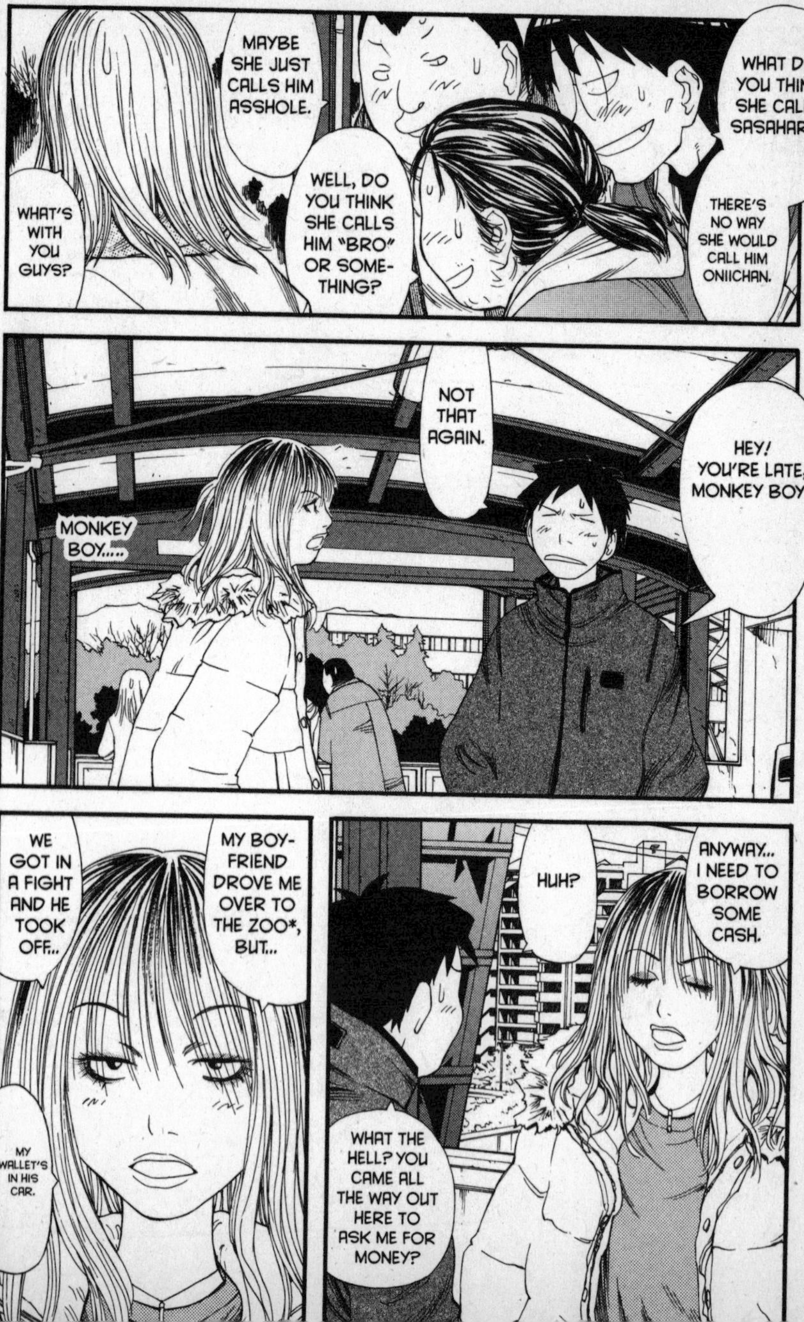
WHAT DO YOU THINK SHE CALLS SASAHARA?
THERE'S NO WAY SHE WOULD CALL HIM ONIICHAN.
WELL, DO YOU THINK SHE CALLS HIM "BRO" OR SOME-THING?
MAYBE SHE JUST CALLS HIM ASSHOLE.
WHAT'S WITH YOU GUYS?
HEY! YOU'RE LATE, MONKEY BOY!
NOT THAT AGAIN.
MONKEY BOY.....
ANYWAY... I NEED TO BORROW SOME CASH.
HUH?
WHAT THE HELL? YOU CAME ALL THE WAY OUT HERE TO ASK ME FOR MONEY?
MY BOY-FRIEND DROVE ME OVER TO THE ZOO*, BUT...
WE GOT IN A FIGHT AND HE TOOK OFF...
MY WALLET'S IN HIS CAR.

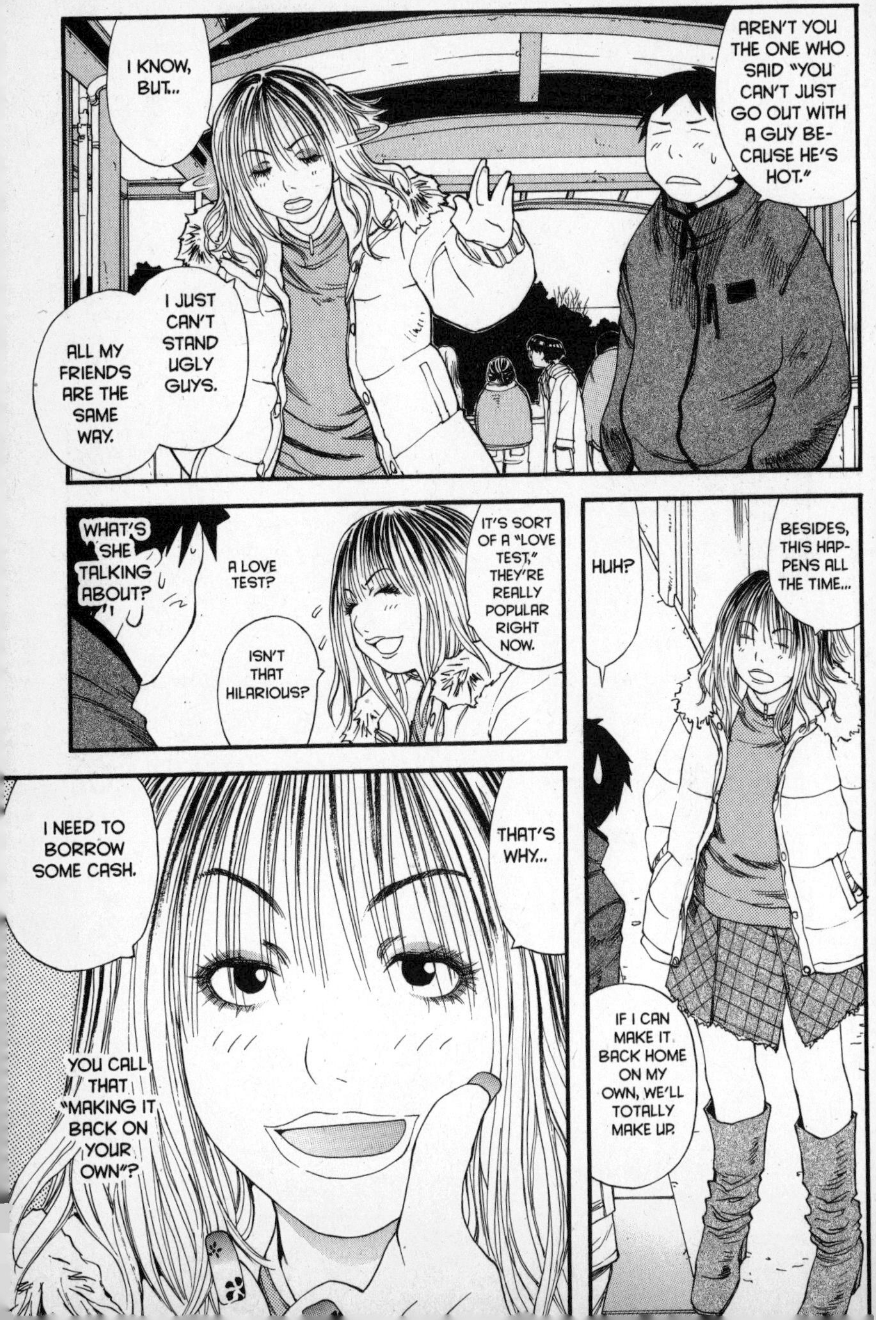
AREN'T YOU THE ONE WHO SAID "YOU CAN'T JUST GO OUT WITH A GUY BE-CAUSE HE'S HOT."
I KNOW, BUT...
I JUST CAN'T STAND UGLY GUYS.
ALL MY FRIENDS ARE THE SAME WAY.
BESIDES, THIS HAP-PENS ALL THE TIME...
HUH?
IF I CAN MAKE IT BACK HOME ON MY OWN, WE'LL TOTALLY MAKE UP.
IT'S SORT OF A "LOVE TEST," THEY'RE REALLY POPULAR RIGHT NOW.
A LOVE TEST?
ISN'T THAT HILARIOUS?
WHAT'S SHE TALKING ABOUT?
THAT'S WHY...
I NEED TO BORROW SOME CASH.
YOU CALL THAT "MAKING IT BACK ON YOUR OWN"?

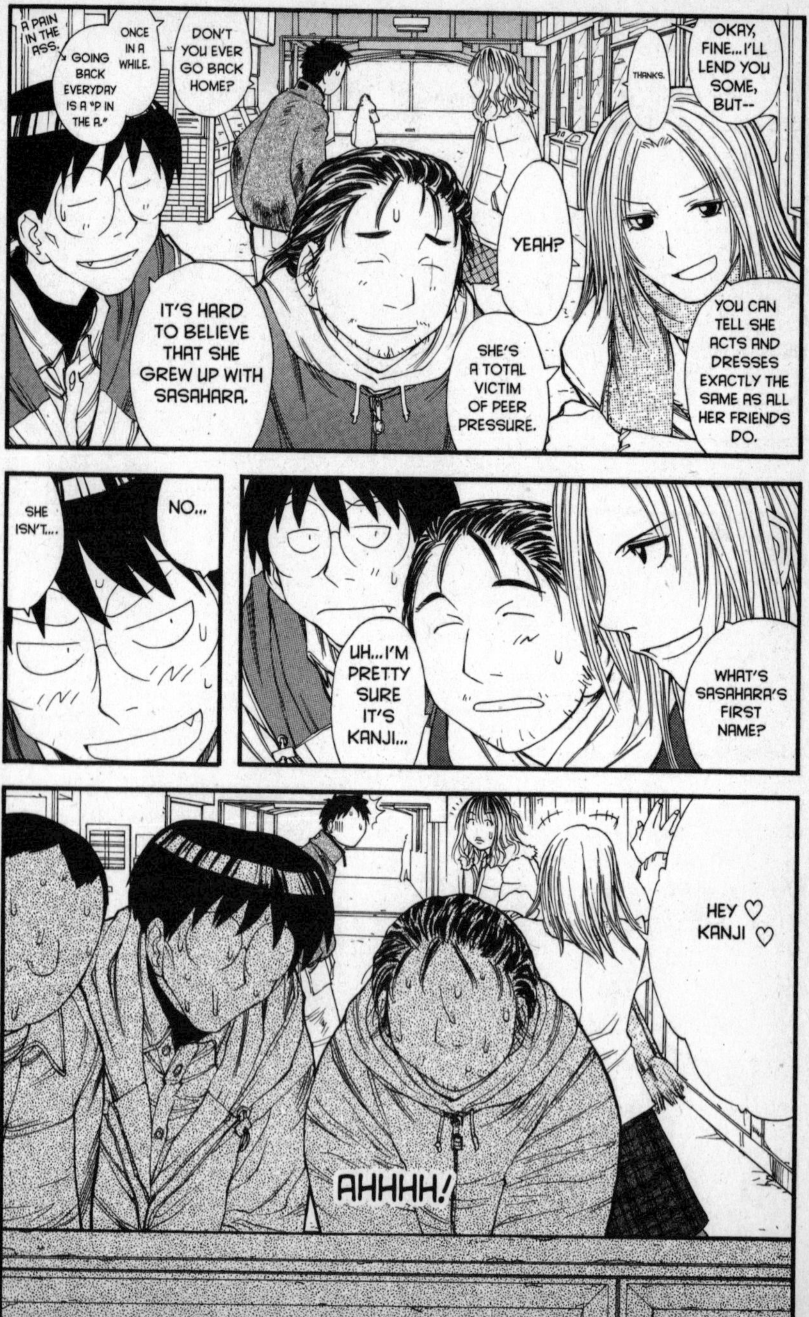
OKAY, FINE...I'LL LEND YOU SOME, BUT--
THANKS.
DON'T YOU EVER GO BACK HOME?
ONCE IN A WHILE.
GOING BACK EVERYDAY IS A "P IN THE A."
A PAIN IN THE ASS.
YOU CAN TELL SHE ACTS AND DRESSES EXACTLY THE SAME AS ALL HER FRIENDS DO.
YEAH?
SHE'S A TOTAL VICTIM OF PEER PRESSURE.
IT'S HARD TO BELIEVE THAT SHE GREW UP WITH SASAHARA.
WHAT'S SASAHARA'S FIRST NAME?
UH...I'M PRETTY SURE IT'S KANJI...
NO...
SHE ISN'T...
HEY ♡ KANJI ♡
AHHHH!

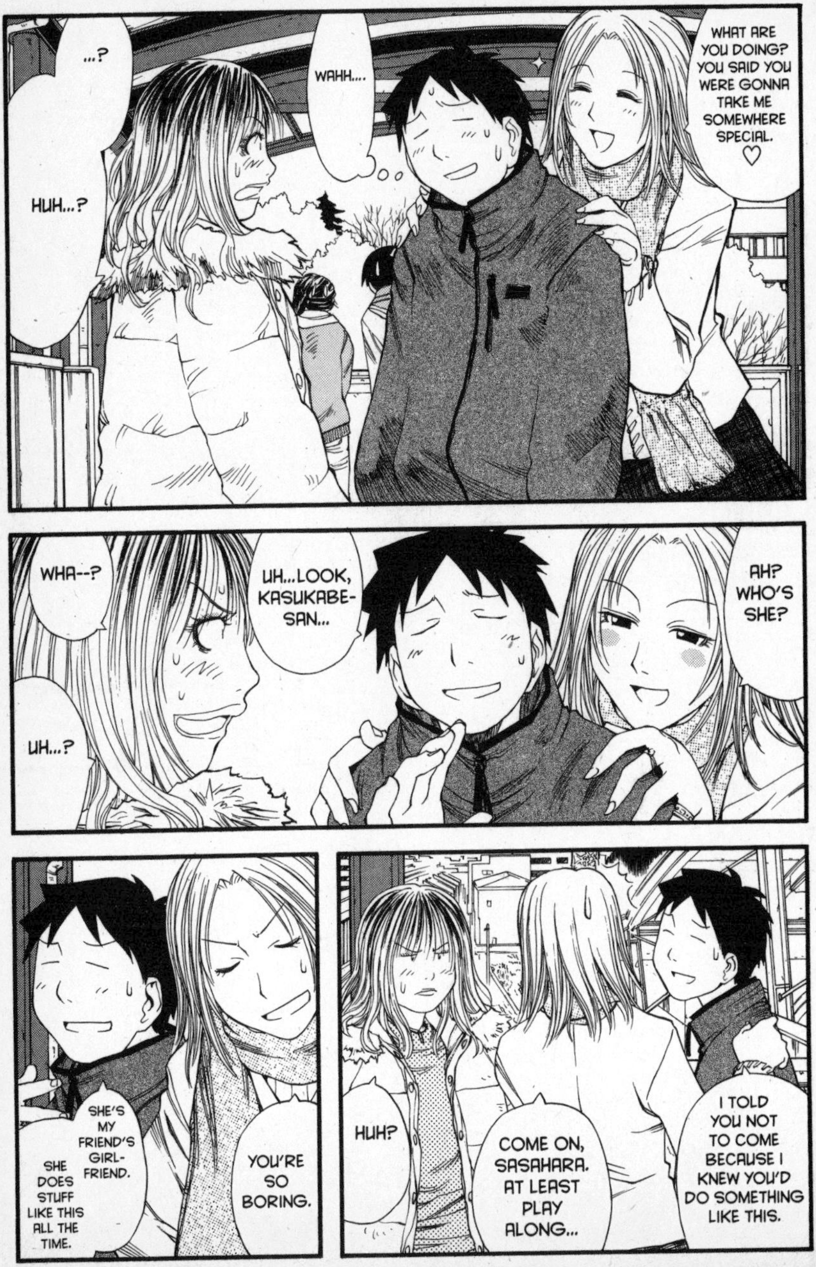
WHAT ARE YOU DOING? YOU SAID YOU WERE GONNA TAKE ME SOMEWHERE SPECIAL. ♡
WAHH....
...?
HUH...?
AH? WHO'S SHE?
UH...LOOK, KASUKABE-SAN...
WHA--?
UH...?
I TOLD YOU NOT TO COME BECAUSE I KNEW YOU'D DO SOMETHING LIKE THIS.
COME ON, SASAHARA. AT LEAST PLAY ALONG...
HUH?
YOU'RE SO BORING.
SHE'S MY FRIEND'S GIRL-FRIEND.
SHE DOES STUFF LIKE THIS ALL THE TIME.

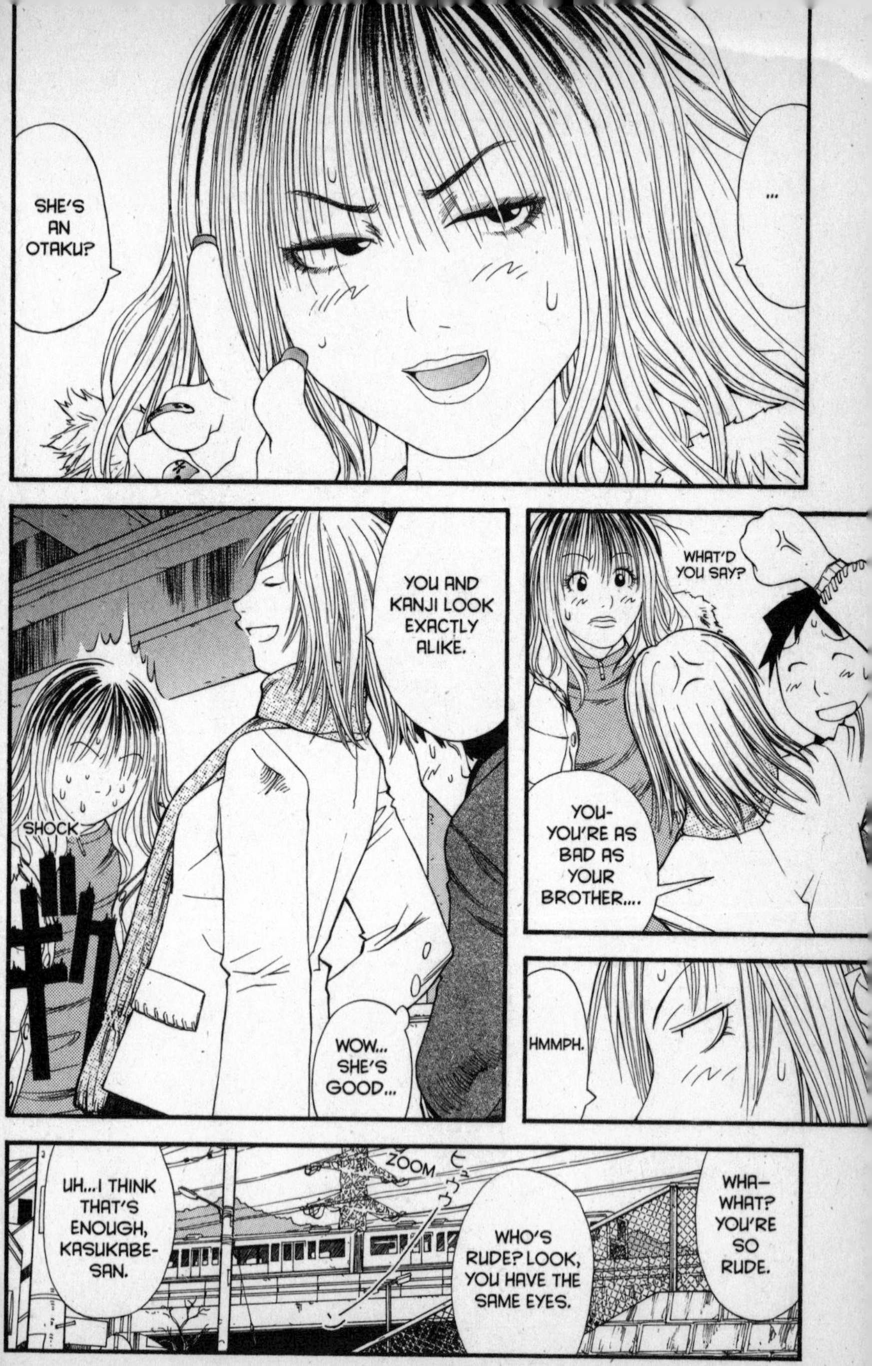
...
SHE'S AN OTAKU?
WHAT'D YOU SAY?
YOU-YOU'RE AS BAD AS YOUR BROTHER....
HMMPH.
YOU AND KANJI LOOK EXACTLY ALIKE.
SHOCK
WOW... SHE'S GOOD...
WHA-WHAT? YOU'RE SO RUDE.
WHO'S RUDE? LOOK, YOU HAVE THE SAME EYES.
ZOOM
UH...I THINK THAT'S ENOUGH, KASUKABE-SAN.

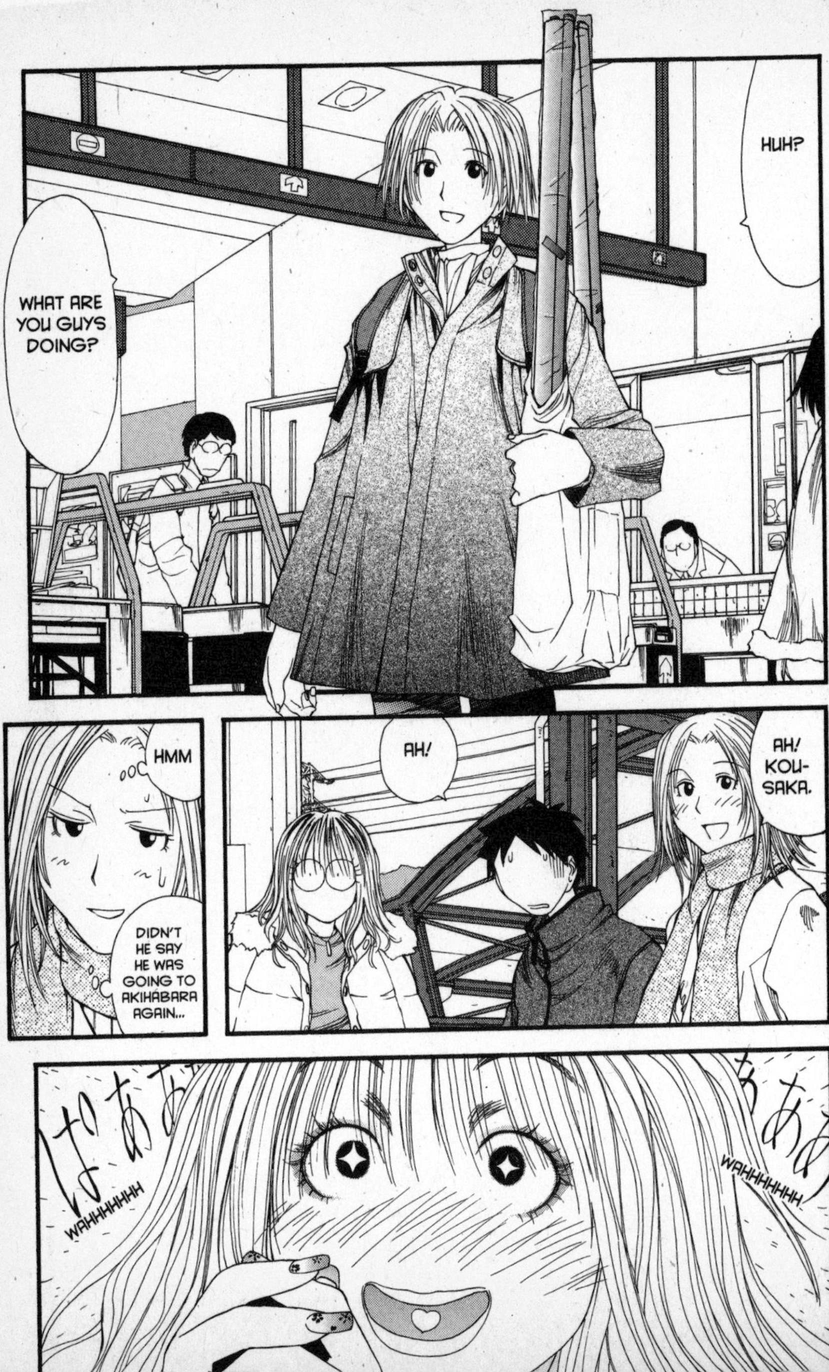
HUH?
WHAT ARE YOU GUYS DOING?
AH! KOU-SAKA.
AH!
HMM
DIDN'T HE SAY HE WAS GOING TO AKIHABARA AGAIN...
WAHHHHHHH
WAHHHHHHH

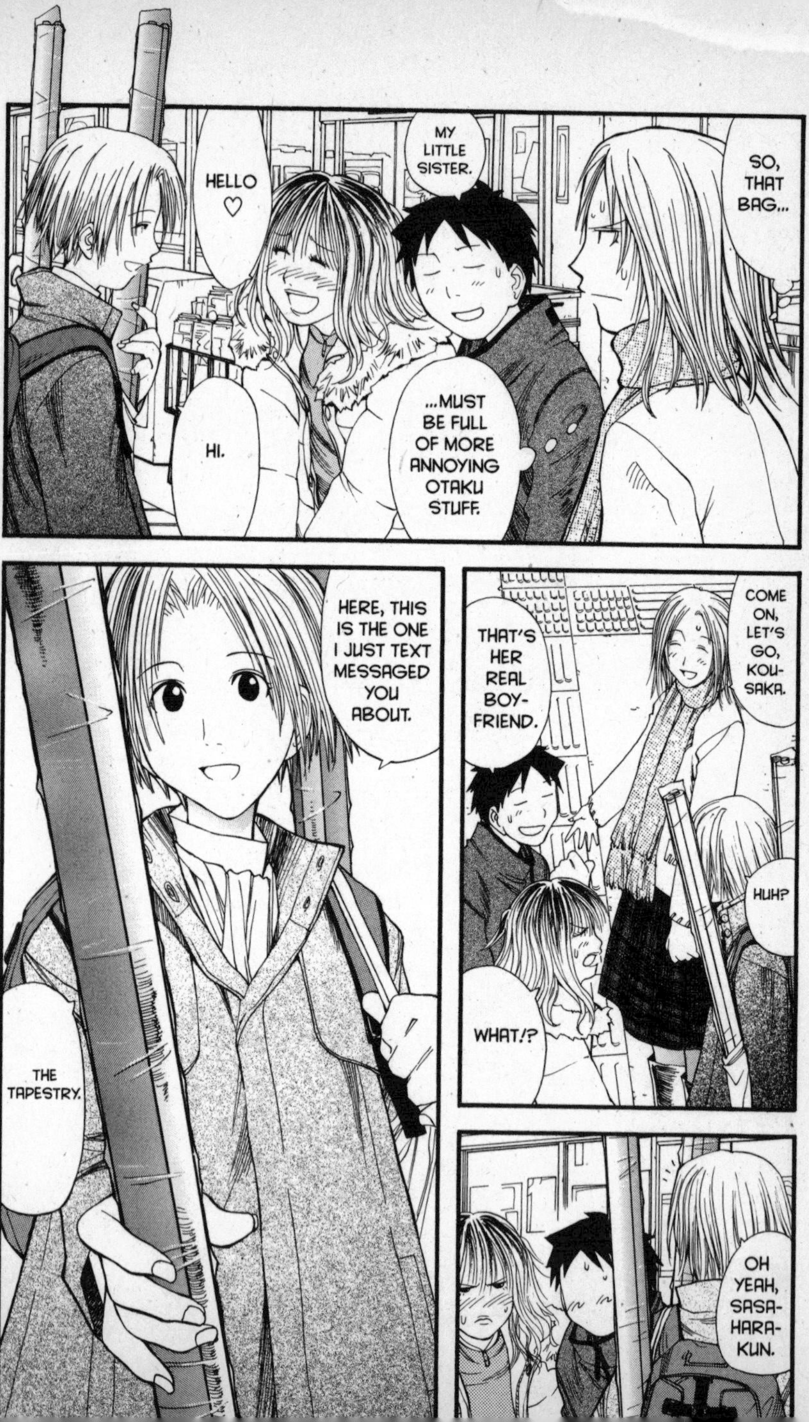
SO, THAT BAG...
MY LITTLE SISTER.
HELLO ♡
...MUST BE FULL OF MORE ANNOYING OTAKU STUFF.
HI.
COME ON, LET'S GO, KOUSAKA.
THAT'S HER REAL BOY-FRIEND.
HUH?
WHAT!?
OH YEAH, SASA-HARA-KUN.
HERE, THIS IS THE ONE I JUST TEXT MESSAGED YOU ABOUT.
THE TAPESTRY.

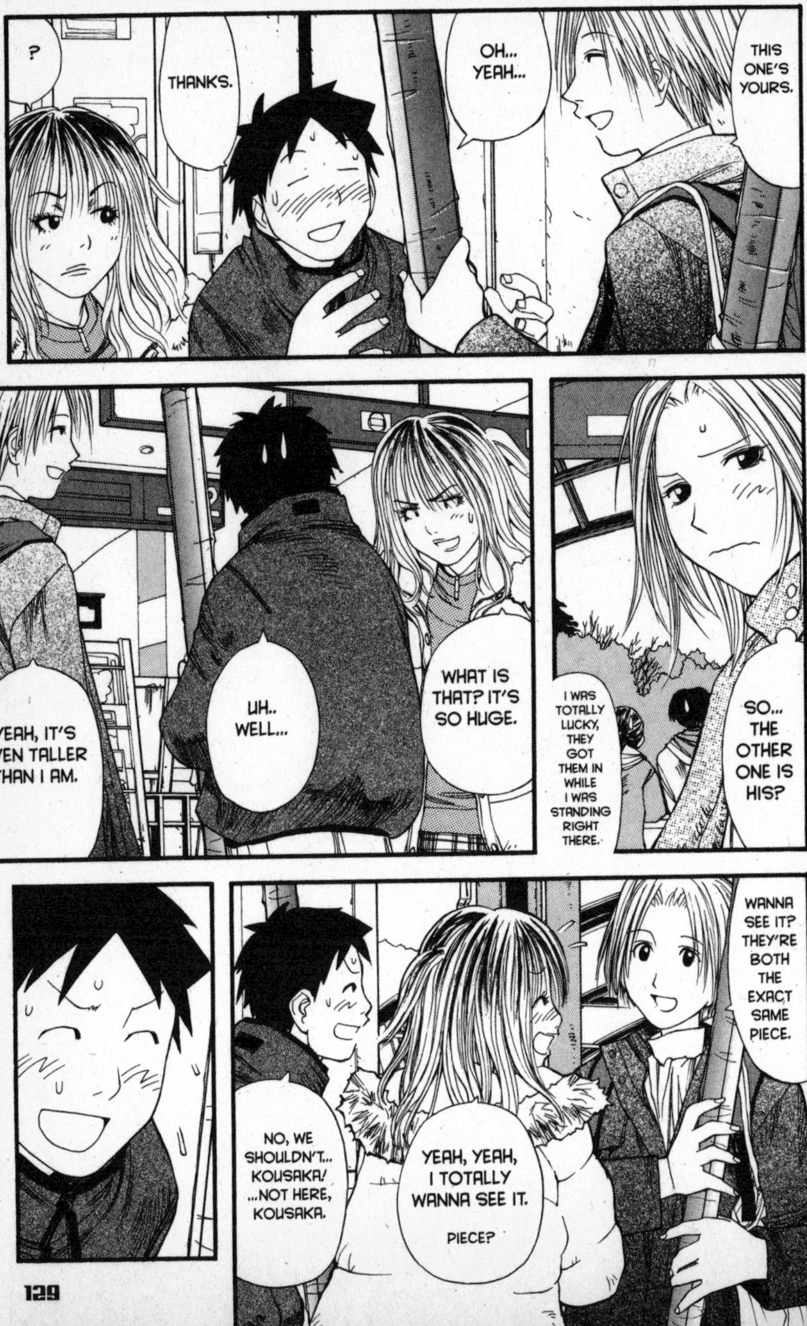
THIS ONE'S YOURS.
OH... YEAH...
THANKS.
?
SO... THE OTHER ONE IS HIS?
I WAS TOTALLY LUCKY, THEY GOT THEM IN WHILE I WAS STANDING RIGHT THERE.
WHAT IS THAT? IT'S SO HUGE.
UH.. WELL...
YEAH, IT'S EVEN TALLER THAN I AM.
WANNA SEE IT? THEY'RE BOTH THE EXACT SAME PIECE.
YEAH, YEAH, I TOTALLY WANNA SEE IT.
PIECE?
NO, WE SHOULDN'T... KOUSAKA! ...NOT HERE, KOUSAKA.

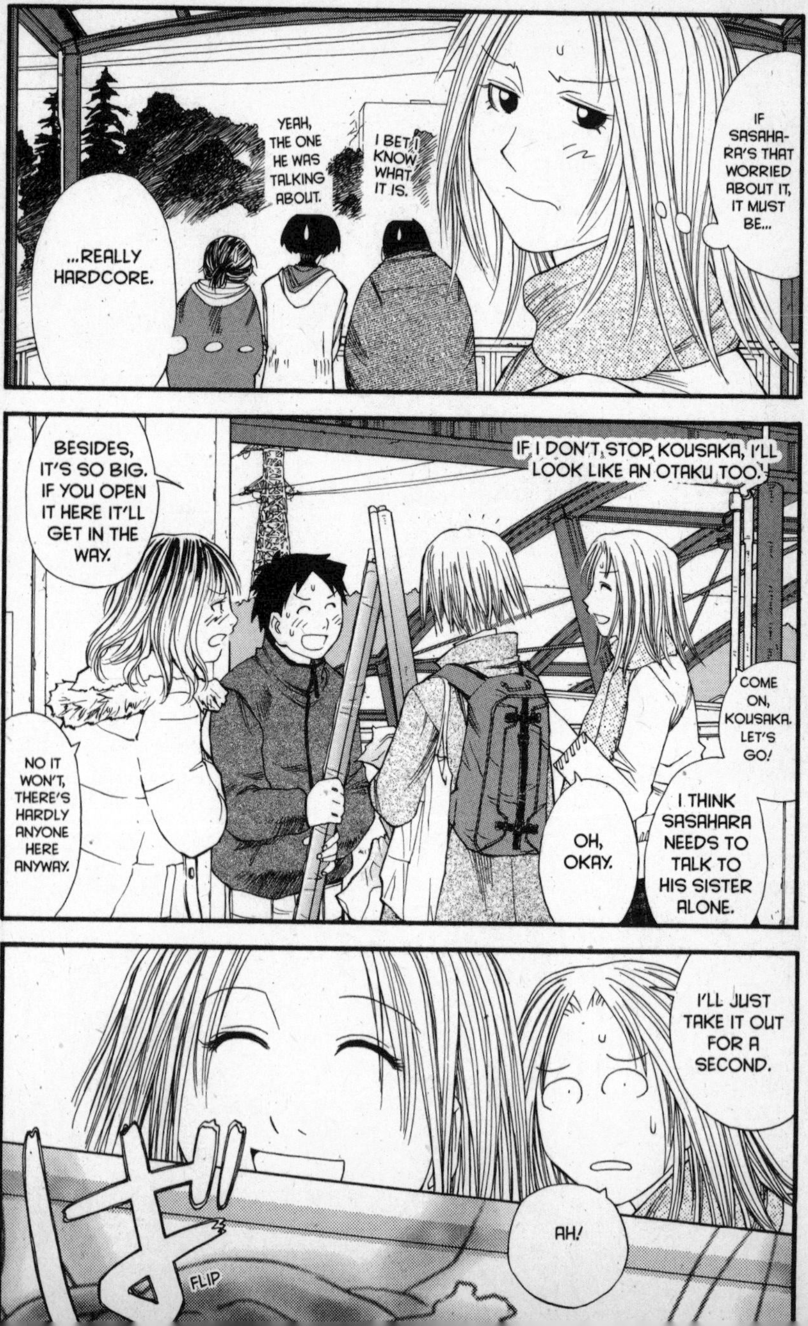
IF SASAHARA'S THAT WORRIED ABOUT IT, IT MUST BE...
I BET I KNOW WHAT IT IS.
YEAH, THE ONE HE WAS TALKING ABOUT.
...REALLY HARDCORE.
IF I DON'T STOP KOUSAKA, I'LL LOOK LIKE AN OTAKU TOO.
COME ON, KOUSAKA. LET'S GO!
I THINK SASAHARA NEEDS TO TALK TO HIS SISTER ALONE.
OH, OKAY.
BESIDES, IT'S SO BIG. IF YOU OPEN IT HERE IT'LL GET IN THE WAY.
NO IT WON'T, THERE'S HARDLY ANYONE HERE ANYWAY.
I'LL JUST TAKE IT OUT FOR A SECOND.
AH!
FLIP

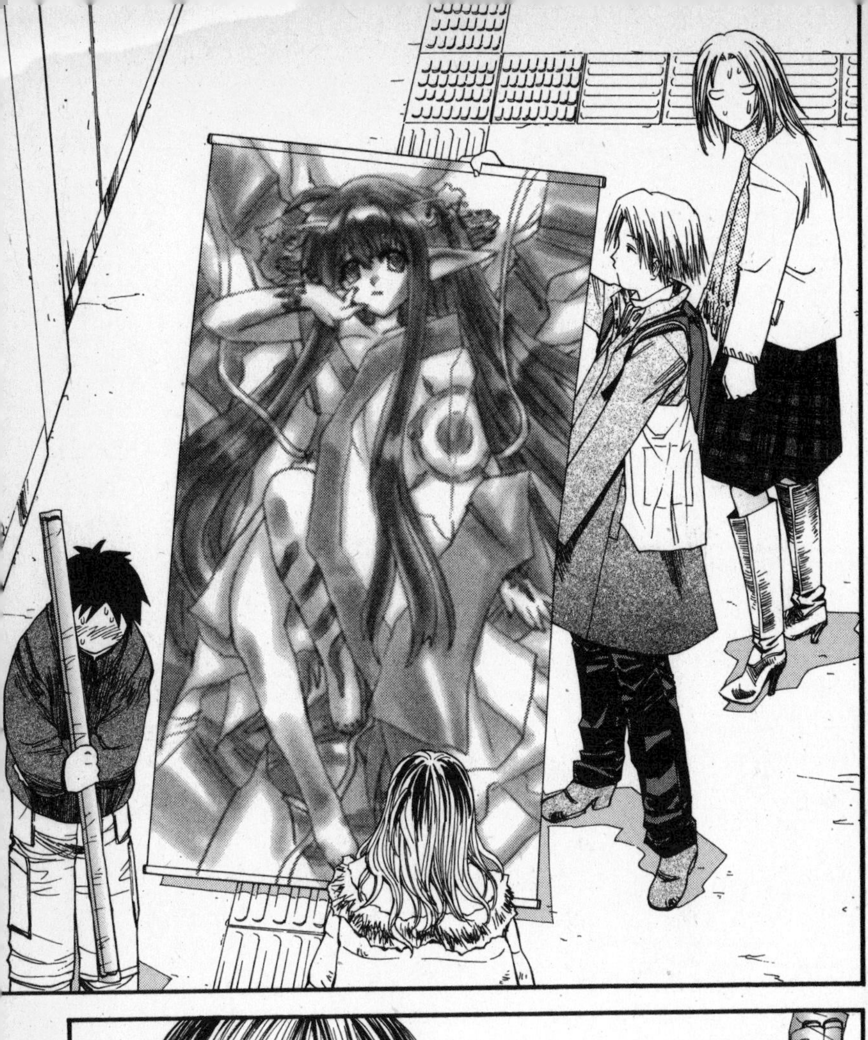
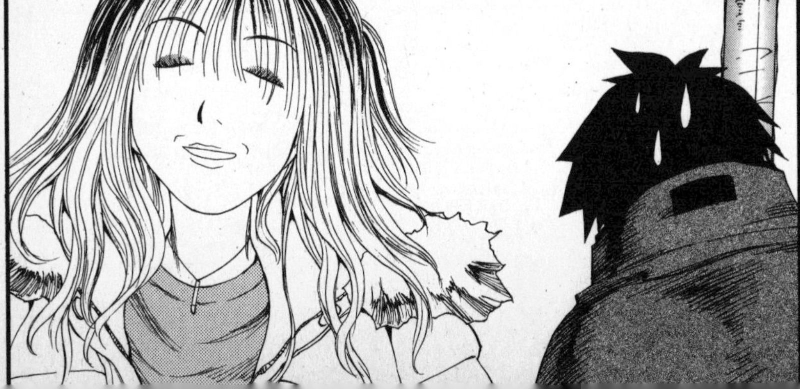

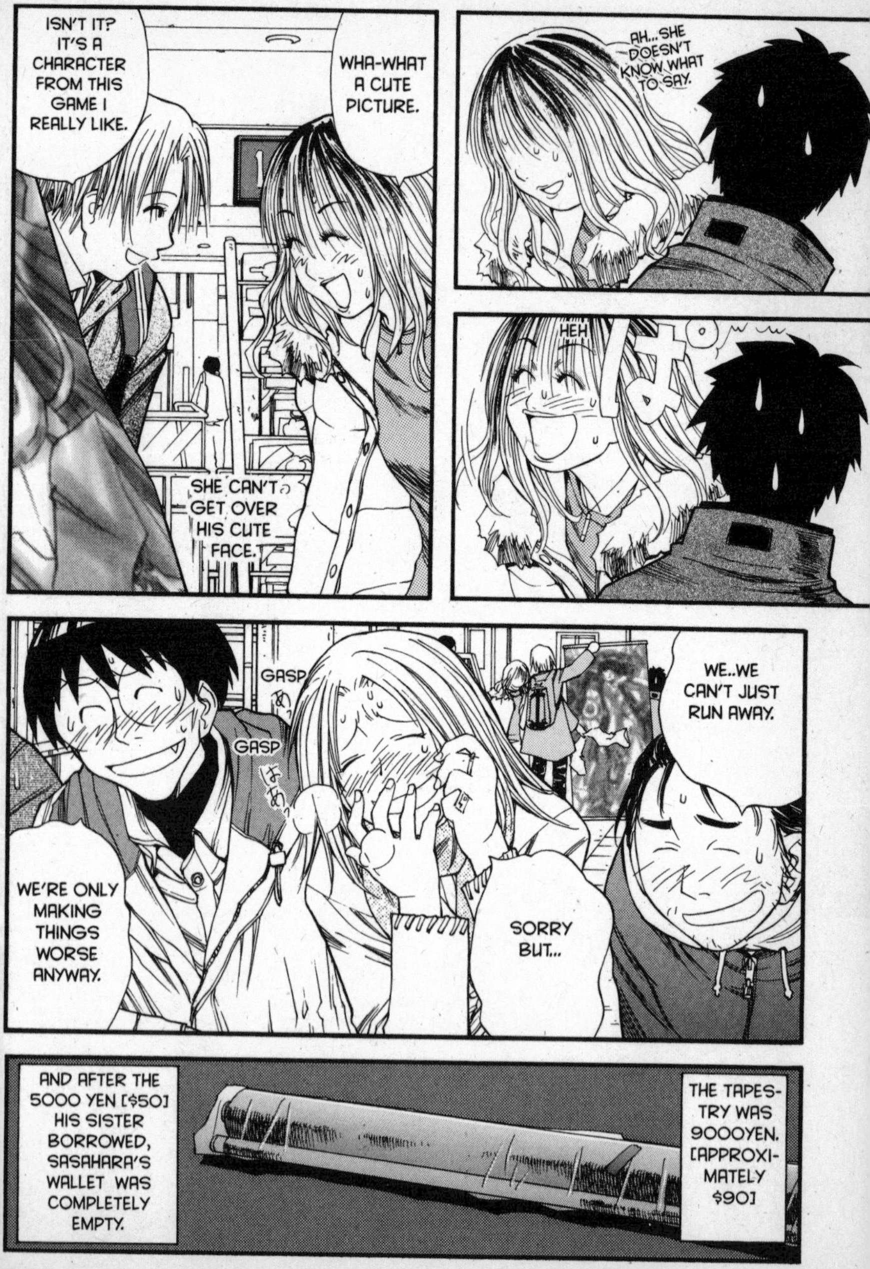
AH...SHE DOESN'T KNOW WHAT TO SAY.
HEH
は
WHA-WHAT A CUTE PICTURE.
ISN'T IT? IT'S A CHARACTER FROM THIS GAME I REALLY LIKE.
SHE CAN'T GET OVER HIS CUTE FACE.
WE..WE CAN'T JUST RUN AWAY.
SORRY BUT...
GASP
GASP
WE'RE ONLY MAKING THINGS WORSE ANYWAY.
THE TAPES-TRY WAS 9000YEN. [APPROXI-MATELY $90]
AND AFTER THE 5000 YEN [$50] HIS SISTER BORROWED, SASAHARA'S WALLET WAS COMPLETELY EMPTY.

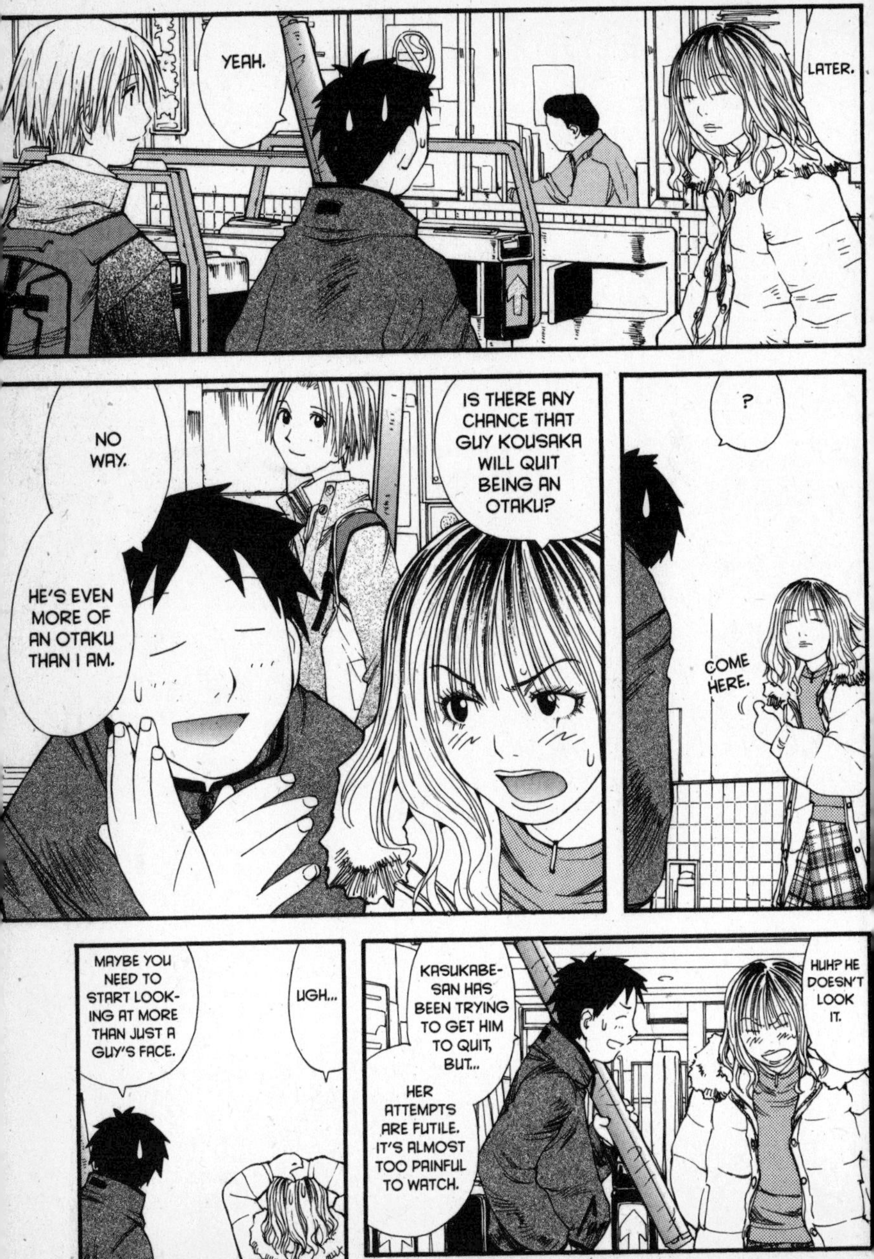
LATER.
YEAH.
?
COME HERE.
IS THERE ANY CHANCE THAT GUY KOUSAKA WILL QUIT BEING AN OTAKU?
NO WAY.
HE'S EVEN MORE OF AN OTAKU THAN I AM.
HUH? HE DOESN'T LOOK IT.
KASUKABE-SAN HAS BEEN TRYING TO GET HIM TO QUIT, BUT...
HER ATTEMPTS ARE FUTILE. IT'S ALMOST TOO PAINFUL TO WATCH.
UGH...
MAYBE YOU NEED TO START LOOKING AT MORE THAN JUST A GUY'S FACE.

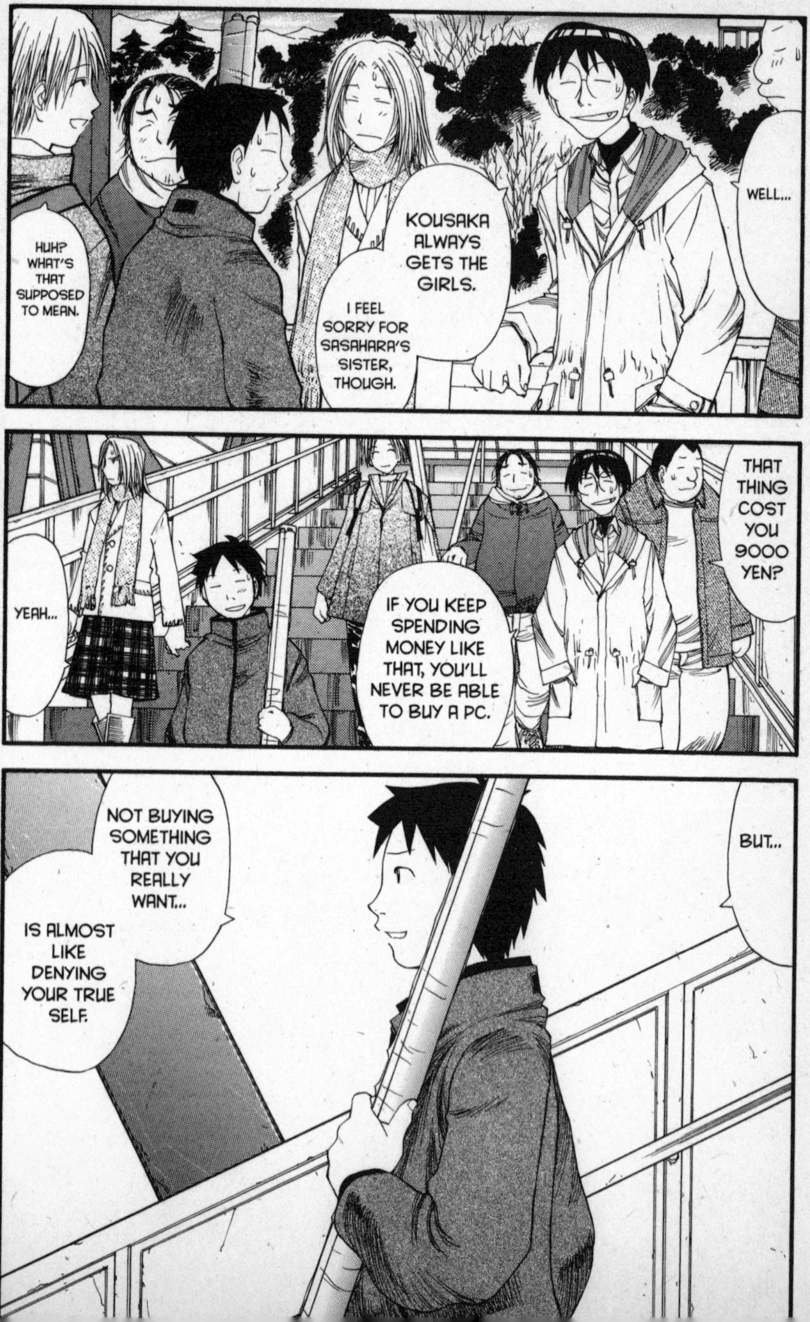
WELL...
KOUSAKA ALWAYS GETS THE GIRLS.
I FEEL SORRY FOR SASAHARA'S SISTER, THOUGH.
HUH? WHAT'S THAT SUPPOSED TO MEAN.
THAT THING COST YOU 9000 YEN?
IF YOU KEEP SPENDING MONEY LIKE THAT, YOU'LL NEVER BE ABLE TO BUY A PC.
YEAH...
BUT...
NOT BUYING SOMETHING THAT YOU REALLY WANT...
IS ALMOST LIKE DENYING YOUR TRUE SELF.

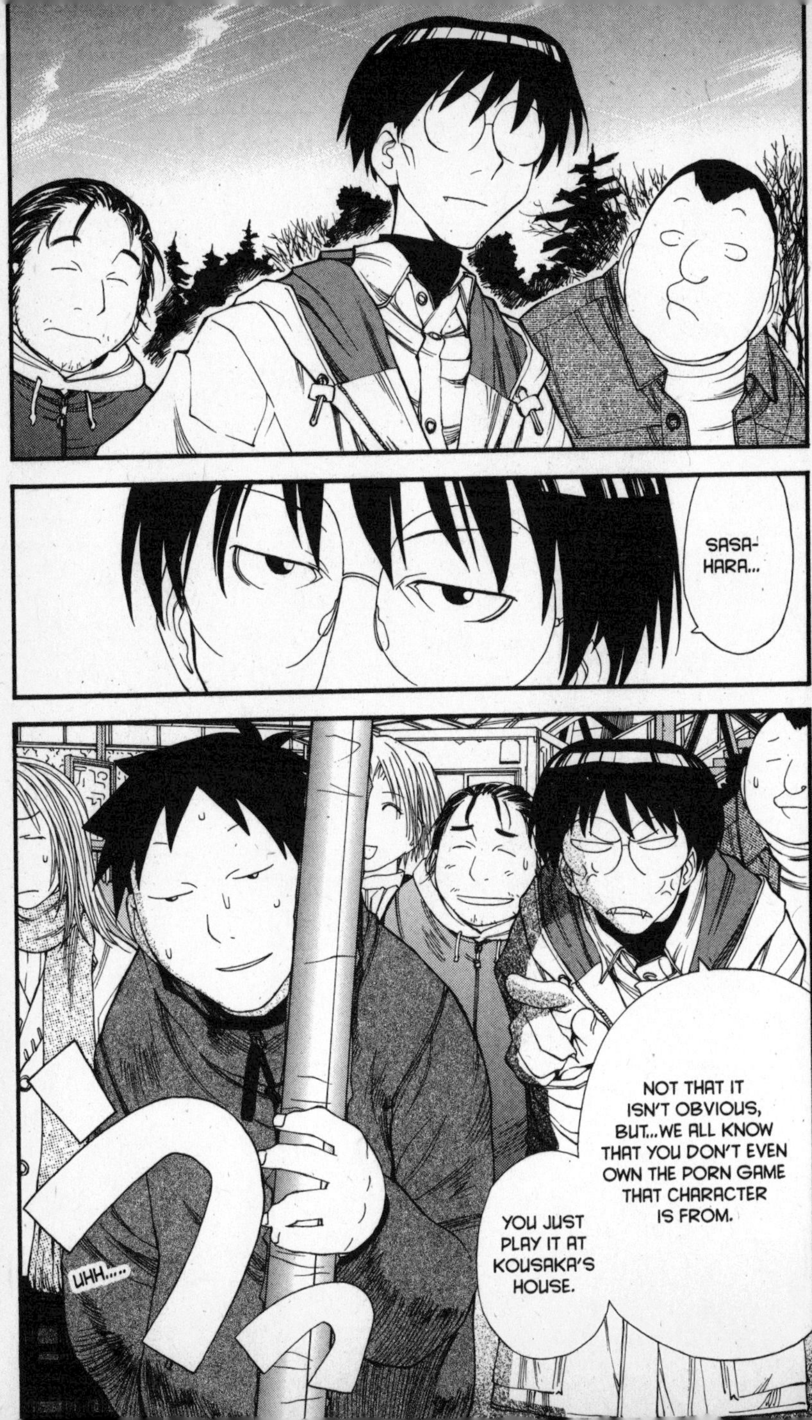
SASA-HARA...
NOT THAT IT ISN'T OBVIOUS, BUT...WE ALL KNOW THAT YOU DON'T EVEN OWN THE PORN GAME THAT CHARACTER IS FROM.
YOU JUST PLAY IT AT KOUSAKA'S HOUSE.
UHH.....

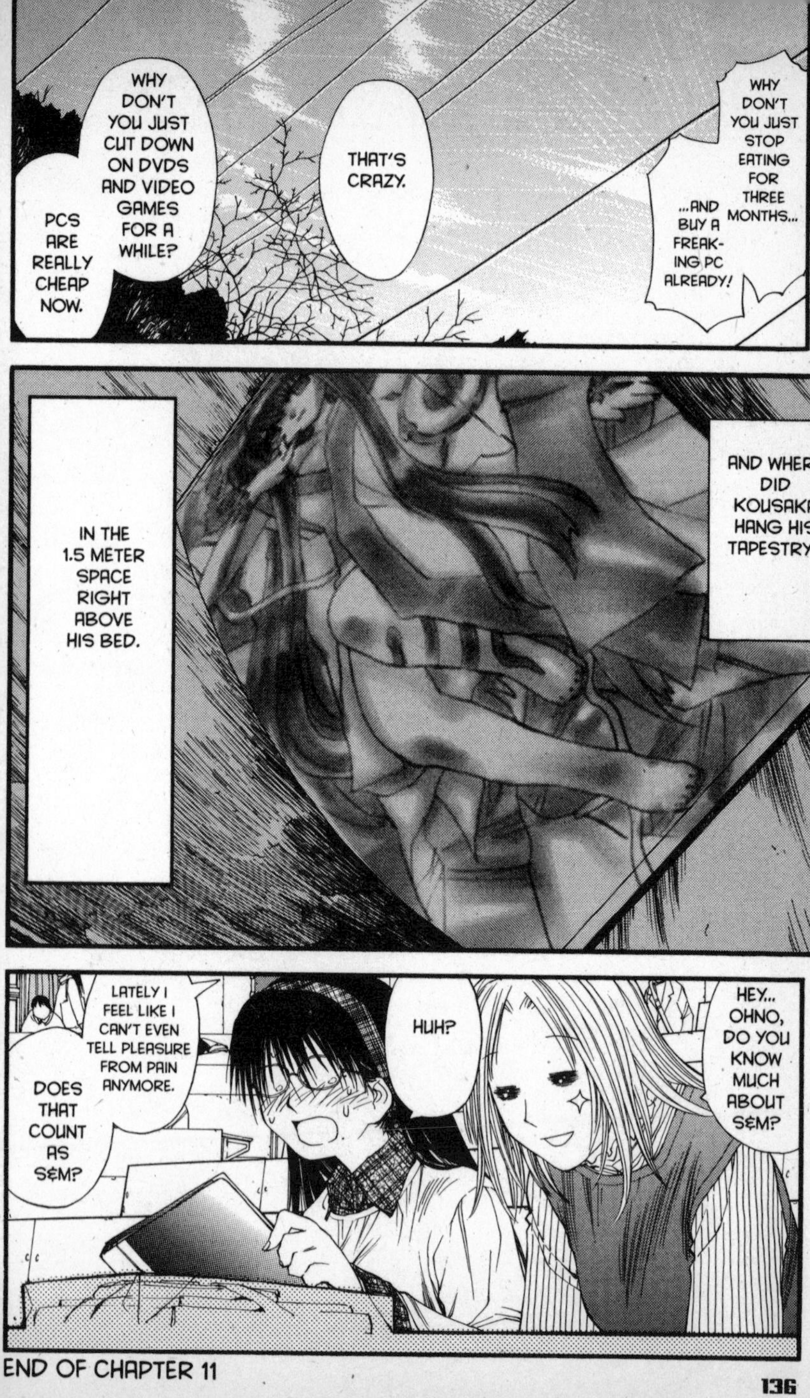
WHY DON'T YOU JUST STOP EATING FOR THREE MONTHS...
...AND BUY A FREAKING PC ALREADY!
THAT'S CRAZY.
WHY DON'T YOU JUST CUT DOWN ON DVDS AND VIDEO GAMES FOR A WHILE?
PCS ARE REALLY CHEAP NOW.
AND WHERE DID KOUSAKA HANG HIS TAPESTRY?
IN THE 1.5 METER SPACE RIGHT ABOVE HIS BED.
HEY... OHNO, DO YOU KNOW MUCH ABOUT S&M?
HUH?
LATELY I FEEL LIKE I CAN'T EVEN TELL PLEASURE FROM PAIN ANYMORE.
DOES THAT COUNT AS S&M?

END OF CHAPTER 11

THE GENSHIKEN MEMBERS PICK...

# KUJI-UN

## ...THE MOST NOTABLE SCENES

TAKEN FROM THE GENSHIKEN'S SPORADICALLY PUBLISHED ZINE "MEBAETAME"

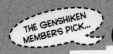

### MY FAVORITE SCENE FROM *KUJI-UN* PART 4 BY "TOSHIZO"

FROM TANKOBON BOOK 4 PG 103

I DIDN'T THINK ANYONE WOULD CHOOSE HER, SO I CHOSE THE HEROINE, TOKINO. EVER SINCE SHINOBU GOT HER SANITY BACK, TOKINO'S CHARACTER HAS GOTTEN PROGRESSIVELY SPACEY...TO THE POINT WHERE PEOPLE KEEP SAYING, "DID SHE LOSE HER MIND AFTER HER HEART WAS BROKEN?" OR "HAS HER CHARACTER CHANGED?" OR "DOES SHE HAVE ALZHEIMER'S OR SOMETHING?" I BELIEVE THE CAUSE IS RELATED TO HER PECULIAR HAIRSTYLE. THIS MATTER HASN'T BEEN CLEARLY SETTLED IN THE ANIME EITHER, AND IT'S LEFT LOYAL VIEWERS FRUSTRATED. IT'S SORT OF LIKE ASTRO GIRL OR NESUO. BY THE WAY, I LIKE THE MANGA VERSION OF THE EQUINOX CASTLE STORY. DURING THE CLIMAX, THE MANGA SHOWS BOGII-CHAN GETTING HIT THREE TIMES IN A SINGLE PANEL. THE ANIME JUST DOESN'T CAPTURE THE SPEED. TOO BAD. [TOSHIZO]

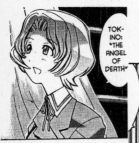

TOK-INO: "THE ANGEL OF DEATH"

BOOK 1 PAGE 31
IT'S NOT TOO BAD HERE. I MEAN, IT STILL LOOKS LIKE NORMAL HAIR.

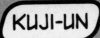

BOOK 2 PAGE 116
IT'S REALLY POINTY. THE ANIME IS LIKE THIS TOO.

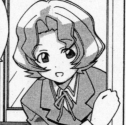

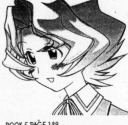

BOOK 5 PAGE 189
IN THIS LATEST DRAWING, SHE LOOKS ALMOST LIKE A CHICKEN OR A BUG. HER SKELETAL STRUCTURE LOOKS REALLY STRONG.

FIRST OF ALL, THIS ISN'T EVEN A SCENE. WHY DID YOU EVEN BOTHER WRITING "MY FAVORITE SCENE FROM KUJI-UN"? MAYBE YOU DID IT ON PURPOSE, BUT...YOU'RE NOT NUMBER 4, YOU'RE NUMBER 5 (LAUGHS). THAT WAS A GOOD ONE...AH...UH-OH...I'VE GOT TO STAY IN CHARACTER. COUGH, COUGH. EVERYBODY KNOWS THIS NOW, BUT "THE ANGEL OF DEATH" IS A NICKNAME FOR A POISONOUS MUSHROOM. APPARENTLY, IT'S A POISONOUS MUSHROOM THAT GROWS ALL OVER JAPAN. MAYBE THE REASON THAT SHE'S SO SPACEY IS THAT SHE ATE TOO MANY OF THOSE MUSHROOMS...HEH HEH. BY THE WAY, I LIKE THE ENDING THEME MUSIC IN THE ANIME VERSION OF THE "TESTUO'S ARMY" STORY. LA LA LA...

WELL...THIS NEXT PASSAGE MIGHT BE THE MOST TROUBLESOME OF THEM ALL (LAUGHS). IT'S YOKO KANNAZUKI-SAN'S TURN. [PIT VIPER]

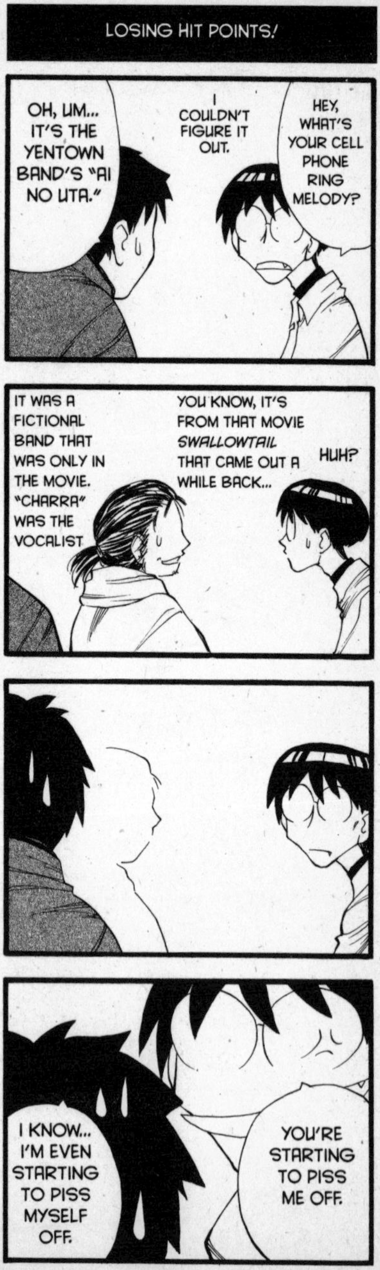
LOSING HIT POINTS!
HEY, WHAT'S YOUR CELL PHONE RING MELODY?
I COULDN'T FIGURE IT OUT.
OH, UM... IT'S THE YENTOWN BAND'S "AI NO UTA."
HUH?
YOU KNOW, IT'S FROM THAT MOVIE *SWALLOWTAIL* THAT CAME OUT A WHILE BACK...
IT WAS A FICTIONAL BAND THAT WAS ONLY IN THE MOVIE. "CHARRA" WAS THE VOCALIST.
YOU'RE STARTING TO PISS ME OFF.
I KNOW... I'M EVEN STARTING TO PISS MYSELF OFF.

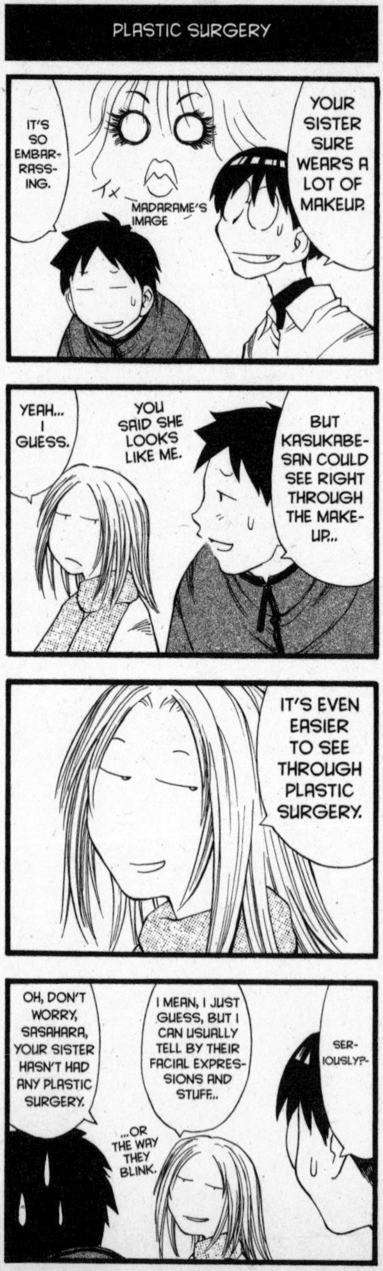
PLASTIC SURGERY
YOUR SISTER SURE WEARS A LOT OF MAKEUP.
MADARAME'S IMAGE
IT'S SO EMBARRASSING.
BUT KASUKABE-SAN COULD SEE RIGHT THROUGH THE MAKE-UP...
YOU SAID SHE LOOKS LIKE ME.
YEAH... I GUESS.
IT'S EVEN EASIER TO SEE THROUGH PLASTIC SURGERY.
SER-IOUSLY?-
I MEAN, I JUST GUESS, BUT I CAN USUALLY TELL BY THEIR FACIAL EXPRESSIONS AND STUFF...
OH, DON'T WORRY, SASAHARA, YOUR SISTER HASN'T HAD ANY PLASTIC SURGERY.
...OR THE WAY THEY BLINK.

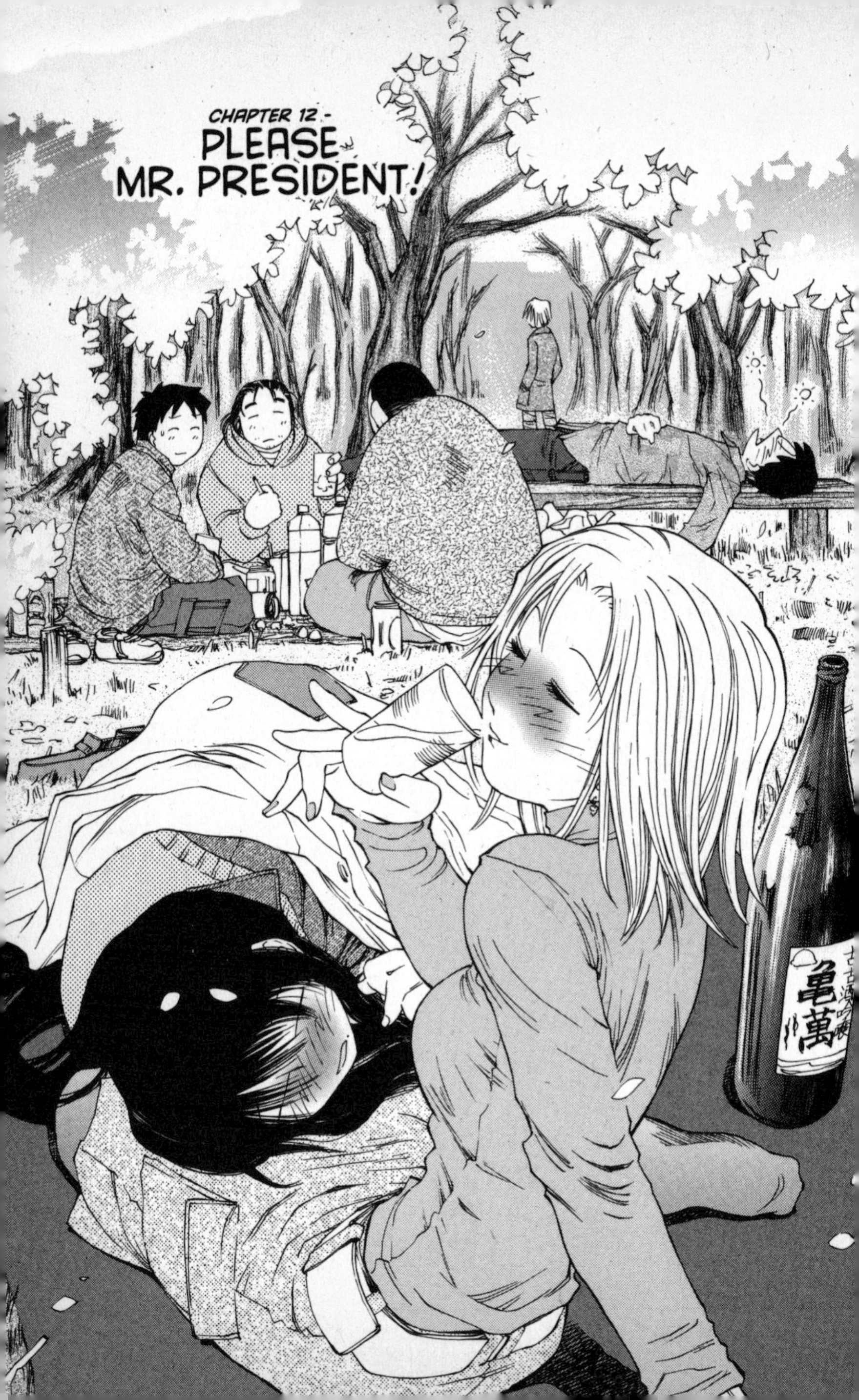
CHAPTER 12 -
PLEASE
MR. PRESIDENT!
亀萬

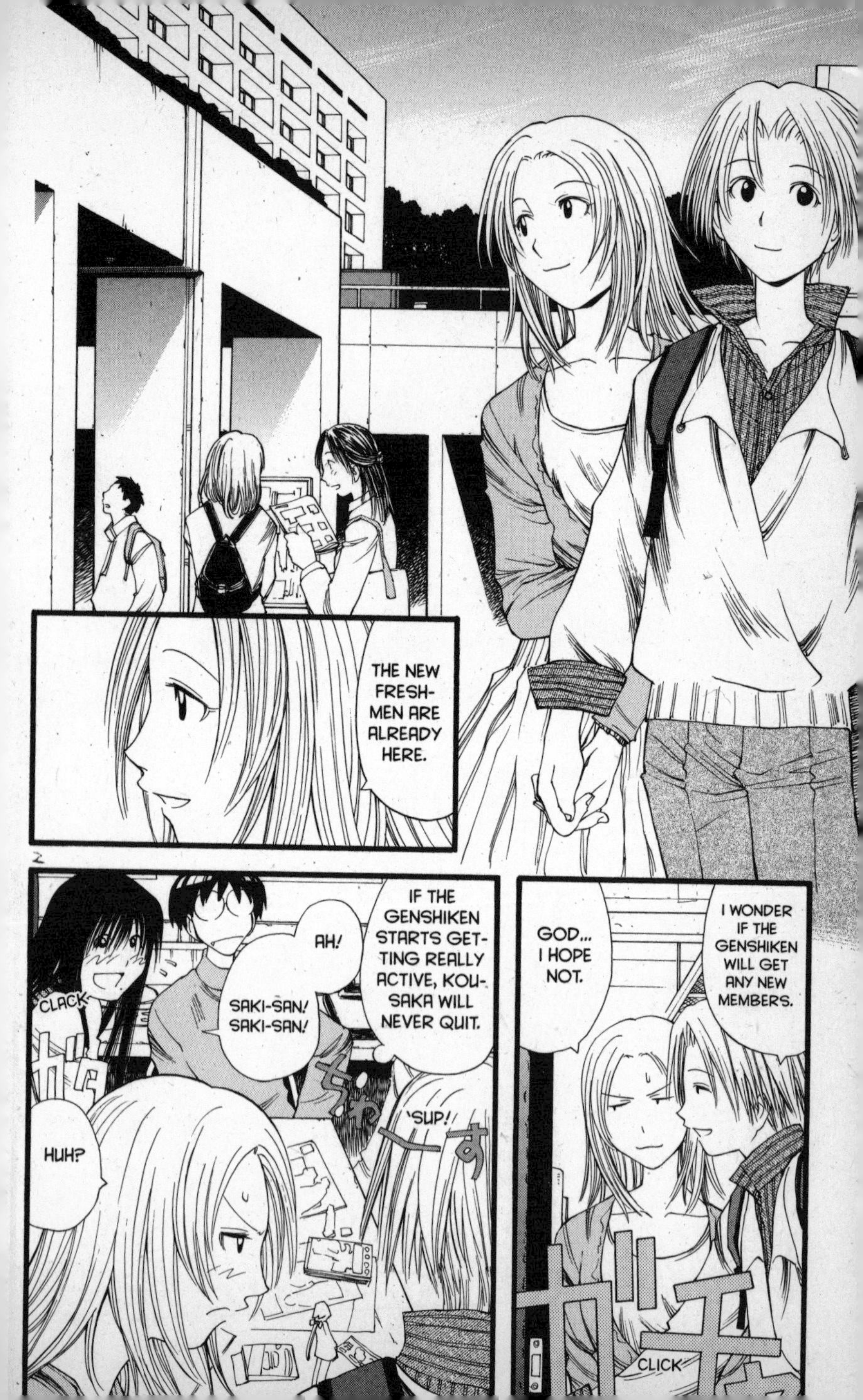
THE NEW FRESH-MEN ARE ALREADY HERE.
I WONDER IF THE GENSHIKEN WILL GET ANY NEW MEMBERS.
GOD... I HOPE NOT.
CLICK
IF THE GENSHIKEN STARTS GET-TING REALLY ACTIVE, KOU-SAKA WILL NEVER QUIT.
AH!
SAKI-SAN! SAKI-SAN!
CLACK
'SUP!
HUH?

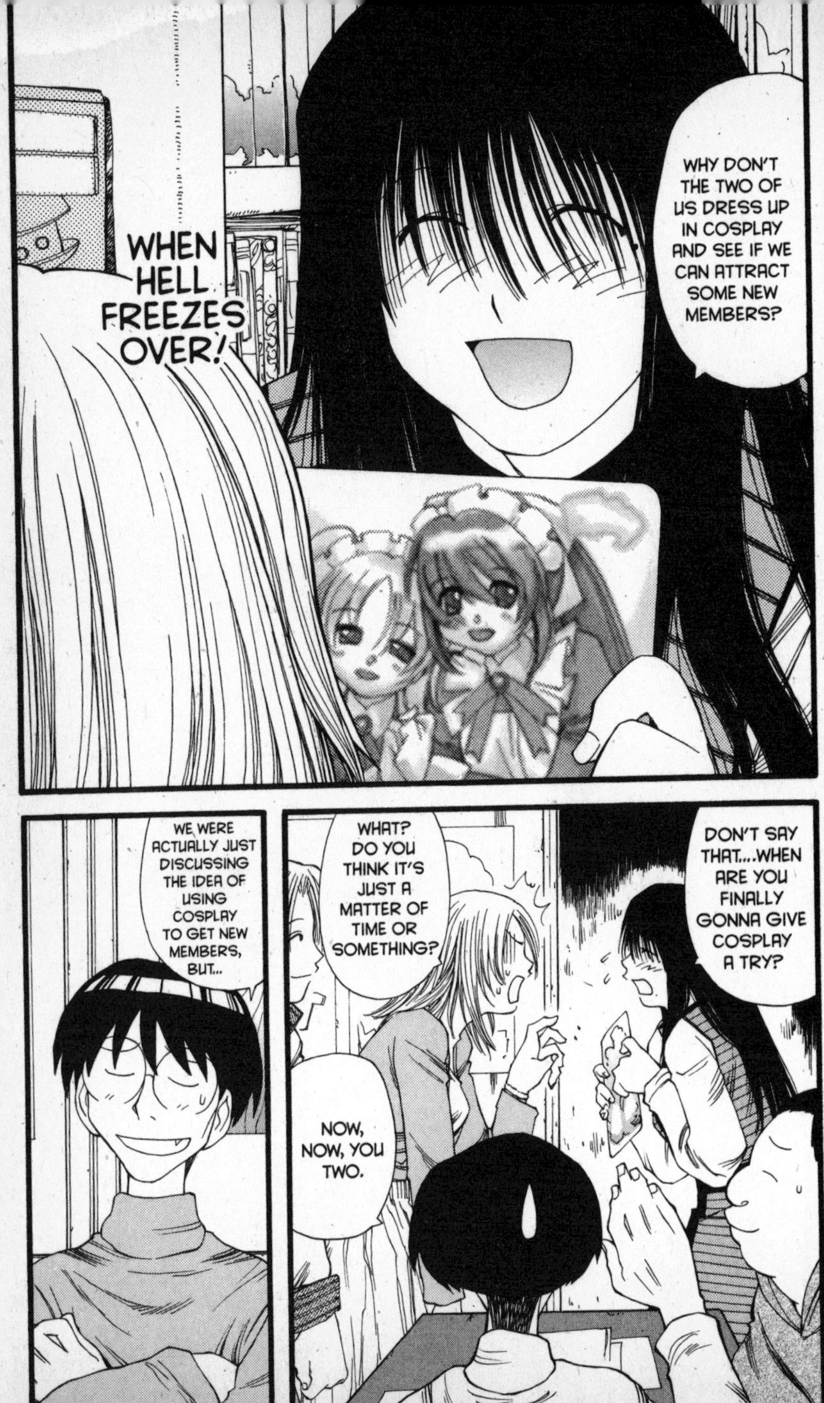
WHY DON'T THE TWO OF US DRESS UP IN COSPLAY AND SEE IF WE CAN ATTRACT SOME NEW MEMBERS?
WHEN HELL FREEZES OVER!
DON'T SAY THAT....WHEN ARE YOU FINALLY GONNA GIVE COSPLAY A TRY?
WHAT? DO YOU THINK IT'S JUST A MATTER OF TIME OR SOMETHING?
NOW, NOW, YOU TWO.
WE WERE ACTUALLY JUST DISCUSSING THE IDEA OF USING COSPLAY TO GET NEW MEMBERS, BUT...

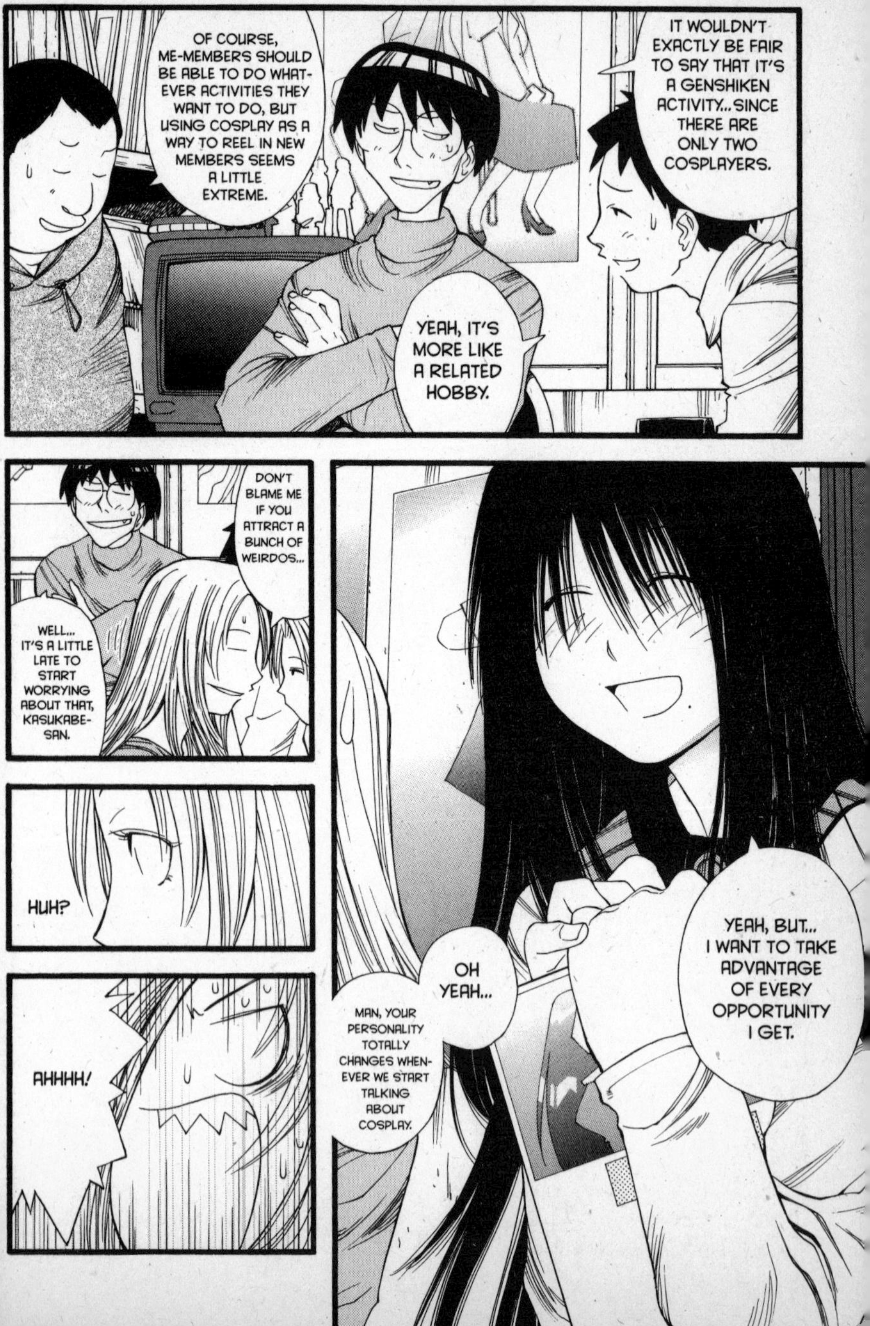
IT WOULDN'T EXACTLY BE FAIR TO SAY THAT IT'S A GENSHIKEN ACTIVITY... SINCE THERE ARE ONLY TWO COSPLAYERS.
OF COURSE, ME-MEMBERS SHOULD BE ABLE TO DO WHATEVER ACTIVITIES THEY WANT TO DO, BUT USING COSPLAY AS A WAY TO REEL IN NEW MEMBERS SEEMS A LITTLE EXTREME.
YEAH, IT'S MORE LIKE A RELATED HOBBY.
YEAH, BUT... I WANT TO TAKE ADVANTAGE OF EVERY OPPORTUNITY I GET.
OH YEAH...
MAN, YOUR PERSONALITY TOTALLY CHANGES WHENEVER WE START TALKING ABOUT COSPLAY.
DON'T BLAME ME IF YOU ATTRACT A BUNCH OF WEIRDOS...
WELL... IT'S A LITTLE LATE TO START WORRYING ABOUT THAT, KASUKABE-SAN.
HUH?
AHHHH!

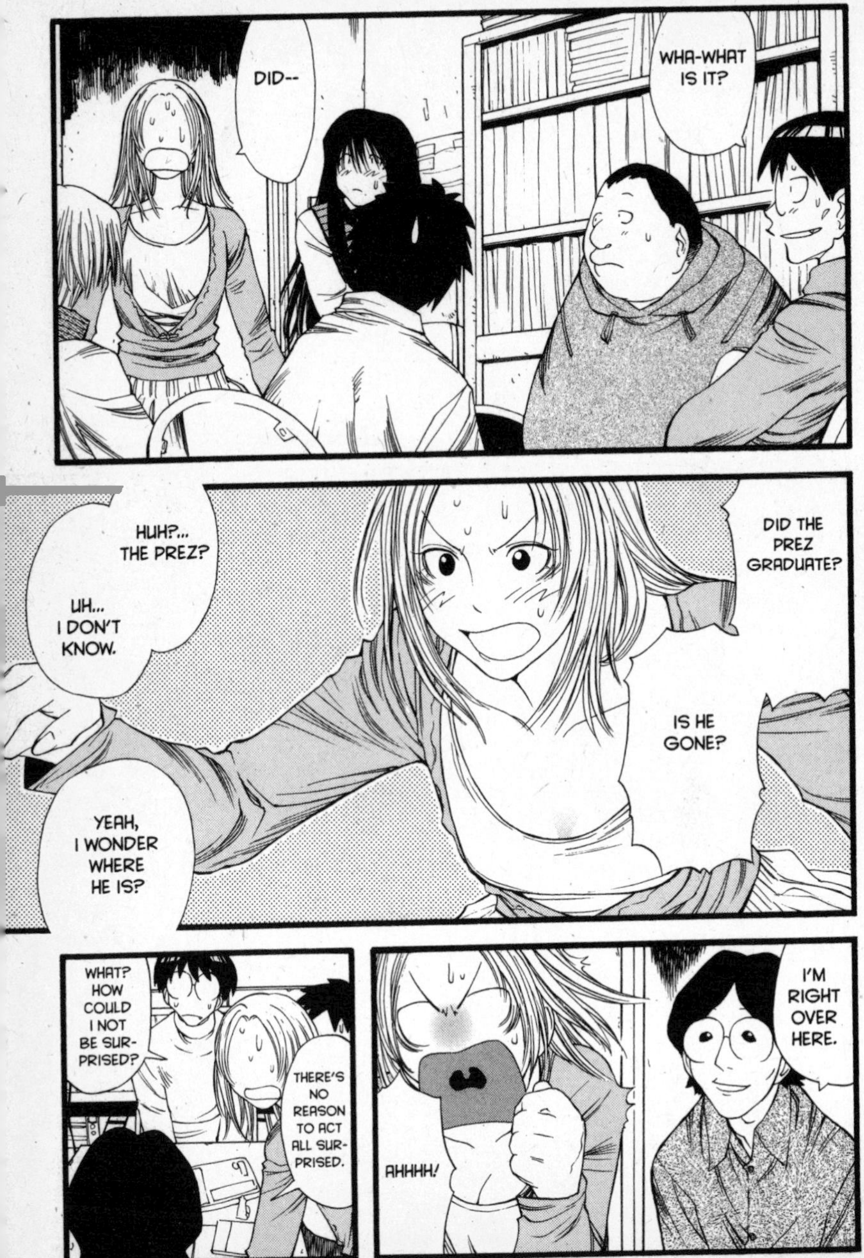
WHA-WHAT IS IT?
DID--
DID THE PREZ GRADUATE?
IS HE GONE?
HUH?... THE PREZ?
UH... I DON'T KNOW.
YEAH, I WONDER WHERE HE IS?
I'M RIGHT OVER HERE.
AHHHH!
THERE'S NO REASON TO ACT ALL SUR-PRISED.
WHAT? HOW COULD I NOT BE SUR-PRISED?

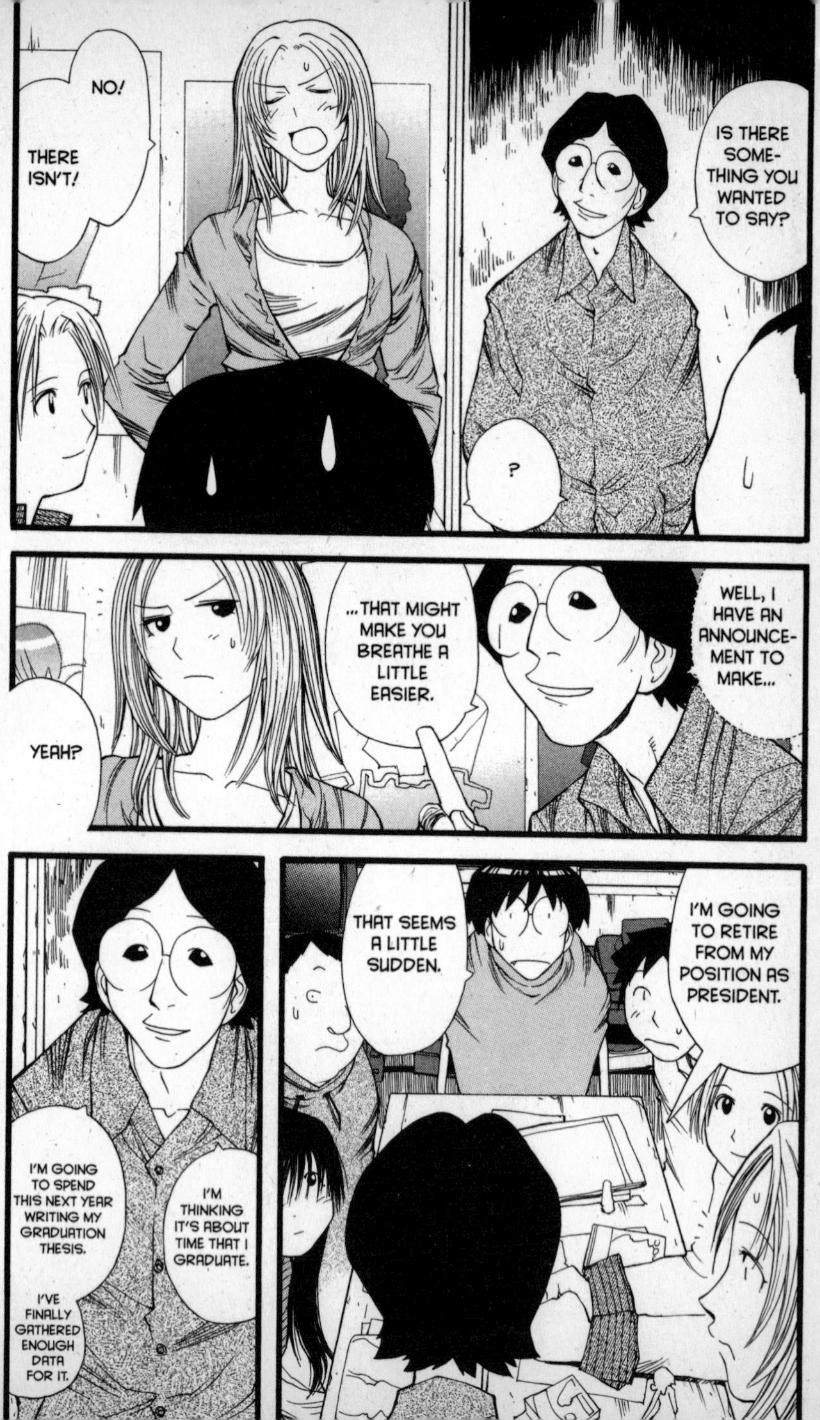
IS THERE SOMETHING YOU WANTED TO SAY?
?
NO!
THERE ISN'T!
WELL, I HAVE AN ANNOUNCEMENT TO MAKE...
...THAT MIGHT MAKE YOU BREATHE A LITTLE EASIER.
YEAH?
I'M GOING TO RETIRE FROM MY POSITION AS PRESIDENT.
THAT SEEMS A LITTLE SUDDEN.
I'M THINKING IT'S ABOUT TIME THAT I GRADUATE.
I'M GOING TO SPEND THIS NEXT YEAR WRITING MY GRADUATION THESIS.
I'VE FINALLY GATHERED ENOUGH DATA FOR IT.

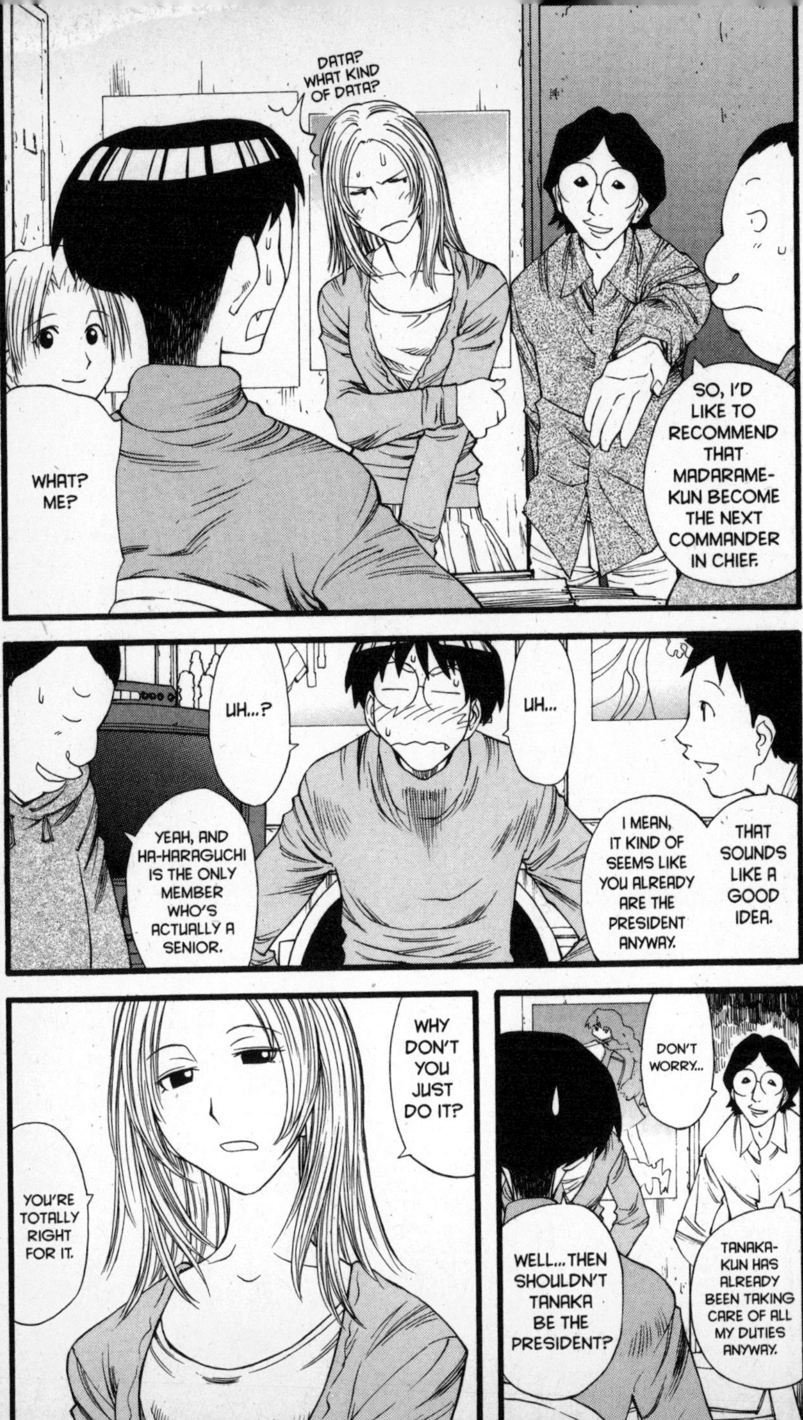
SO, I'D LIKE TO RECOMMEND THAT MADARAME-KUN BECOME THE NEXT COMMANDER IN CHIEF.
DATA? WHAT KIND OF DATA?
WHAT? ME?
THAT SOUNDS LIKE A GOOD IDEA.
I MEAN, IT KIND OF SEEMS LIKE YOU ALREADY ARE THE PRESIDENT ANYWAY.
UH...
UH...?
YEAH, AND HA-HARAGUCHI IS THE ONLY MEMBER WHO'S ACTUALLY A SENIOR.
DON'T WORRY...
TANAKA-KUN HAS ALREADY BEEN TAKING CARE OF ALL MY DUTIES ANYWAY.
WELL...THEN SHOULDN'T TANAKA BE THE PRESIDENT?
WHY DON'T YOU JUST DO IT?
YOU'RE TOTALLY RIGHT FOR IT.

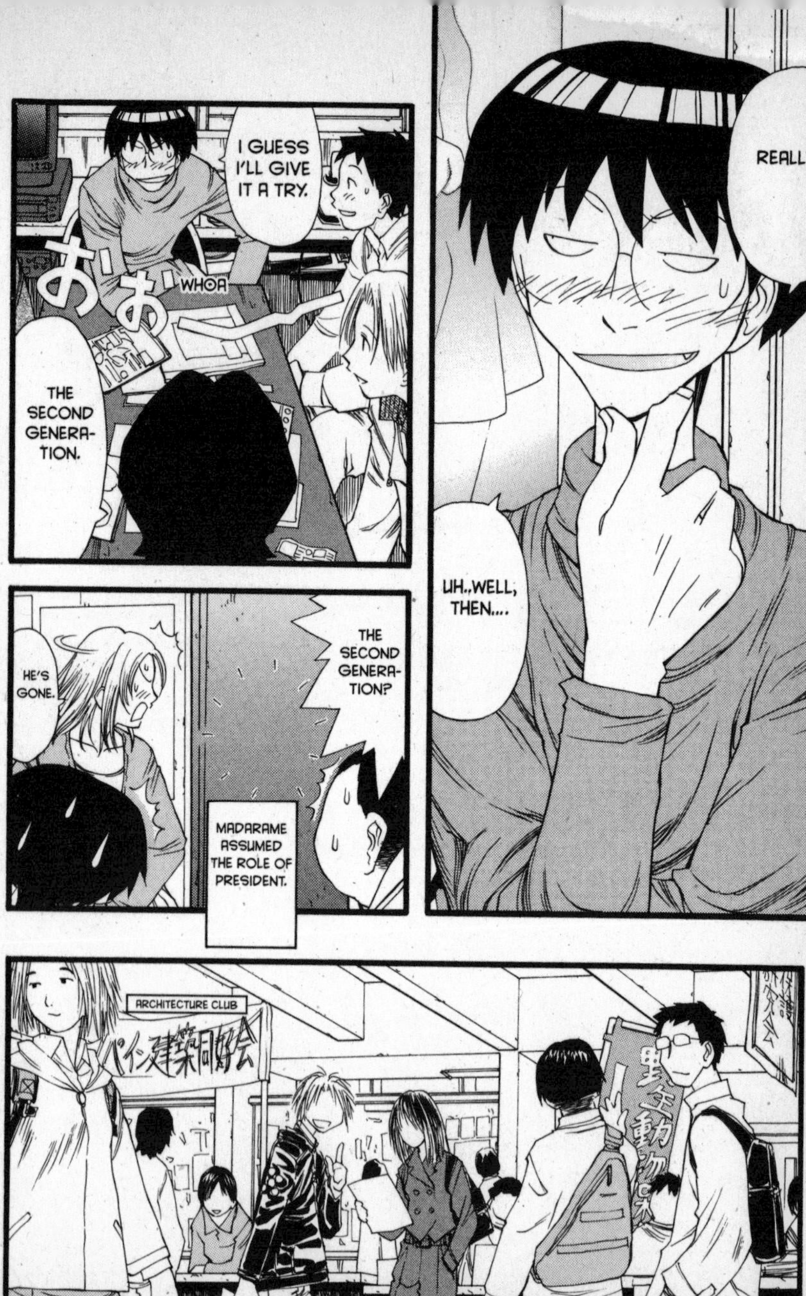
REALLY?
UH..WELL, THEN....
I GUESS I'LL GIVE IT A TRY.
WHOA
THE SECOND GENERATION.
THE SECOND GENERATION?
HE'S GONE.
MADARAME ASSUMED THE ROLE OF PRESIDENT.
ARCHITECTURE CLUB

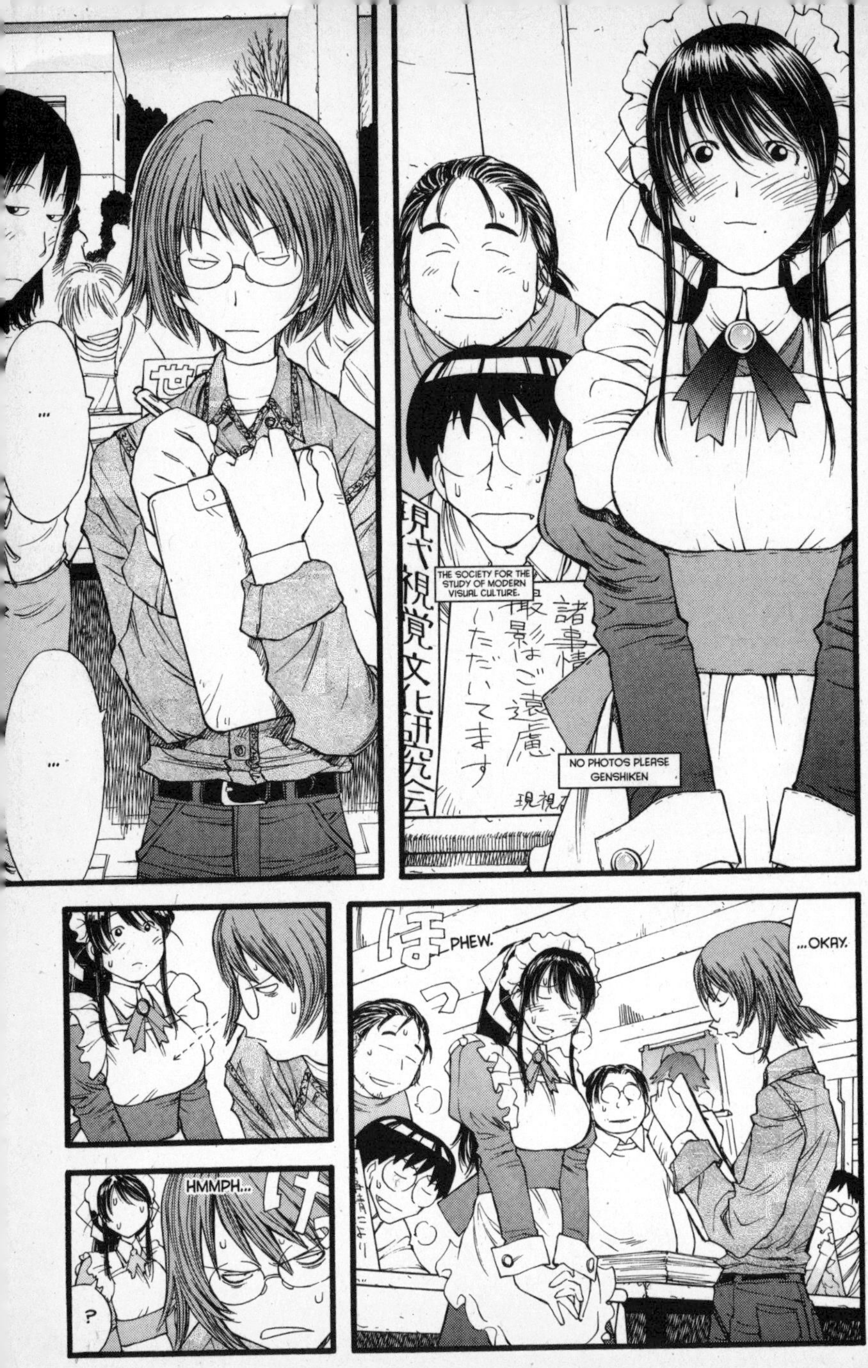
現代視覚文化研究会
THE SOCIETY FOR THE STUDY OF MODERN VISUAL CULTURE.
諸事情 撮影はご遠慮いただいてます
NO PHOTOS PLEASE GENSHIKEN
...
...
ほっ
PHEW.
...OKAY.
HMMPH...
?

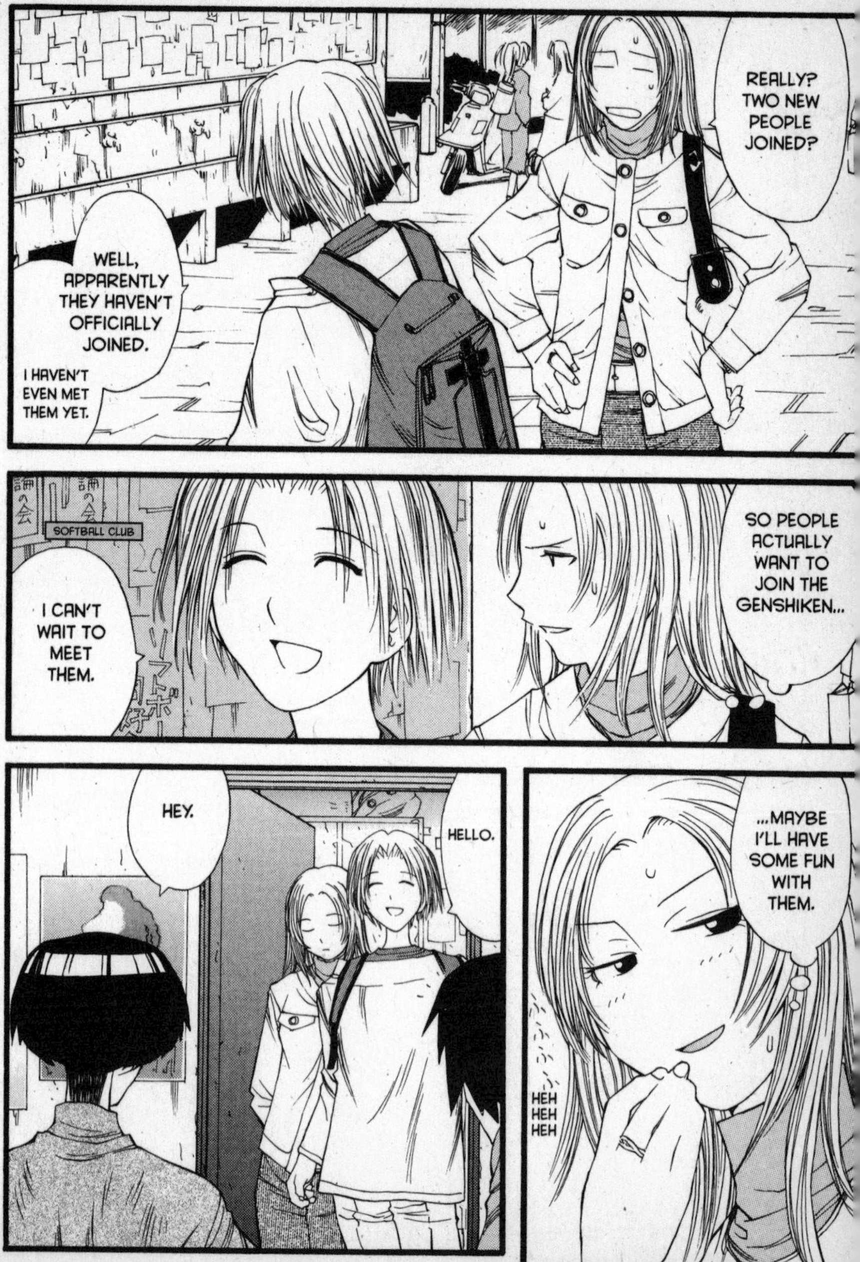
REALLY? TWO NEW PEOPLE JOINED?
WELL, APPARENTLY THEY HAVEN'T OFFICIALLY JOINED.
I HAVEN'T EVEN MET THEM YET.
SO PEOPLE ACTUALLY WANT TO JOIN THE GENSHIKEN...
SOFTBALL CLUB
I CAN'T WAIT TO MEET THEM.
...MAYBE I'LL HAVE SOME FUN WITH THEM.
HEH HEH HEH
HELLO.
HEY.

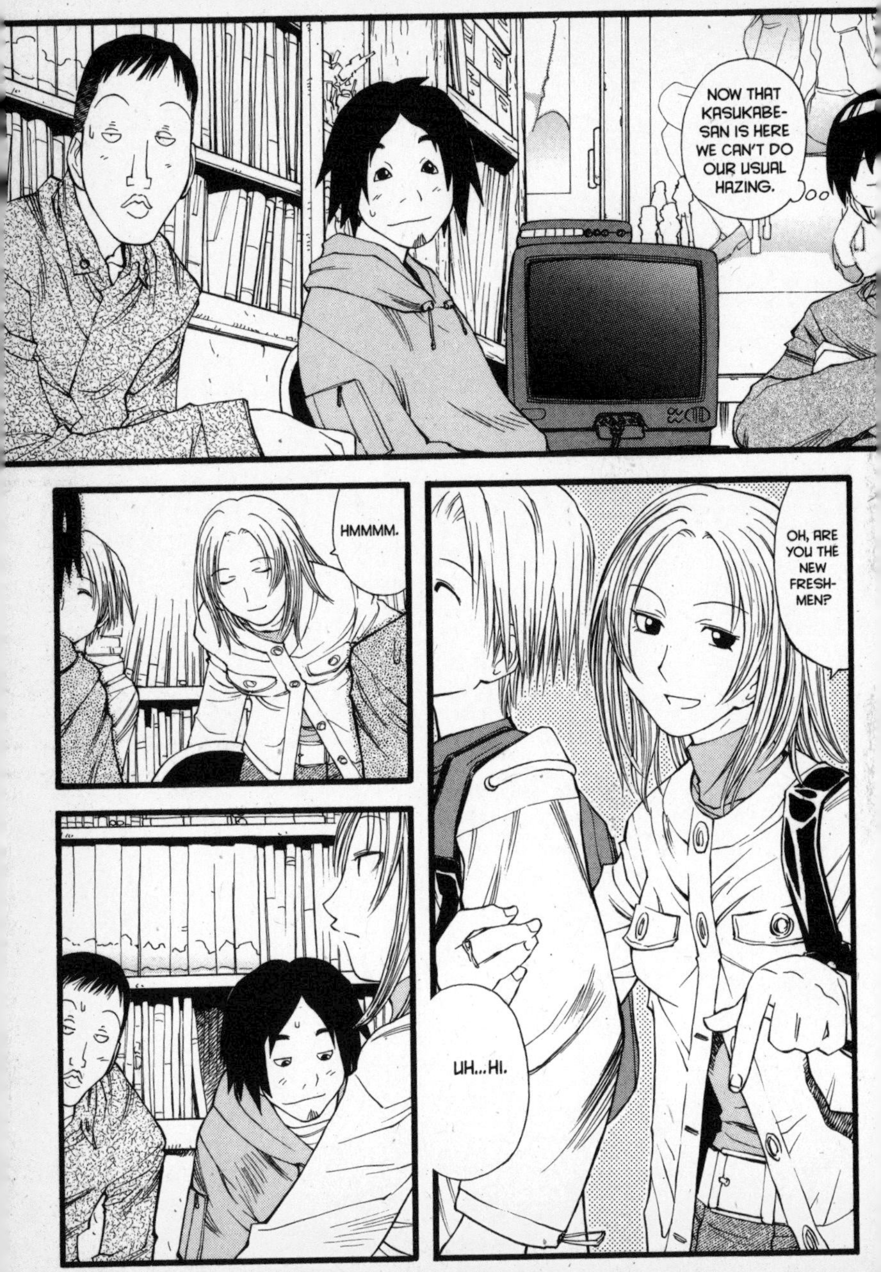
NOW THAT KASUKABE-SAN IS HERE WE CAN'T DO OUR USUAL HAZING.
OH, ARE YOU THE NEW FRESH-MEN?
UH...HI.
HMMMM.

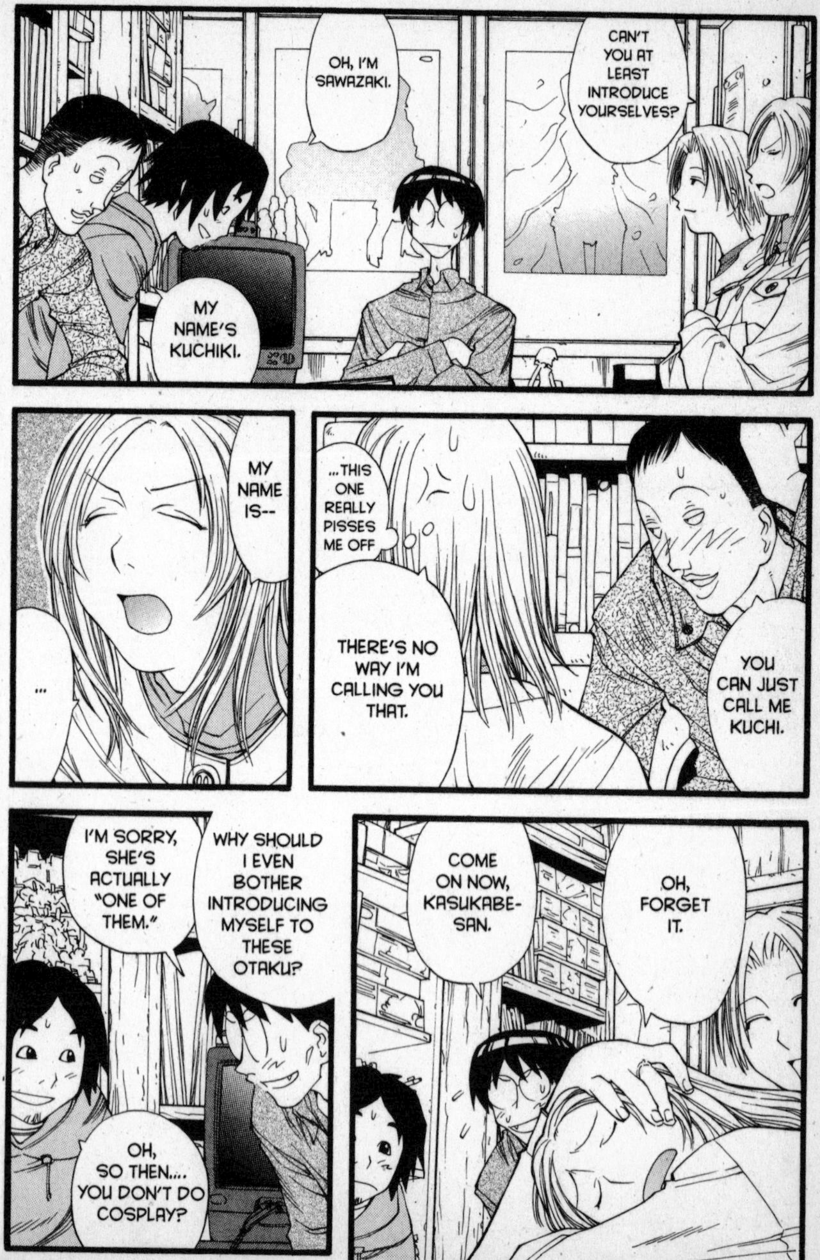
CAN'T YOU AT LEAST INTRODUCE YOURSELVES?
OH, I'M SAWAZAKI.
MY NAME'S KUCHIKI.
YOU CAN JUST CALL ME KUCHI.
...THIS ONE REALLY PISSES ME OFF
THERE'S NO WAY I'M CALLING YOU THAT.
MY NAME IS--
...
OH, FORGET IT.
COME ON NOW, KASUKABE-SAN.
WHY SHOULD I EVEN BOTHER INTRODUCING MYSELF TO THESE OTAKU?
I'M SORRY, SHE'S ACTUALLY "ONE OF THEM."
OH, SO THEN.... YOU DON'T DO COSPLAY?

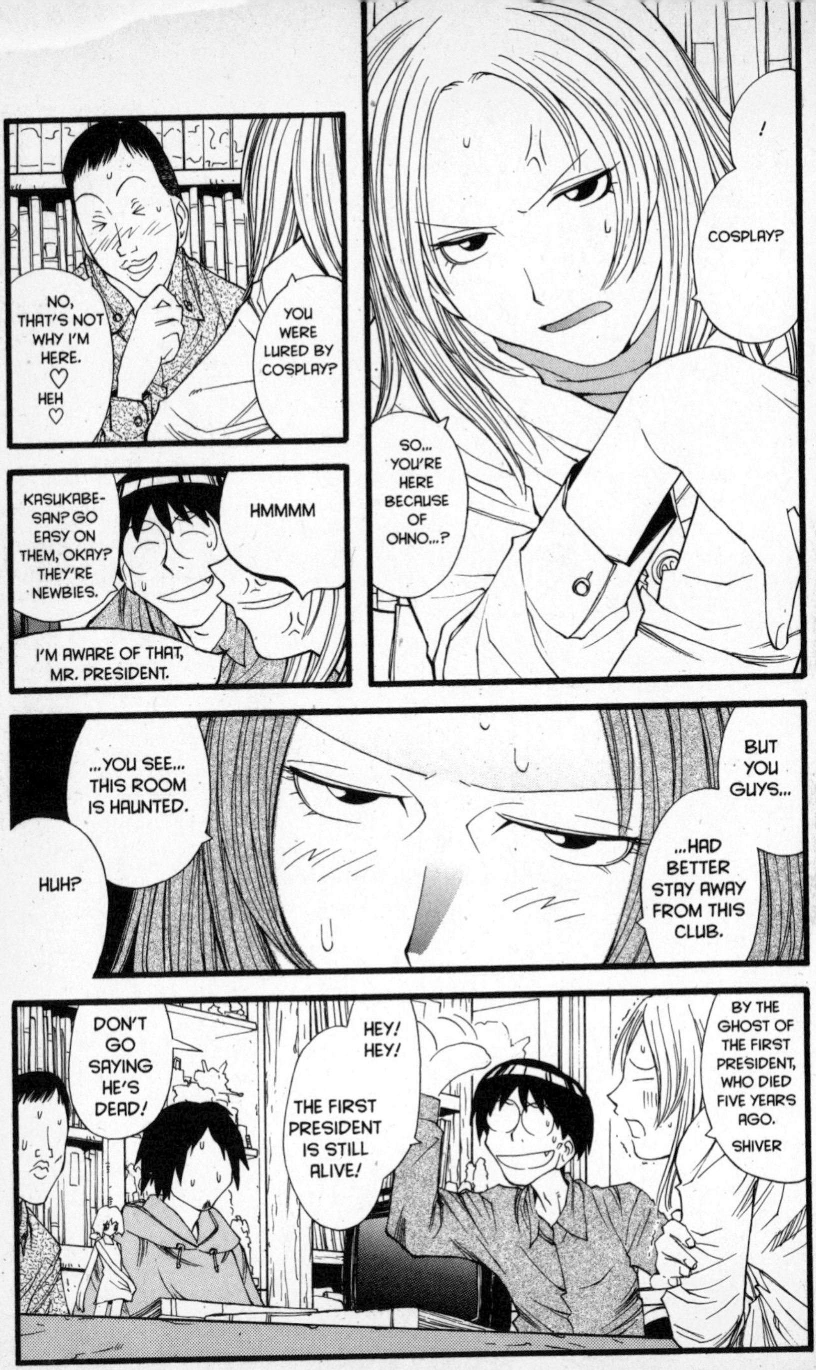
!
COSPLAY?
SO... YOU'RE HERE BECAUSE OF OHNO...?
YOU WERE LURED BY COSPLAY?
NO, THAT'S NOT WHY I'M HERE. ♡ HEH ♡
HMMMM
KASUKABE-SAN? GO EASY ON THEM, OKAY? THEY'RE NEWBIES.
I'M AWARE OF THAT, MR. PRESIDENT.
BUT YOU GUYS...
...HAD BETTER STAY AWAY FROM THIS CLUB.
...YOU SEE... THIS ROOM IS HAUNTED.
HUH?
BY THE GHOST OF THE FIRST PRESIDENT, WHO DIED FIVE YEARS AGO.
SHIVER
HEY! HEY!
THE FIRST PRESIDENT IS STILL ALIVE!
DON'T GO SAYING HE'S DEAD!

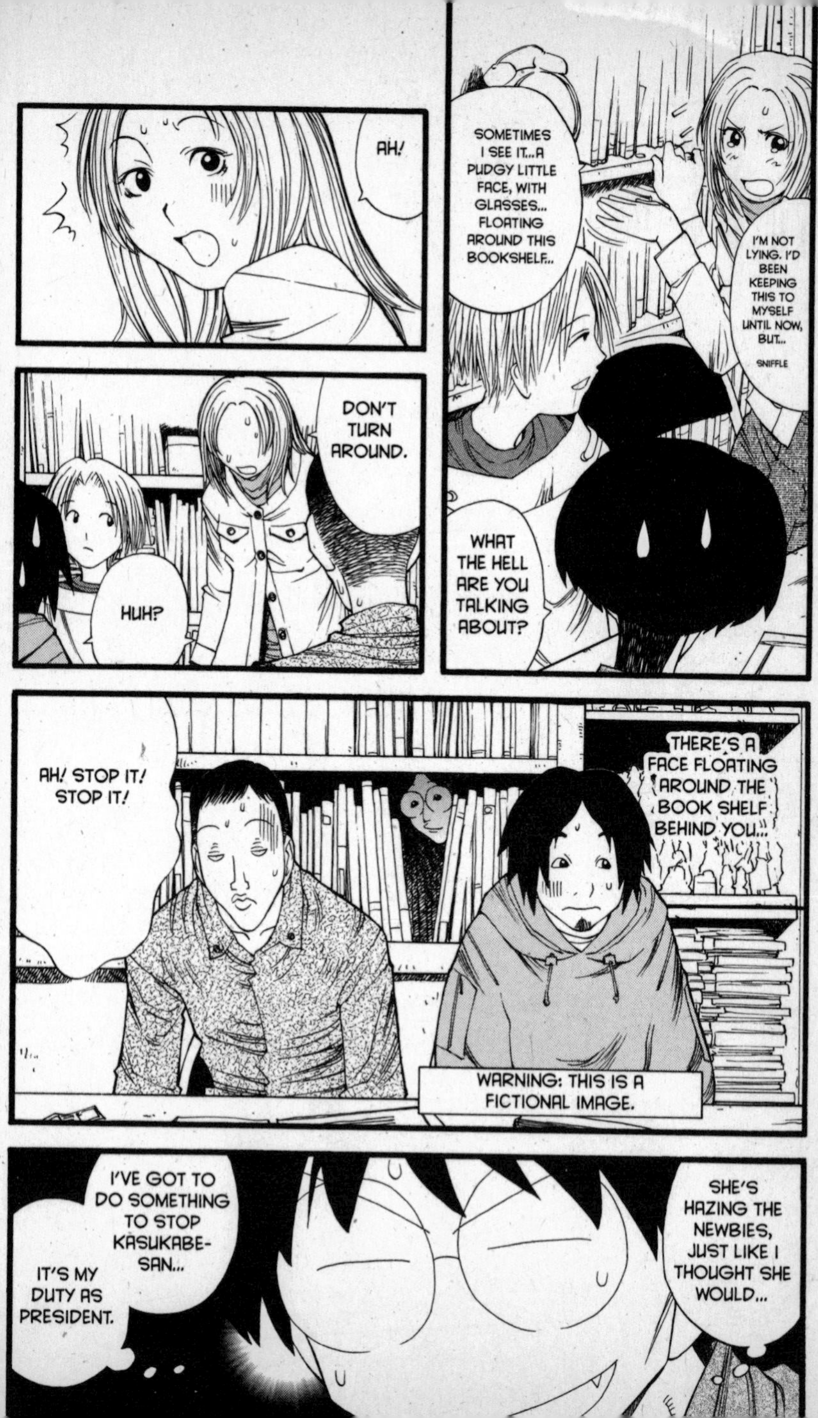

I'M NOT LYING. I'D BEEN KEEPING THIS TO MYSELF UNTIL NOW, BUT...
SNIFFLE
SOMETIMES I SEE IT...A PUDGY LITTLE FACE, WITH GLASSES... FLOATING AROUND THIS BOOKSHELF...
WHAT THE HELL ARE YOU TALKING ABOUT?
AH!
DON'T TURN AROUND.
HUH?
THERE'S A FACE FLOATING AROUND THE BOOK SHELF BEHIND YOU...
AH! STOP IT! STOP IT!
WARNING: THIS IS A FICTIONAL IMAGE.
SHE'S HAZING THE NEWBIES, JUST LIKE I THOUGHT SHE WOULD...
I'VE GOT TO DO SOMETHING TO STOP KASUKABE-SAN...
IT'S MY DUTY AS PRESIDENT.

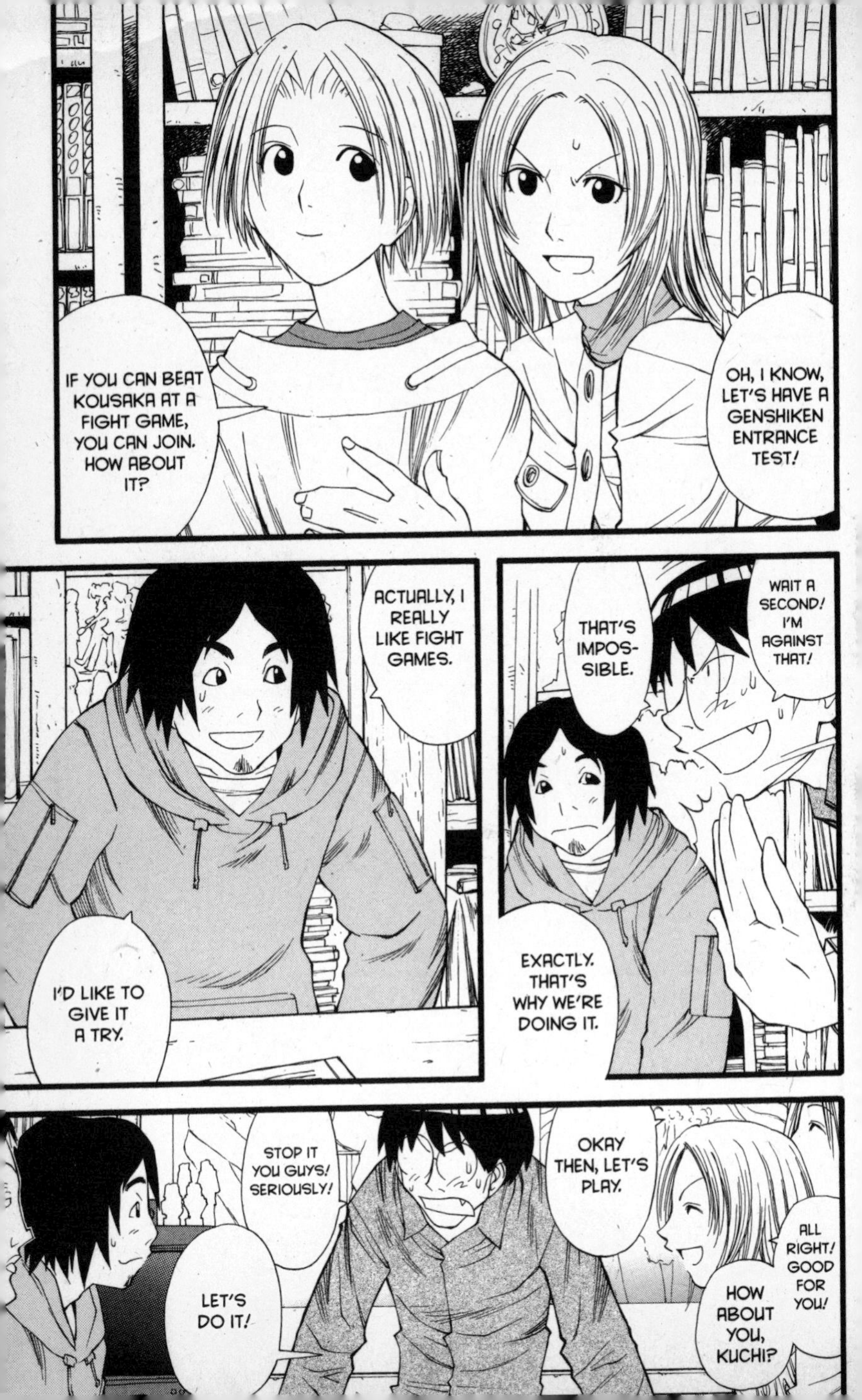
OH, I KNOW, LET'S HAVE A GENSHIKEN ENTRANCE TEST!
IF YOU CAN BEAT KOUSAKA AT A FIGHT GAME, YOU CAN JOIN. HOW ABOUT IT?
WAIT A SECOND! I'M AGAINST THAT!
THAT'S IMPOS-SIBLE.
EXACTLY. THAT'S WHY WE'RE DOING IT.
ACTUALLY, I REALLY LIKE FIGHT GAMES.
I'D LIKE TO GIVE IT A TRY.
ALL RIGHT! GOOD FOR YOU!
HOW ABOUT YOU, KUCHI?
OKAY THEN, LET'S PLAY.
STOP IT YOU GUYS! SERIOUSLY!
LET'S DO IT!

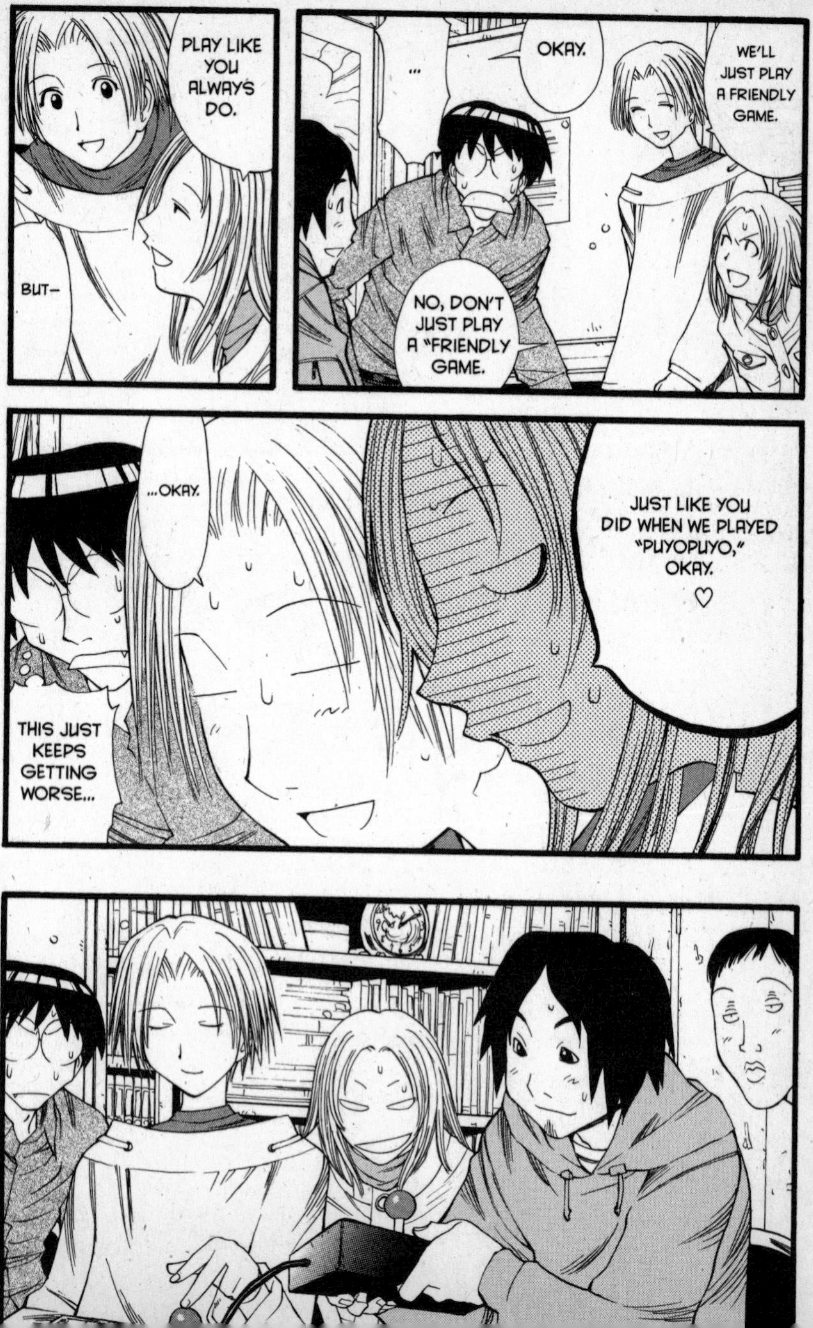
WE'LL JUST PLAY A FRIENDLY GAME.
OKAY.
...
NO, DON'T JUST PLAY A "FRIENDLY GAME.
PLAY LIKE YOU ALWAYS DO.
BUT—
JUST LIKE YOU DID WHEN WE PLAYED "PUYOPUYO," OKAY. ♡
...OKAY.
THIS JUST KEEPS GETTING WORSE...

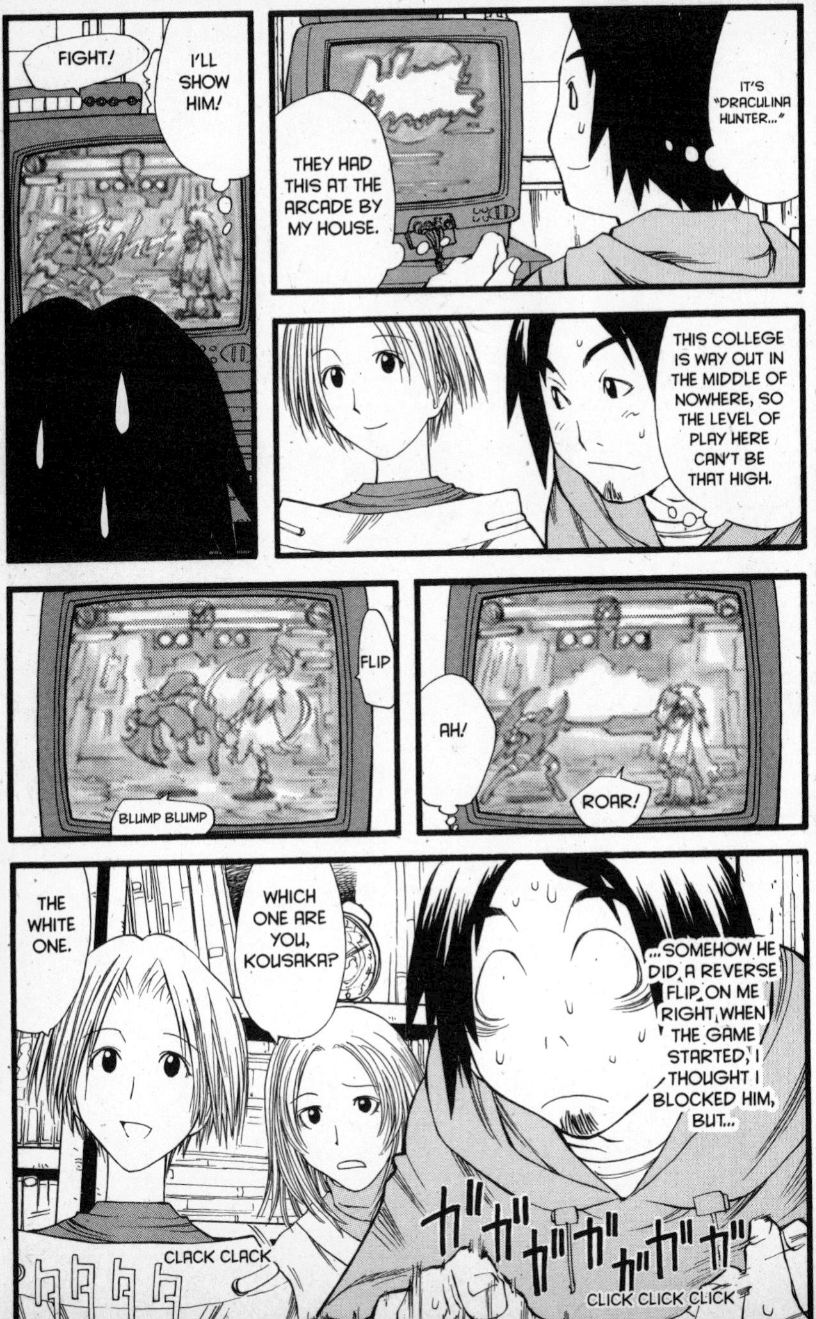
IT'S "DRACULINA HUNTER..."
THEY HAD THIS AT THE ARCADE BY MY HOUSE.
THIS COLLEGE IS WAY OUT IN THE MIDDLE OF NOWHERE, SO THE LEVEL OF PLAY HERE CAN'T BE THAT HIGH.
I'LL SHOW HIM!
FIGHT!
AH!
ROAR!
FLIP
BLUMP BLUMP
...SOMEHOW HE DID A REVERSE FLIP ON ME RIGHT WHEN THE GAME STARTED, I THOUGHT I BLOCKED HIM, BUT...
WHICH ONE ARE YOU, KOUSAKA?
THE WHITE ONE.
ガガガガガガガ
CLICK CLICK CLICK
タタタタ
CLACK CLACK

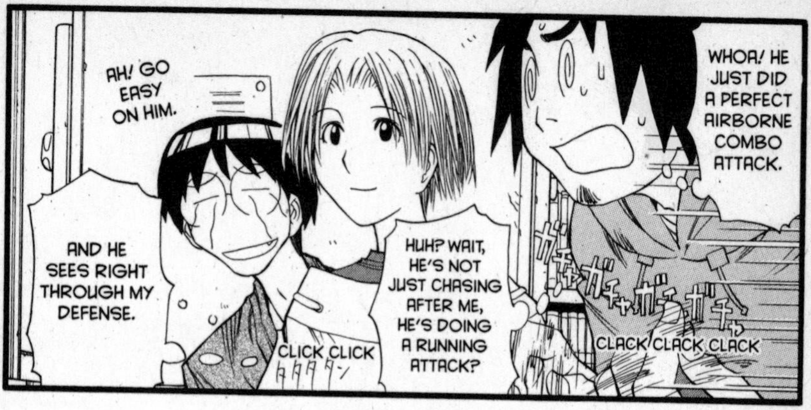
WHOA! HE JUST DID A PERFECT AIRBORNE COMBO ATTACK.
CLACK CLACK CLACK
HUH? WAIT, HE'S NOT JUST CHASING AFTER ME, HE'S DOING A RUNNING ATTACK?
CLICK CLICK
AH! GO EASY ON HIM.
AND HE SEES RIGHT THROUGH MY DEFENSE.

## K•O

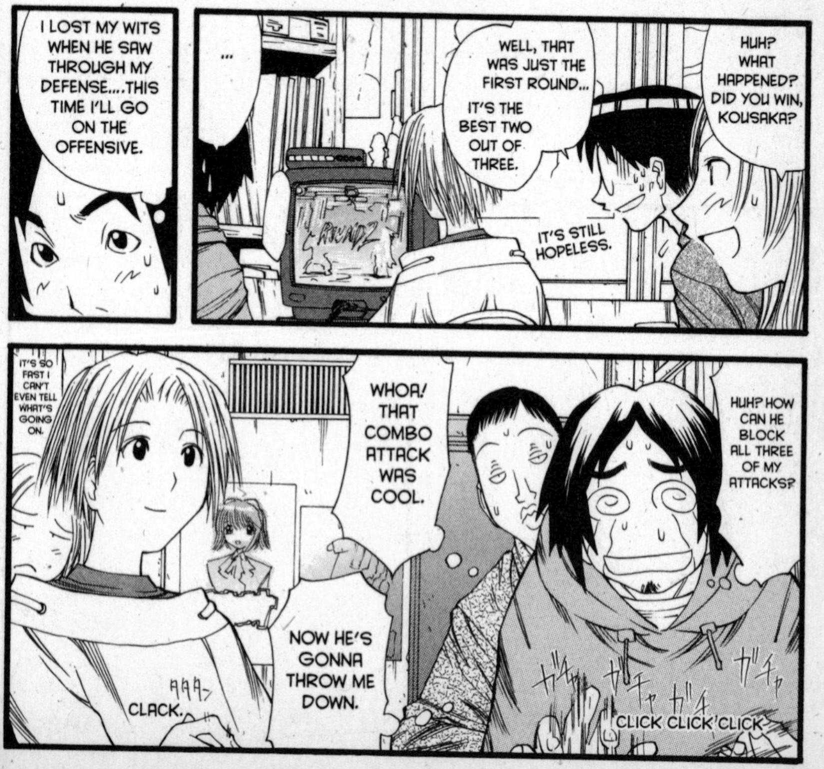
HUH? WHAT HAPPENED? DID YOU WIN, KOUSAKA?
WELL, THAT WAS JUST THE FIRST ROUND...
IT'S THE BEST TWO OUT OF THREE.
IT'S STILL HOPELESS.
...
I LOST MY WITS WHEN HE SAW THROUGH MY DEFENSE....THIS TIME I'LL GO ON THE OFFENSIVE.
HUH? HOW CAN HE BLOCK ALL THREE OF MY ATTACKS?
CLICK CLICK CLICK
WHOA! THAT COMBO ATTACK WAS COOL.
NOW HE'S GONNA THROW ME DOWN.
IT'S SO FAST I CAN'T EVEN TELL WHAT'S GOING ON.
CLACK.

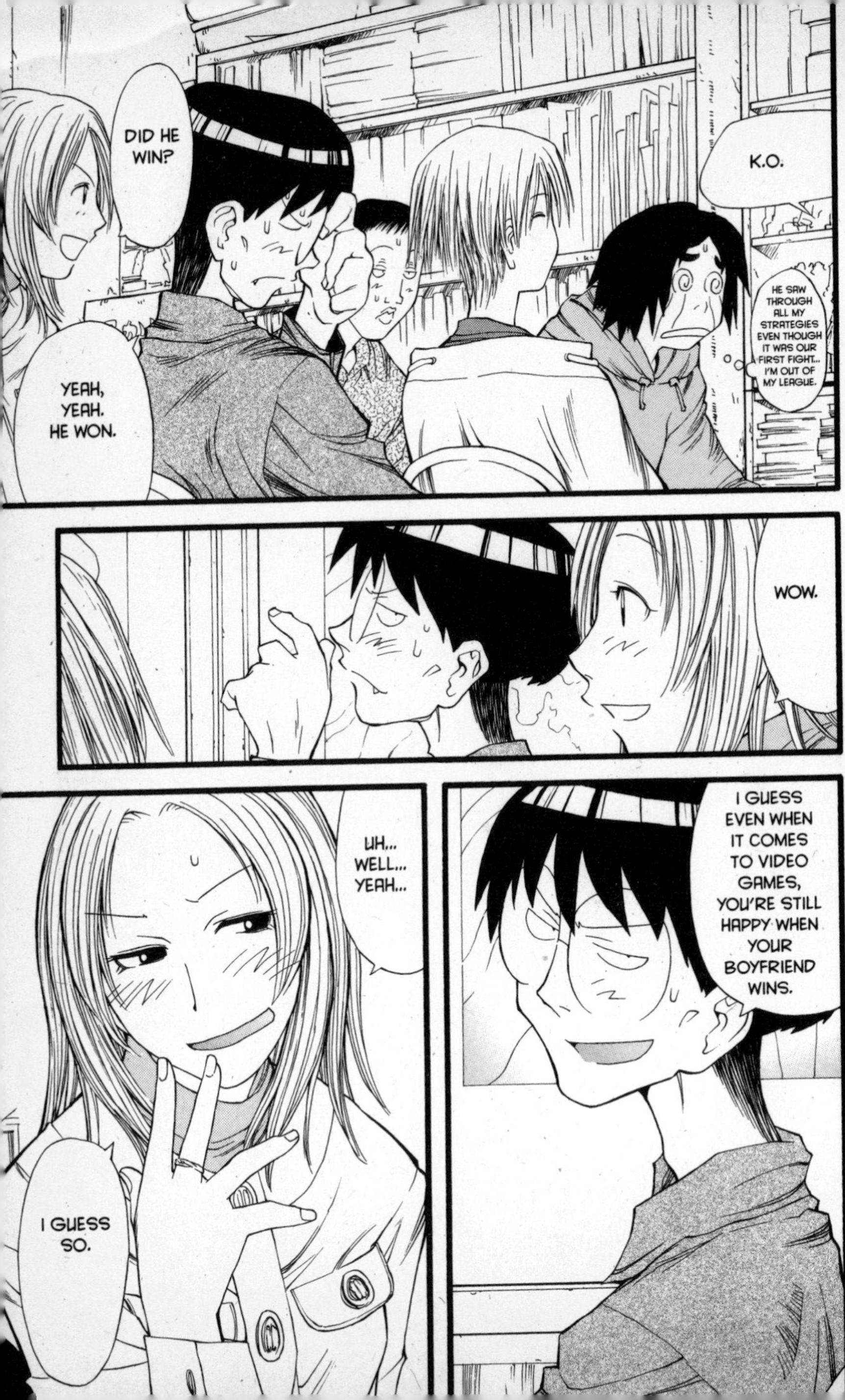
K.O.
HE SAW THROUGH ALL MY STRATEGIES EVEN THOUGH IT WAS OUR FIRST FIGHT... I'M OUT OF MY LEAGUE.
DID HE WIN?
YEAH, YEAH. HE WON.
WOW.
I GUESS EVEN WHEN IT COMES TO VIDEO GAMES, YOU'RE STILL HAPPY WHEN YOUR BOYFRIEND WINS.
UH... WELL... YEAH...
I GUESS SO.

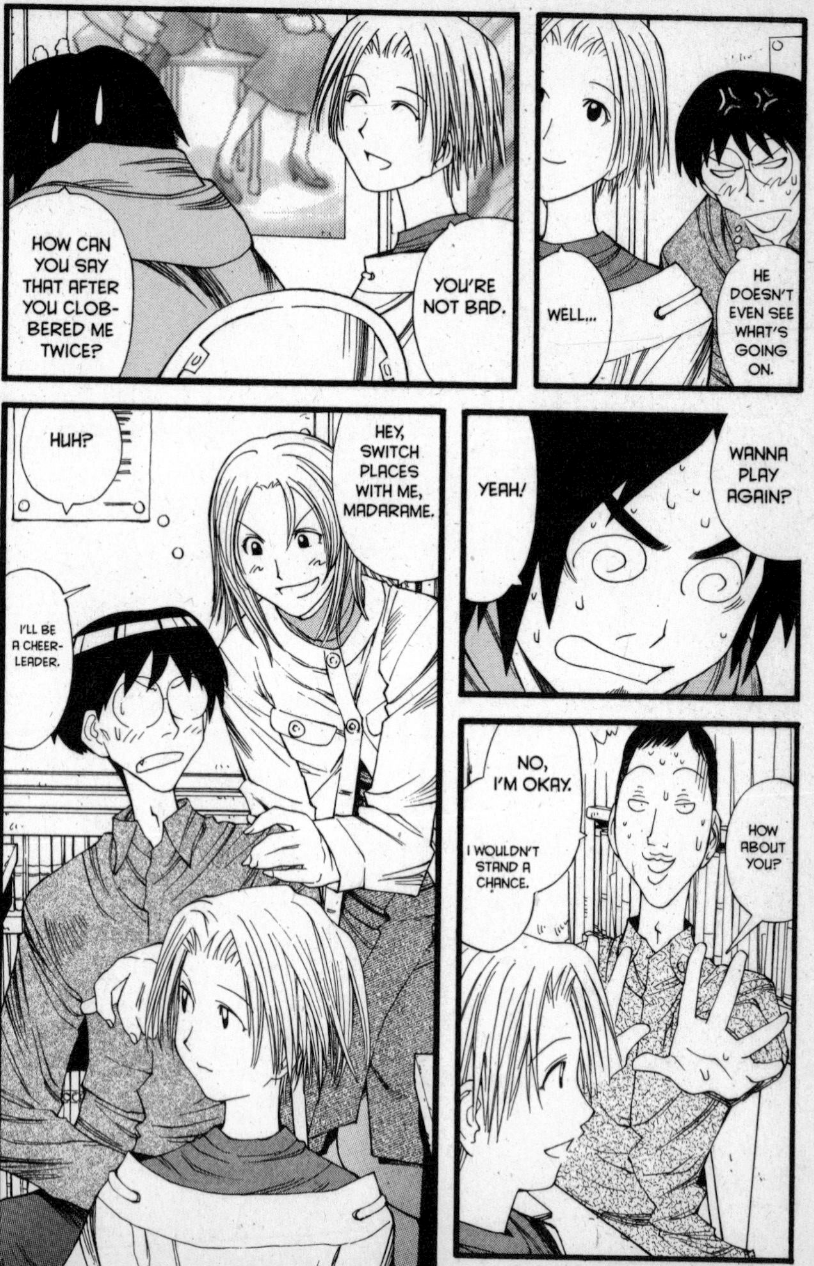
HE DOESN'T EVEN SEE WHAT'S GOING ON.
WELL...
YOU'RE NOT BAD.
HOW CAN YOU SAY THAT AFTER YOU CLOBBERED ME TWICE?
WANNA PLAY AGAIN?
YEAH!
HOW ABOUT YOU?
NO, I'M OKAY.
I WOULDN'T STAND A CHANCE.
HEY, SWITCH PLACES WITH ME, MADARAME.
HUH?
I'LL BE A CHEERLEADER.

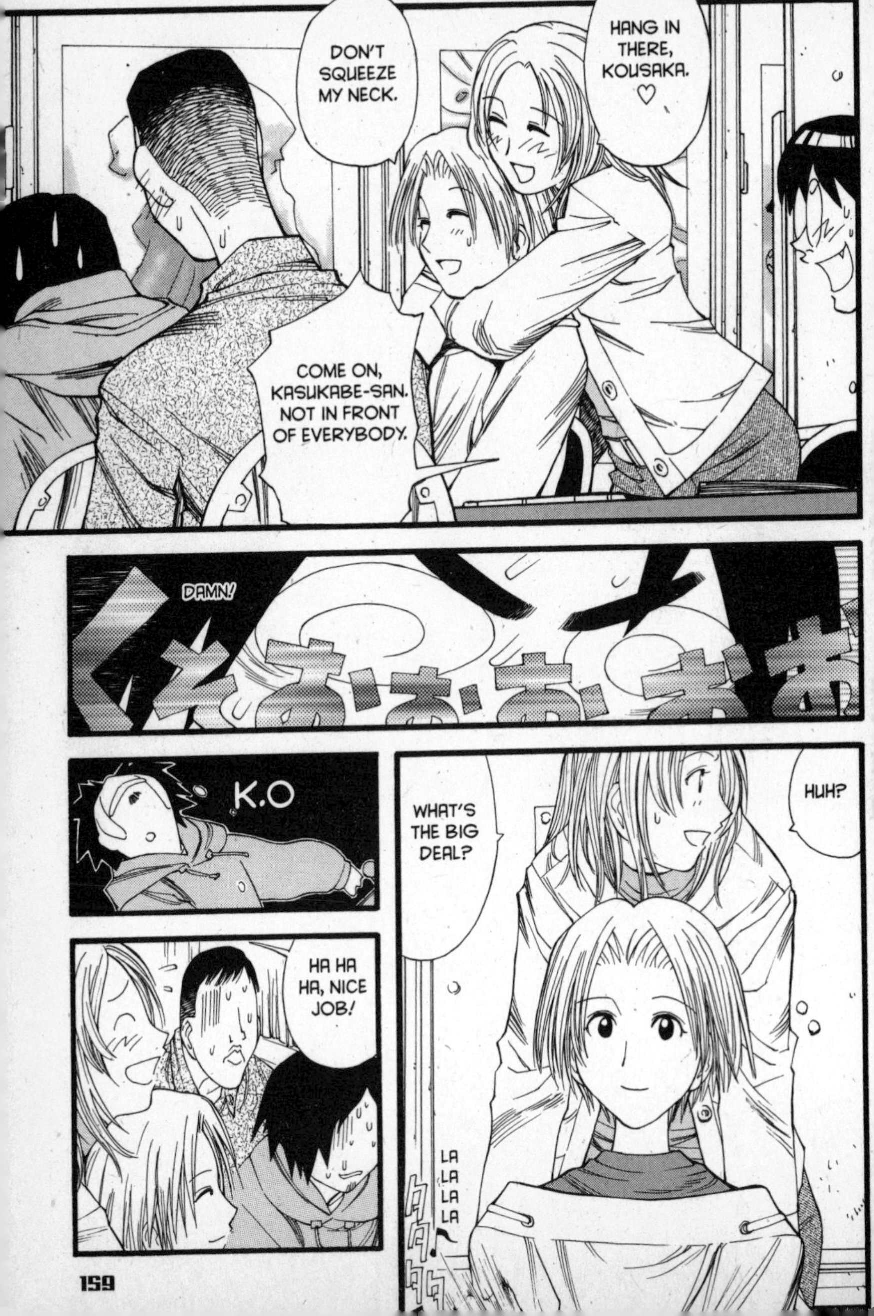
HANG IN THERE, KOUSAKA. ♡
DON'T SQUEEZE MY NECK.
COME ON, KASUKABE-SAN. NOT IN FRONT OF EVERYBODY.
DAMN!
HUH?
WHAT'S THE BIG DEAL?
LA LA LA LA
K.O
HA HA HA, NICE JOB!

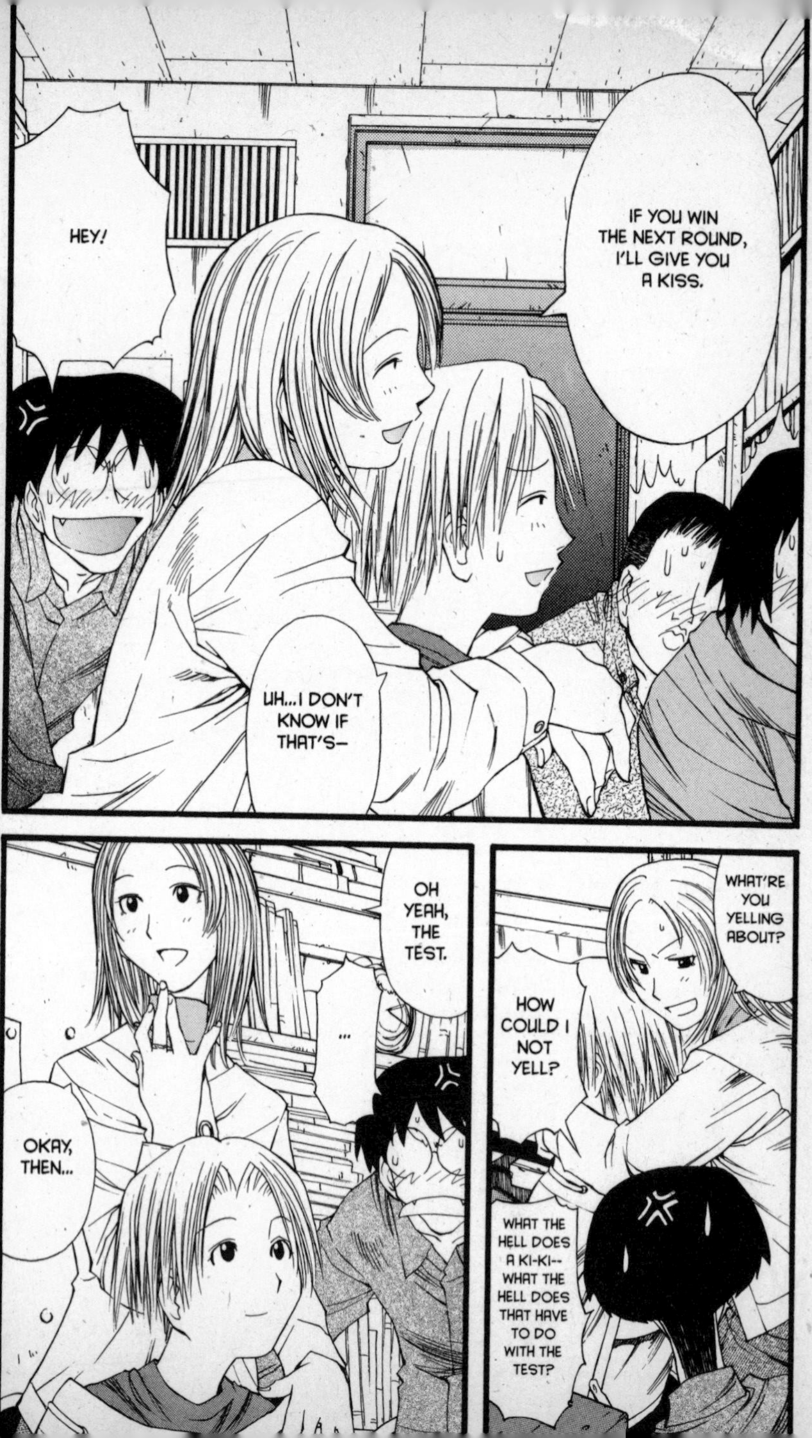
IF YOU WIN THE NEXT ROUND, I'LL GIVE YOU A KISS.
HEY!
UH...I DON'T KNOW IF THAT'S—
WHAT'RE YOU YELLING ABOUT?
HOW COULD I NOT YELL?
WHAT THE HELL DOES A KI-KI-- WHAT THE HELL DOES THAT HAVE TO DO WITH THE TEST?
OH YEAH, THE TEST.
...
OKAY, THEN...

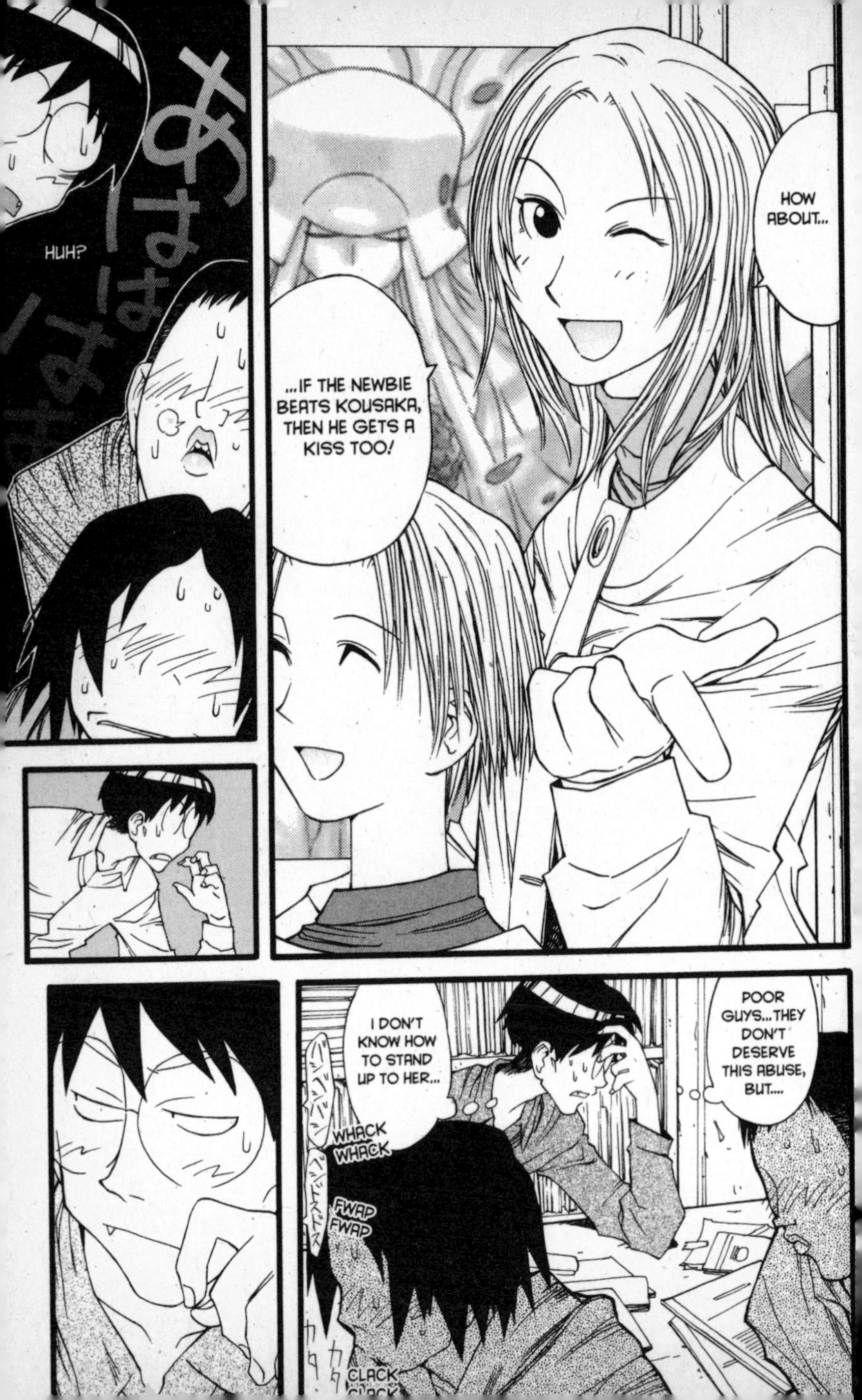

HOW ABOUT...
...IF THE NEWBIE BEATS KOUSAKA, THEN HE GETS A KISS TOO!
あははは
HUH?
POOR GUYS...THEY DON'T DESERVE THIS ABUSE, BUT....
I DON'T KNOW HOW TO STAND UP TO HER...
WHACK WHACK
FWAP FWAP
CLACK

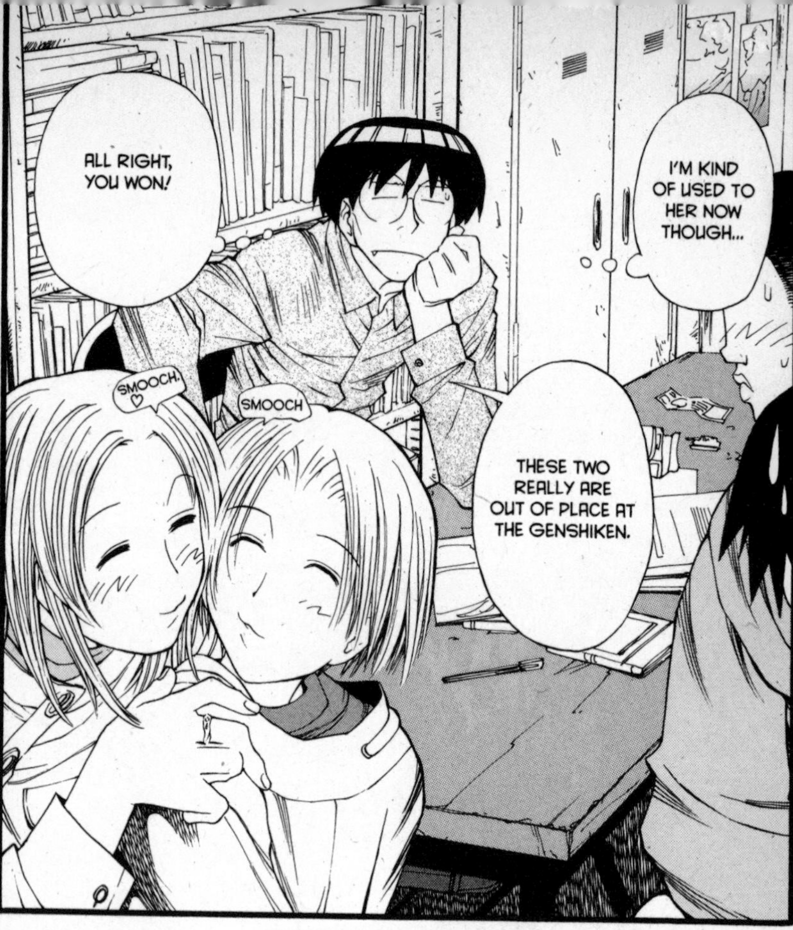
I'M KIND OF USED TO HER NOW THOUGH...
ALL RIGHT, YOU WON!
SMOOCH
SMOOCH. ♡
THESE TWO REALLY ARE OUT OF PLACE AT THE GENSHIKEN.

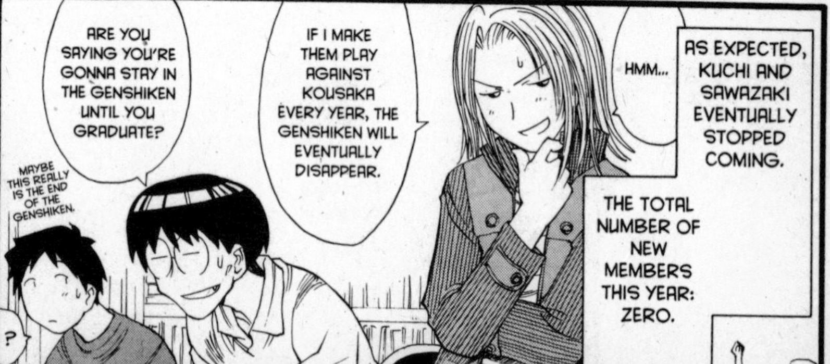
AS EXPECTED, KUCHI AND SAWAZAKI EVENTUALLY STOPPED COMING.
THE TOTAL NUMBER OF NEW MEMBERS THIS YEAR: ZERO.
HMM...
IF I MAKE THEM PLAY AGAINST KOUSAKA EVERY YEAR, THE GENSHIKEN WILL EVENTUALLY DISAPPEAR.
ARE YOU SAYING YOU'RE GONNA STAY IN THE GENSHIKEN UNTIL YOU GRADUATE?
MAYBE THIS REALLY IS THE END OF THE GENSHIKEN.
?

END OF CHAPTER 12

THE GENSHIKEN MEMBERS PICK...

# KUJI-UN

**...THE MOST NOTABLE SCENES**

TAKEN FROM THE GENSHIKEN'S SPORADICALLY PUBLISHED ZINE "MEBAETAME"

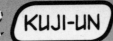

## MY FAVORITE SCENE FROM *KUJI-UN* PART 6 BY "YOKO KANNAZUKI"

NOT IN THE TANKOBON BOOK

SHOW YOURSELF!
SLAM

I WANT TO SEE MORE OF THE GUY ON THE RIGHT AND THE GUY ON THE LEFT ♡. [YOKO]

...THIS IS EXACTLY THE KIND OF SCENE I THOUGHT YOU'D CHOOSE...I MEAN, IT'S EXACTLY WHAT I'D EXPECTED. I CAN'T TELL IF YOU'RE KIDDING OR IF YOU'RE SERIOUS. IF THIS IS A JOKE, I DON'T EVEN KNOW IF IT'S FUNNY OR NOT. IN THIS SCENE, THE VICE-PRESIDENT'S FIANCÉ (WHO WAS PROBABLY ABOUT 12 AT THE TIME) IS ABOUT TO BE CAPTURED BY THE GANG IN BLACK AFTER COMMITTING VARIOUS ACTS OF MISCHIEF. OBVIOUSLY, THE ONE IN THE MIDDLE IS THE VICE-PRESIDENT'S GRANDFATHER. BUT WHY THE GUY ON THE RIGHT, AND NOT THE GRANDFATHER? IS IT BECAUSE HE LOOKS LIKE HE'D APPEAR IN "CHINDAN"?

...WELL, THE ONLY PERSON WHO HASN'T WRITTEN ANYTHING YET IS THE GENSHIKEN'S MOST DANGEROUS CREATURE, CRASHER HANAYAMA-SAN (I NAMED HER THAT). WELL...WHEN I TRIED TO GIVE HER THE FIVE KUJI-UN TANKOBON, SHE TORE THEM TO PIECES. JUST KIDDING. SHE THREW THEM ON THE FLOOR. THAT'S THE TRUTH. [PIT VIPER].

DATAMAN

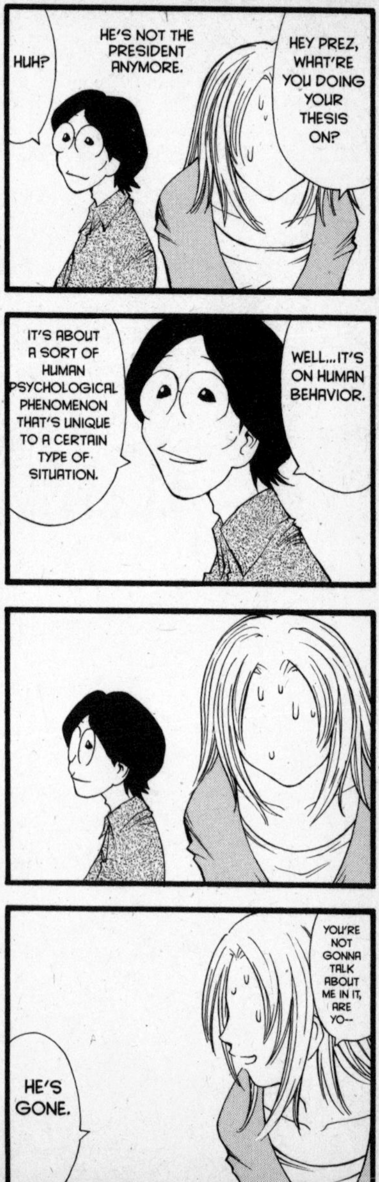
HEY PREZ, WHAT'RE YOU DOING YOUR THESIS ON?
HE'S NOT THE PRESIDENT ANYMORE.
HUH?
WELL...IT'S ON HUMAN BEHAVIOR.
IT'S ABOUT A SORT OF HUMAN PSYCHOLOGICAL PHENOMENON THAT'S UNIQUE TO A CERTAIN TYPE OF SITUATION.
YOU'RE NOT GONNA TALK ABOUT ME IN IT, ARE YO--
HE'S GONE.

WHAT THE HELL WERE YOU DOING?

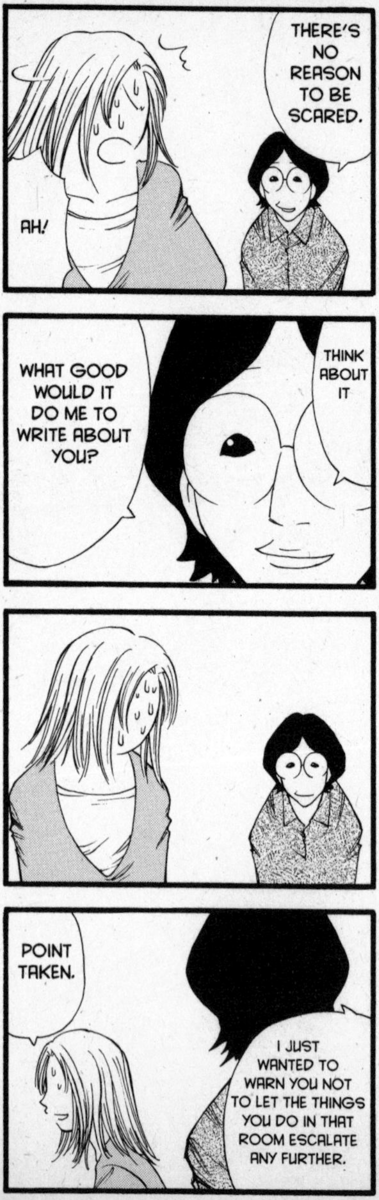
THERE'S NO REASON TO BE SCARED.
AH!
THINK ABOUT IT
WHAT GOOD WOULD IT DO ME TO WRITE ABOUT YOU?
I JUST WANTED TO WARN YOU NOT TO LET THE THINGS YOU DO IN THAT ROOM ESCALATE ANY FURTHER.
POINT TAKEN.

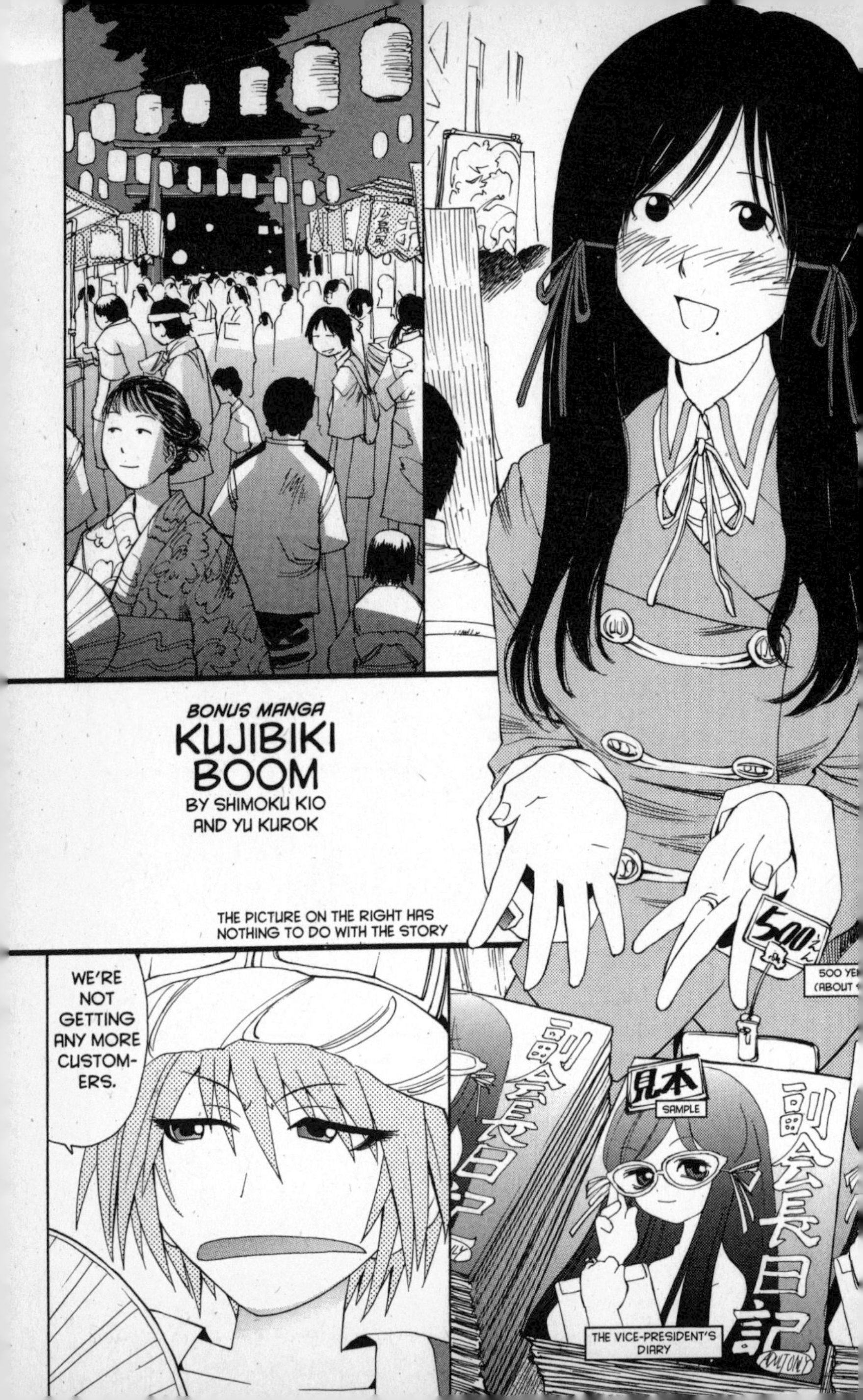
BONUS MANGA
KUJIBIKI BOOM
BY SHIMOKU KIO AND YU KUROK
THE PICTURE ON THE RIGHT HAS NOTHING TO DO WITH THE STORY
500えん
500 YE
(ABOUT
見本
SAMPLE
副会長日記
THE VICE-PRESIDENT'S DIARY
ADULT ONLY
WE'RE NOT GETTING ANY MORE CUSTOM-ERS.

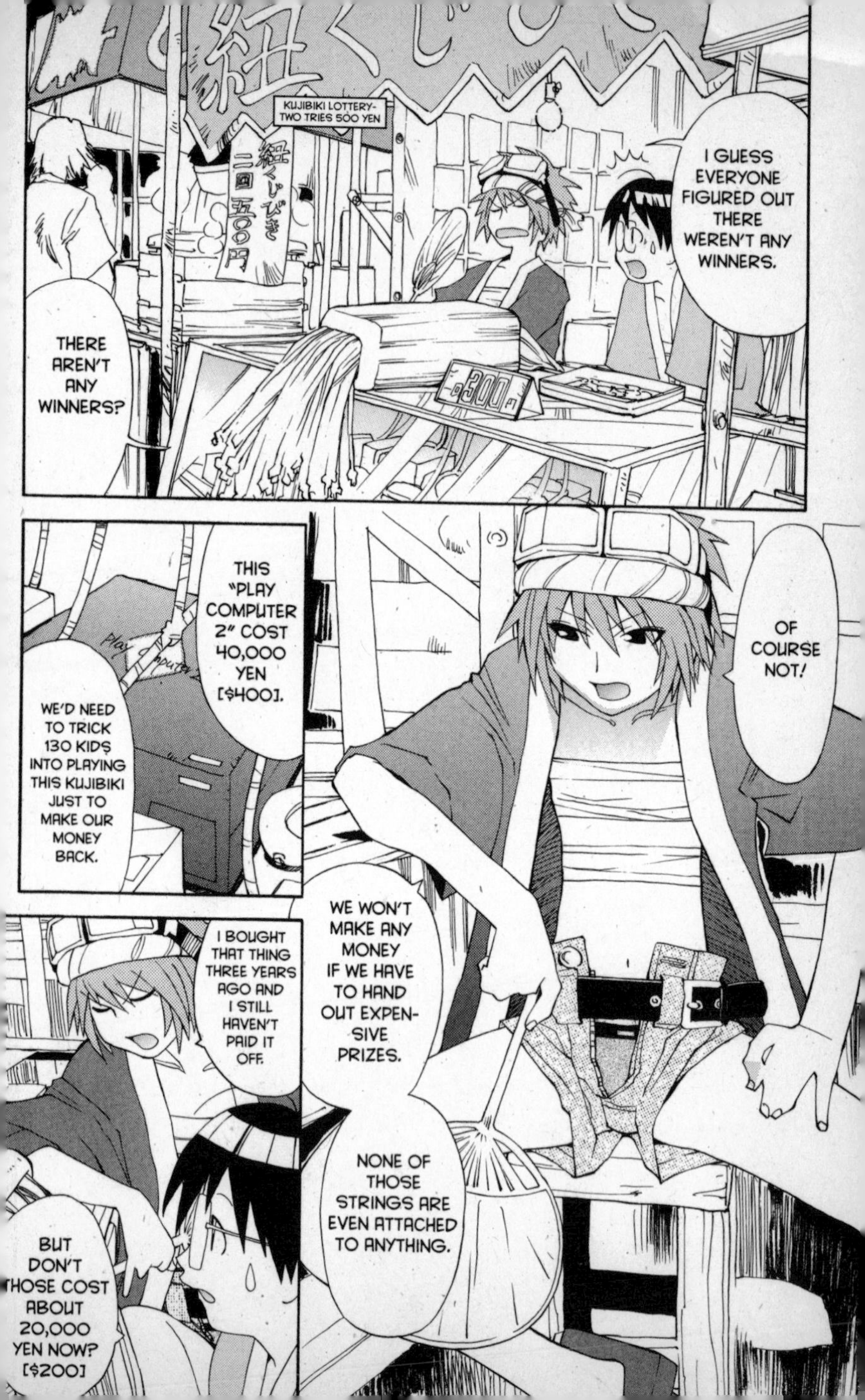
I GUESS EVERYONE FIGURED OUT THERE WEREN'T ANY WINNERS.
KUJIBIKI LOTTERY- TWO TRIES 500 YEN
THERE AREN'T ANY WINNERS?
OF COURSE NOT!
WE WON'T MAKE ANY MONEY IF WE HAVE TO HAND OUT EXPEN- SIVE PRIZES.
NONE OF THOSE STRINGS ARE EVEN ATTACHED TO ANYTHING.
THIS "PLAY COMPUTER 2" COST 40,000 YEN [$400].
WE'D NEED TO TRICK 130 KIDS INTO PLAYING THIS KUJIBIKI JUST TO MAKE OUR MONEY BACK.
I BOUGHT THAT THING THREE YEARS AGO AND I STILL HAVEN'T PAID IT OFF.
BUT DON'T THOSE COST ABOUT 20,000 YEN NOW? [$200]

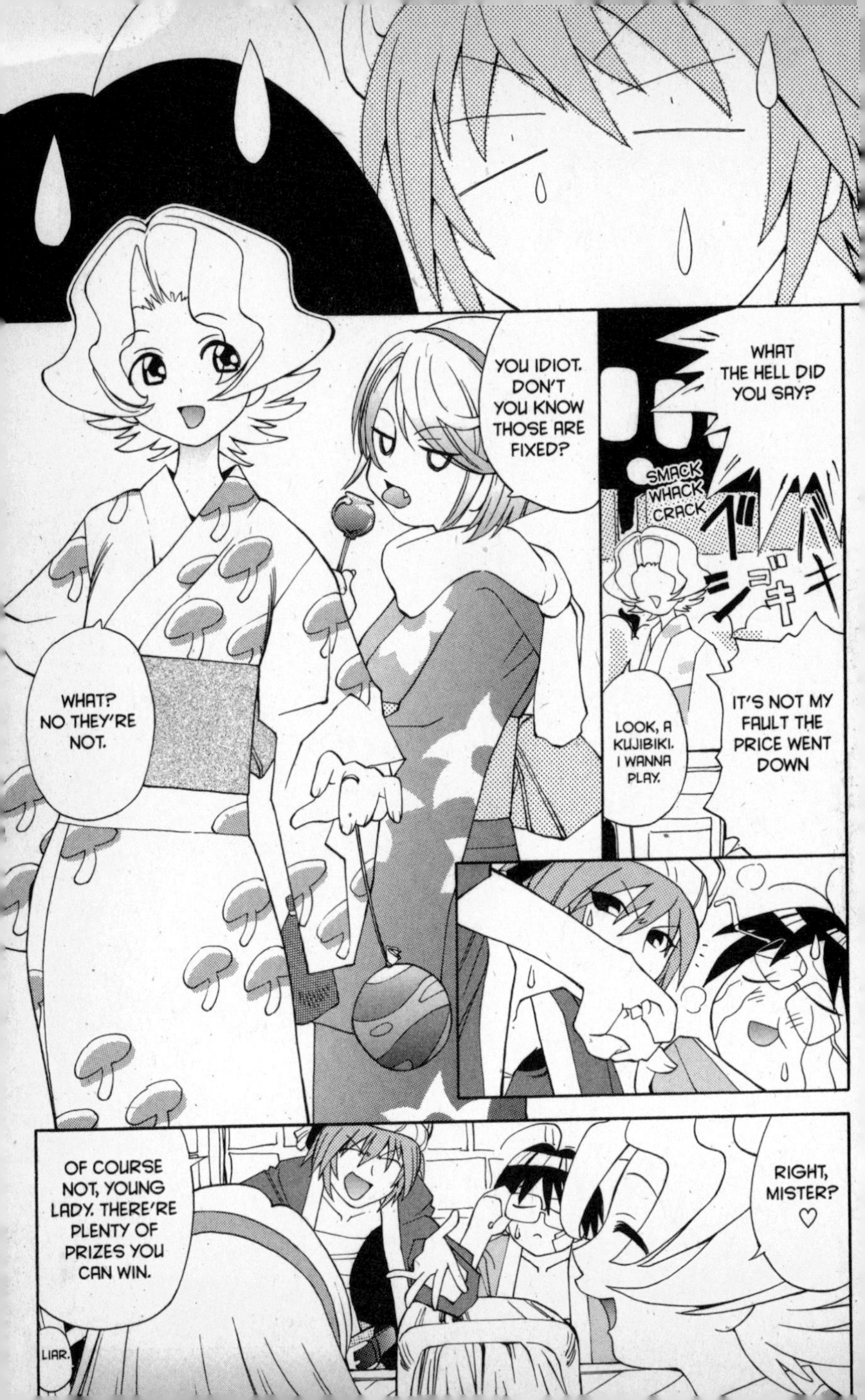
WHAT THE HELL DID YOU SAY?
SMACK WHACK CRACK
IT'S NOT MY FAULT THE PRICE WENT DOWN
LOOK, A KUJIBIKI. I WANNA PLAY.
YOU IDIOT. DON'T YOU KNOW THOSE ARE FIXED?
WHAT? NO THEY'RE NOT.
RIGHT, MISTER? ♡
OF COURSE NOT, YOUNG LADY. THERE'RE PLENTY OF PRIZES YOU CAN WIN.
LIAR.

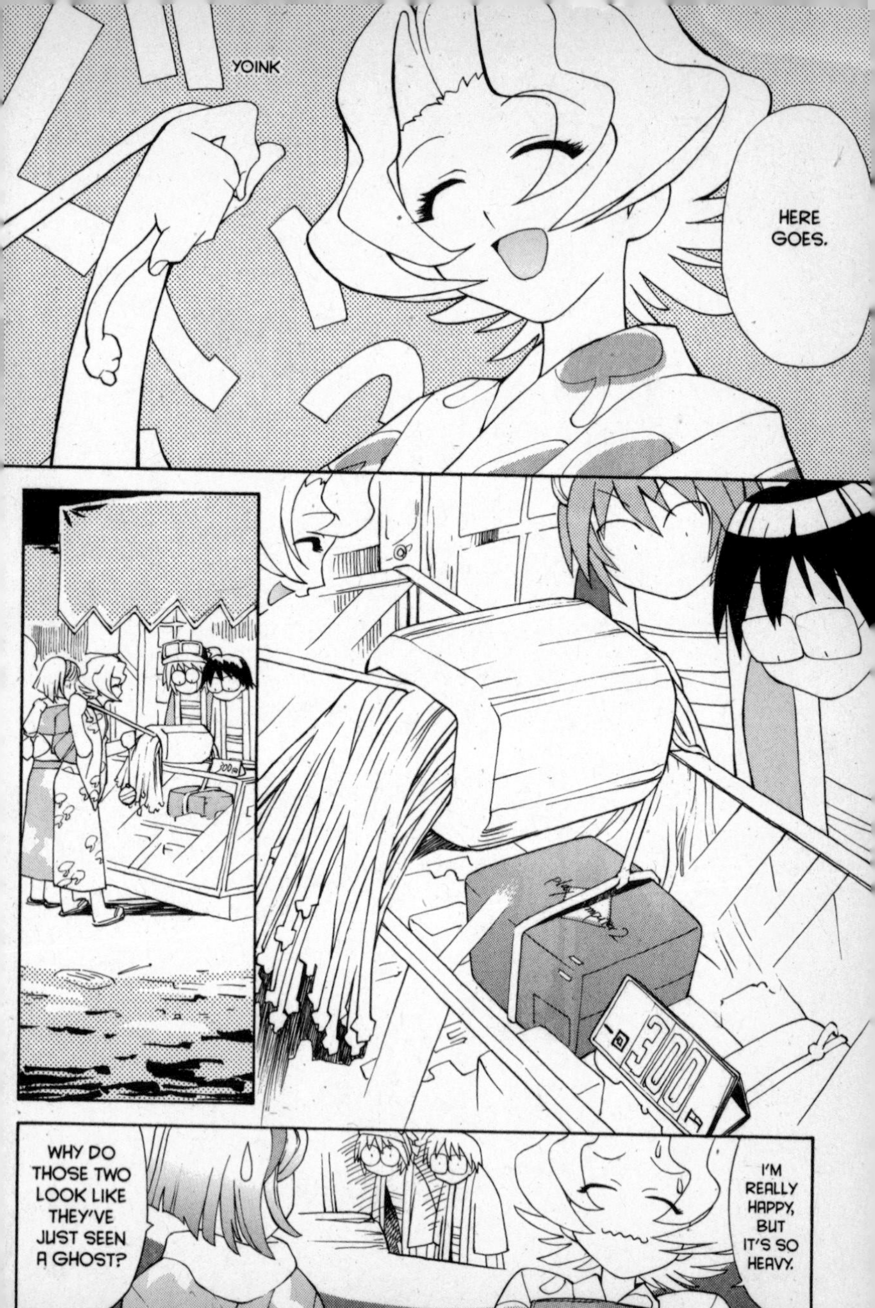
HERE GOES.
YOINK
I'M REALLY HAPPY, BUT IT'S SO HEAVY.
WHY DO THOSE TWO LOOK LIKE THEY'VE JUST SEEN A GHOST?

END OF GENSHIKEN BOOK 2

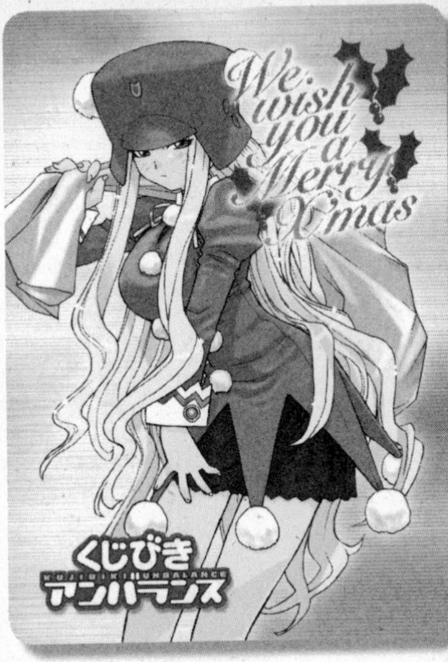
We wish you a Merry X'mas
くじびき
KUJIBIKI UNBALANCE
アンバランス

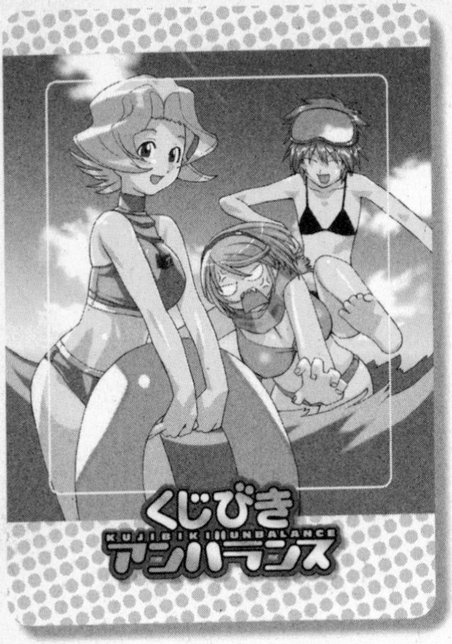
くじびき
KUJIBIKI UNBALANCE
アンバランス

くじびき KUJIBIKI UNBALANCE アンバランス

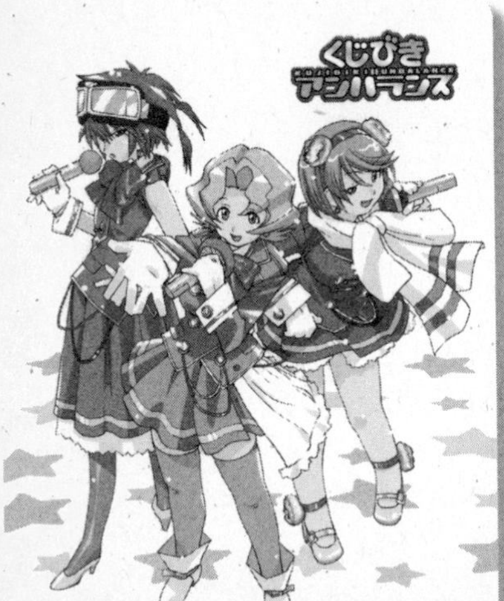
くじびき
KUJIBIKI UNBALANCE
アンバランス

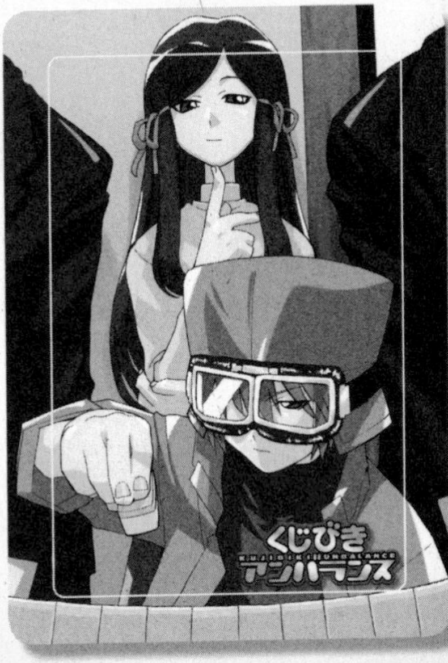
くじびき
KUJIBIKI UNBALANCE
アンバランス

くじびき KUJIBIKI UNBALANCE アンバーランス

# About the Author

Kio Shimoku was born in 1974.
In 1994 his debut work, *Ten No Ryoiki*, received
second place in the "Afternoon Shiki Prize"
contest. Other past works include *Kagerounikii*,
*Yonensei*, and *Gonensei*, all of which
appeared in *Afternoon* magazine.
He has been working on Genshiken
since 2002.

# Translation Notes

Japanese is a tricky language for most Westerners, and translation is often more art than science. For your edification and reading pleasure, here are notes on some of the places where we could have gone in a different direction in our translation of the work, or where a Japanese cultural reference is used.

### *Zasae-san, page 5*

"Zasae-san" is a play on the popular manga and anime series "Sazae-san."

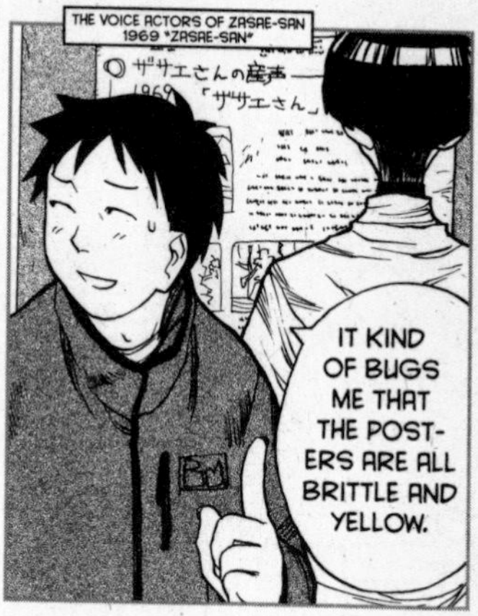
THE VOICE ACTORS OF ZASAE-SAN
1969 "ZASAE-SAN"
IT KIND OF BUGS ME THAT THE POSTERS ARE ALL BRITTLE AND YELLOW.

### *Michael Schumacher, page 18*

Michael Schumacher is a German race car driver.

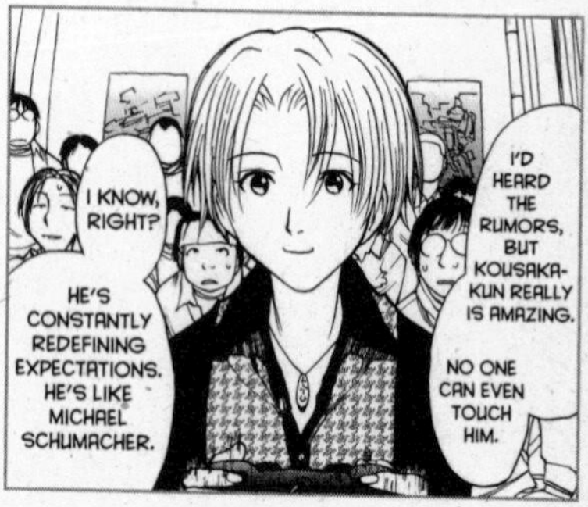
I'D HEARD THE RUMORS, BUT KOUSAKA-KUN REALLY IS AMAZING.
NO ONE CAN EVEN TOUCH HIM.
I KNOW, RIGHT?
HE'S CONSTANTLY REDEFINING EXPECTATIONS. HE'S LIKE MICHAEL SCHUMACHER.

## *Candid camera, page 58*

The Prez is indicating that he may have hidden cameras in the girls' bathrooms. Perverts are occasionally nabbed in Japan (and in the U.S.) for this crime.

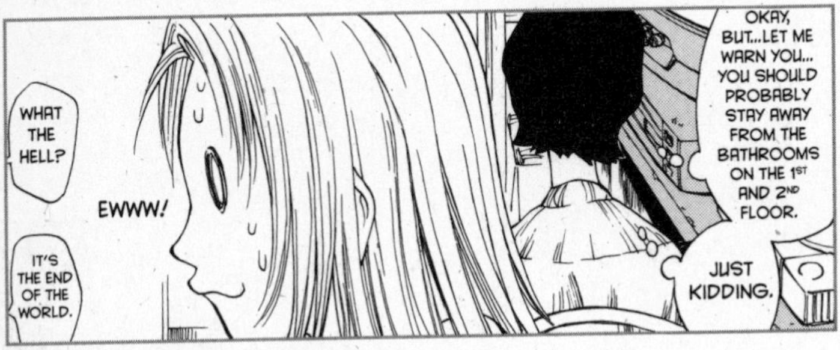
OKAY, BUT...LET ME WARN YOU... YOU SHOULD PROBABLY STAY AWAY FROM THE BATHROOMS ON THE 1ST AND 2ND FLOOR.
JUST KIDDING.
WHAT THE HELL?
EWWW!
IT'S THE END OF THE WORLD.

## *Manga cafés, page 62*

Manga cafés, called manga kissaten in Japanese, are coffee-houses with large manga libraries. Patrons pay for a drink and sit and read the manga of their choice.

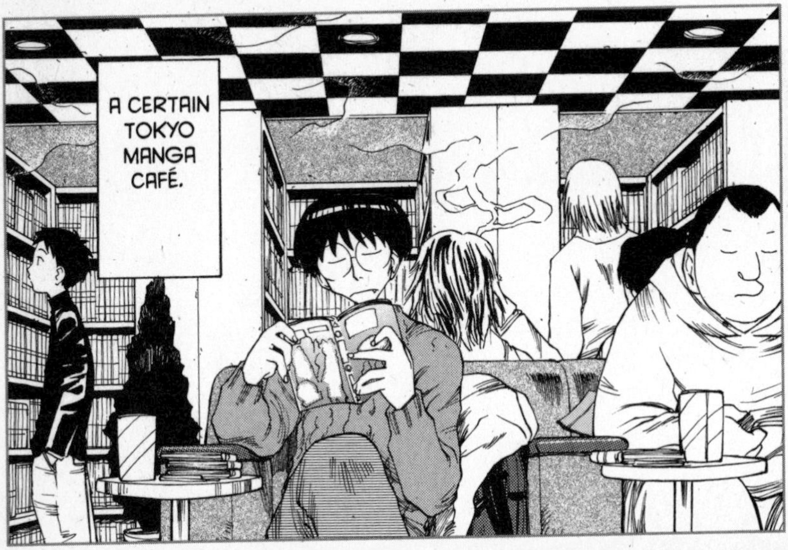
A CERTAIN TOKYO MANGA CAFÉ.

## *Garage kit, page 63*

A "garage kit" is a type of highly detailed large-scale model. These models originated in Japan but are now popular all over the world.

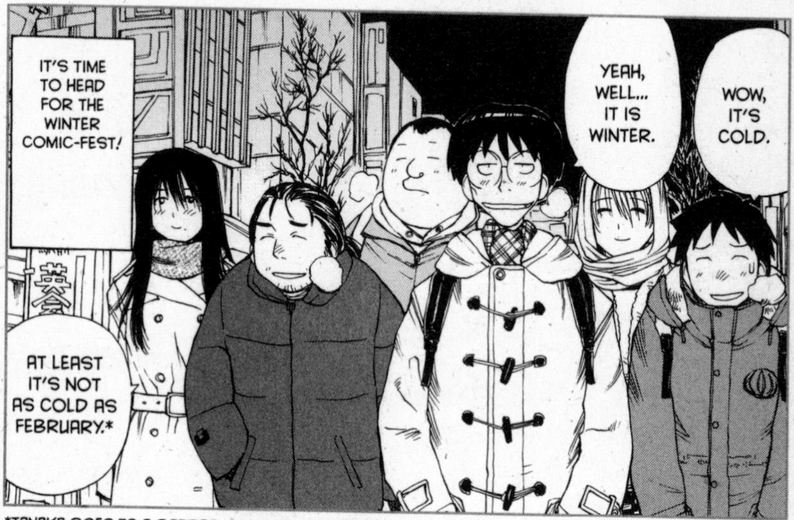
WOW, IT'S COLD.
YEAH, WELL... IT IS WINTER.
IT'S TIME TO HEAD FOR THE WINTER COMIC-FEST!
AT LEAST IT'S NOT AS COLD AS FEBRUARY.*

*TANAKA GOES TO A GARAGE KIT MODEL CONVENTION EVERY FEBRUARY.

## *J cup, page 95*

Japan's domestic soccer league is called the "J League." Based on Saki's remark, Madarame is guessing that Ohno wears a "J" cup bra size. Kanji thinks of the soccer World Cup and guesses that Ohno might wear a "W" cup.

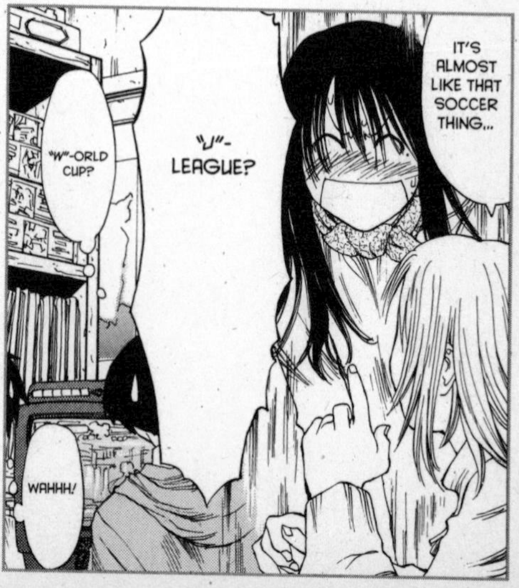
IT'S ALMOST LIKE THAT SOCCER THING...
"J"-LEAGUE?
"W"-ORLD CUP?
WAHHH!

### Puyopuyo, page 103

Puyopuyo is a game similar to Tetris.

AFTER CAREFUL CONSIDERATION SHE DECIDED ON THE GAME "PUYOPUYO."
THE OBJECT OF THIS FAMOUS GAME IS TO ARRANGE THE "PUYO" BLOCKS INTO LINES AS THEY FALL.

### Puyo vs. Puyopuyo, page 112

The individual pieces in the game Puyopuyo are called "puyo." Kousaka is distracted by the fact that Saki is saying she's dressed as "puyopuyo" when, more precisely, she is dressed as a "puyo."

### Dragon, page 113

The chapter title and the character costumes are a reference to the role-playing game "Dragon Quest."

CHAPTER 11
SASAHARA GAINS SOME HIT POINTS, BUT LOSES INTELLIGENCE POINTS.

### *Girly girl, page 118*

Kanji refers to his sister as a "gyaru," which we translated as "girly girl." A "gyaru" is actually a word for a subculture of young Japanese girls who typically wear extreme fashions, dyed hair and heavy makeup.

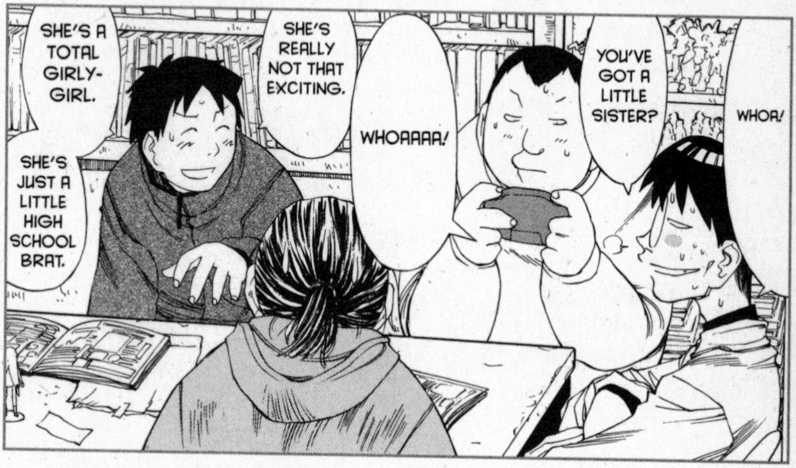
WHOA!
YOU'VE GOT A LITTLE SISTER?
WHOAAAA!
SHE'S REALLY NOT THAT EXCITING.
SHE'S A TOTAL GIRLY-GIRL.
SHE'S JUST A LITTLE HIGH SCHOOL BRAT.

### *Oniichan, page 122*

"Oniichan" is a casual variant of "oniisan," the honorific term for older brother. It can also be used to refer to young men in general. The female variant is "oneesan" or "oneechan."

### *Last names, page 122*

In Japan people call each other by their last names, especially in formal situations. In casual situations people may use first names, but all of the Genshiken guys go by their last names.

### *Nesuo, page 137*

Nesuo is a play on the character Suneo, from the anime "Doraemon."

### *Ai No Uta, page 138*

"Ai No Uta" means "The song of love." *Swallowtail Butterfly* is the movie's full name. It was directed by Shunji Iwai and starred the J-pop star Charra.

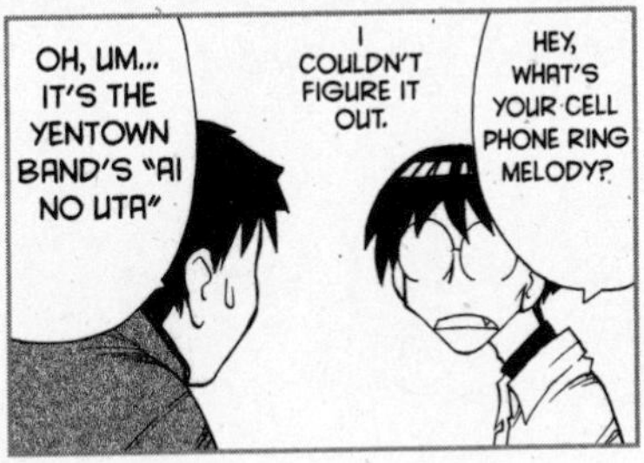
HEY, WHAT'S YOUR CELL PHONE RING MELODY?
I COULDN'T FIGURE IT OUT.
OH, UM... IT'S THE YENTOWN BAND'S "AI NO UTA"

### *Kujibiki lottery, page 166*

This is a kujibiki lottery. The box is full of small pieces of rope. Winning pieces are supposed to be attached to a prize.

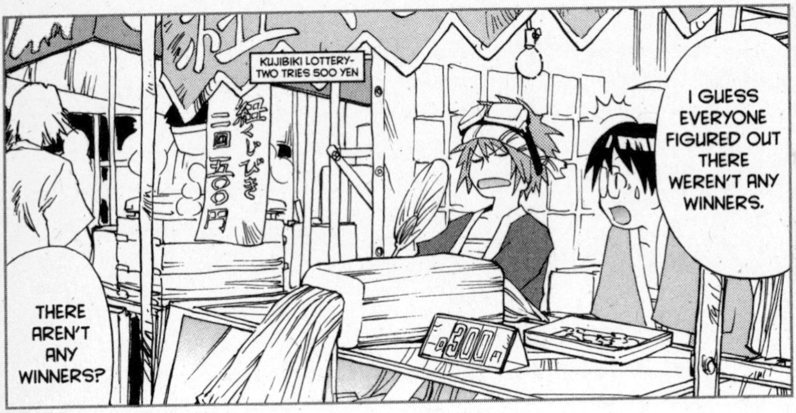
KUJIBIKI LOTTERY- TWO TRIES 500 YEN
I GUESS EVERYONE FIGURED OUT THERE WEREN'T ANY WINNERS.
THERE AREN'T ANY WINNERS?

# Honorifics

Throughout the Del Rey Manga books, you will find Japanese honorifics left intact in the translations. For those not familiar with how the Japanese use honorifics and, more importantly, how they differ from American honorifics, we present this brief overview.

Politeness has always been a critical facet of Japanese culture. Ever since the feudal era, when Japan was a highly stratified society, use of honorifics—which can be defined as polite speech that indicates relationship or status—has played an essential role in the Japanese language. When addressing someone in Japanese, an honorific usually takes the form of a suffix attached to one's name (example: "Asuna-san"), or as a title at the end of one's name or in place of the name itself (example: "Negi-sensei," or simply "Sensei!").

Honorifics can be expressions of respect or endearment. In the context of manga and anime, honorifics give insight into the nature of the relationship between characters. Many translations into English leave out these important honorifics, and therefore distort the "feel" of the original Japanese. Because Japanese honorifics contain nuances that English honorifics lack, it is our policy at Del Rey not to translate them. Here, instead, is a guide to some of the honorifics you may encounter in Del Rey Manga.

**-san:** This is the most common honorific and is equivalent to Mr., Miss, Ms., or Mrs. It is the all-purpose honorific and can be used in any situation where politeness is required.

**-sama:** This is one level higher than "-san" and is used to confer great respect.

**-dono:** This comes from the word "tono," which means "lord." It is an even higher level than "-sama" and confers utmost respect.

**-kun:** This suffix is used at the end of boys' names to express familiarity or endearment. It is also sometimes used by men among friends, or when addressing someone younger or of a lower station.

**-chan:** This is used to express endearment, mostly toward girls. It is also used for little boys, pets, and even among lovers. It gives a sense of childish cuteness.

**Bozu:** This is an informal way to refer to a boy, similar to the English term "kid" or "squirt."

**Sempai:** This title suggests that the addressee is one's senior in a group or organization. It is most often used in a school setting, where underclassmen refer to their upperclassmen as "sempai." It can also be used in the workplace, such as when a newer employee addresses an employee who has seniority in the company.

**Kohai:** This is the opposite of "sempai" and is used toward underclassmen in school or newcomers in the workplace. It connotes that the addressee is of a lower station.

**Sensei:** Literally meaning "one who has come before," this title is used for teachers, doctors, or masters of any profession or art.

**[blank]:** Usually forgotten in these lists, but perhaps the most significant difference between Japanese and English. The lack of honorific means that the speaker has permission to address the person in a very intimate way. Usually, only family, spouses, or very close friends have this kind of permission. Known as *yobisute*, it can be gratifying when someone who has earned the intimacy starts to call one by one's name without an honorific. But when that intimacy hasn't been earned, it can also be very insulting.

# Preview of Volume 3

We're pleased to present you a preview from Volume 3.
This volume will be available in English on October 25, 2005,
but for now you'll have to make do with Japanese!

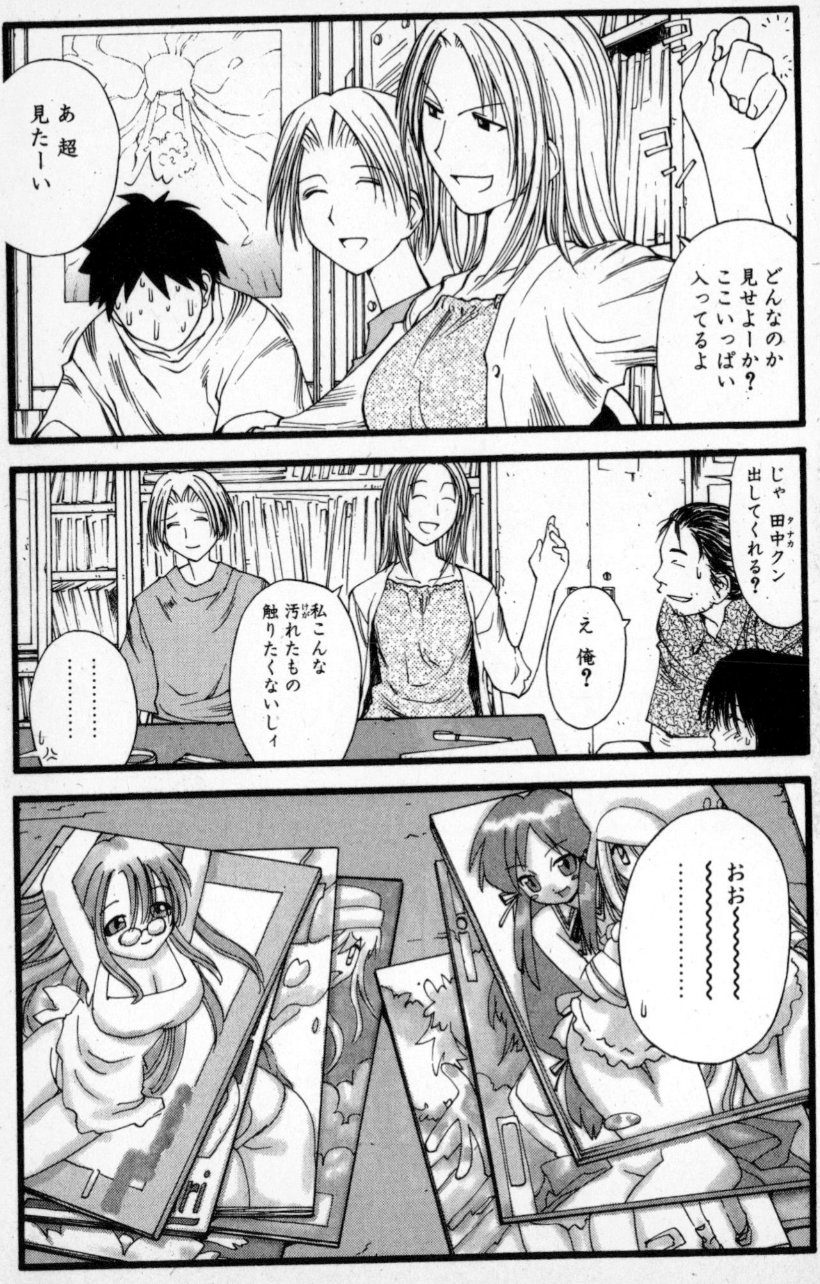
どんなのか
見せよーか？
ここいっぱい
入ってるよ
あ 超
見たーい
じゃ 田中クン
出してくれる？
え 俺？
私こんな
汚れたもの
触りたくないしィ
……
おお〜〜〜……

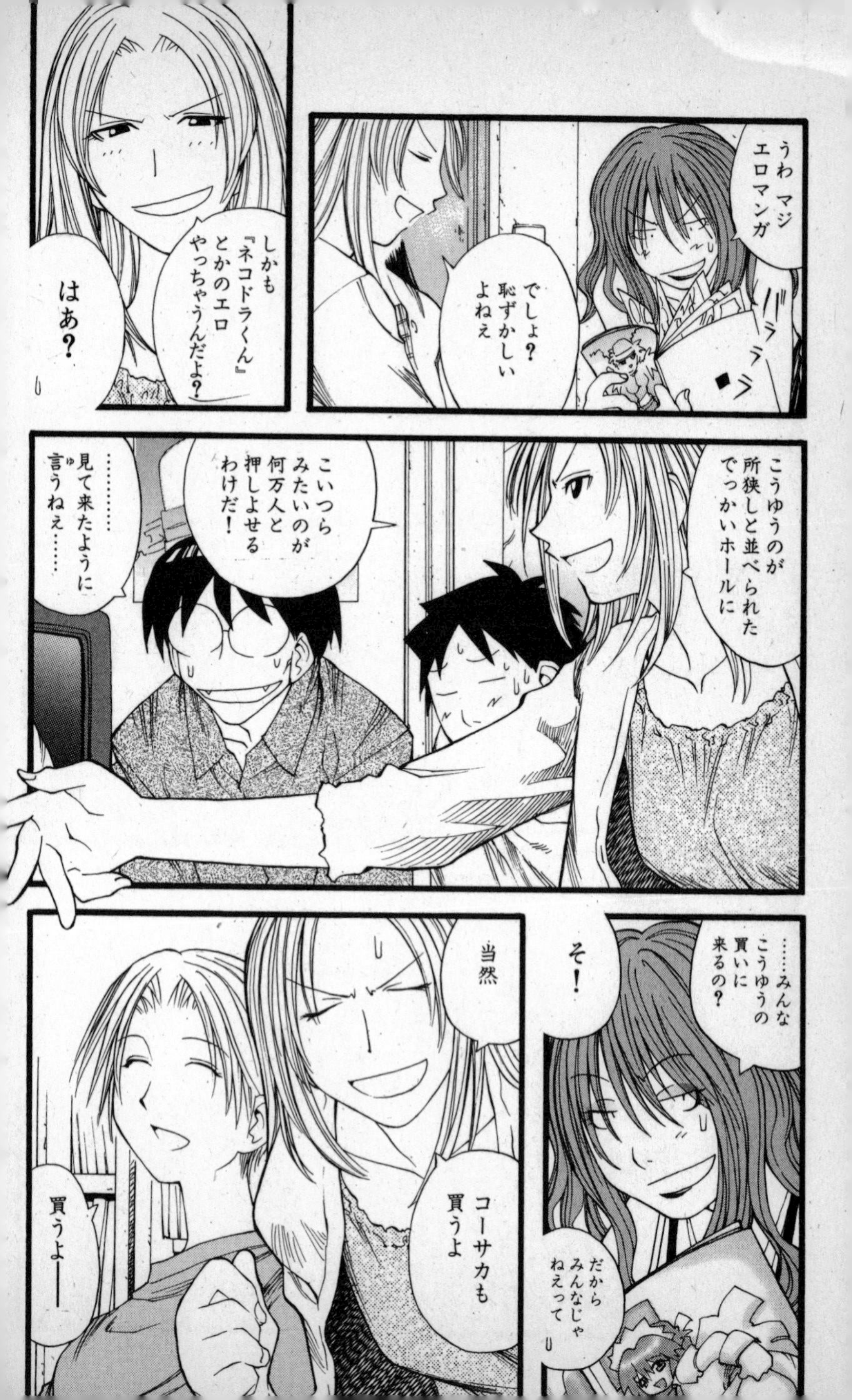
うわ マジ エロマンガ
バラララ
でしょ？恥ずかしいよねえ
しかも『ネコドラくん』とかのエロやっちゃうんだよ？
はあ？
こうゆうのが所狭しと並べられたでっかいホールに
こいつらみたいのが何万人と押しよせるわけだ！
……見て来たように言うねえ……
……みんなこうゆうの買いに来るの？
そ！
だからみんなじゃねえって
当然
コーサカも買うよ
買うよー

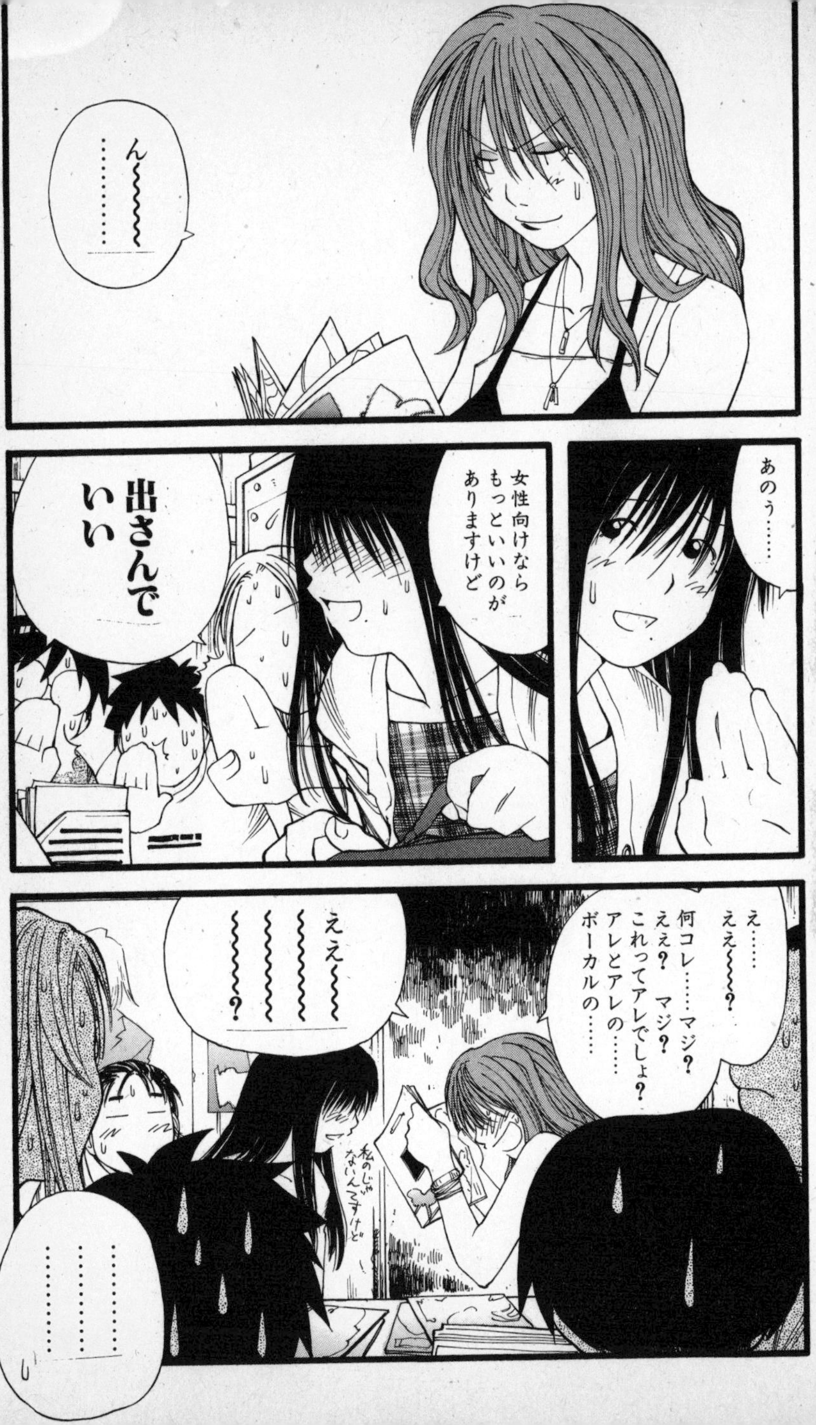
ん〜〜〜〜……
あのう……
女性向けなら もっといいのが ありますけど
出さんでいい
え…… ええ〜〜〜？ 何コレ……マジ？ ええ？ マジ？ これってアレでしょ？ アレとアレの…… ボーカルの……
ええ〜〜〜〜〜〜〜〜？
私のじゃないんですけど
………………

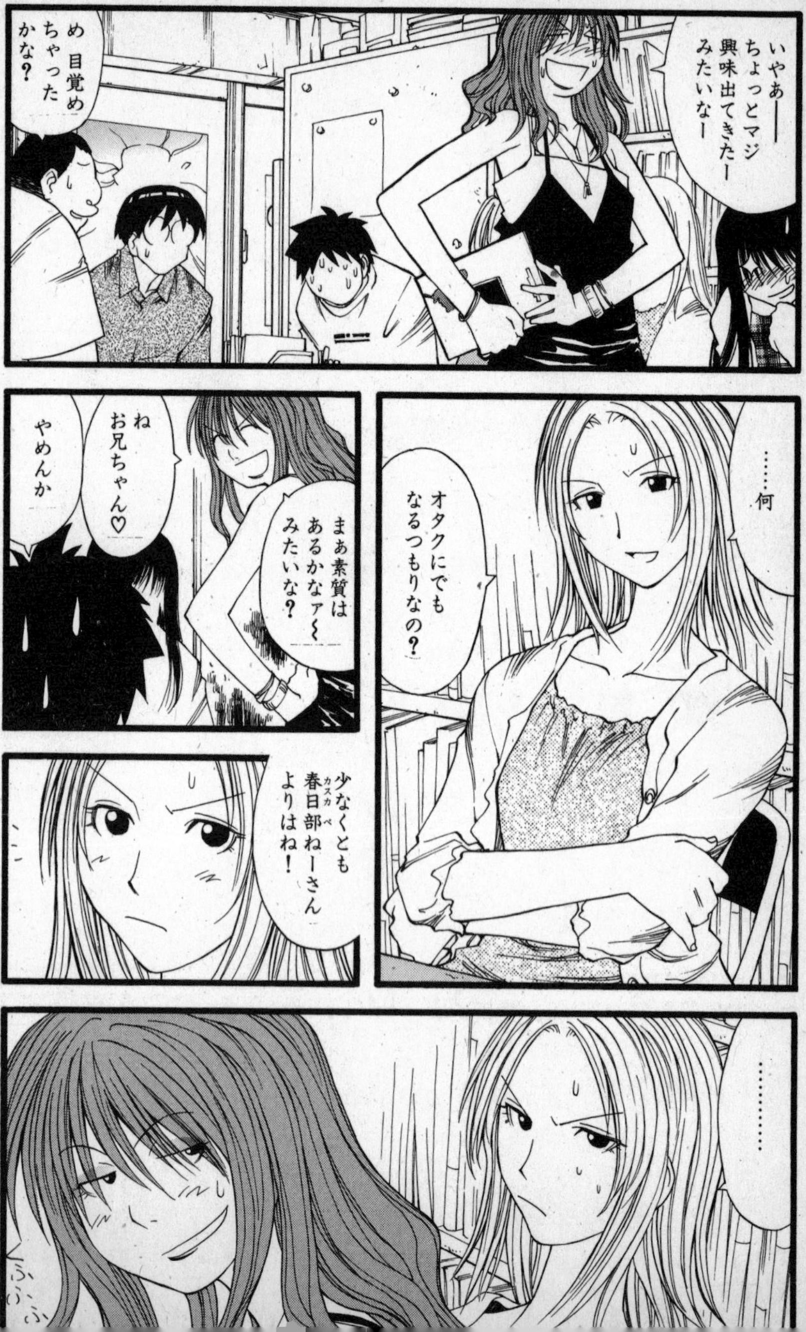
いやあー ちょっとマジ 興味出てきたー みたいなー
め 目覚めちゃった かな？
……何
オタクにでも なるつもりなの？
まぁ素質は あるかなァ〜 みたいな？
ね お兄ちゃん♡
やめんか
少なくとも 春日部ねーさん よりはね！
……
くふふふ

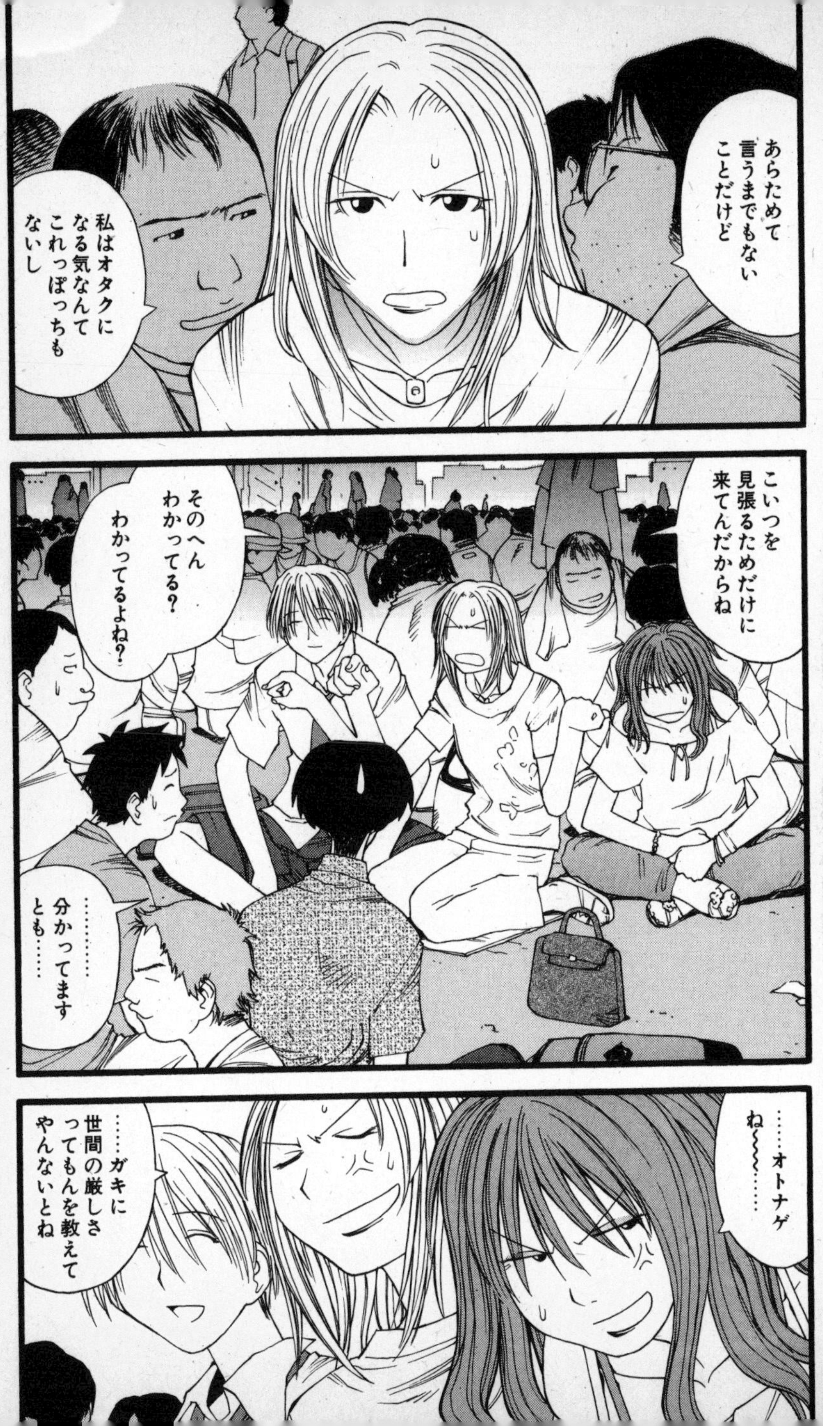
あらためて言うまでもないことだけど
私はオタクになる気なんてこれっぽっちもないし
こいつを見張るためだけに来てんだからね
そのへんわかってる?
わかってるよね?
……………分かってますとも……
……オトナゲね～～～……
……ガキに世間の厳しさってもんを教えてやんないとね

# NEGIMA!™ VOLUME 6

## BY KEN AKAMATSU

### *KIDNAPPED IN KANSAI!*

The chaotic class trip continues as Negi Springfield and his thirty-one beautiful female students explore the historic cities of Kyoto and Nara. Negi's special headache is Konoka, the headmaster's granddaughter, who turns out to have her own magical abilities! Although she's not aware of them, others certainly are . . . and Konoka is kidnapped by a group of wizards who plan to corrupt her budding talents. Negi is going to need all the help he can get—even if it comes from a former foe. . . .

6
NEGIMA!™
MAGISTER NEGI MAGI
KEN AKAMATSU
CREATOR OF LOVE HINA!

**Ages: 16+**

*Includes special extras after the story!*

**VOLUME 6: On sale June 28, 2005**

DEL REY

*For more information and to sign up for Del Rey's manga e-newsletter, visit www.delreymanga.com*

# Nodame Cantabile

## VOLUME 2

### BY TOMOKO NINOMIYA

There's a new kid in town, and Nodame had better be on her guard. The new rival plays timpani like a dream—and not only that, has the hots for Nodame's crush, Shinichi Chiaki. Plus a wretched old man has an eye (and hand) out for Nodame. It's a lot to handle, for a girl who has trouble just keeping her room clean . . . .

Shinichi has his own problems. A famous conductor starts a new orchestra at school, and Shinichi finally gets his chance to conduct. But he soon discovers there's more to the craft than just following notes on a page. Could this hard lesson unexpectedly turn his life around and change his destiny?

Ages: 13 +

**Includes special extras after the story!**

**VOLUME 2: On sale July 26, 2005**

*For more information and to sign up for Del Rey's manga e-newsletter, visit www.delreymanga.com*

# VOLUME 4

## BY TOMOKO HAYAKAWA

Ignoring all attempts by her four handsome housemates to make her into a proper lady, Sunako Nakahara is enjoying her reclusive existence of horror films and solitude. However, when her aunt decides that Sunako should have a romantic life, her haven is endangered. Her aunt is coming home to arrange a relationship for her!

Kyohei and the other guys must teach Sunako how to behave on a date—fast—or their free-rent arrangement is over. But with a girl who has explosive nosebleeds whenever she meets anyone attractive, it's going to take more than just coaching to get her through her big day! Will Sunako learn what it takes to have a normal romantic life?

Ages: 16+

**Includes special extras after the story!**

**VOLUME 4: On sale June 28, 2005**

*For more information and to sign up for Del Rey's manga e-newsletter, visit www.delreymanga.com*